The
Garland Library
of
War and Peace

The
Garland Library
of
War and Peace

Under the General Editorship of
Blanche Wiesen Cook, *John Jay College, C.U.N.Y.*
Sandi E. Cooper, *Richmond College, C.U.N.Y.*
Charles Chatfield, *Wittenberg University*

The Future of War
in Its Technical, Economic
and Political Relations

by

Jean De Bloch
(Ivan Bliokh)

Translated by

R. C. Long

with a conversation
with the author by

William T. Stead

and an introduction by

Edwin D. Mead

with a new introduction
for the Garland Edition by

Sandi E. Cooper

Garland Publishing, Inc., New York & London
1972

Library of Congress Cataloging in Publication Data

Bloch, Jan Gotlib, 1836-1902.
The future of war in its technical, economic, and
political relations.

(The Garland library of war and peace)
Translation of v. 6 of Budushchaia voĭna.
1. Military art and science. 2. War. I. Title.
II. Series.
U102.B646 1972   355.02   75-147466
ISBN 0-8240-0257-1

Introduction

In the last decade of the nineteenth century, Ivan Bliokh (Jean de Bloch), a self-made Polish railway magnate turned his attention to the problem of war and military preparedness in his contemporary Europe. The major fruit of his engagement was a six volume study of war which was published in Polish, Russian, French and German. Only the last volume, a summary and conclusion of the whole, was translated into English.

Allegedly, Tsar Nicholas II's decision in 1898 to call for an arms limitation conference among the powers — which led to the convocation of the Hague Conference of 1899 — was influenced in part by Bliokh's work. But beyond that, Bliokh's massive analysis of war merits respect and study for its often uncanny predictions of the shape and impact of a major war among "civilized" states have been borne out between 1914 and the present. Bliokh analyzed war in a truly "interdisciplinary" manner. His charts, graphs, statistics and descriptive researches examined all aspects of the economic capabilities of European states. His study of modern weaponry explored the current and future potential of armed confrontation. His conclusions tied together the economic and technological data to demonstrate that victory, as

5

conceived by military experts, was an impossibility. His apprehension was that

> *any attempt . . . made to demonstrate the inaccuracy of my assertions by putting the matter to a test on a great scale . . . [would inevitably] result in a catastrophe which would destroy all existing political organizations.*

What Bliokh envisioned was nothing less than the total destruction of western civilization proceeding from a major war among the great powers. From this position, he argued the futility of the contemporary obsession with military preparedness which served only to impoverish nations and aggravate social tensions. Technologically, the war being prepared would be an incredible slaughter between adversaries who were so roughly equal that no advance or "victory" could be expected. Battlefields would resemble Sebastopol where a spade was as valuable as a rifle as men would dig in and only then shoot at each other.

Fighting would not be contained in isolated fields alone. In fact, its weight would be directly borne by civilian populations. In the future war that was being prepared, Bliokh saw hamlets, towns and villages destroyed to prevent sanctuary and refuge. In the new kind of war, everyone was the potential enemy.

For Bliokh, such a war was impossible because it defeated the purpose of war − victory. Limited engagements of troops on clearly delineated fields of battle was a thing of the past. Entire nations would be deeply and irrevocably involved – from shouldering the burden of production, sharing fewer and fewer goods, to directly experiencing attack.

Given the revolutionary improvement in tools of combat, Bliokh reasoned that a few half-trained militia defending small territories were as useful as the most highly skilled professional armies that Europe could produce. The Boer War substantiated his contention that the revolution in warfare rendered well equipped armies nearly useless against committed raw recruits who were defending their homeland. Thus, he questioned why nations should expend vast sums to train armies and restock arsenals. The expenses of preparedness were eroding the economies and public finances of every European nation. Eventually, the result would be social convulsion. Either war itself or the preparation for war would destroy the social and political order.

Who then are the utopians, Bliokh wondered? Those who asserted that war or its preparation could provide neither security nor social stability? Or those who insisted that the arms race and the conscripted army were the only form of security – si vis pacem, para bellum? For Bliokh, the so-called "practical" men who insisted on preparing for a war in which there could be no victory were "the real Utopians of our time, [who were] wasting the resources of civilizations."

The basic contours of Bliokh's case against the

INTRODUCTION

resort to warfare by modern states was not original with him. Anyone familiar with the position taken by peace thinkers and organizations in his period has frequently encountered versions of the argument. None, however, had laced it with the detailed analysis of costs, of production requirements, of man and technical power that Bliokh introduced. He apparently came to his conclusions after vast researches undertaken in his leisure time and not through contact with pacifist views. The publication of his work, of course, brought him into contact with peace activists who hailed him. His ideas made their way into western Europe with the French and German translations, and with his articles and lectures against the Boer War, he developed a reputation in Britain. While no English edition of the entire six volumes ever appeared, the final volume (reprinted here) was translated with the addition of a special preface by the noted English peace activist and writer, William T. Stead. Stead, a journalist, chose to present Bliokh in an informal, conversational transcript which remains a lively, albeit brief, introduction to the author and his ideas.

Sandi E. Cooper
Division of Social Sciences
Richmond College – C.U.N.Y.

The
Future of War

The

FUTURE OF WAR
IN ITS TECHNICAL
ECONOMIC AND
POLITICAL
RELATIONS

BY

I. S. BLOCH

TRANSLATED BY R. C. LONG, AND WITH A CONVERSATION
WITH THE AUTHOR BY W. T. STEAD, AND AN
INTRODUCTION BY EDWIN D. MEAD

BOSTON
GINN & COMPANY
1902

CONTENTS

PAGE

INTRODUCTION, BY EDWIN D. MEAD.
CONVERSATIONS WITH THE AUTHOR, BY W. T.
STEAD vii

AUTHOR'S PREFACE lxiii

PART I

MILITARY AND NAVAL DEVELOPMENTS

CHAP.   PAGE

I. HOW WAR WILL BE WAGED ON LAND . . 3

II. PLANS OF CAMPAIGN : POSSIBLE AND IMPOSSIBLE 63

III. THE FUTURE OF NAVAL WARFARE. . . 93

IV. DOES RUSSIA NEED A NAVY ? . . . 113

V. WHAT WARS HAVE COST IN THE NINETEENTH
CENTURY 128

VI. WHAT THEY WILL COST IN THE FUTURE . . 140

VII. THE CARE OF THE WOUNDED . . . 146

CONTENTS

PART II
ECONOMIC DIFFICULTIES IN TIME
OF WAR

CHAP.   PAGE

I. In Russia 163

II. In Britain 251

III. In Germany 266

IV. In France 277

V. Effect of War on the Vital Needs of Peoples 294

VI. Probable Losses in Future Wars . . 319

VII. Militarism and its Nemesis . . 347

LIST OF MAPS AND DIAGRAMS

PAGE

Map of Russian Defensive System 74
Map of Paths of Advance of the Austro-German Armies from
   Points of Concentration to the Vistula-Bug-Narev Theatre
   of War 77
Map of Paths of Advance of the German and Austrian Armies on
   the Vistula-Bug-Narev Theatre of War, from Pierron and
   Brailmont . . . , ... 78
Plan of Invasion by Russia of Prussian Territory . . . 89
Diagram of Expenditure on the Crimean War 129
Diagram of Expenditure on the War of 1859 130
Diagram of Expenditure by Russia on the War of 1877-78 . . 131
Diagram of Expenditure of Europe on War in the second half
   of the Nineteenth Century 132
Diagram of Increase per cent. of Military Expenditure between
   1874 and 1896 134
Diagrams of Probable Daily Expenditure on a Future War 142-144
Diagram of Percentage Distribution of the Revenues . . . 145
Diagram of Result of Firing from an 11-mil. Rifle . . 149-150
Plate showing effect of a Bullet fired from a distance of 3500
   metres on the Human Tibia, and on the Bone of an Ox . 153
Diagram showing Depreciation of Russian Securities at the Out-
   break of War 168
Plan showing Expenditure by Russia, per Inhabitant, on Army
   and Navy . . . , ... 170
Diagram of Russian Exports and Imports (1889-94) . , . 172
Diagram of Percentage of Russian Export to Production (1890-94) 175
Plan of Russian Grain Production per Inhabitant . . . 176
Diagram of Classification of Russian Imports 178
Plan of Russian Commercial Undertakings in 1892, per 100,000 of
   the Population 180
Plan of Russian Expenditure on Posts and Telegraphs per In-
   habitant 181
Plan of Output of Russian Factories 183
Diagram of Percentage Comparison of Wages in Russia, Great
   Britain, and North America 186

LIST OF MAPS AND DIAGRAMS

PAGE

Plan of Percentage Growth of Russian Population between 1885 and 1897 189

Plan of Average Number of Houses in a Russian Settlement . 191

Plan of Average Value of one Property destroyed by Fire in Russia, between 1860–87 194

Plan of Average Losses by Fire in Russia per 100 Inhabitants (1860–68) 195

Plan of Number of Large Cattle in Russia, per 1000 desaytins (1888) 199

Plan of Comparative Yields of Agricultural Countries of Europe 200

Plan of Comparative Number of Large Cattle in Agricultural Countries of Europe 201

Diagram of Russian Harvest in 1893 205

Diagram of Growth of the Orthodox Population in Russia, and the General Population of other Countries, per 1000 . . 207

Diagram of the Number of Marriages, per 1000, of the Population of the Countries of Europe 208

Diagram of the Number of Births, per 1000, of the Population of the Countries of Europe 208

Diagram of the Mortality, per 1000, of the Population of the Countries of Europe 209

Diagram of Percentage Mortality of Children under one year, in the Countries of Europe 210

Diagram of the Number of Survivors out of 1000 Children born at all ages up to 75 212

Diagram of the Value of Human Life at Various Ages . . 214

Plan of Outlay on Instruction in Russia in 1887, per Inhabitant . 215

Diagram of Percentage of Illiterates accepted for Military Service in chief European Countries 217

Diagrams showing Number of Students in Higher and Intermediate Russian Educational Institutions, per 100,000 of the Population 218–219

Diagram of Number of Doctors in European Countries, per 100,000 of the Population 220

Diagram of Number of Quadratic Kilometres for every Doctor . 221

Plan of Outlay on Medicine in Russia, per Inhabitant . . 222

Plan of Number of Deaths from Typhus in Russia, per 1000 Cases 224

Diagram of Number of Illegitimates in 1000 Births, in chief European Countries 225

Diagram of Number of Suicides per 100,000 of the Population, in chief European Countries 226

Diagram of Consumption of Spirits per 100 of the Population, in chief European Countries, in 1868 and 1888 . . . 229

Diagram of Number of Deaths from Drunkenness per Million of the Population, in chief European Countries . . . 230

Diagram of Average Number of Convictions per 200,000 of the Population of Russia 231

LIST OF MAPS AND DIAGRAMS

PAGE

Diagrams of Numbers of Various Classes condemned for Murder per Million of the corresponding Population in chief European Countries . . . . . , . . . 232

Diagrams of Numbers of Various Classes convicted for Theft per Million of the corresponding Population in chief European Countries 233

Diagrams of Numbers convicted for Highway Robbery per Million of the corresponding Population in chief European Countries 234

Diagrams of Numbers convicted for Swindling per Million of the corresponding Population, in chief European Countries . 235

Diagram of Percentage Relation of Men and Women convicted in chief European Countries 236

Diagram of Percentage Increase in Russia in the Fifteen Chief Forms of Crime 236

Diagram of Number of Convictions in Great Britain per 100,000 of the Population 237

Diagram of Comparative Convictions in France and Austria . 237

Diagram of Number of Convictions per 100,000 of Population in Germany 238

Plan of Expenditure on Justice and Prisons in Russia per Inhabitant 239

Plan of Percentage of Grown Horses in Russia 241

Plan of Amount of Production of Iron and Steel in Russia . . 243

Diagram of Number of Native and Imported Cattle in England . 256

Diagram of Classification by Occupation of 1000 of the Population of Great Britain . . , ... 259

Diagram of Distribution of the Income of the Population of England 260

Diagram of State of Savings in Great Britain in 1895 . . . 261

Diagram of Expenditure of England on Armed Forces between 1864 and 1895 264

Diagram of Classification of Workers in Germany according to Wages 273

Diagram of Emigration from Germany to America (1891-1894) . 274

Diagram of Value of Foreign Securities stamped in Germany . 276

Diagram of French Imports and Exports (1860-1894) . . . 278

Diagram of French Trade (1860-1894) 279

Diagram of French Trade (1883-1894) 280, 281

Diagram of French Revenue and Expenditure (1861-1893) . 281

Diagram of French Debt (1852-1895) 282

Diagram of French Savings (1869-1895) 282

Diagram of Average Value of Properties, in Francs, passing by Legacy 283

Diagram of the Distribution of the French Population according to Occupation in 1886 284

LIST OF MAPS AND DIAGRAMS

PAGE

Diagram of Assistance given to the Poor in France in 1889 . 288

Diagram of Number of Old Men and Children in Percentage
Relation to Population in chief European Countries . . 289

Diagram of Number of Bachelors in Percentage Relation to
Population in chief European Countries 290

Diagram of Increase or Decrease of the Population in France
and Germany per 1000 291

Diagram of Number of Population in chief European Countries
in 1788 and 1888 in Millions 292

Diagram of Value by Growth of Population in France and Germany, from 1788 to 1888 293

Diagram showing the Number of Days on which Food would be
Lacking in Time of War in chief European Counties . . 296

Diagram showing the Number of Days on which Oats would be
Lacking in time of War in chief European Countries . . 298

Diagram of Superfluity or Deficiency of Meat in chief European
Countries 304

Diagram of Superfluity or Deficiency of Salt in chief European
Countries 305

Diagram of Superfluity or Deficiency of Kerosene in chief
European Countries 306

Diagram of Superfluity or Deficiency of Stone Coal in chief
European Countries 306

Chart showing Comparative Development of Socialists and Freethinkers in Germany according to the Elections of 1891 . 312

Diagram of Percentage of Horses which would be taken for
Military Purposes in chief European Countries . . . 316

Diagram showing Amount of Living Force of a Bullet . . 320

Diagram showing Penetrative Power of the Mauser Bullet on
Numbers of Horses' Carcases 321

Diagram of Rotation and Weight of Bullets of various Rifles . 322

Diagram of Zone of Effective Fire against Infantry by Chassepot
and Mannlicher Rifles respectively 323

Diagram of Breadth of Zone of Effective Fire against Cavalry by
the Chassepot and Mannlicher Rifles respectively . . 324

Diagram of Distance of Useful Fire 325

Diagrams of Percentage of Hits in Fire at One Infantryman by
French and German Soldiers 326-327

Diagram of the Deviation of the Paskevitch Instrument . . 327

Diagram of the Number of Cartridges Carried by One Soldier
with Different Rifles 328

Diagram of Number of Sappers to 100 Infantrymen in Various
European Countries 333

Diagram of Losses in the German Army in the War of 1870 . 336

Diagram showing Influence of the Quality of Firearms on the
Relations of Killed to Wounded 343

INTRODUCTION

The death of M. Jean de Bloch, which occurred at Warsaw just as the year (1902) began, is a misfortune for the whole world. It is peculiarly so at this immediate juncture; for the imperative problem with the world at this time is how to get rid of war and substitute for it a rational way of settling international differences, and no other man in our time has studied this problem so scientifically or contributed so much to its solution as Jean de Bloch. Indeed, I think it is not too much to say that M. Bloch was the most thorough and important student of the question of War in all its details and upon its many sides who has ever lived, and that his great book upon "The Future of War" will remain the chief armory from which the men of the twentieth century who are warring against war will continue to draw until their sure victory comes, and all national and international disputes are settled in the courts, as to-day personal disputes are settled.

I think that no book ever written in the cause of the peace and order of the world, save Hugo Grotius's great work alone, has rendered or is likely to render such influential practical service as Bloch's "Future of War," supplemented as it has been by his articles in the various reviews during the years since the work was first published. Dante's "De Monarchia," the "Great Design" of Henry IV, William Penn's "Plan for the Peace of Europe," Immanuel Kant's "Eternal Peace," the essays of LaCroix, Saint Pierre, Bellers and Bentham, Sumner's "True Grandeur of Nations," —these high appeals and such as these have pierced to the hearts of thinking men in the successive centuries, and their general and cumulative effect in ele-

INTRODUCTION

vating the tone and broadening the outlook of society upon the question of War and its evils has been immense. It would be hard, however, to lay the hand upon any distinct practical reform or progress wrought by any of them in its own day or days that followed. But Grotius's "Rights of War and Peace" wrought almost a revolution, and it did it almost at once. With it, it may be said with a high degree of justice, international law was born into the world almost full grown; and from the time of its appearance war, horrible at its best, has been in its usages a very different thing from what it was before. Equally definite, distinct and practical has been the influence of Bloch's "Future of War"; and I believe that it will be seen at the end of this twentieth century that its influence has been equally powerful and far-reaching.

Bloch's monumental work upon "The Future of War," in six volumes, was published in Russian five or six years ago. It was the result of a decade's special study by this eminent financier and economist, whose whole life's experience had fitted him to understand so well those phases of the question which he felt it most important to emphasize to Europe. Editions of the complete work have been brought out in German and in French, under the distinguished author's own supervision. No edition has yet appeared in English; only this translation of the last volume, in which the conclusions are summarized, has been published for popular use. It is a pleasure, however, to be able to state that the preparation of a complete English edition is about to be undertaken. No library in America or England, no university or college, no editorial room or minister's study should be without it. Meantime it is a satisfaction to know and to assure the public that the present volume contains the gist of the whole work, the clear statement of all its important principles. It will always be the best thing for the ordinary reader, giving all which he requires. I count it a peculiar benefaction that a cheap edition of this work is now given to the public by a publisher whose heart is in it, making it possible for

INTRODUCTION

all men to possess it and for the friends of peace to circulate it by the thousand. I trust that they will earnestly unite to do it. The Peace cause has suffered because so much of its best literature is not available in attractive and cheap form and is not widely circulated. This need we are assured is now to be effectively met; and the present publication is surely a good beginning.

The matter of really greatest moment in our time for the student of War and the worker for Peace has not been the war in South Africa nor the war in the Philippines, but the Hague Conference. The Hague Conference did not come into existence without ancestry, without intellectual forces which made it imperative and certain. It came not simply because the Czar sent out his Rescript; it was because the Czar himself had been converted, that commanding intellectual forces had been in operation in Russia. I think there was none of these intellectual forces more potent than that exerted by Jean de Bloch. Bloch's book was an epoch-making book. It startled the Czar and his ministers; it startled all serious thinkers in Europe; it was one of the cardinal forces that compelled the Conference at the Hague. At that Conference, in a private and unofficial capacity, Bloch himself was present throughout. He always declined the honor paid 1 im of having suggested the Conference to the Czar by his book; the idea he declared was the result of general evolution, which was forcing upon all serious minds the conviction of the folly and impossibility of continuing the war system.

If ever a man is born under conditions which naturally compel him to think of the tragedies of war, of its horrors and burdens, and of the evils of those race antagonisms which so often lead to war, I think it must be a Polish Jew. The very word Jew brings up the thought of the sufferings, the social and political ostracism, the injustices and wrongs of every sort, which have been the lot of the Jew through all these centuries. The name of Poland reminds us equally impressively of those scarce slumbering hatreds and

INTRODUCTION

antagonisms there still after a hundred years, a monument to the cruelty and wickedness of the wars which ended Poland's national life, as the close of one of the most mournful and shameful chapters in human history.

Jean de Bloch was a Polish Jew, a poor Polish Jew, beginning his life as a pedlar, hawking his wares about the streets of Warsaw. Finally getting through good fortune a sum of money, he resolved that he would push out of the ignorance and narrowness into which he was born, and he found his way to Berlin. There he studied for three years, largely with French and English tutors, and then went back to Warsaw. He was a man if immense energy and a devoted student. He rapidly acquired a fortune as a banker and also obtained a high reputation as a sociologist and an economist. He married a rich and talented woman, and their home became a notable intellectual centre. He wrote exhaustive works in many volumes upon Russian railways, Russian finance, and Russian local government. It was to him presently that the Russian commercial folk and the Russian government itself were turning to finance their operations. He became the leading banker of Poland—a sort of Polish Rothschild—and he became the president of important railway systems. He was led as a result of all this to understand what were the menaces to the economy of states of the war system obtaining in Europe. Seeing that war lay at the root of the trouble, he devoted himself for years to the preparation of his exhaustive work upon "The Future of War," the most powerful arraignment of war and the most powerful argument for the peace of the world which has been written in our time, or perhaps in any time. From his youth he had studied war, and he had written many pamphlets on military subjects; but "The Future of War" was his supreme effort.

With that work Bloch came to the Hague Conference. He came, he said, as a learner; but he came also as a teacher and a helper. He came to bring his book, to distribute it, to explain it, and to acquire in-

INTRODUCTION

formation and education for himself. He sincerely believed that his book was the Bible of this cause. He was not a vain nor an opinionated man, but he had the profoundest confidence in his insight and in the things which he had learned. His argument was, on the whole, and in the place where he laid the emphasis, a new one. The peace societies had in the main appealed to the moral side of this matter; Jean de Bloch appealed to the business side. The appeals of the apostles of peace have been for the most part to the world's humanity and piety; although it would be a mistake and a wrong not to remember that from William Penn's time to Charles Sumner's they have not failed to urge again and again the economic argument and point out what would result if the world would apply to constructive ends what it wastes on war. Jean de Bloch said: We must appeal to the purse, to common sense, and make men see that this war system is the most stupid thing in creation. That was where he directed almost his whole argument. He said that if it came to a great European war, that war could only cease with the annihilation of one combatant and the financial ruin of the other. He said that, so far from this question of an international court being a Utopian thing, it was the men who were going on with their schemes for wars who were really dealing in chimeras; that the time has come when we should apply our resources, not to the things which waste and devastate, but to the things that build up states and the industries and the social welfare of men. He appealed to the facts of war as they unrolled themselves before the eyes of Europe; he showed what the real results of the Franco-Prussian War were; he drew the lessons from the Russo-Turkish War. The destructiveness of modern warfare, with its frightful new weapons, becomes so appalling that a general European war would bring the universal bankruptcy of nations. The present armed peace, indeed, is so costly that the burdens of it already threaten social revolution in almost every country in Europe.

INTRODUCTION

Bloch, unlike most peace men, was one of the most critical students of military affairs; he met the military men upon their own ground. He lectured last summer to the United Service Institution in London, a body of military experts, with a major-general in the chair; and he proved himself the superior of those practical and learned military men upon every technical point, and worsted them in the debate.

In the last years of Bloch's life he was engaged chiefly in drawing from the South African War the warning lessons which the world needs to learn. He has shown that the Boers have been so successful not, as has been often said, because of the topography of the country or because they are particularly good marksmen, but because they have profited by the utterly changed conditions of war. Bloch shows that the fundamental change came in with the American Civil War. The American Civil War, he was never tired of telling the people of Europe, settled it that the alleged superiority of disciplined armies over volunteer troops amounts to nothing; that the ordinary military training is often a positive disadvantage in preparing for modern warfare. War is no longer the clash of solid phalanxes with solid phalanxes in showy, heroic combat upon battlefields. Cavalry and artillery are rapidly becoming useless. Soldiers cannot be compacted, but must be spread apart, and each must rely upon himself as never before. One man in defence is a match for ten in offence; the methods of guerilla warfare become more and more common and necessary; and the civilian soldier, the simple volunteer, is as good as the regular, and often better.

This is a thing of immense moment; for if it is true it makes the whole effort to maintain great armaments a vain thing. Robert Peel said with discernment that, instead of wasting the resources of a country to maintain great armies and navies, the sensible nation in the future will rely upon its own latent energies, perfectly sure that if it has inherent energy it can always improvise powers necessary for any de-

INTRODUCTION

fence at very short notice. There is no practical demand or excuse longer for costly armies and navies; all this great armament is waste. Bloch has shown that thing to the modern world,—that from the scientific point of view armies and navies are not a source of strength to any nation, but rather a source of weakness; that they do not defend, but rather drain and endanger. He has not been answered; I do not believe he can be answered. We are his debtors,—the foolish and long-suffering world is his debtor,—for the thoroughness and power with which he has taught this great lesson.

"The Future of War" was but the culmination of M. Bloch's remarkable activities in his life's campaign for peace and an organized world. His articles in the reviews and magazines—Russian, French, German and English—were innumerable. His impressive article upon "Militarism in Politics," in the last December number of the *Contemporary Review*, should be read by all Americans as well as by all Englishmen, at this time. His earlier article in the same review (September, 1901) on "The Wars of the Future" is the most striking statement in brief of the main principles of his great book; it should be printed as a tract and scattered broadcast up and down the land. Another powerful statement of his position has appeared in our own *North American Review* since his death (April, 1902).

Bloch was not only present at the Hague during the Conference, but at Paris during the Exposition, always indefatigable in his work of enlightenment. When necessary he took the platform; and so it was that we had the privilege of seeing and meeting him when he came to London last summer to deliver his lectures on the Transvaal War before the Royal United Service Institution, to which I have referred. After one of these lectures he invited us to a personal meeting; and at this meeting he unfolded with great earnestness his scheme for having established at several of the world's leading centres what he called War and Peace Institutions. These were to be large mu-

INTRODUCTION

seums, in which, by pictures, panoramas, models, charts and many means, the real character and significance of modern warfare should be brought home to the actual perception of men and women, who now for the most part have no adequate comprehension of what war is. Especially did he wish to have the practical and economic aspects emphasized, to make men see how and why, in the changed military conditions, a really successful war on the part of one great power upon another really great power is impossible.

At the time of his death M. Bloch was actually engaged in the establishment of the first of these remarkable museums at Lucerne; and he provided for its generous endowment. He chose Lucerne as a point to begin, since it is a place so much visited, and he felt that the knowledge of the work would spread thence to all the world, and the work be largely copied. He had secured a large and imposing building at Lucerne and was prosecuting the work of preparation at large personal expense; for M. Bloch was a man of great wealth, and put much money, as well as thought and zeal, into his peace propaganda.

He was anxious that what he was planning in Lucerne should also be done in London; and he gave me a long typewritten outline of his scheme to submit to William Mather, George Cadbury and other leading peace men in England, whose coöperation might be enlisted. I believe that London will yet have such an institution. I sincerely hope that America will have such a one; and this was M. Bloch's earnest desire. He spoke of New York and Washington as appropriate locations; and in one of these cities, through the munificence of some one of our haters of war and lovers of peace, who could certainly put a half million dollars to no more useful or necessary service to-day, this institution should surely rise and continue to teach its lessons until they are no longer needed.

I wish that it might be founded now, while the workers for peace through all the world are mourning for Bloch, as a strong assurance that his work and

INTRODUCTION

influence shall be perpetuated and shall grow. I wish that in memory of him it might be called simply *The Bloch Institution*. I wish that the things which he suggests in the outline which he prepared, and which I hope will soon be published, might all be carried out; and I wish that, in sympathetic hands, catching his great inspiration, the institution might be developed with a fulness of which even he hardly dreamed. I wish that one great hall might be devoted to copies of all of Verestchagin's pictures, and that other halls might serve similar ends. I wish that year by year addresses might be given at the institution by the world's best thinkers in behalf of a rationally organized world; that peace and arbitration conferences might there be regularly held; that from that centre all the world's best literature upon this commanding interest might be widely circulated; and that useful publications might there have their source. I can think of no institution that would be of greater service in America at this time. I can think of no worthier monument which we could rear to Jean de Bloch. His noblest and immortal monument he has himself created in his great work on "The Future of War."

EDWIN D. MEAD.

CONVERSATIONS WITH M. BLOCH

By William T. Stead

"*The Future of War*" *is the title of M. de Bloch's voluminous cyclopædia on the art of war, past, present, and to come. But that is a mistake. For M. Bloch's thesis is that there is no war to come, that war indeed has already become impossible.*

It would really have been clearer therefore to call this translation of the sixth and concluding volume of his immense book "Is War Now Impossible?"—as in the English edition,—for this title gives a much clearer idea of the contents. For M. Bloch contends in all sober seriousness that war—great war in the usual acceptation of the word—has already, by the natural and normal development of the art or science of warfare, become a physical impossibility!

That is what this book was written to prove.

PREFACE

But, before reading the chapters crammed with statistics and entering upon the arguments of the great Polish economist, the reader may find it convenient to glance over, as a preliminary introduction to the book, the following free rendering of the conversations which I have had the privilege of enjoying with the author at St. Petersburg and in London.

"UTOPIANS," said M. Bloch; "and they call us Utopians, idealists, visionaries, because we believe that the end of war is in sight? But who are the Utopians, I should like to know? What is a Utopian, using the term as an epithet of opprobrium? He is a man who lives in a dream of the impossible; but what I know and am prepared to prove is, that the real Utopians who are living in a veritable realm of phantasy are those people who believe in war. War has been possible, no doubt, but it has at last become impossible, and those who are preparing for war, and basing all their schemes of life on the expectation of war, are visionaries of the worst kind, for war is no longer possible."

"That is good news, M. Bloch," I replied; "but is it not somewhat of a paradox? Only last year we had the Spanish-American war; the year before, the war between Turkey and Greece. Since when has war become impossible?"

"Oh," replied M. Bloch, with vivacity, "I do not speak of such wars. It is not to such frontier brawls, or punitive operations such as you in England, for instance, are perpetually engaging in on the frontiers of your extended empire, that I refer when I say that war has become impossible. When soldiers and statesmen speak about the War of the Future, they do not refer to such trumpery expeditions against semi-barbarous peoples. The war of the future, the war which has become impossible, is the war that has haunted the imagination of mankind for the last thirty years, the war in which great nations armed to the teeth were to fling themselves with all their resources into a struggle for life and death This is the war that every day becomes more and more impossible. Yes, it is in preparations against that impossible war that these so-called practical men, who are the real Utopians of our time, are wasting the resources of civilisation."

" Pray explain yourself more clearly, M. Bloch."

"Well," said he, "I suppose you will admit that war has practically become impossible for the minor States. It is as impossible for Denmark or for Belgium to make war to-day as it would be for you or for me to assert the right of private war, which our forefathers possessed. We cannot do it. At least, we could only try to do it, and then be summarily suppressed and punished for our temerity. That is the position of the minor States. For them war is practically forbidden by their stronger neighbours. They are in the position of the descendants of the feudal lords, whose right of levying war has vanished owing to the growth of a strong central power whose interests and authority are incompatible with the exercise of what used to be at one time an almost universal right. For the minor States, therefore, war is impossible."

"Admitted," I replied. "Impossible, that is to say, without the leave and licence of the great Powers."

" Precisely," said M. Bloch ; " and hence, when we discuss the question of future war, we always deal with it as a war between great Powers. That is to say, primarily, the long talked-of, constantly postponed war between France and Germany for the lost provinces; and, secondly, that other war, the thought of which has gradually replaced that of the single-handed duel between France and Germany, viz., a war between the Triplice and the Franco-Russian Alliance. It is that war which constantly pre-occupies the mind of statesmen and sovereigns of Europe, and it is that war which, I maintain, has become absolutely impossible."

" But how impossible, M. Bloch ? Do you mean morally impossible ? "

" No such thing," he replied. " I am dealing not with moral considerations, which cannot be measured, but with hard, matter-of-fact, material things, which can be esti-mated and measured with some approximation to absolute accuracy. I maintain that war has become impossible alike from a military, economic, and political point of view. The very development that has taken place in the mechanism of war has rendered war an impracticable operation. The dimensions of modern armaments and the organisation of society have rendered its prosecution an economic impossibility, and, finally, if any attempt were made to demonstrate the inaccuracy of my assertions by putting the matter to a test on a great scale, we should find the inevitable result in a catastrophe which would destroy all existing political organisations. Thus, the great war cannot be made, and any attempt to make it would result in suicide. Such, I believe, is the simple demonstrable fact."

" But where is the demonstration ? " I asked.

M. Bloch turned and pointed to his encyclopædic work upon "The Future of War," six solid volumes, each containing I do not know how many quarto pages, which stood piled one above the other.

"Read that," he said. "In that book you will find the facts upon which my demonstration rests."

"That is all very well," I said; "but how can you, M. Bloch, an economist and a banker, set yourself up as an authority upon military matters?"

"Oh," said M. Bloch, "you have a saying that it is often the outsider that sees most; and you must remember that the conclusions arrived at by military experts are by no means inaccessible to the general student. In order to form a correct idea as to the changes that have taken place in the mechanism of war, it is quite conceivable that the bystander who is not engaged in the actual carrying out of the evolution now in progress may be better able to see the drift and tendency of things than those who are busily engaged in the actual detail of the operation. I can only say that while at first hand I have no authority whatever, and do not in any way pose as a military or naval expert, I have taken all imaginable pains in order to master the literature of warfare, especially the most recent treatises upon military operations and the handling of armies and fleets, which have been published by the leading military authorities in the modern world. After mastering what they have written, I have had opportunities of discussing personally with many officers in all countries as to the conclusions at which I have arrived, and I am glad to know that in the main there is not much difference of opinion as to the accuracy of my general conclusions as to the nature of future warfare."

"But do they also agree with you," I said, "that war has become impossible?"

"No," said M. Bloch, "that would be too much to expect. Otherwise Othello's occupation would be gone. But as they have admitted the facts, we can draw our own conclusions."

"But I see in your book you deal with every branch of the service, armaments of all kinds, manœuvres, questions of strategy, problems of fortification—everything, in fact, that comes into the consideration of the actual conduct of modern war. Do you mean to tell me that military men generally think you have made no mistakes?"

"That would be saying too much. The book was referred by the Emperor of Russia at my request to the Minister of War, with a request that it should be subjected to examination by a council of experts. The results of that council were subsequently communicated to the Emperor in the shape of a report, which set forth that while in dealing with so very many questions it was impossible to avoid some mistakes, it was their opinion that the book was a very useful one, and that it was most desirable that it should be placed in the hands of all staff officers. They also added an expression of opinion that no book could contribute so much to the success of the Conference or to the information of those who were to take part in its deliberations.

"The one question upon which strong difference of opinion existed was that concerning the use of the bayonet. I have arrived at the conclusion, based upon a very careful examination of various authorities, that the day of the bayonet is over. In the Franco-German war the total mortality of the Germans from cold steel amounted to only one per cent. The proportion on the

French side was higher, but I think it can be mathe-matically demonstrated that, in future, war will be decided at ranges which will render the use of the bayonet impos-sible. General Dragomiroff, however, a veteran of the old school, cannot tolerate this slight upon his favourite weapon. In his eyes the bayonet is supreme, and it is cold steel which at the last will always be the deciding factor in the combats of peoples. He therefore strongly condemns that portion of my book ; but it stands on its own merits, and the reader can form his own judgment as to the probability of the bayonet being of any practical use in future war."

" General Dragomiroff's devotion to the bayonet," I remarked, " reminds me of our admirals' devotion to sails in our navy. Fifteen years ago it was quite obvious that the fighting ship of the future had no need for sails—that, indeed, sails were an encumbrance and a danger ; but all the admirals of the old school attached far more importance to the smartness in furling and unfurling sail than they did to proficiency in gunnery or in any of the deciding factors in naval battles. They clung to masts and yards for years after all the younger officers in the service knew that they might as well have clung to bows and arrows ; and I suppose you will find the same thing in regard to the bayonet."

" Yes," said M. Bloch, " the bayonet seems to me alto-gether out of date. No doubt it is a deadly enough weapon, if you can get within a yard of your enemy ; but the problem that I have been asking myself is whether in future combatants will ever be able to get within one hundred yards of one another, let alone one yard."

" But then," I rejoined, " if that be so, wars will be much less deadly than they were before."

"Yes and no," said M. Bloch; "they will become less deadly because they have become more deadly. There is no kind of warfare so destructive of human life as that in which you have bodies of men face to face with each other, with nothing but cold steel to settle the issue. The slaughter which took place in the old wars between barbarians, or between the Romans and the barbarian tribes on their frontiers, was simply appalling. There is nothing like it in modern warfare, and this diminution of the mortality in battle has been, paradoxically enough, produced by the improved deadliness of the weapons with which men fight. They are, indeed, becoming so deadly that before long you will see they will never fight at all."

"That," I replied, "was the faith of Rudyard Kipling, who wrote me a few months ago saying that he relied for the extinction of war upon the invention of a machine which would infallibly slay fifty per cent. of the combatants whenever battle was waged. 'Then,' he said, 'war would cease of itself.' The same idea was expressed by Lord Lytton in his novel of 'The Coming Race,' in which he attributed the final disappearance of war from the planet to the discovery of vril, a destructive so deadly that an army could be annihilated by the touch of a button by the finger of a child."

"Yes," said M. Bloch; "that is so; but until mankind has made experience of the deadliness of its weapons there will be terrible bloodshed. For instance, at Omdurman the destruction inflicted upon the forces of the Khalifa came very near the fifty per cent. standard of Rudyard Kipling. That one experience was probably sufficient even for the Dervishes. They will never again face the fire of modern rifles. The experience which they have learned is rapidly becoming generalised throughout the armies of Christendom, and although there may be some frightful scenes of wholesale slaughter, one or two experiences of that kind will rid our military authorities of any desire to come to close quarters with their adversaries."

"What a paradox it is!" I replied. "We shall end by killing nobody, because if we fought at all we should kill everybody. Then you do not anticipate increased slaughter as the result of the increased precision in weapons?"

"You mistake me," said M. Bloch. "At first there will be increased slaughter—increased slaughter on so terrible a scale as to render it impossible to get troops to push the battle to a decisive issue. They will try to, thinking that they are fighting under the old conditions, and they will learn such a lesson that they will abandon the attempt for ever. Then, instead of a war fought out to the bitter end in a series of decisive battles, we shall have as a substitute a long period of continually increasing strain upon the resources of the combatants. The war, instead of being a hand-to-hand contest in which the combatants measure their physical and moral superiority, will become a kind of stalemate, in which neither army being able to get at the other, both armies will be maintained in opposition to each other, threatening each other, but never being able to deliver a final and decisive attack. It will be simply the natural evolution of the armed peace, on an aggravated scale."

"Yes," said M. Bloch, "accompanied by entire dislocation of all industry and severing of all the sources of supply by which alone the community is enabled to bear the crushing burden of that armed peace. It will be a multiplication of expenditure simultaneously accompanied by a diminution of the sources by which that expenditure can be met. That is the future of war—not fighting, but famine, not the slaying of men, but the bankruptcy of nations and the break-up of the whole social organisation."

"Now I begin to perceive how it is that we have as a prophet of the end of war a political economist, and not a soldier."

"Yes," said M. Bloch, "it is as a political economist that I discovered the open secret which he who runs may read. The soldier by natural evolution has so perfected the mechanism of slaughter that he has practically secured his own extinction. He has made himself so costly that mankind can no longer afford to pay for his maintenance, and he has therefore transferred the sceptre of the world from those who govern its camps to those who control its markets."

"But now, M. Bloch, will you condescend to particulars, and explain to me how this great evolution has been brought about?"

"It is very simple," said M. Bloch. "The outward and visible sign of the end of war was the introduction of the magazine rifle. For several hundred years after the discovery of gunpowder the construction of firearms made little progress. The cannon with which you fought at Trafalgar differed comparatively little from those which you used against the Armada. For two centuries you were content to clap some powder behind a round ball in an iron tube, and fire it at your enemy.

"The introduction of the needle gun and of breech-loading cannon may be said to mark the dawn of the new era, which, however, was not definitely established amongst us until the invention of the magazine rifle of very small calibre. The magazine gun may also be mentioned as an illustration of the improved deadliness of firearms ; but, as your experience at Obdurman showed, the deciding factor was not the Maxim, but the magazine rifle."

"Yes," I said ; "as Lord Wolséley said, it was the magazine rifle which played like a deadly hose spouting leaden bullets upon the advancing enemy."

"Yes," said M. Bloch, "and the possibility of firing half a dozen bullets without having to stop to reload has transformed the conditions of modern war."

" Do you not exaggerate the importance of mere rapidity of fire ? " I asked.

" No," said M. Bloch ; " rapidity of fire does not stand alone. The modern rifle is not only a much more rapid firer than its predecessors, but it has also an immensely wider range and far greater precision of fire. To these three qualities must be added yet a fourth, which completes the revolutionary nature of the new firearm, and that is the introduction of smokeless powder."

" The Spanish-American campaign," I said, " illustrated the importance of smokeless powder ; but how do you think the smokelessness of the new explosives will affect warfare in the future ?"

" In the first case," said M. Bloch, " it demolishes the screen behind which for the last 400 years human beings have fought and died. All the last great battles have been fought more or less in the dark. After the battle is joined, friends and foes have been more or less lost to sight in the clouds of dense smoke which hung heavy over the whole battlefield. Now armies will no longer fight in the dark. Every soldier in the fighting line will see with frightful distinctness the havoc which is being made in the ranks by the shot and shell of the enemy. The veil which gun-powder spread over the worst horrors of the battlefield has been withdrawn for ever. But that is not the only change. It is difficult to over-estimate the increased strain upon the nerve and *morale* of an army under action by the fact that men will fall killed and wounded without any visible or audible cause. In the old days the soldier saw the puff of smoke, heard the roar of the gun, and when the shell or shot ploughed its way through the ranks, he associated cause and effect, and was to a certain extent prepared for it. In the warfare of the future men will simply fall and die without either seeing or hearing anything."

"Without hearing anything, M. Bloch?"

"Without hearing anything, for although the smokeless powder is not noiseless, experience has proved that the report of a rifle will not carry more than nine hundred yards, and volley-firing cannot be heard beyond a mile. But that brings us to the question of the increased range of the new projectiles. An army on march will suddenly become aware of the comparative proximity of the foe by seeing men drop killed and wounded, without any visible cause; and only after some time will they be able to discover that the invisible shafts of death were sped from a line of sharp-shooters lying invisible at a distance of a mile or more. There will be nothing along the whole line of the horizon to show from whence the death-dealing missiles have sped. It will simply be as if the bolt had come from the blue. Can you conceive of anything more trying to human nerves?"

"But what is the range of the modern rifle?"

"The modern rifle," said M. Bloch, "has a range of 3000 or 4000 metres—that is to say, from two to three miles. Of course, I do not mean to say that it will be used at such great distances. For action at long range, artillery is much more effective. But of that I will speak shortly. But you can fairly say that for one mile or a mile and a half the magazine rifle is safe to kill anything that stands between the muzzle and its mark ; and therein," continued M. Bloch, " lies one of the greatest changes that have been effected in modern firearms. Just look at this table " (see page 4). " It will explain better than anything I can say the change that has been brought about in the last dozen years.

" In the last great war, if you wished to hit a distant mark, you had to sight your rifle so as to fire high up into the air, and the ball executing a curve descended at the range at which you calculated your target stood. Between the muzzle and the target your bullet did no execution. It was soaring in the air, first rising until it reached the maximum height, and then descending it struck the target or the earth at one definite point some thousand yards distant. Contrast this with the modern weapon. There is now no need for sighting your gun so as to drop your bullet at a particular range. You aim straight at your man, and the bullet goes, as is shown in the diagram, direct to its mark. There is no climbing into the air to fall again. It simply speeds, say, five feet from the earth until it meets its mark. Anything that stands between its object and the muzzle of the rifle it passes through. Hence whereas in the old gun you hit your man only if you could drop your bullet upon the square yard of ground upon which he was standing, you now hit him so long as you train your rifle correctly on every square yard of the thousand or two thousand which may intervene between the muzzle of your gun and the end of the course of the shot. That circumstance alone, even without any increase in the rapidity of the fire, must enormously add to the deadliness of the modern firearms."

" Could you give me any exact statistics as to the increased rapidity of fire ? "

"Certainly," said M. Bloch. " That is to say, I can give you particulars up to a comparatively recent time, but the progress of the science of firearms is so rapid that no one can say but that my statistics may be old before you print your report of this talk. The ordinary soldier will fire twelve times as many shots per minute as he was able to do in 1870, and even this is likely to be rapidly improved upon. But you may take it that what with increased rapidity of fire, greater penetrative power, and the greater precision that the gun which the soldier will carry into the battle will possess, the rifle of to-morrow will be forty times as effective as the chassepot was in the Franco-Prussian war. Even the present gun is five times as deadly."

"But do not you think that with this rapid firing a soldier will spend all his ammunition and have none left ? "

" There, again," said M. Bloch, " the improvement in firearms has enormously increased the number of cartridges which each man can carry into action. In 1877, when we went to war with Turkey, our soldiers could only carry 84 cartridges into action. When the calibre of the rifle was reduced to 5 mm. the number which each soldier was furnished with rose to 270. With a bullet of 4 mm. he will carry 380, and when we have a rifle of 3 mm. calibre he will be able to take 575 into action, and not have to carry any more weight than that which burdened him when he carried 84, twenty years ago. At present he carries 170 of the 7·62 mm."

" But we are a long way off 3 mm. calibre, are we not, M. Bloch ? "

" Not so far. It is true that very many countries have not yet adopted so small a bore. Your country, for instance, has between 7½ and 8 mm. The United States have adopted one with 6; Germany is contemplating the adoption of 5; but the 3 mm. gun will probably be the gun of the future, for the increased impetus of the small bore and its advantage in lightness will compel its adoption."

" You speak of the increased penetrative power of the bullet. Do you think this will add considerably to the deadliness of rifle-fire ? "

" Oh, immensely," said M. Bloch. " As you contract the calibre of the gun you increase the force of its projectile. For instance, a rifle with a calibre of only 6·5 mm. has 44 per cent. more penetrative power than the shot fired by an 8 mm. rifle. Then, again, in previous wars, if a man could throw himself behind a tree he felt comparatively safe, even although the bullets were hurtling all round. To-day the modern bullet will pierce a tree without any difficulty. It also finds no obstacle in earthworks such as would have turned aside the larger bullets. There is therefore less shelter, and not only is there less shelter, but the excessive rapidity with which the missile travels (for it is absurd to call the slender projectile, no thicker than a lead pencil, a ball) will add enormously to the destructive power of the shot. Usually when a bullet struck a man, it found its billet, and generally stopped where it entered; but with the new bullet this will not be the case. At a near range it will pass through successive files of infantry, but what is more serious is that should it strike a bone, it is apt to fly upwards or sideways, rending and tearing everything through which it passes. The mortality will be much greater from this source than it has been in the past."

" But is this not all very much theory ? Have you any facts in support of your belief that the modern bullet will be so much more deadly than its predecessor ? In England quite the opposite impression prevailed, owing to the experience which we gained in Jameson's raid, when many of the combatants were shot through and seemed none the worse, even although the bullet appeared to have traversed a vital part of the body."

M. Bloch replied : " I do not know about the Jameson raid. I do know what happened when the soldiers fired recently upon a crowd of riotous miners. It is true that they fired at short range, not more than thirty to eighty paces. The mob also was not advancing in loose formation, but, like most mobs, was densely packed. Only ten shots were fired, but these ten shots killed outright seven of the men and wounded twenty-five, of whom six afterwards died. Others who were slightly wounded concealed their injuries, fearing prosecution. Each shot, therefore, it is fair to estimate, must have hit at least four persons. But ignoring those unreported cases, there were thirty-two persons struck by bullets. Of these, thirteen died, a proportion of nearly 40 per cent., which is at least double the average mortality of persons hit by rifle-bullets in previous wars. It has also been proved by experiments made by firing shots into carcases and corpses, that when the bullet strikes a bone it acts virtually as an explosive bullet, as the point expands and issues in a kind of mushroom shape. Altogether I take a very serious view of the sufferings," continued M. Bloch, " and of the injury that will be inflicted by the new weapons."

" Is the improvement in the deadliness of weapons confined to small-arms ?   Does it equally extend to artillery
firing ? "

" There," said M. Bloch, " you touch upon a subject
which I have dealt with at much length in my book.   The
fact is that if the rifle has improved, artillery has much more
improved.   Even before the quick-firing gun was introduced into the field batteries an enormous improvement
had been made.   So, indeed, you can form some estimate
of the evolution of the cannon when I say that the French
artillery to-day is held by competent authorities to be at
least one hundred and sixteen times more deadly than the
batteries which went into action in 1870."

" How can that be ? " I asked.   " They do not fire one
hundred and sixteen times as fast, I presume ? "

" No ; the increased improvement has been obtained
in many ways.   By the use of range-finders it is possible
now to avoid much firing into space which formerly prevailed.   An instrument weighing about 60 lb. will in three
minutes give the range of any distance up to four miles,
and even more rapid range-finders are being constructed.
Then, remember, higher explosives are used ; the range
has been increased, and even before quick-firing guns were
introduced it was possible to fire two and a half times as
fast as they did previously.   The effect of artillery-fire
to-day is at least five times as deadly as it was, and being
two or three times as fast, you may reckon that a battery
of artillery is from twelve to fifteen times as potent an
instrument of destruction as it was thirty years ago.   Even
in 1870 the German artillerists held that one battery was
able absolutely to annihilate any force advancing along a
line of fire estimated at fifteen paces in breadth for a distance
of over four miles.

"If that was so then, you can imagine how much more deadly it is now, when the range is increased and the explosive power of the shell has been enormously developed. It is estimated that if a body of 10,000 men, advancing to the attack, had to traverse a distance of a mile and a half under the fire of a single battery, they would be exposed to 1450 rounds before they crossed the zone of fire, and the bursting of the shells fired by that battery would scatter 275,000 bullets in fragments over the mile and a half across which they would have to march. In 1870 an ordinary shell when it burst broke into from nineteen to thirty pieces. To-day it bursts into 240. Shrapnel fire in 1870 only scattered thirty-seven death-dealing missiles. Now it scatters 340. A bomb weighing about 70 lb. thirty years ago would have burst into forty-two fragments. To-day, when it is charged with peroxilene, it breaks up into 1200 pieces, each of which is hurled with much greater velocity than the larger lumps which were scattered by a gunpowder explosion. It is estimated that such a bomb would effectively destroy all life within a range of 200 metres of the point of explosion. The artillery also benefits by the smokeless powder, although, as you can easily imagine, it is not without its drawbacks."

"What drawbacks?"

"The fact that the artillerymen can be much more easily picked off, when they are serving their guns, by sharp-shooters than was possible when they were enveloped in a cloud of smoke of their own creation. It is calculated that one hundred sharp-shooters, who would be quite invisible at a range of five hundred yards, would put a battery out of action in four minutes if they could get within range of one thousand yards. At a mile's

range it might take one hundred men half an hour's shooting to put a battery out of action.   The most effective
range for the sharp-shooter is about eight hundred paces.
At this range, while concealed behind a bush or improvised
earthwork, a good shot could pick off the men of any
battery, or the officers, who could not avail themselves of
the cover to which their men resort."

" How will your modern battle begin, M. Bloch ? "

" Probably with attempts on outposts made by sharp-
shooters to feel and get into touch with each other.
Cavalry will not be of much use for that purpose.   A
mounted man offers too good a mark to a sharp-shooter.
Then when the outposts have felt each other sufficiently
to give the opposing armies knowledge of the whereabouts
of their antagonists, the artillery duel will commence at a
range of from four to five miles.   As long as the artillery
is in action it will be quite sufficient to render the nearer
approach of the opposing forces impossible.   If they are
evenly matched, they will mutually destroy each other,
after inflicting immense losses before they are put out of
action.   Then the turn of the rifle will come.   But the
power of rifle-fire is so great that it will be absolutely
impossible for the combatants to get to close quarters
with each other.   As for any advance in force, even in
the loosest of formations, on a front that is swept by the
enemies' fire, that is absolutely out of the question.   Flank
movements may be attempted, but the increased power
which a magazine rifle gives to the defence will render
it impossible for such movements to have the success
that they formerly had.   A small company can hold its
own against a superior attacking force long enough to
permit of the bringing up of reinforcements.   To attack
any position successfully, it is estimated that the attack-

ing force ought to outnumber the assailants at least by 8 to 1. It is calculated that 100 men in a trench would be able to put out of action 336 out of 400 who attacked them, while they were crossing a fire-zone only 300 yards wide."

"What do you mean by a fire-zone?"

"A fire-zone is the space which is swept by the fire of the men in the trench."

"But you assume that they are entrenched, M. Bloch?"

"Certainly, everybody will be entrenched in the next war. It will be a great war of entrenchments. The spade will be as indispensable to a soldier as his rifle. The first thing every man will have to do, if he cares for his life at all, will be to dig a hole in the ground, and throw up as strong an earthen rampart as he can to shield him from the hail of bullets which will fill the air."

"Then," I said, "every battlefield will more or less come to be like Sebastopol, and the front of each army can only be approached by a series of trenches and parallels?"

"Well, that, perhaps, is putting it too strongly," said M. Bloch, "but you have grasped the essential principle, and that is one reason why it will be impossible for the battle of the future to be fought out rapidly. All digging work is slow work, and when you must dig a trench before you can make any advance, your progress is necessarily slow. Battles will last for days, and at the end it is very doubtful whether any decisive victory can be gained."

"Always supposing," I said, "that the ammunition does not give out."

"Ammunition will not give out. Of powder and shot there is always plenty."

"I doubt that," I replied. "The weak point of all this argument as to the impossibility of war implies that the modern mechanism of war, which is quite sufficient to prevent armies coming into close contact, also possesses qualities of permanence, or rather of inexhaustibility. What seems much more probable is that with the excessive rapidity of fire, armies will empty their magazines, and the army that fires its last cartridge first will be at the mercy of the other. Then the old veteran Dragomiroff will rejoice, for the bayonet will once more come into play."

M. Bloch shook his head.

"I do not think that armies will run short of ammunition. All my arguments are based upon the assumption that the modern war is to be fought with modern arms. I do not take into account the possibility that there will be a reversion to the primitive weapons of an earlier day."

"Well, supposing that you are right, and that ammunition does not run short, what will happen?"

"I have quoted in my book," said M. Bloch, "the best description that I have ever seen of what may be expected on a modern battlefield. I will read it to you, for it seems to convey, more vividly than anything that I could say, just what we may expect:—

"The distance is 6000 metres from the enemy. The artillery is in position, and the command has been passed along the batteries to 'give fire.' The enemy's artillery replies. Shells tear up the soil and burst; in a short time the crew of every gun has ascertained the distance of the enemy. Then every projectile discharged bursts in the air over the heads of the enemy, raining down hundreds of fragments and bullets on his position. Men and horses are overwhelmed by this rain of lead and iron. Guns destroy one another, batteries are mutually annihilated, ammunition cases are emptied. Success will be with those whose fire does not slacken. In the midst of this fire the battalions will advance.

"Now they are but 2000 metres away. Already the rifle-bullets whistle round and kill, each not only finding a victim, but penetrating files, ricocheting, and striking again. Volley succeeds volley, bullets in great handfuls, constant as hail and swift as lightning, deluge the field of battle.

"The artillery having silenced the enemy is now free to deal with the enemy's battalions. On his infantry, however loosely it may be formed, the guns direct thick iron rain, and soon in the position of the enemy the earth is reddened with blood.

"The firing lines will advance one after the other, battalions will march after battalions ; finally the reserves will follow. Yet with all this movement in the two armies there will be a belt a thousand paces wide, separating them as by neutral territory, swept by the fire of both sides, a belt which no living being can stand for a moment. The ammunition will be almost exhausted, millions of cartridges, thousands of shells will cover the soil. But the fire will continue until the empty ammunition cases are replaced with full.

"Melinite bombs will turn to dust farmhouses, villages, and hamlets, destroying everything that might be used as cover, obstacle, or refuge.

"The moment will approach when half the combatants will be mowed down, dead and wounded will lie in parallel rows, separated one from the other by that belt of a thousand paces which will be swept by a cross fire of shells which no living being can pass.

" The battle will continue with ferocity. But still that thousand paces unchangingly separate the foes.

" Who shall have gained the victory ? Neither.

" This picture serves to illustrate a thought which, since the perfection of weapons, has occupied the minds of all thinking people. What will take place in a future war ? Such are constrained to admit that between the combatants will always be an impassable zone of fire deadly in an equal degree to both the foes.

" With such conditions, in its application to the battles of the future, the saying of Napoleon seems very questionable: ' The fate of battle is the result of one minute, of one thought, the enemies approach with different plans, the battle becomes furious ; the decisive moment arrives, and a happy thought sudden as lightning decides the contest, the most insignificant reserve sometimes being the instrument of a splendid victory.'

" It is much more probable that in the future both sides will claim the victory."

" Pleasant pictures, certainly ; and if that authority is right, you are indeed justified in believing that there will be no decisive battles in the war of the future."

" There will be no war in the future," said M. Bloch ; " for it has become impossible, now that it is clear that war means suicide."

" But is not everything that you are saying an assumption that people will make war, and that therefore war itself *is* possible ? "

" No doubt," said M. Bloch ; "the nations may endeavour to prove that I am wrong, but you will see what will happen. Nothing will be demonstrated by the next war if it is made, in spite of warnings, but the impossibility of making war, except, of course, for the purpose of self-destruction. I do not for a moment deny that it is possible for nations to plunge themselves and their neighbours into a frightful series of catastrophes which would probably result in the overturn of all civilised and ordered government. That is, of course, possible; but when we say that war is impossible we mean that it is impossible for the modern State to carry on war under the modern conditions with any prospect of being able to carry that war to a conclusion by defeating its adversary by force of arms on the battlefield. No decisive war is possible. Neither is any war possible, as I proceed to show, that will not entail, even upon the victorious Power, the destruction of its resources and the break-up of society. War therefore has become impossible, except at the price of suicide. That would, perhaps, be a more accurate way of stating the thesis of my book."

"I understand; but do you think you have proved this?"

"Certainly," said M. Bloch. "So far I have only spoken about the improvements that have been wrought in two branches of the service, viz., in the magazine rifle and the greater efficiency of artillery. Taken by themselves, they are sufficiently serious to justify grave doubt as to whether or not we have not reached a stage when the mechanism of slaughter has been so perfected as to render a decisive battle practically impossible; but these two elements are only two. They are accompanied by others which are still more formidable to those who persist in contemplating war as a practical possibility."

"To what are you referring?" I asked.

"Chiefly to the immensity of the modern army. The war of 1870–71 was a contest of giants, but the German armies operating in France did not exceed half a million men, whereas if war were to break out to-day, the Germans would concentrate over a million men on their front, while the French would be no whit behind them in the energy with which they would concentrate all their available fighting men on the frontier. In a war between the Triple and the Dual Alliance there would be ten millions of men under arms."

"How would you make up the total of ten millions which you say would be mobilised in case of a war between the Dual and Triple Alliance?"

"The figures in millions are briefly: Germany, 2,500,000; Austria, 1 3–10ths millions; Italy, 1 3–10ths millions, making a total of 5,100,000 for the Triple Alliance. France would mobilise 2½ millions, and Russia 2,800,000, making 5,300,000—10,400,000. It has yet to be proved that the human brain is capable of directing the movements and providing for the sustenance of such immense masses of human beings. The unwieldiness of the modern army has never been adequately taken into account. Remember that those millions will not be composed of veterans accustomed to act together. More than half of the German and French troops which will be confronting each other on mobilisation in case of war will be drawn from the reserves. In Russia the proportion of reserves would be only three hundred and sixty, in Italy two hundred and sixty, per thousand; but even this proportion is quite sufficient to indicate how large a mass of men, comparatively untrained, would find their place in the fighting front."

"But have not great generals in the past commanded

armies of millions ?—Xerxes, for instance, and Tamerlane, and Attila at the head of his Huns ? "

" No doubt," said M. Bloch, " that is quite true ; but it is one thing to direct a horde of men living in the simplest fashion, marching shoulder to shoulder in great masses, and it is an altogether different thing to manœuvre and supply the enormously complex machine which we call a modern army.   Remember, too, that in the old days men fought in masses, whereas the very essence of modern war is that you must advance in loose order and never have too big a clump of soldiers for your enemy to fire at. Hence the battle will be spread over an enormous front, and every mile over which you spread your men increases the difficulties of supply, of mutual co-operation, and of combined effort."

" But has not the training of officers kept pace with the extension and development of modern armaments ? "

" Yes," said M. Bloch, " and no.   It is true, no doubt, that an effort has been made to bring up the technical training of officers to the necessary standard ; but this is quite impossible in all cases.   A very large proportion of the officers who will be in command in a general mobilisation would be called from the reserve, that is to say, they would be men who are not familiar with the latest developments of modern tactics, and who would find themselves suddenly called upon to deal with conditions of warfare that were almost as different from those with which they were trained to deal as the legionaries of Cæsar would have been if they had been suddenly summoned to face the musketeers of Frederic the Great."

" Is that not an exaggeration, M. Bloch ? Do you think that the art of war has changed so much ? "

" Changed ? " said M. Bloch ; " it has been so thoroughly

revolutionised in the last thirty years, that if I had a son who was preparing for a military career, I would not let him read a book on tactics or strategy that had not been written in the last fifteen years, and even then he would find that great changes had taken place within that period. It is simply appalling to contemplate the spectacle of millions of men, half of whom have been hurriedly summoned from the field, the factory, and the mine, and the whole placed under command of officers not one in a hundred of whom has ever been under fire, and half of whom have been trained in a more or less antiquated school of tactics. But even then that is not the worst. What we have to recognise is the certainty that even if all officers were most efficient when the war began, the war would not last many weeks before the majority of the officers had been killed off."

"But why?" I said.

"The percentage of officers killed and wounded in action was much greater even in 1870 than the proportion of privates killed and wounded. The Germans, for instance, lost two officers killed and three wounded to each private who was similarly disabled. But that was before the improved weapon came into play. In the Chilian war the proportion of officers killed was 23 per cent. and 75 per cent. wounded, whereas among the men only 13 per cent. were killed and 60 per cent. wounded."

"To what do you attribute this?" I asked.

"The cause is very simple. The officers are compelled to expose themselves much more than the men under their orders. They have to be up and about and moving, while the men are lying in the shelter of the trenches. This is so well recognised that every Continental army pays special attention to the training of sharp-shooters, whose word of command is that they should never waste a shot upon any one but an officer. Hence the general conviction on the part of the officers abroad that if the great war broke out they would never survive to see the conclusion of peace."

"When I was in Paris, M. Bloch, that conviction did not seem to be very general on the part of the French officers."

"It is different in Germany," said M. Bloch, "and in Austria-Hungary, and the French would not be long in finding it out. Again and again officers have said to me that while they would of course do their duty if they were ordered to the front, they would take their place at the head of their men knowing that they would never return. So general is this conviction that you will find very little trace of any war party among the officers in Germany. They know too well what war would mean to them. But I am not thinking so much of the fate of the individuals as the result which will inevitably follow when this massed million of men found themselves deprived of their commanders.

"An army is a very highly specialised organisation. Without competent officers, accustomed to command, it degenerates into a mere mob, and of all things in the world nothing is so helpless as a mob. It can neither march, fight, manœuvre, nor feed itself. An army without leaders is not only a mob, but it is apt to degenerate into a very cowardly mob. Remember that every man is not naturally brave. It was said long ago that a very good fighting army consisted of three sorts of soldiers: only one-third of the men in the ranks were naturally brave, another third were naturally cowards, while the last third was capable of being brave under

circumstances when it was well led and kept up to its
work. Take away the officers, and this middle third
naturally gravitate to the cowardly contingent, with
results which have been seen on many a stricken field.
Hence, under modern conditions of warfare every army
will tend inevitably to degenerate into such a mob. It is
for those practical military men who persist in regarding war as a possibility to explain how they hope to
overcome the difficulty created by the very magnitude
and unwieldiness of the machine which they have
created."

"But do not you think, M. Bloch, that if the nations
discover that their armies are too big to be used, they
will only fight with such manageable armies as they can
bring to the front, manoeuvre, feed, and supply with the
munitions of war?"

M. Bloch shook his head. "The whole drift and
tendency of modern tactics," he said, "is to bring up the
maximum number of men to the front in the shortest
possible loss of time and to hurl them in the largest
possible numbers upon the enemy's position. It is absolutely necessary, if you take the offensive, to have a
superior force. It is from a military point of view an
impossibility to attack a superior force with an inferior,
and the effect of the improvement in modern weapons has
been to still further enhance the necessity for superiority
of force in attacking. There will, therefore, be no
question of fighting with small armies. The largest
possible force will be brought to the front, and this effort
will inevitably result in the breakdown of the whole
machine.

"You must have the maximum ready to hand at
the beginning. Remember the fighting force of an army

weakens with every mile that it advances from its base Napoleon entered Russia with 400,000 men ; but although he had only fought one battle, he had only 130,000 men with him when he entered Moscow. The Germans, when they were in France, employed one-sixth of their infantry in covering their communications and defending their rear. This proportion is likely to be much increased in future wars. The opportunity for harassing the line of communications in the rear of an invading army has been enormously multiplied by the invention of smokeless powder. The *franc tireur* in the Franco-German war took his life in his hand, for the range of his gun was not very great in the first place, and in the second his where-abouts was promptly detected by the puff of smoke which showed his hiding-place. Now the whole line of com-munications will be exposed to dropping shots from marks-men who, from the security of thicket or hedge, will deal out sudden death without any tell-tale smoke to guide their exasperated and harassed enemy to the hiding-place.

"I have now dealt," said M. Bloch, "with the difficulties in the way of modern war, arising first from the immense improvement that has been wrought in the mechanism of slaughter, and secondly with the unmanageability of the immense masses of men who will be mobilised at the out-break of war. Let us now proceed to the third, and what to my mind constitutes far the most serious obstacle in the way of modern war—viz., the economic impossibility of waging war upon the scale on which it must be waged if it is waged at all.

"The first thing to be borne in mind is that the next war will be a long war. It was the declared opinion of Moltke that the altered conditions of warfare rendered it impossible to hope that any decisive result could be arrived at before two years at the least. The Franco-German war lasted seven months, but there is no hope of any similar war being terminated so rapidly. Of course this is assuming that war is to be terminated by fighting. In reality the war of the future, if ever it takes place, will not be fighting ; it will be terminated by famine."

" Why should wars be so excessively prolonged ? "

" Because all wars will of necessity partake of the character of siege operations. When we invaded Turkey in 1877 we were detained for months behind the impro- vised earthworks of Plevna. If war were to break out in Europe to-day, each combatant would find itself con- fronted, not by an isolated and improvised Plevna, but by carefully prepared and elaborately fortified networks of Plevnas. It is so on all frontiers. The system of defence has been elaborated with infinite skill and abso- lute disregard of financial considerations. Whether it will be a German army endeavouring to make its way into Moscow and St. Petersburg, or a Russian army striking at Berlin or at Vienna, or a German army invading France—in every case the invading army would find itself confronted by lines upon lines of fortresses and fortified camps, behind which would stand arrayed forces equal or superior in number to those which it could bring into the field against them. These fortresses would have to be taken or masked.

" Now it is calculated that to take a modern fortress adequately defended, even by superior forces, is an opera- tion which cannot be put through in less than one hundred and twenty days—that is, supposing that everything goes well with the assailants. Any reverse or any interruption of the siege operations would, of course, prolong this period. But it is not merely that each fortress would have to be reduced, but every field would more or less become an improvised fortified camp. Even when an army was defeated it would retreat slowly, throwing up earthworks, behind which it would maintain a harassing fire upon its pursuers; and the long line of invisible sharp-shooters, whose presence would not be revealed even by the tell-tale puff of smoke, would inevitably retard any rapid advance on the part of the victors. It is indeed maintained by many competent authorities that there is no prospect of the victorious army being able to drive the defeated forces from the field of battle so completely as to establish itself in possession of the spoils of war. The advantage is always with the defending force, and every mile that the assailants advance from their base would increase their difficulties and strengthen their opponents. Long and harassing siege operations in a war of blockade would wear out the patience and exhaust the resources of armies."

"But armies have stood long sieges before now," I objected.

"Yes," said M. Bloch, "in the past; but we are talking of the future. Do not forget that the wear and tear would be terrible, and the modern man is much less capable of bearing it than were his ancestors. The majority of the population tends more and more to gravitate to cities, and the city dweller is by no means so capable of lying out at nights in damp and exposed positions as the peasant. Even in comparatively rapid campaigns sickness and exhaustion slay many more than either cold steel or rifle-bullets. It is inevitable that this should be the case. In two weeks' time after the French army is mobilised, it is the expectation of the best authorities that they would have 100,000 men in hospital, even if never a shot had been fired."

"That I can well understand. I remember when reading Zola's 'La Debàcle' feeling that if the Germans had kept out of the way altogether and had simply made the French march after them hither and thither, the whole Napoleonic army would have gone to pieces before they ever came within firing distance of their foes."

"Yes," said M. Bloch. "The strain of marching is very heavy. Remember that it is not mere marching, but marching under heavy loads. No infantry soldier should carry more than one-third of his own weight; but instead of the average burden of the fully accoutred private being 52 lb. it is nearer 80 lb., with the result that the mere carrying of weight probably kills more than fall in battle. The proportion of those who die from disease and those who lose their lives as the consequence of wounds received in fighting is usually two or three to one. In the Franco-German war there were four times as many died from sickness and exhaustion as those who lost their lives in battle. In the Russo-Turkish war the proportion was as 16 to 44. In the recent Spanish war in Cuba the proportion was still greater. There were ten who died from disease for one who fell in action. The average mortality from sickness tends to increase with the prolongation of the campaign. Men can stand a short campaign, but when it is long it demoralises them, destroys the spirit of self-sacrifice which sustained them at the first in the opening weeks, and produces a thoroughly bad spirit which reacts upon their physical health. At present there is some regard paid to humanity, if only by the provision of ambulances, and the presence of hospital attendants, nurses, and doctors. But in the war of the future these humanities will go the wall."

"What!" I said, "do you think there will be no care for the wounded?"

"There will be practically no care for the wounded," said M. Bloch, "for it will be impossible to find adequate shelter for the Red Cross hospital tent or for the hospital orderlies. It will be impossible to take wounded men out of the zone of fire without exposing the Red Cross men to certain death. The consequence is they will be left to lie where they fall, and they may lie for days. Happy they will be if they are killed outright. Why, even in the last great war the provision for attendance on the wounded was shamefully inadequate. After Gravelotte there were for some time only four doctors to attend to 10,000 wounded men, and the state of things after Sadowa was horrible in the extreme. It is all very well to inveigh against this as inhumanity, but what are you to do when in the opinion of such a distinguished army physician as Dr. Billroth it would be necessary to have as many hospital attendants as there are soldiers in the fighting line? What is much more likely to be done is that the dying and the dead will be utilised as ramparts to strengthen the shelter trenches. This was actually done at the battle of Worth, where Dr. Porth, chief military physician of the Bavarian army, reported that he found in some places in the battlefield veritable ramparts built up of soldiers who had fallen by the side of their comrades, and in order to get them out of the way they had piled them one upon the top of the other, and had taken shelter behind their bodies. Some of these unfortunates built into this terrible rampart were only wounded, but the pressure of the superincumbent mass soon relieved them from their sufferings."

" What a horrible story ! "

" Yes," said M. Bloch ; " but I believe that war will be decided not by these things—not even by fighting-men at all, but by the factors of which they at present take far too little account."

" And what may those factors be ? " I asked.

" Primarily, the quality of toughness or capacity of endurance, of patience under privation, of stubbornness under reverse and disappointment. That element in the civil population will be, more than anything else, the deciding factor in modern war. The men at the front will very speedily be brought to a deadlock. Then will come the question as to how long the people at home will be able to keep on providing the men at the front with the necessaries of life. That is the first factor. The second factor, which perhaps might take precedence of the moral qualities, is whether or not it is physically possible for the population left behind to supply the armies in front with what they need to carry on the campaign."

" But have they not always done it in the past ? "

M. Bloch shook his head impatiently. " What is the use of talking about the past when you are dealing with an altogether new set of considerations ? Consider for one moment what nations were a hundred years ago and what they are to-day. In those days before railways, telegraphs, steamships, &c., were invented, each nation was more or less a homogeneous, self-contained, self-sufficing unit. Europe was built in a series of water-tight compartments. Each country sufficed for its own needs, grew its own wheat, fattened its own cattle, supplied itself for its own needs within its own frontiers. All that is

changed ; with the exception of Russia and Austria there
is not one country in Europe which is not absolutely
dependent for its beef and its bread supplies from beyond
the frontiers. You, of course, in England are absolutely
dependent upon supplies from over sea. But you are
only one degree worse off than Germany in that respect.
In 1895, if the Germans had been unable to obtain any
wheat except that which was grown in the Fatherland,
they would have lacked bread for one hundred and two
days out of the three hundred and sixty-five. Every year
the interdependence of nations upon each other for the
necessaries of life is greater than it ever was before.
Germany at present is dependent upon Russia for two
and a half months' supply of wheat in every year. That
supply would, of course, be immediately cut off if Russia
and Germany went to war ; and a similar state of things
prevails between other nations in relation to other com-
modities. Hence the first thing that war would do would
be to deprive the Powers that made it of all opportunity
of benefiting by the products of the nations against whom
they were fighting."

"Yes," I objected, "but the world is wide, and would
it not be possible to obtain food and to spare from neutral
nations ? "

"That assumes," said M. Bloch, "first that the
machinery of supply and distribution remains unaffected
by war. Secondly, that the capacity for paying for
supplies remains unimpaired. Neither of those things is
true. For you, of course, it is an absolute necessity
that you should be able to bring in food from beyond
the seas ; and possibly with the aid of your fleet you may
be able to do it, although I fear the rate of war premium
will materially enhance the cost of the cargoes. The

other nations are not so fortunate. It was proposed some time ago, I know, in Germany, that in case of war they should endeavour to replace the loss of Russian wheat by importing Indian wheat through the Suez Canal—an operation which in the face of the French and Russian cruisers might not be very easy of execution. But even supposing that it was possible to import food, who is to pay for it? And that is the final crux of the whole question."

"But," again I objected, "has the lack of money ever prevented nations going to war? I remember well when Lord Derby, in 1876, was quite confident that Russia would never go to war on behalf of Bulgaria because of the state of the Russian finances; but the Russo-Turkish war took place all the same, and there have been many great wars waged by nations which were bankrupt, and victories won by conquerors who had not a coin in their treasury."

"You are always appealing to precedents which do not apply. Modern society, which is organised on a credit basis, and modern war, which cannot be waged excepting at a ruinous expenditure, offer no points of analogy compared with those times of which you speak. Have you calculated for one moment what it costs to maintain a soldier as an efficient fighting man in the field of battle? The estimate of the best authorities is that you cannot feed him and keep him going under ten francs a day—say, eight shillings a day. Supposing that the Triple and Dual Alliance mobilise their armies, we should have at once confronting us an expenditure for the mere maintenance of troops under arms of £4,000,000 a day falling upon the five nations. That is to say, that in one year of war under modern conditions the Powers would spend

£1,460,000,000 sterling merely in feeding their soldiers, without reckoning all the other expenses that must be incurred in the course of the campaign. This figure is interesting as enabling us to compare the cost of modern wars with the cost of previous wars. Take all the wars that have been waged in Europe from the battle of Waterloo down to the end of the Russo-Turkish war, and the total expenditure does not amount to more than £1,250,000,000 sterling, a colossal burden no doubt, but one which is nearly £200,000,000 less than that which would be entailed by the mere victualling of the armies that would be set on foot in the war which we are supposed to be discussing. Could any of the five nations, even the richest, stand that strain ? "

" But could they not borrow and issue paper money ? "

" Very well," said M. Bloch, " they would try to do so, no doubt, but the immediate consequence of war would be to send securities all round down from 25 to 50 per cent., and in such a tumbling market it would be difficult to float loans. Recourse would therefore have to be had to forced loans and unconvertible paper money. We should be back to the days of the assignats, a temporary expedient which would aggravate the difficulties with which we have to deal. Prices, for instance, would go up enormously, and so the cost, 8s. a day, would be nearer 20s. if all food had to be paid for in depreciated currency. But, apart from the question of paying for the necessary supplies, it is a grave question whether such supplies could be produced, and if they could be produced, whether they could be distributed."

" What do you mean by ' distributed ' ? " I asked.

" Distributed ? " said M. Bloch. " Why, how are you to get the food into the mouths of the people who want it if you had (as you would have at the beginning of the war) taken over all the railways for military purposes? Even within the limits of Germany or of Russia there would be considerable difficulty in securing the transit of food-stuffs in war time, not merely to the camps, but to the great industrial centres. You do not seem to realise the extent to which the world has been changed by the modern industrial system. Down to the end of the last century the enormous majority of the population lived in their own fields, grew their own food, and each farm was a little granary. It was with individuals as it was with nations, and each homestead was a self-contained, self-providing unit. But nowadays all is changed. You have great industrial centres which produce absolutely nothing which human beings can eat. How much, for instance, do you grow in the metropolitan area for the feeding of London? Everything has to be brought by rail or by water to your markets. So it is more or less all over the Continent, especially in Germany and France. Now it so happens (and in this I am touching upon the political side of the question) that those districts which produce least food yield more Socialists to the acre than any other part of the country. It is those districts, rife with all elements of political discontent, which would be the first to feel the pinch of high prices and of lack of food. But this is a matter on which we will speak later on."

"But do you think," I said, "that the railways would be so monopolised by the military authorities that they could not distribute provisions throughout the country?"

"No," said M. Bloch. "It is not merely that they would be monopolised by their military authorities, but that they would be disorganised by the mobilisation of troops. You forget that the whole machinery of distribution and of production would be thrown out of gear by mobilisation ; and this brings me to the second point upon which I insist—viz., the impossibility of producing the food. At the present moment Germany, for instance, just manages to produce sufficient food to feed her own population, with the aid of imports from abroad, for which she is able to pay by the proceeds of her own industry. But in the case of war with Russia she would not be able to buy two and a half months' supply of wheat from Russia, and therefore would have to pay much more for a similar supply of food in the neutral markets, providing she could obtain it. But she would have to buy much more than two and a half months' from Russia, because the nine months' corn which she produces at present is the product of the whole labour of all her able-bodied agricultural population ; and how they work you in England do not quite realise. Do you know, for instance, that after the ' Büsstag,' or day of penitence and prayer, at the beginning of what we call the farmers' year or summer season, the whole German agricultural population in some districts work unremittingly fifteen hours a day seven days a week, without any cessation, without Sundays or holidays, until the harvest is gathered in ; and even with all that unremitting toil they are only able to produce nine months' supply of grain. When you have mobilised the whole German army, you will diminish at least by half the strong hands available for labour in the field. In Russia we should not, of course, be in any such difficulty, and in the scrupulous observance of Sunday we have a reserve which would enable us to recoup ourselves for the loss of agricultural labour. We should lose, for instance, 17 per cent. of our peasants ; but if those who were left worked on Sunday, in addition to weekdays, we should just be able to make up for the loss of the men who were taken to war.   Germany has no such reserves, nor France ; and hence it is that, speaking as a political economist, I feel extremely doubtful as to whether it would be possible for either Germany or France to feed their own population, to say nothing of their own soldiers, when once the whole machine of agricultural production had been broken up by the mobilisation *en masse* of the whole population."

"But has this point never been considered by the sovereigns and statesmen of Europe ? " I inquired.

"You know," replied M. Bloch, " how it is with human beings.   We shall all die, but how few care to think of death ?   It is one of the things inevitable which no one can alter by taking thought.   So it is with this question. War once being regarded as unavoidable, the rulers shut their eyes to its consequences.   Only once in recent history do I remember any attempt on the part of a European Government gravely to calculate the economic consequences of war under modern conditions.   It was when. M. Burdeau was in the French Ministry.   He appointed a committee of economists for the purpose of ascertaining how the social organism would continue to function in a time of war, how from day to day their bread would be given to the French population.   But no sooner had he begun his investigation than a strong objection was raised by the military authorities, and out of deference to their protests the inquiry was indefinitely suspended.   Hence we are going forward blindfold, preparing all the while for a war without recognising the fact that the very fundamental first condition of being able to wage it does not exist.   You might as well prepare for a naval war without being sure that you have a sea in which your ships can float as to continue to make preparations for a land war unless you have secured in advance the means by which your population shall live. Every great State would in time of war be in the position of a besieged city, and the factor which always decides sieges is the factor which will decide the modern war. Your soldiers may fight as they please ; the ultimate decision is in the hands of *famine*."

"Well, it is an old saying that 'armies always march upon their bellies,'" said I. "'Hunger is more terrible than iron, and the want of food destroys more armies than battles,' was a saying of the first Napoleon, which holds good to-day."

"But," interrupted M. Bloch, "I am not speaking so much of the armies, I am speaking of the population that is behind the armies, which far outnumbers the armies and which is apt to control the policy of which the armies are but the executive instrument. How long do you think the populations of Paris or of Berlin or of the great manufacturing districts in Germany would stand the doubling of the price of their food, accompanied, as it would be, by a great stagnation of industry and all the feverish uncertainty and excitement of war ?

"What is the one characteristic of modern Europe ? Is it not the growth of nervousness and a lack of phlegmatic endurance, of stoical apathy ? The modern European feels more keenly and is much more excitable and impressionable than his forefathers. Upon this highly excitable, sensitive population you are going to inflict the miseries of hunger and all the horrors of war. At the same time you will enormously increase their taxes, and at the same time also you will expose your governing and directing classes to more than decimation at the hands of the enemy's sharp-

d

shooters. How long do you think your social fabric will remain stable under such circumstances ? Believe me, the more the ultimate political and social consequences of the modern war are calmly contemplated, the more clearly will it be evident that if war is possible it is only possible, as I said before, at the price of suicide."

"From which, therefore, it follows, in your opinion, M. Bloch, that the Peace Conference has not so much to discuss the question of peace as to inquire into whether or not war is possible ? "

" A committee of experts, chosen from the ablest representatives of the Powers sent to the Hague," replied M. Bloch, "would have very little difficulty in coming to a conclusion upon the facts which I have just set forth in my book. Those experts might be soldiers and political economists, or the inquiry might be divided into two heads, and the two questions relegated to different committees of specialists. I am quite sure that, as the result of such a dispassionate international investigation into the altered conditions of the problem, they could only arrive at one conclusion—viz., that the day when nations could hope to settle their disputes by appealing to the arbitrament of war has gone by : first, because from that tribunal no definite decision can speedily be secured ; and secondly, the costs of the process are ruinous to both the suitors."

" It is rather a happy idea, that of yours, M. Bloch," said I, "that of the last Court of Appeal of nations having broken down by the elaboration of its own procedure, the excessive costliness of the trial, and, what is much more serious than anything else, the impossibility of securing a definite verdict. Hitherto the great argument in favour of war is that it has been a tribunal capable of giving unmistakably a decision from which there was no appeal."

"Whereas, according to my contention," said M. Bloch, "war has become a tribunal which by the very perfection of its own processes and the costliness of its methods can no longer render a decision of any kind. It may ruin the suitors, but the verdict is liable to be indefinitely postponed.

"Therefore the ultimate Court of Appeal having broken down," I said, "it is necessary to constitute another, whose proceedings would not be absolutely inconsistent with economic necessity or with the urgent need for prompt and definite decision. But if this be admitted, what immense world-wide consequences would flow from such a decision."

"Yes," said M. Bloch, "the nations would no longer go on wasting £250,000,000 sterling every year in preparing to wage a war which can only be waged at the price of suicide, that is to say, which cannot be waged at all, for no nation willingly commits suicide. Then we may hope for some active effort to be made in the direction of ameliorating the condition of the people. The fund liberated from the war-chest of the world could work marvels if it were utilised in the education of the people. At present, as you will see from the tables which I have compiled in my book, the proportion of money spent on education compared with that spent on war is very small. In Russia, for instance, we have an immense deal to do in that direction. In some provinces no fewer than 90 per cent. of the recruits are illiterate. In fact, as you will see from what I have written, I have been as much attracted to this subject from the desire to improve the condition of the people as from any other source. Hence my book took in part the shape of an investigation of the moral, social, and material conditions in which the masses of the Russian peasants pass their lives. It is a painful picture, and one that cannot fail profoundly to touch the hearts of all those who have followed the results of my investigation. The condition of the mass of the people in every country leaves much to be desired, but especially is this the case in my own country, where the resources of civilisation have hardly been drawn upon for the improvement of the condition of the peasants."

" Yet, M. Bloch, I think I gather from you that Russia was better able to support a war than more highly organised nations."

" You are quite right," said M. Bloch. " It is true that Russia can, perhaps better than all other countries, contemplate the dangers or impossibilities of modern war ; but that is precisely because she is not so highly organised and so advanced or developed in civilisation as her neighbours. Russia is the only country in Europe which produces sufficient food for her own people. She is not only able to produce enough grain to feed her own people, but she exports at present four millions of tons every year. A war which stopped the export trade would simply place this immense mass of food at the disposal of our own people, who would be more in danger of suffering from a plethora of food than from a scarcity. But nevertheless, although this is the case, the very backwardness of Russia renders it more important that she should avoid exposing her nascent civilisation to the tremendous strain of a great war. Practically we may be invulnerable, but if, when having beaten back our invaders, we were to endeavour in turn to carry the war across our frontiers, we should find ourselves confronted by the same difficulties which make offensive war increasingly difficult, not to say impossible. Neither is there any conceivable territorial or political result attainable by force of arms here or in Asia which would be any adequate compensation for the sacrifices which even a victorious war would entail."

"All this may be true, but nations do not always count the cost before going to war."

"No," said M. Bloch ; "if they did, they would very seldom go to war. Take, for instance, the civil war in the United States of America. According to some calculations it would have cost the United States four milliards of francs, that is to say £160,000,000 sterling, to have bought up all their slaves at £200 a head, and emancipated them. Instead of taking that method of solving a dangerous and delicate problem, they appealed to the sword, with the result that it is estimated that the war occasioned the country losses of one kind and another amounting to twenty-five milliards of francs, or £1,000,000,000 sterling, to say nothing of all the bloodshed and misery entailed by that war. The cost of emancipation thus ciphered out at £1200 a head per slave instead of £200 per head, at which the bargain could easily have been arranged. The economic condition of our peasants in many of our provinces," continued M. Bloch, "is heartrending. Their ignorance, their innocence, their simplicity, render them an easy prey to money-lenders, who have in many cases succeeded in establishing a veritable system of slave labour."

"How could that be ? " I asked. "The serfs were emancipated in 1861."

"Yes," said M. Bloch, "they were emancipated, but their emancipation without education left them an easy prey to the Kulaks, who advance money upon their labour. A peasant, for instance, has to pay his taxes, say, in winter time, and the Kulak will advance the twenty or thirty roubles which he may have to pay in return for what is called his 'summer labour.' The price of labour in Russia in summer is twice or thrice as much as it is in winter. The Kulak buys the summer labour at the winter rates, and then having purchased in advance the summer labour of the unfortunate peasant, he collects his chattels in droves and farms them out wherever he can dispose of them. It is veritable slavery. But even this is less terrible than that which can be witnessed in some provinces, where parents sell their children to speculators, who buy them up and send them to St. Petersburg and Moscow as calves are sent to market, where they are sold out for a term of years as apprentices to those who have no scruples against securing cheap labour on those terms.

"No one who has seen anything of the squalor and wretchedness, the struggle with fever and famine, in the rural districts of Russia, especially when there has been a failure of harvest, can be other than passionate to divert for the benefit of the people some of the immense volume of wealth that is spent in preparing for this impossible war. The children of most Russian peasants come into the world almost like brute beasts, without any medical or skilled attendance at childbirth, and they are brought up hard in a way that fortunately you know little of in wealthy England. Can you imagine, for instance," said M. Bloch, speaking with great fervour and feeling, "the way in which infants are left inside the home of most Russian peasants, whose mothers have to leave them to labour in the fields? The child is left alone to roll about the earthen floor of the hut, and as it will cry for hunger, poultices of chewed black bread are tied round its hands and feet, so that the little creature may have something to suck at until its mother comes back from the fields. At every stage in life you find the same deplorable lack of what more prosperous nations regard as indispensable to human existence. In some provinces we have only thirty-seven doctors per million inhabitants, and as for nurses, school-masters, and other agents of civilisation, there are whole vast tracts in which they are absolutely unknown. All this makes our population hardy, no doubt—those who survive ; but the infant mortality is frightful, and the life which the survivors lead is very hard and sometimes very terrible."

" The contrasts between the vital statistics of Russia and of France are, I suppose, about as wide as could be imagined."

" Yes," said M. Bloch. " But although the French system of limiting the family and keeping infant mortality down to a minimum has some great advantages, it has great disadvantages. In a limited family much greater pains are taken to preserve the life of the sickly children. Hence, instead of allowing them to be eliminated by natural process, whereby the race would be preserved from deterioration, they are sedulously kept alive, and the vitality of the nation is thereby diminished. In other respects our Russian people are very different from what you imagine. For instance, it may surprise you, but it is undoubtedly true, that the amount of spirit consumed by our people is very much less per head than that which is drunk in England, and also that the number of illegitimate births in Russia is lower per thousand than in an other country in Europe. This is due to the prevalence of early marriages, for our people marry so early that when our young men are taken for the army from 30 to 60 per cent. are married before they enter the ranks. You may smile," said M. Bloch, " at me for thinking that those questions must be considered in a discussion of the future war ; but it is the moral stamina of a population which will ultimately decide its survival, and I therefore could not exclude the discussion of all the elements which contribute to the well-being of a population in endeavouring to forecast the future of war."

"Now, M. Bloch, let us turn to another subject. We have talked hitherto about armies, and only about armies. What is your idea about navies ? "

" My idea about a navy," said M. Bloch, " is that unless you have a supreme navy, it is not worth while having one at all, and that a navy that is not supreme is only a hostage in the hands of the Power whose fleet is supreme. Hence, it seems to me that for Russia to spend millions in the endeavour to create a deep-sea fleet of sea-going battleships is a great mistake. The money had much better be used for other purposes."

"What ! " said I, "then, do you not think that Russia needs a navy ? "

"A navy, yes," said M. Bloch, "a navy for coast defence, perhaps, and also cruisers, but a fighting fleet of battleships, no. It is a folly to attempt to create such a navy, and the sooner that is recognised the better."

"But," I persisted, "do you not agree with Captain Mahan in thinking that sea-power is the dominant factor in the destiny of nations ? "

"Do not let us theorise; let us look at facts," said M. Bloch. "What I see very plainly is that the navy may be almost ignored as a vital factor in a war to the death between Russia and any of her neighbours. Suppose, for instance, that we had a war with Germany. What would be the good of our fleet ? Suppose that it is inferior to that of Germany, it will be either captured, or shut up in harbour, unable to go out. If it is superior to that of Germany, what better are we? Here we have history to guide us. We cannot hope to have such an unquestioned superiority at sea over the Germans as the French had in the war of 1870; but what use was the naval supremacy of France to the French in their death-grapple with the Germans? Why, so far from finding them useful, they absolutely laid their ironclads up in harbour and sent their crews to Paris to assist in the defence of the capital—and they did right. Germany was striking at the heart of France when she struck at Paris, and no amount of superiority over the German fleet on the part of the French could be counted for a moment as a set-off against the loss of their capital. So it will always be."

"But," I objected, "could the German fleet not be utilised for the purpose of landing an expedition on the Russian coast?"

"No doubt," said M. Bloch, "it might. But here again I may quote Count Moltke. When, in 1870, we were discussing the possibility of a French expedition to the shores of the Baltic, Moltke declared that, so far from regarding such an expedition with alarm, he would rather welcome it, because any diversion of French forces from the point where the decisive blow must be delivered would increase the German chances of success. Hence, if the Germans were to send an expeditionary force to Russian waters, it would only represent the subtraction of so many fighting men from the seat of war, where the real issue of the campaign would be decided. No; Russia would have no reason to fear any serious attack from the sea. That being so, what is the use of wasting all our resources upon ironclads which we could not use?

It would have been much better to have gone on piling up expenditure on our army much more rapidly than we have upon our fleet. In 1876 we spent twenty-seven million roubles on the navy, and twenty years later we were spending sixty-seven millions, so that the naval expenditure had more than doubled, while the expenditure on the army had only increased fifty per cent."

" Do you not think that a German, British, or Japanese fleet might seriously injure Russia by bombarding the coast towns ? "

" No," said M. Bloch. " Such coast towns as we have, and they are not many, are for the most part well defended, too well defended to be seriously attacked by an enemy's fleet. The experience of Crete does not increase our dread of the bombarding ironclad as a method likely to affect the issues of a campaign. Why, is it not true that the international fleet on one occasion fired 70 shells and only killed three men and wounded 15 ? "

" And what about the protection of your commerce, M. Bloch ? "

" The protection of our commerce would have to be undertaken (if undertaken at all) by cruisers and not by battleships. Besides, there should be some regard paid to the value of the thing protected, and the insurance which you pay for it. At this moment our oversea mercantile marine is small, so small compared with that of England that, although you are spending twice as much on your navy as we do, your naval insurance rate (if we may so call it) only amounts to 16 francs per ton of merchant shipping, whereas with us the rate is as high as 130 francs ; or if it is reckoned by a percentage upon the trade, our naval expenditure is twice as high as yours. And to what purpose ? "

" But, M. Bloch, supposing that our fleet is inferior in strength to the German fleet, and that it is wiped off the face of the sea. What then ? "

" What then ? " said M. Bloch. " Why, we shall just be in the position that the Italians were in when they lost their fleet at Lissa to the Austrians. But what effect had that decisive naval victory upon the fortunes of the campaign ? The fate of Austria was sealed by the battle of Sadowa, and all naval losses which we might incur would naturally be charged for in the indemnity which we should impose upon our defeated enemy if we came off victorious, and if we were beaten on land our defeat at sea would not be a material aggravation of our position."

" But, M. Bloch, do not you think that you need a strong fleet in order to keep your channels of trade open ? "

" I do not believe," said M. Bloch, " that you can keep your channels of trade open, even with the strongest fleet. I grant that if you have a supreme fleet, you may at least have a chance of keeping the trade routes open, but if you have not a supreme fleet (and for Russia this is out of the question) you can do nothing, and Russia, fortunately being self-contained and self-supporting, could manage to subsist better, if her oversea trade were cut off, than any other country."

" Then how would you apply your reasoning to England ? "

" England," said M. Bloch, " is in a different category from all the other nations. You only grow enough bread in your own country to feed your people for three months in the year. If you do not command the seas, if you cannot bring to your markets the food of the world, you

are in the position of a huge beleaguered fortress with
only three months' rations for the whole people. If you
ask my opinion, I tell you frankly that I do not think
your position is very enviable, not because of any danger
from invasion, for I recognise the superiority of your fleet,
but because it seems to me that any nation is in a very
precarious position which has to depend for so much of
its food upon countries across the sea. A single cruiser
let loose upon one of your great trade routes would send
up the price of provisions enormously, and although no
one could hope to blockade the English ports, any interruption in the supply of raw material, any interference
with the stream of food products which are indispensable
for the sustenance of your people, would endanger you
far more than the loss of a pitched battle.

"It is true that you are prosperous ; but there are many
elements in your population the material condition of
which leaves much to be desired, and with the stress and
strain of industrial stagnation, caused by the closing of
markets abroad and the rise in the price of food which
would be inevitable under any circumstances, you might
have as considerable internal difficulties as any of those
which threaten your neighbours. But, there again, if
(which God forbid) England should find herself at war,
the factor which will decide the issue will not be the
decisive battle ; it will be pressure of want, the lack of
food, in short, the economic results which must inevitably
follow any great war in the present complex state of
human civilisation.

"In short," said M. Bloch, "I regard the economic
factor as the dominant and decisive element in the matter.
You cannot fight unless you can eat, and at the present
moment you cannot feed your people and wage a great

war. To a certain extent this is already recognised, so much so that there are a few general principles that it is worth while mentioning. First, you may take it for granted that the great war, if it ever breaks out, will not take place until after the harvest has been gathered. To mobilise in spring, or in early summer, would bring starvation too closely home to the population for any statesman to think of it. Secondly, whenever there is a bad harvest you may be sure there will be no war. Even with a full granary it will be very difficult for any nation to feed its troops, to say nothing of its home population. With a bad harvest it would be impossible. Hence, if ever you should see a rapid buying-up of bread-stuffs on the part of any nation, you may feel sure that there is danger ahead ; but so long as there is no attempt made to secure reserve supplies of grain, you may regard with comparative equanimity the menaces of war."

"Then, on the whole, you are hopeful concerning the future, M. Bloch ? "

"Yes," said he ; "hopeful with the hope that is born not of fantasy or of Utopian dreaming, but from the painstaking examination of hard, disagreeable facts. The soldier is going down and the economist is going up. There is no doubt of it. Humanity has progressed beyond the stage in which war can any longer be regarded as a possible Court of Appeal. Even military service has lost much of its fascination. At one time war appealed to the imagination of man, and the poets and painters found no theme so tempting as depicting the heroism of the individual warrior, whose courage and might often turned the tide of battle and decided the destiny of nations. All that has long gone by the board. War has become more and more a matter of mechanical arrangement. Modern battles will be decided, so far as they can be decided at all, by men lying in improvised ditches which they have scooped out to protect themselves from the fire of a distant and invisible enemy. All the pomp and circumstance of glorious war disappeared when smokeless powder was invented. As a profession militarism is becoming less and less attractive. There is neither booty to be gained, nor promotion, with an ever increasing certainty of a disagreeable death, should war ever take place."

"The old toast in the British Army used to be," I said, "'Bloody war and quick promotion.'"

"Yes," said M. Bloch, "as long as bloody war only killed out a certain percentage it meant more rapid promotion for the rest, but if it kills out too many the attraction fails, for there is no promotion to a dead man. Side by side with the drying up of the attractiveness of a military career there has gone on an increasing agitation against the whole system, an agitation which finds its most extreme exponents among the Socialists, whose chief stock-in-trade is to dwell upon the waste of industrial resources caused by the present organisation of society on a competitive basis, which they maintain naturally and necessarily results in the excessive burdens of our armed peace. What the Governments will all come to see soon more or less clearly is that if they persist in squandering the resources of their people in order to prepare for a war which has already become impossible without suicide, they will only be preparing the triumph of the socialist revolution."

AUTHOR'S PREFACE

NATURAL philosophers declare that the atmosphere reveals at times the presence of a certain so-called cosmic dust. It influences the change of colours in the sky, it colours the sunlight with a bloody line, it penetrates our dwellings and our lungs, acts injuriously upon living organisms, and, falling even upon the summits of hills, leaves its traces upon their mantles of virgin snow.

In the public and private life of modern Europe something of the same kind reveals itself. A presentiment is felt that the present incessant growth of armaments must either call forth a war, ruinous both for conqueror and for conquered, and ending perhaps in general anarchy, or reduce the people to the most lamentable condition.

Is this unquiet state of mind the consequence of a mistaken or sickly condition of the nervous system of the modern man? Or is it justified by possible contingencies?

Such questions cannot be answered categorically. All would desire that the dangers caused by armaments were but a symptom which time will destroy. But even an unanimous desire cannot have the power to change the great concatenation of circumstances which are the cause of armaments, until the time shall come when, in the words of Von Thünen, the interests of nations and the interests of humanity shall cease to contend with one another, and culture shall have awakened a sense of the solidarity of the interests of all.

Such a state of affairs is unhappily still distant. It is true that the ruinousness of war under modern conditions is apparent to all. But this gives no sufficient guarantee that war will not break forth suddenly, even in opposition to the wishes of those who take part in it. Involuntarily we call to mind the words of the great Bacon, that " in the vanity of the world a greater field of action is open for folly than for reason, and frivolity always enjoys more influence than judgment." To-day these words are even more apposite than in the past. For Reason itself it is harder than before to find a path in the field of circumstances which change for ever. The speed with which relations change is a characteristic feature of our time. In modern times a few years see greater changes in the material and moral condition of masses than formerly took place in the course of centuries. This greater mobility of contemporary life is the consequence of better education, the activity of parliaments, of associations, and of the press, and the influence of improved communications. Under such influences the peoples of the world live lives not only their own, but the lives of others also ; intellectual triumphs, economic progress, materialised among one people, react at once on the condition of others ; the intellectual outlook widens as we ascend, as the seascape widens from a hill, and, like the sea, the whole world of culture drifts and fluctuates eternally.

Every change in conditions or disposition is affirmed only after a struggle of elements. An analysis of the history of mankind shows that from the year 1496 B.C. to the year 1861 of our era, that is, in a cycle of 3357 years, were but 227 years of peace and 3130 years of war : in other words, were thirteen years of war for every year of peace. Considered thus, the history of the lives of peoples presents a picture of uninterrupted struggle. War, it would appear, is a normal attribute to human life.

The position now has changed in much, but still the new continues to contend with the

e

remnants of the old.   The old order has changed
and given place to the new.   Siéyes compared
the old order of things with a pyramid standing
upon its apex, declaring that it must be given a
more natural position and placed upon its base.
This demand has been fulfilled in this sense, that
the edifice of state has been placed upon foundations incomparably wider than before, affirmed on
the rights and wills of millions of men, the so-
named middle order of society.

It is natural that the greater the number of
voices influencing the course of affairs the more
complex is the sum of interests to be considered.
The economic revolution caused by the application of steam has been the cause of entirely new
and unexpected conditions between the different
countries of the world and between the classes
inhabiting them, enriching and strengthening
some, impoverishing and weakening others, in
measure as the new conditions permitted to each
participation in the new distribution of revenues,
capital, and influence.

With the innumerable voices which are now
bound up in our public opinion, and the many
different representatives of its interests, naturally
appear very different views on militarism and its
object, war.   The propertied classes, in particular
those whose importance and condition was

established during the former distribution of power and former methods of acquisition, precisely those classes whom we call Conservatives, are inclined to confuse even the intellectual movement against militarism with aspirations for the subversion of social order. In this is sometimes given, they attribute, too great an importance to single and transitory phenomena, while no sufficient attention is turned·on the dangerous fermentation of minds awakened by the present and constantly growing burdens of militarism.

On the other hand, agitators, seeking influence on the minds of the masses, having deduced from the new conditions with recklessness and even intentional misrepresentation the most extreme conclusions, deny all existing rights, and promise to the masses more than the most perfect institutions could give them. In striving to arouse the masses against militarism such agitators unceremoniously ascribe to every thinker who does not share their views selfish impulses, although in reality he may be following sincere convictions.

And although the masses are slow to surrender themselves to abstract reasoning, and act usually only under the influence of passion or disaster, there can be no doubt that this agitation, ceaselessly carried on in parliaments, on platforms, and in the press, penetrates more and more deeply

the people, and awakens in it those feelings which
in the midst of the disasters called forth by war
might easily lead them to action. The evil of
militarism serves to-day as the chief instrument of
the activity of agitators, and a tangible object for
attack, while in reality these agitators strive not
only for the suppression of militarism, but for the
destruction of the whole social order.

With such a position of affairs—that is, on the
one hand, the ruinous competition in constantly
increasing armaments, and, on the other, the
social danger for all which grows under a general·
burden — it is necessary that influential and
educated men should seriously attempt to give
themselves a clear account of the effect of war
under modern conditions; whether it will be
possible to realise the aims of war, and whether
the extermination of millions of men will not be
wholly without result.

If, after consideration of all circumstances, we
answer ourselves, "War with such conditions is
impossible; armies could not sustain those cata-
clysms which a future war would call forth; the
civil population could not bear the famine and
interruption of industry," then we might ask the
general question : "Why do the peoples more
and more exhaust their strength in accumulating
means of destruction which are valueless even to

accomplish the ends for which they are prepared?"

It is very natural, that even a long time ago, in many Western European countries, in all ranks of society, many attempts have been made, partly theoretical and partly practical, to eliminate war from the future history of humanity. Philosophers and philanthropists, statesmen and revolutionaries, poets and artists, parliaments and congresses, more strongly and strongly every day insist upon the necessity of avoiding the bloodshed and disasters of war.

A time was when it seemed protests against war were assuming practical importance. But the desire for revenge awakened by the events of 1870 turned the disposition of peoples in another direction. Nevertheless the idea remains and continues to operate on minds. The voices of scholars and the efforts of philanthropists directed against war naturally found an echo among the lower orders of populations. In the twilight of imperfect knowledge fantastic visions appeared, of which agitators took advantage. This agitation increased every year.

In recent times war has become even more terrible than before in consequence of perfected weapons of destruction and systems of equipment and training utterly unknown in the past. What is graver still, the immensity of armies and the training of soldiers in entrenchment must call forth difficulties in provisioning and defence from climatic conditions.

It is true that certain military authors think that the bloodshed of the battlefield will be decreased in consequence of the greater distance between the combatants, that attacks by cavalry and with the bayonet are improbable in the present conditions of firearms, while retreat will be facilitated for a defeated army. But, even admitting this, which is by no means proved, there can be no doubt that with modern firearms the impression which battle makes on armies will be incomparably greater than before, while smokeless powder will change even the nature of these impressions. Infantry and artillery fire will have unprecedented force, while aid to the wounded will be made more difficult by the great range both of small-arms and of artillery. Smoke will no longer conceal from the survivors the terrible consequences of the battle, and every advance will be made with full appreciation of the probabilities of extermination. From this, and from the fact that the mass of soldiers will have but recently been called from the field, the factory, and the workshop, it will appear that even the psychical conditions of war have changed. Thus in the armies of Western states the agitation against war may extend even so far as the materialisation of socialistic theories subverting the bases of monarchies.

The thought of those convulsions which will be called forth by a war, and of the terrible means prepared for it, will hinder military enterprise, notwithstanding the passionate relations of the people to some of the questions in dispute among them. But, on the other hand, the present conditions cannot continue to exist for ever. The peoples groan under the burdens of militarism. Europe is ever confronted with the necessity of drawing from the productive forces of the peoples new and new millions for military purposes. Hardly was the small-calibre rifle adopted when invention made a new advance, and there can be no doubt that soon the Great Powers will be compelled to adopt a weapon of still smaller calibre with double the present energy, allowing soldiers to carry a greater number of cartridges. At the same time we see in France and Germany preparation of new artillery to turn to the best advantage the new smokeless powder. Millions are expended on the construction of new battleships and cruisers. But every year brings such radical improvements in guns, in speed, and in coal-carrying capacity that vessels hardly launched

are obsolete, and others must be built to replace
them.   In view of what we see in Germany,
Italy, and Austria, we are compelled to ask, Can
the present incessant demands for money from
Parliament for armaments continue for ever
without social outbreaks?   And will not the
present difficulty of carrying on war at last be
replaced by an absolute impossibility, at least in
those countries where high culture has increased
the value of the life of every citizen?   Thus, in
the war of the future will appear not only quanti-
tative differences in the number of armies but
also qualitative differences which may have immense importance.

But what is still graver are the economic and
social convulsions which war will call forth in
consequence of the summons under the flag of
almost the whole male population, the interruption of maritime communications, the stagnation
in industry and trade, the increase in the price of
the necessaries of life, and the destruction of
credit.   Will these convulsions not be so great
that governments will find it impossible in the
course of time indicated by military specialists as
the probable duration of war to acquire means for
maintaining their armies, satisfy the requirements
of budgets, and at the same time feed the destitute remainder of the civil population?

Within the last twenty-five years such changes have taken place in the very nature of military operations that the future war will in no way be like its predecessors. In consequence of the adoption of improved artillery, explosive shells, and small-arms which allow the soldier to carry an immense number of cartridges, in consequence of the absence of concealing smoke, in consequence of the immense proportions which military operations must take as a result of the vastness of armies, such unquestioned authorities on military affairs as Moltke and Leer and many other eminent military writers declare that a future war will last many years.

But with modern political, social, and economic conditions it would be strange if there did not arise in England, Italy, Austria, Russia, Germany, and France—in one country from one reason, in another from another—factors which will disarrange the apparatus of war and prevent its continuance before the ends desired shall have been attained. This is a question of the first gravity, yet military writers entirely ignore it, attending only to the technical side of war.

In consequence of alliances concluded, all plans of activity are founded on the combined operations of allied armies. What will happen to combinations founded on united action when one

or another of the allies is compelled to cease
operations through insufficient means for resisting
the social influences of war?

Thus we find that military questions are bound
up with questions of economy. But military
writers look on the future war only from the
point of view of attaining certain objects by
destroying the armies of the enemy; the economic
and social consequences of war, if they are considered at all, are considered only as secondary
objects. Even economists, in consequence of the
difficulty of such a question, have made no single
investigation resulting in a complete picture of
the consequences of war. But this is in no way
surprising.

Without acquaintance with the technicalities of
warfare it is impossible to understand what will
be its precise conditions, or to define the limits
where the operation of defined laws will cease
and accidental phenomena appear. A result could
only be obtained by careful study of the very
nature of war in all its phenomena. Twenty
years ago such a task would have been comparatively easy. But the last two decades have
witnessed immense changes equal to revolutions.
First of all a fundamental change has taken place
in the very elements which take part in war and
from which its course depends. In a future war

on the field of battle, instead of professional soldiers, will appear whole peoples with all their peculiar virtues and failings.

A full appreciation of the conditions of a future war is all the more difficult since on the one hand new methods of attack and defence, as yet insufficiently tested, will be employed, and, on the other hand, because former wars were carried on by means of long-service professional soldiers. But not only will a future war take the character of a struggle of whole nations living a wide and complex life, with military problems corresponding in complexity, but the arms and apparatus of destruction are the very finest result of the inventiveness and creative activity of mankind.

The elements contending in a future war will be all the moral and intellectual resources of nations, all the forces of modern civilisation, all technical improvements, feelings, characters, minds and wills—the combined fruit of the culture of the civilized world. It is thus that this question demands the attention of all society. In Western states, especially from the adoption of conscription, interest in military affairs has spread through all ranks of society.

Reasoning on the basis of future wars, military writers declare that the chief elements of warfare, although only in their general character, must be made known to the population, which in the event of war constitutes the army, and from whose activity depends the issue of campaigns. It is not enough that officers and soldiers actually on service know what they are to meet in a future war. In the ranks of armies in time of war will appear an immense proportion of officers and men from the reserves, who for many years have taken no part in military exercises. As a consequence of this, in every state appear popular compositions with the object of informing the public of the technique of modern war, all, almost without exception, neglecting the economic side of the question. Some prejudge a future war from the example of history. Such neglect, as a rule, the improvement of weapons and the increased complexity of strategy and tactics. Others, well informed as to the improvement of weapons, but neglecting inevitable conclusions, assume that war will last but a short time, and therefore pay no attention to the financial and economic perturbation which it will cause or its effects on the moral condition of the people.

The late General Fadeleff very justly pointed out the danger arising from such a state of affairs. " The opinion of the people of their strength has immense influence on the course of politics ; this opinion is often frivolous and unfounded, though

from it may depend the destiny of nations. Yet
it is generally agreed that even the elements of
military affairs constitute a speciality which must
remain unknown by the public. But when the
moment comes to express its opinion on war and
peace, to balance the chances of success, it may
be assumed that of ten military specialists whose
authority is accepted nine will adopt the opinions
of the social medium in which they live. Thus a
public, entirely ignorant of military questions,
often becomes the deciding factor in decision.
To free oneself from the influence of public
opinion in such matters is impossible." It was
with the object of making accessible in some
degree information accumulated on all matters
directly or indirectly connected with war that the
present work was undertaken, of which this
volume is but an abridgment.

It is but a slight service to diagnose an illness
and pronounce it incurable. The position of the
European world, the organic strength of which is
wasted, on the one hand, in the sacrifice of
millions on preparations for war, and, on the
other, in a destructive agitation which finds in
militarism its apology and a fit instrument for
acting on the minds of the people, must be admitted to be abnormal and even sickly. Is it
possible that there can be no recovery from this?

We are deeply persuaded that a means of recovery exists if the European states would but set themselves the question—in what will result these armaments and this exhaustion, what will be the nature of a future war, can resource be had to war even now for the decision of questions in dispute, and is it possible to conceive the settlement of such questions by means of the cataclysm which, with modern means of destruction, a war between five Great Powers with ten millions of soldiers would cause?

Delay in the practical settlement of this question is impossible. And when a settlement is arrived at it will be shown that for twenty, forty years millions have been wasted yearly on fruitless armaments which cannot be employed, and by means of which the decision of international disputes is inconceivable. But then it will be too late; then such immense losses will have been sustained that Europe generally will be in a worse position than Italy to-day. Then, instead of the dangers of international war, other threatening symptoms will have appeared.

That war will become impossible in time—this is indicated by all. Its apparatus grows more rapidly than the productiveness of European states, and preparations will continue to swallow more and more of the in ome of peoples. Meantime the relations of the nations become closer and closer, their interdependence more plain, and their solidarity in any great convulsion will constantly grow.

That war will finally become impracticable is apparent. The question is more apposite—when will the recognition of this inevitable truth be spread among European governments and peoples ? When the impossibility of resorting to war for the decision of international quarrels is apparent to all, other means will be devised.

PART I

MILITARY AND NAVAL DEVELOPMENTS

CHAPTER I

HOW WAR WILL BE WAGED ON LAND

In former times bullets, for a great part of their course, flew over the heads of the combatants, and were effective only for an insignificant distance. The modern bullet will strike all it meets for a distance of 660 yards, and after the introduction of the more perfect arms now in course of preparation the effective distance will be as great as 1210 yards. And as it is most improbable that on the field of battle it will not meet with a single living being in such a distance, we may conclude that every bullet will find its victim.

The old powder was a mechanical mixture of nitre, sulphur, and charcoal, upon the ignition of which were liberated many elements which did not enter into new combinations. The new powder is a chemical combination which gives scarcely any smoke and produces no empyreuma in the barrel. At the same time the explosive force of the new powder is much greater than that of the old, and its quality of smokelessness or of giving little smoke, in the first place, renders it impossible to judge of the position and forces of an enemy by smoke, and, in the second, frees the marksmen from the clouds of smoke which formerly were an obstacle to aiming. And as in the opinion of many authorities the last word concerning explosives has not yet been said, in the war of the future, especially if it should take place some years from now, explosives of such strength will be employed that the concentration of armies in the open field, or even under the cover of fortifications, will be almost impossible, so that the apparatus of war prepared at the present time may prove itself useless.

The improvement of small arms goes forward with incredible speed. By the almost unanimous testimony of competent persons, the changes which took place in the course of five centuries cannot be compared in importance with those which have been made since the wars of 1870 and 1877–78. The well-known specialist, Professor Gebler, made a comparison, expressed in figures, between different modern small arms, taking as his standard of effectiveness at 100 degrees the Mauser rifle, 11 mil., of 1871. On this basis he worked out the effectiveness of modern weapons as follows:

The modern French rifle	433
The modern German rifle	474
The new rifles in use in Italy and Spain . .	580
The 6-mil. rifle adopted by the United States .	1000
The 5-mil. rifle now undergoing test . . .	1337

Therefore, if in the war of 1870 the German and French armies had been armed with weapons of modern type, speaking theoretically, the losses in that war would have been 4⅓ to 4¾ times greater than they actually were. Had they been armed with the 6-mil. rifle used in the United States of America the losses would have been ten times greater.

Nevertheless, specialists declare that the new weapons adopted in European armies, and even the 6 mil. rifle, are already obsolete, and that the future will see a self-loading weapon made out of an alloy of aluminium, from which a series of shots may be fired without taking the rifle from the shoulder or losing time and energy in reloading.

Experiments made in Belgium with the new self-charging rifles and pistols of the Mauser system show that (firing only such a number of cartridges as will fit into the magazine) a trained soldier can fire from six to seven times a second; upon shooting a greater number of cartridges from a gun, which requires reloading, the maximum number of shots with the 6-mil. gun is:

Without aiming	.	.	.	78 per minute.
Aiming	.	.	.	60 ,,

But the efforts to improve small arms do not stop there, and governments will continue to strive to lessen calibres, as is maintained by Professor Gebler, General Wille, Professor Pototski, and other authorities, to 4 and, it may be, even to 3 millimetres. It is true that there are great difficulties in the utilisation of such small calibres, but the successes already achieved by technical science may be taken to guarantee that these also will be surmounted.

Such a weapon will excel the present in efficiency even more than the present rifle excels the past. The diminution of the calibre of rifles to 5 mil. makes it possible for a soldier to carry 270 cartridges, instead of the 84 which he carried in 1877; the reduction of the calibre to 4 mil. would enable him to carry 380 cartridges; while with the reduction of the calibre to 3 mil. the number of cartridges borne would increase to 575. In addition, the levelling of the trajectory of the bullet would give to shooting such dead-liness that it would be practically impossible to strengthen the fighting line with reserves.

Professor Gebler declares that these improved weapons will be forty times more effective than those used in 1870. From this must result the complete re-armament of all armies, if before that time limits be not placed upon the rivalry of the nations in preparation for war. For the re-armament of their infantry, Germany, France, Russia, Austria, and Italy would, by our calculation, be compelled to spend the immense sum of £150,800,000.

But, apart from future improvements in arms, it is easy to see with existing improvements the following consequences: (1) The opening of battles from much greater distances than formerly; (2) the necessity of loose formation in attack; (3) the strengthening of the defence; (4) the increase in the area of the battlefield; and (5) the increase in casualties.

It is enough here to cite some statistics as to the action of modern arms as compared with the arms of 1870–71 and 1877–78. Thus, the bullet of the Chassepot, the

Berdan, or the Prussian needle-gun fired from a distance of 1760 yards could not penetrate a human skull, whereas the bullet of modern low-calibre rifles at a distance of 3850 yards will penetrate the hard bones of an ox.

But many military writers declare that the improvement in small arms will be neutralised by the fact that rapidity of fire will deprive the soldier of coolness and capacity to turn to account the superiority of the modern weapon.

Let us admit for the moment that modern long-range rifles, even with their future improvements, will not prove more deadly in battle than their predecessors. Such an improbable and apparently unfounded proposition is directly refuted by the experience of the Chilian war of 1894. In that war the armies of the Congress were armed, partly with old, partly with modern weapons, and it was proven that each company of soldiers armed with rifles of a modern type put out of action 82 men in the armies of the President-Dictator, while a company of soldiers armed with obsolete weapons, put out of action only 34 men. The absence of smoke alone must increase immensely the deadliness of modern arms. The history of past battles relates that at a distance of sixty paces combatants often could not see one another, and that their fire proved ineffective. And even if long-range rifles do not prove more deadly than their predecessors, it will still be absurd to deny that a certain number of projectiles will disable a certain number of men. And as, in the wars of the present century, the number of shots fired for every disablement has fluctuated between $8\frac{1}{2}$ and 164, it is plain that the supply of cartridges now carried by each soldier is sufficient to disable at least one opponent ; while the supply of 380 cartridges with the 4-mil. rifle, and of 575 with the 3-mil. rifle, will be more than enough to disable two or three of the enemy. In other words, even supposing the effectiveness of modern arms to be in no way increased, the fire of one rifle may disable two or three of the enemy. From this it is plain that, even with the weapons now adopted, the effectiveness of fire presents the possibility of total mutual annihilation.

Such is the comparison when regard is had alone to the increase in the supply of cartridges arising from the reduction of the calibre of rifles.

But in addition we must take into account the rapidity with which modern weapons may be fired. In a given time twelve times as many shots may be fired as in 1867, while the chances of missing fire and of injury to the powder by damp have been removed. In addition to this must be borne in mind the long range of modern weapons, the absence of the accumulations in the barrel of the rifle, the adoption by officers of instruments for precisely ascertaining distances, the use by under-officers of field-glasses, and finally, the substitution of the old powder by smokeless powder. All these conditions will undoubtedly increase the number of losses, and if the operation of each were considered as a factor in multiplying past losses, we should attain almost incredible but technically and mathematically trustworthy figures.

To this must be added the improvement, since 1870, in the instruction of soldiers in firing. In the training of soldiers every year an immense quantity of ammunition is expended. In addition, mechanical means are employed to show the direction of the barrel on aiming and firing. These are new conditions entirely, or in a great degree, unknown in the time of the last great wars. If we take into account the fact that 500 cartridges are prepared for every rifle, the expenditure of which, of course, is not stinted, we are confronted with a direct denial of the possibility, even for armies of millions of men, in the event of equal strength, to sustain such losses.

In addition to small arms the power of artillery has increased in a measure incomparable with the past.

A glance backward at the development of field artillery shows that from the date of the invention of powder improvements in arms took place very slowly. In imperfect weapons, it would seem, it would have been much easier to effect improvements. Nevertheless, to within a recent date, the effect of artillery fire remained very inconsiderable.

In 1891 Professor Langlois estimated the increase of

the power of artillery fire since the war of 1870 in the following manner : With an equal number of discharges, modern artillery will be five times more effective than the artillery of 1870. But as modern field guns are capable of discharging in a given time from two to two and a half more projectiles than the old guns, it follows that the power of artillery fire has multiplied since 1870 no less than from twelve to fifteen times.

The calculations made by Professor Langlois in 1891 are already out of date. In France, in Germany, and in Russia quick-firing guns are being made, and from the testimony of such authoritative writers as General Wille, Professor Pototski, and Captain Moch, we find that the fire of these new guns is at least twice as powerful as that of the gun of 1891, of which Langlois speaks in the following terms : " We have before us a whole series of improvements of the greatest importance, and must admit that munitions of war are entirely different from those in use in the past." So that in order to form some idea as to the total losses in a future war it is necessary to compare the action of the latest perfected arms with the action of the old guns employed up to the present time. Such a comparison only shows that, as in the case of quick-firing rifles, the past can give no precise forecast as to the effect of artillery in future wars.

With the introduction of smokeless powder and the employment of nickel steel on the one hand, and the strengthening by wire of the barrels of guns on the other, arms of tremendous power are being made.

A comparison of the result of the firing of a thousand rifle bullets by soldiers attacking in loose formation with the action of shrapnel, shows that one round of shrapnel is effective over a space double the length of that covered by a thousand rifle bullets, and not less in width. Experiment has also shown that the fragments of shrapnel disperse themselves over a space 880 yards in length and 440 yards in breadth. Prince Hohenlohe, commander of the German artillery in the war of 1870, in the most emphatic manner declared that " a battery placed against

a road fifteen paces in width might annihilate a whole
mass of infantry on this road for a distance of 7700 yards,
so that no one would even think of standing there."

Not less are the successes attained in the improvement
of projectiles. The use of steel in their manufacture
permitted their being charged with a greater number
of bullets. The use of explosives four times more powerful than were formerly employed gave to each splinter
and bullet immense force. The flight of bullets and
splinters may be likened to the action of a sieve from
which drops of water are driven. Imagine such a sieve
revolving at great speed, and some idea will be gained of
the manner in which the fragments of shells would be
dispersed.

In the war of the future, shell, which is much less effective
than shrapnel, will be employed less than formerly.
Shrapnel will be the chief ammunition of artillery, although
if we believe French reports, it is proved that all in the
vicinity of a bursting Brisant shell will be knocked down by
the agitation of the atmosphere and sustain serious internal
injuries, while in the case of the shell bursting in a covered
space every one there will be killed either by the action of
mechanical forces, or by the poisonous gases liberated by
the explosion.

By a comparison of the effect of artillery ammunition
with the effect of that employed in 1870, it is shown that,
on the average, shells burst into 240 pieces instead or
19–30 as was the case in 1870. The shrapnel employed
in 1870 burst into 37 pieces, now it gives as many as 340.
An iron bomb weighing 82 pounds, which, with the old
powder gave 42 fragments, filled with peroxylene gives
1204 pieces. With the increase in the number of bullets
and fragments, and in the forces which disperse them,
increases also the area which they affect. Splinters and
bullets bring death and destruction not only, as in 1870, to
those in the vicinity of the explosion, but at a distance of
220 yards away, and this though fired from a distance of
3300 yards.

With such improved ammunition the destruction pro-

duced in the ranks of armies will be immense. From
the statistics furnished by the Prussian General Rohne,
we have estimated the losses which would be sustained
by a body of 10,000 men attacking in loose formation
a fortified position. From this estimate it is shown that
before the attacking party succeeded in covering 2200
yards in the direction of the defenders' trenches every
individual composing it may be struck by bullets and
fragments of shells, as the defenders' artillery in that time
will have succeeded in firing 1450 rounds, scattering
275,000 bullets and fragments, of which 10,330 will
take effect in the attacking lines.

But artillery fire will be directed not only against the
attacking troops, which, when within range of the trenches
may be destroyed by rifle fire, but also, to a greater extent,
against supporting bodies which must follow in closer
order, and among which, therefore, the action of artillery
fire will be even more deadly.

And as at the same time the quantity of artillery in all
armies has considerably increased, we may well ask the
question whether the nerves of short-service soldiers will
stand the terrible destructiveness of its fire.

The improvement, in all respects, of fire-arms, and
the high degree of perfection achieved in artillery and
artillery ammunition are by no means all that the
mind of man has contrived as weapons of destruction. The whole series of auxiliary instruments
which in a future war may have immense importance
has, since the last war, been improved. Velocipedes,
carrier pigeons, field telegraphs and telephones, apparatus for signalling by day and by night, and for illuminating the field of battle, photographic apparatus
for the survey of positions from great distances, means of
observing the movements of armies by the use of observation scaffolding, ladders, watch towers and balloons—all
in a great degree do away with that insufficiency of information which formerly prevented united and successful
operations.

As a necessary consequence of the increase in the

power of fire, we find the more frequent and more extended adoption of defences, and cover for protection in attack and for hampering the enemy. Even in times of peace, positions are prepared for the defence of certain points of the railways and main roads and of water communications.

In addition to this in the future war every body of men appointed for defence, and even for attack—if it is not to attack at once—must immediately entrench itself. It must dig, so to speak, in the earth its line of battle, and, if time permit, must raise a whole series of defensive points, taking advantage of natural obstacles, and perfecting them with defensive works. Sheltered behind such works, and in a position to devote all their energy to fire against the enemy, the defenders will sustain losses comparatively slight, only their heads and hands—that is, an eighth part of their height—being exposed, while the attacking bodies will be exposed to the uninterrupted fire of the defenders, and deprived almost of all possibility of replying to their fire. For the construction of such trenches and earthworks, each division of an army is now furnished with the requisite tools.

In the opinion of competent military writers the war of the future will consist primarily of a series of battles for the possession of fortified positions. In addition to field fortifications of different kinds, the attacking army will have to deal with auxiliary obstacles which will be met with in the neighbourhood of fortifications, that is, in the very position where they will be subjected to the greatest danger from the enemy's fire—obstructions formed of beams, networks of wire, and pit-falls. To overcome these obstacles great sacrifices must be made.

The part of cavalry in a future war presents this primary difference with its part in the past. At the very beginning of war, and even before the attacking army has passed the frontier, it will be sent to make irruptions on the territory of the enemy, penetrating the country as far as possible, destroying communications, depôts, and telegraphs, seizing government resources, and preventing the concentration of

troops.   After this the cavalry which follows as part of
the constitution of the regular army will be employed in the
making of reconnaisances.   In a future war such duties
will be undoubtedly more difficult than before, owing to
the adoption of smokeless powder.   Even after having
determined the general position of an enemy, cavalry will
hardly be in a condition to acquire any precise information,
to determine his strength, and even the distance of his
advanced posts.   The pickets of the enemy will not stand
in the open field, but under cover, behind eminences,
groups of trees, and hedges.   From a distance of a quarter
of a mile the fire from the concealed pickets of the enemy
will be very effective, yet the pickets themselves will be
invisible.   In all probability pickets will open fire at the
distance of half a mile, to prevent the closer approach of the
reconnoitring party, and as with modern arms horsemen
may be picked from the saddle from a great distance, the
patrol will be unable to determine the distance of the
enemy by the effect of his fire.   With modern arms and
smokeless powder a single marksman in a sheltered position may cause serious loss to a body of troops, as witness
the case cited in the " Military Album," when in an attack
by Bavarians on a French battalion sheltered behind a low
wall, a Bavarian soldier climbed into a tree, and picked off
the French at will, while no smoke betrayed him, and
several volleys failed to kill the daring marksman.

Thus scouting parties will be forced to move with great
caution, and will not always be able to collect sufficient
information, all the more so because, having come under
the fire of insignificant posts, and having been obliged to
withdraw, they will naturally not wish to admit that they
were engaged with small numbers of the enemy.   More
precise information may be attained only by means of
infantry commands which are more easily sheltered, and
which can approach more closely the positions of the
enemy.   Such a definition of the duties in reconnaissances
of cavalry patrols and infantry commands is laid down in
the Instructions for Infantry elaborated by the French
technical committee : " Cavalry may obtain only general,

approximate information as to the position and strength of the enemy; for the acquiring of detailed and precise information infantry must be employed." And actually, in the French military manœuvres, cavalry are now kept at some distance, and close reconnaissances are made by infantry. Nevertheless, the reconnoitring importance of cavalry, in the strategical sense, has increased. It must be taken into account that the territory of the enemy will be sown with a multitude of permanent and improvised fortified positions and points, and an army will not attack without having around itself, and more particularly in advance, a network of cavalry detachments split up into small parts and patrols. To a large extent such cavalry will operate independently, as when crossing the frontier in the beginning of war. It must alarm the enemy, destroy or seize provisions, guard the bridges, seize despatches, collect information as to the enemy's movements, and protect the communications of the army in its rear.

The greater the importance played in modern war by railways, telegraphs, and improvised entrenchments, the more essential has become this strategical employment of cavalry. Military writers generally assume that the chief strength of cavalry must be sent forward for investigation, and for the protection of the advanced guards of armies, as Germans expressed by the German saying, "Die Reiterei allzeit voran!" (Horsemen always to the front). In view of the power of modern arms, and the resulting practice of disposing troops behind natural and artificial defences, and in view of the great network of defensive points prepared in advance, an attacking army will more than ever find it necessary to feel its way, and to reconnoitre the country into which it is advancing. Thus the capacity of cavalry as the "feelers" of an army has become especially important.

As to the part cavalry should play in actual battle, military writers differ in a remarkable degree. Some, as the French Captain Nigot, believe that the desperate massed attacks of cavalry, which prove so effective in manœuvres, are impossible, as with the great increase in the power of fire, cavalry will not be able to strike at infantry even when weakness is observed. From his calculations it appears that a battalion of 800 rifles, with one volley fired at a range of 330 yards, would unhorse 424 troopers, and if a battalion were to open fire at 880 yards, and continue firing, at a distance of 110 yards 2656 men would have been put out of action, that is several battalions of cavalry, attacking one after another.

Such is not the view of all military writers. Thus one author, relying on the fact that cavalry will cover a given distance at twice the speed of infantry, contends that although cavalry is subjected to treble the possibility of disablement, yet one factor neutralises the other, and therefore the loss of cavalry will be no greater than the loss of infantry in the same distance.

Of one thing there is not the slightest doubt, that is, that cavalry is threatened with treble probability of being struck. In France it was shown that under equal conditions cavalry losses under fire are from two and a half to three times as great as infantry losses, and that cavalry cannot, therefore, remain immovable under fire. Therefore, in France it is considered proven that in time of battle cavalry must keep at a distance of not less than 3850 yards from the enemy, and may draw nearer only towards the close of the battle. Otherwise it would be swept away by rifle and artillery fire.

The speed at which cavalry may attack is taken by some at 550 yards a minute, but most authorities limit it to 440, even to 374, yards a minute. But even if, notwithstanding inequalities of the battlefield and the close formation which lowers the general speed to the speed of the slowest horses, the speed of attack is taken as half a mile in two minutes—almost racing speed—nevertheless, in the course of these two minutes' exposure to effective fire before it can get to close quarters with infantry, cavalry must suffer immense losses which will force it to disperse or make its attack feeble.

It must be understood that for the consideration of this question we have only the opinions of different military specialists. The German author of the " Militärische

Essays" says that modern conditions in no way involve the fascination which surrounds cavalry in the traditions of the Seven Years War, and that the German army would enter upon war with from 30,000 to 40,000 superfluous cavalry, which would only create difficulties in concentration and to the Commissariat. But other authorities declare that the smokelessness of the battlefield will be favourable for cavalry attack, since it will be easier seen at what points the enemy's infantry is weak, while it will be more difficult for infantry to await from afar, without the covering of smoke, the impetuous shock of masses of cavalry.

This moment when weakening is observed in the enemy's infantry is relied upon by the advocates of cavalry attack in battle. One even goes so far as to say that upon the clash of cavalry upon infantry "it will matter nothing what may be in the hands of the trembling infantry—magazine rifles, flint-locks, or simply pitch-forks." But, as Von der Goltz observes, weakness may be very plain in the ranks of an army and yet not be seen by the enemy. Such weakness can only be seen from advanced positions, and while the information is being conveyed to the proper quarter and cavalry is being sent to attack, the auspicious moment may have passed. On the other hand, the movement of masses of cavalry is always visible owing to the dust it raises, and all the fire of the enemy may be concentrated on these masses, artillery fire against cavalry being effective from a long range, as the mass presents an immense target.

In comparison with the times of the Seven Years War cavalry has itself made progress. It is furnished with stronger and swifter horses. But this improvement can in no way be compared with the increase in range and rapidity of fire. In addition to this, as the same author observes, in former times it was sufficient to break up thick masses of infantry and their opposition was at an end ; now infantry begins the battle in loose formation, each individual command constitutes a unit fit for battle, and even the solitary soldier will not lose his wits while a cartridge remains upon him.   Thus the relations between cavalry and infantry have entirely changed.

It is questionable, indeed, whether in the future cavalry will have that importance which formerly belonged to it, as a force deciding battle and afterwards completing the overthrow of the enemy by pursuit.   Even in the wars of 1870 and 1877 this importance of cavalry seemed diminished, although, on the other hand, its importance in the reconnoitring of occupied territory, the protection of armies, and its value in independent action have increased.

In addition to this, a new function for cavalry has been created—immediate irruption into the   territory of an enemy, and the destruction of his arrangements for mobilisation, and his communications.   To what extent such action of cavalry in the moment of the declaration of war will prove successful is still to be proven by experience.   In the event of success such action would cause disorganisation in the enemy's arrangements, and force him to accelerate them.   And as operations, considering the immensity of modern armies, may be successfully carried on only by the precise execution of strategical plans elaborated in advance, then the disorganisation caused by sudden cavalry irruptions might have the most important results.

As concerns the *rôle* of cavalry in pursuit, it is more important to consider this *rôle* in the pursuit of retreating armies to their farthest movement than in the pursuit of armies in their actual retreat from the field of battle. Doubts have been expressed as to the decisiveness of future battles.   It is very probable that in the majority of cases the road selected for retreat will be guarded by defences constructed in advance, the retreating army falling back upon the nearest position and offering fresh resistance to the victors, who, on their side, will be weakened by the storming of the first positions.   In such case the most important *rôle* of cavalry may be to prevent the retreating army drawing reinforcement from other sections of the army which, owing to the vastness of the field of battle, may find themselves at considerable distance from the main army.

In any case it will be seen that the duties of cavalry in war remain very important, although the fulfilment or non-fulfilment of some of the tasks appointed for it has still to be shown by experience.

Quite otherwise is the case of artillery.

It is an accepted axiom that without the aid of artillery it is impossible to drive infantry, even infantry considerably weaker in numbers, out of a fortified position ; and as all infantry when acting on the defensive will be entrenched, then armies in future will find themselves mainly dependent upon artillery.

The successful employment of artillery will depend upon the opposition it meets from the artillery fire of the enemy. The artillery of the attacking side will begin by attempting to silence, or at least to weaken the artillery fire of the defenders, which object being accomplished, it will be able to turn its attention to the enemy's infantry. The artillery of the defending army, possessing as it will many advantages, will attempt to prevent this. The result of such a duel, if the defenders have artillery of nearly equal strength and quality, in all probability will be the annihilation of the attacking artillery ; while if the superiority of the attacking artillery be substantial, the result will more probably be mutual annihilation.

The increase in the artillery of all armies, the improvement of ammunition, the adoption of smokeless powder and of new explosives, the improvement in tactics, all these must lead to such great losses in the artillery service that their action will be paralysed, or the losses in the armies will become so tremendous that war itself will be impossible.

Such a conclusion may seem risky, but it is founded on the investigations of the most competent artillerists, and in the justice of their conclusions it is difficult not to concur, when we consider the changes which have taken place since the time of the last great war.

As relates to the employment of artillery, it may first of

B

all be noted that the adoption of new powders has changed for the worse the position of artillerymen. In former times a thick cloud of smoke hampered the aim of the artilleryman. But on the other hand it prevented the enemy's artillery and infantry from taking accurate aim.

As long as ordinary powder was used there was no especial need for increase in accuracy and rapidity of fire, for quick firing produced so much smoke that after a short time it was necessary to slacken fire, except on those occasions when there was a favourable wind ; and accuracy also was not as important as it is at the present day. With smokeless powder it is possible to discharge more shots in a few minutes favourable for fire than were formerly discharged in a day's battle. In this connection the accuracy of modern fire must again be insisted upon. Cannon at a distance of 2011 yards has placed shot in the same hole four times in succession.*

It must be borne in mind that against the enemy's artillery the defending army will make use also of sharp-shooters. Using the new powder, sharpshooters will have full possibility to approach the batteries of the enemy, and concealing themselves behind inequalities of the field of battle, with no smoke to betray them, may pick off all the enemy's gunners and horses.

Manœuvres in which smokeless powder has been used confirm the opinion that from a distance of 440 yards it is impossible to discover marksmen hidden behind trees or bushes. But from this distance every shot of a skilful marksman will claim its victim. In addition to this, all armies now possess specially organised bodies of chas-seurs, trained to fire from great distances, and accustomed stealthily to approach their mark. It is plain that for such commands there can be no especial difficulty in stealing up to a battery and picking off the artillerymen. The French, German, and Austrian armies dispose of sufficient numbers of such soldiers. It is well known that Germany, France, Austria, and Switzerland yearly expend considerable sums

* Löbell, " Militärische Jahresberichte," 1894.

on the encouragement of good shooting, and that among
the population of those states there is a considerable
number of first-rate shots. In the Russian army chasseur
commands are also found with the different army divisions.

According to the data of the Prussian General Rohne
100 sharpshooters will put a battery out of action, firing
from a distance of—

880 yards in the course of			2.4	minutes.
1100 ,,	,,	,,	4	,,
1320 ,,	,,	,,	7.5	,,
1650 ,,	,,	,,	22	,,

But even if the destruction of the gunners be not accomplished by sharpshooters, it is very probable that it will
soon be done by the artillery of the enemy.

The quantity and power of artillery in all armies has
been multiplied many times. If the figures which represent these increased quantity and increased power be
multiplied it will be shown that in comparison with 1870
the strength of the French artillery has been multiplied
116 times, and of the German 42 times. But after the
introduction of the improved artillery now being accomplished the strength of artillery will be again redoubled.

If, to form some idea how losses in a future war from the
action of artillery alone will exceed the corresponding
losses in 1870-71, we multiply the figure of these latter
losses by the figures which represent the increased force
of modern artillery, the result would be incredible, for it
would show that there could not be an army large enough
to sustain such losses. But for the purpose of giving an
idea as to the power of modern artillery these figures have
a theoretical value, resulting as they do from simple arithmetical calculation.

In one sense calculation will not be uninstructive.
What number of soldiers will be disabled by the use
of that quantity of shots which is found in the ammunition cases of the batteries of different countries, taking
into account the conditions for marksmanship less favourable in war than in peace ? When we make this calculation,

on the figures of the Prussian general and well-known
military writer Müller, we find that the ammunition carried
by the batteries of the French and Russian armies, taken
together, would put out of action six millions of soldiers.
Continuing our calculations upon the data of the same
authority we find that the Franco-Russian artillery, with
its ready supply of ammunition, would be capable of withstanding the attack of double that number, or twelve
millions of men.   The ready supply of ammunition in the
united German, Austrian and Italian armies would disable
five millions of men, and successfully repulse the attack
of ten millions of infantry.

A writer no less authoritative, a professor of the chief
artillery school in France, Colonel Langlois, speaking as to
the character of future battles, expresses the opinion that
for one field-piece up to 500 rounds will be required.   If
we estimate the quantity of artillery, and the number of
fragments produced by explosion, it is shown that these
are sufficient for the destruction of forces eight times
stronger than the armies opposed to them.   It is necessary
to mention here that modern projectiles, filled with powerful
explosives, will be dangerous not only to the enemy, but
also to the army which employs them.   The storing,
transport, and employment of such explosives under the
well-directed fire of an enemy may lead to catastrophes
which will still further increase the horrors of war.   In
France *fougasse* shells, containing 4 pounds of melinite,
have been adopted.   The majority of writers are agreed
that in view of the possible premature explosion of melinite
shells, *fougasse* shells are very dangerous, as in such
event, the bursting of the gun seems inevitable.   But the
danger is not limited to the possible bursting of guns.
Against entrenched armies, mortars and siege artillery of
great size will be employed.   The projectiles of these will
be filled with strong explosives, such as peroxylene and
melinite.   Now these explosives are capable of exploding
unexpectedly on certain changes of temperature and from
other causes not yet ascertained.   The agitation of the air
caused by the enemy's shells may also cause explosions.

It is enough to note that explosions are by no means uncommon during experiments, although these experiments are carried on by trained men under the supervision of picked officers. The very mystery with which not only the experiments but the accidents which arise therefrom are surrounded, proves recognition of the difficulties that arise and the uncertainty of success. England is the only country where circumstantial accounts of accidents in dealing with explosives are published. In the yearly memoranda of inspectors we usually find a long list of accidents in the making or transport of explosive substances, and this, among other things, shows that notwithstanding all measures of precaution, armies are sometimes supplied with dangerously defective ammunition. For the sake of safety in many armies explosive projectiles are painted various colours, and, in order to distinguish them at night, are given a different form. In addition to that they must be transported separately, and the very fitting of the tube into the projectile is done at the time of loading.

It is very natural to find that in time of battle, when armies are in a state of tension, perfect coolness is found only among exceptional natures. During the American Civil War thousands of rifles were found upon the battle-fields doubly and trebly loaded, and sometimes charged to the very muzzle. If in such a simple matter as the loading of a rifle such mistakes are made, what is to be expected in the use of highly explosive ammunition, the safe handling of which demands the greatest precision and caution ?

. Even if we were able to assume that cartridges will always be furnished with explosive tubes only when operations begin, or on the very position on which they are to be employed, and that guns will always be loaded with due caution and regularity, even in that case we find the possibility of a new and even greater danger.

Fougasse cartridges consist of a long steel cylinder, of which the smooth interior is filled with melinite, roburite, ecrasite, or some other explosive. All these substances differ from one another by admixtures and mode of preparation.   It is obvious that the thinner the case of the cartridge the greater the quantity of explosives it will contain.

In the opinion of experts, the direct action of gases on explosion is limited to a comparatively small space— 16½ yards—but their explosion develops such force that for a certain distance it will drag gun, gunners, and horses. It cannot but be observed that if in the manufacture of the ammunition any faults were to escape detection, the very gravest consequences might ensue.   In one of the latest English compositions on artillery the following sentences occur : " The founding of ordinary shells demands great care in order to prevent premature explosion in the barrel of the gun.   Shells must not have on their internal surface any roughness which might cause explosion."

On the explosion of such a shell in the barrel of a gun the body of the latter was shattered into more than twenty bits, the carriage was completely destroyed, and the wheels turned into a heap of splinters.   Individual fragments of the destroyed weapon weighed 363 pounds, and were flung 99 yards forward and backward from the place on which the gun had stood, and nearly 108 yards on either side.   Notwithstanding the distance between guns, a single explosion might embrace several guns with all their ammunition.

Not far from the battery ammunition cases will be placed.   If these be not exploded by the concussion of the atmosphere they may very easily be exploded by some of the heavy fragments which fall upon them.   Is there any one who can declare that all such accidents will be obviated by perfection of technical construction and, with the present constitution of armies, by the careful selection of those who are to deal with explosives ?

All this leads to the conclusion that even if we do not consider the dangers proceeding from explosions, the artillery and ammunition already prepared is sufficient for the destruction of much larger armies than will be moved on the field of battle.   But such destruction may not take place for the very simple reason that the artillery of each combatant may in a very short time silence the fire of its adversary. And as the quantity of artillery, their quality, and the training of their crews will, in the opinion of most authorities, be almost equal on both sides, then common sense tells us that in the artillery duel with which battles will commence either the attacking side, having less protection, will be destroyed, or mutual extermination will result. Thus the problem might arise for infantry to attack without the support of artillery, and as this, as we shall hereafter show, is impossible without terrible losses, tactics would probably be changed, and with the remnants of its artillery the side having the advantage in the artillery duel must await the attack of the enemy ; conditions which would probably result in a repetition of the events of 1632 at Nuremburg, when Gustavus Adolphus and Wallenstein entrenched themselves and laid all their hopes of victory on the exhaustion of the enemy.

As concerns the operations of infantry in the future war there is no settled opinion even on the chief question, that is, the deciding influence in battle of an infantry attack. If war were to break out to-morrow all armies in this respect would find themselves under the influence of the contradiction between instructions, manœuvres, and the views of the more noted military writers, General Skugarevski, Müller, Von Rohne, Janson, and others. There is no reason to be surprised at this, as the introduction of smokeless powder, improved rifles ten times more effective than the rifles of the old type, better instruction of soldiers, and their equipment with instruments for the construction of earthworks have changed in every respect the conditions of war.

Modern tactics are primarily the result of our experience of the last great war. As long as the progress of military technical science was comparatively slow it was not difficult to rely upon the experience of the past. At the present day the state of affairs is entirely different ; in former times re-armament took place after hundreds of years, then after many decades, now it takes place in a very short time.

But not only the change in armament will influence the action of infantry. The smokelessness of the battlefield, the perfection of rifles, artillery, and explosives, and at the same time the employment of army hordes consisting largely of short-service soldiers, have created entirely new conditions for the war of the future.

In battle a combatant may from a distance three to four times greater than before inflict serious losses on attacking troops. The killing off of the officers and consequent weakening in leadership, will be direct consequences of a smokeless battlefield, and of the precision of modern small arms which makes it possible for marksmen to select their victims at will.

Meantime, the *rôle* which will be played by infantry has become more complex. In preliminary operations infantry must take a far larger part than formerly. The close reconnoitring of an enemy's position has become the duty of infantry scouts, who will be obliged to advance stealthily in order to obtain the information necessary for any successful attack. Without such service by infantry scouts an immense superiority would remain on the defensive side which, having studied the locality in advance, and occupying a commanding position, would simply with the aid of field-glasses direct all its blows successfully.

For the carrying out of such reconnaissances and the collecting of information, not only daring but skilful and sagacious soldiers are required, and with the modern composition of armies it will be very difficult to find such men. The determining of positions by smoke is no longer possible ; while to determine positions by sound is extraordinarily difficult. Experiments carried out on French shooting ranges show that the sound caused by the explosion of smokeless powder does not penetrate as far as that of sulphur powder ; a single rifle shot is heard no farther than 880 yards, and volleys, according to the number of rifles, no farther than from 1320 to 1540 yards. Yet knowledge of the strength and position of an enemy is much more essential than before, as the losses from an unexpected encounter will be very great.

From modern infantry men much more endurance also will be required. Marches will be made in deep columns in consequence of the growth of armies; while the number of these marches, as a consequence of the massiveness of modern armies, will increase in comparison with former times, since, owing to considerations of space and commissariat, modern armies must be split up and the individual sections must reunite with the main body on drawing near to an enemy superior in numbers.

Thus the conditions surrounding advance to battle and battle itself have become extraordinarily complicated. Yet on mobilisation for every hundred soldiers serving with the colours under present arrangements from 26 men (Italy) to 361 men (Russia) will be drawn from the reserve. The majority of these men will have long forgotten what they learnt during their period of service, while of their officers only a fraction will be in a high state of efficiency.

With such conditions it would seem necessary that field instructions and regulations must be elaborated in time of peace, giving precise directions as to tactics in all contingencies. But in this very respect in every army we find deficiencies of different kinds. Theoretical instructions do not correspond to practical necessities and are constituted from a limited standpoint. Colonel Mignol says that the tactics recommended in the latest French official instructions in essence differ very little from those introduced after the invention of firearms and the adoption of bayonets, that is, when firearms were about forty times less effective than they are to-day. At that time in the first line of battle marched musketeers who opened the combat, followed by pikemen who carried out the actual assault. Now battle is opened by moving forward lines of riflemen, after which storming columns will advance. But are these two forms of tactics in essence the same? Is it possible that all the progress in ballistics which has strengthened the defensive power of infantry and increased the mobility and strength of artillery, has not led to a change in the very nature of war? Is it possible that war remains the same as in the time of matchlocks, flintlocks, and ramrods with the mere difference that musketeers have been replaced by sharpshooters, and pikemen by reserves and the *masse ?* The inadequacy of the recommended systems is so obvious that as soon as new instructions appear they are submitted to criticism and changed. In truth, the views concerning the duties of infantry present a labyrinth of irreconcilable contradictions, one incompatible with another.

The reader must not think that these contradictions are apparent only to the layman. General Luset, a very well-informed specialist, speaking of French tactics, asks : " Who has not been astonished by the differences of view found in the text-books of our schools on questions touching the actual condition of tactics ? Can we admit that the teaching of infantry officers in the lower schools agrees with that which they receive in the highest military training institutions ? The teaching of this higher school does not correspond to the courses of the *Ecole d'Appli-cation*. The ideas insisted upon in the teaching of the higher military school change continually. There is a chaos of contending ideas and principles, and out of the general confusion not a ray of light appears. Is it surprising that officers ask, ' What is the use of study ? ' Let teachers first agree among themselves ! "

Attentive study of German writers will reveal differences no less great. But for many obvious reasons they are expressed with greater caution. Many German military writers are restrained from a too frank admission of the dangers and difficulties of war under modern conditions by the fear of giving food to the agitation against militarism.

Rules hasten after rules, supplementary explanations are constantly added, and in the result of results we find a chaos of inconsistencies. It could not be otherwise. When all units of infantry are furnished with trenching tools in such quantities that in the course of a very short time earthworks may be thrown up, each attacking body is subjected to eight times the danger of their sheltered opponents. But in addition to rifle fire, attacking forces will be subjected to fire from the protected artillery of the defenders.

It is not surprising therefore that, concerning the character of the future employment of infantry, the views of different authorities present numberless and grave contradictions.

A considerable number of military writers, judging from the experience of past wars, conclude that the main points in the employment of infantry in battle have not changed. Infantry will be employed in battle as in the past, but in loose formation, and the command of infantry will not be especially difficult not only for experienced officers, but even for those who have been taken from the reserve. On the other hand, other writers declare that for the command of infantry on the battlefield even more ability will be required than for the command of artillery and cavalry. For 300 officers who are capable of learning to command a battery or a squadron not 100 will be found in any army capable of leading infantry under fire. What, then, shall we expect from the officers of the reserve? In one thing, however, all are agreed—that whatever be the tactics adopted, their successful execution will require great skill in taking advantage of cover and in overcoming obstacles, knowledge when to seek shelter on the ground and to advance again at the proper moment. Will the reservists only just summoned to the colours be in a condition to fulfil these duties? But even suppose that a considerable part will consist of perfectly trained and enduring officers and soldiers, what in such event will be their losses?

Some say that there is no reason for supposing that in a future war armies will sustain greater losses than in the past. Others, no less authoritative, declare that attacks having with their object the occupation of an enemy's position in a future war will be so difficult and bloody that neither side will be in a condition to celebrate the victory. Before the defended position will be formed a belt 1100 yards wide, for both sides equally inaccessible, limited by human bodies over which will fly thousands of bullets and shells, a belt over which no living being will be able to pass to decide the battle with the bayonet.

But another view is expressed. All this, some writers say, would be true in view of the small-calibre rifles and improved artillery now in use if the field of battle were a drill-ground where distances were known and marksmen guaranteed that they would not be struck by the enemy's fire, and if the field of battle were a perfectly level space ; but in nature such positions are rarely met with, and armies will take advantage of the shelter of woods and under-growth, eminences and depressions. Hidden behind the first line of riflemen who will constitute the *Kugelfang* the succeeding lines will advance with much less losses.

To this is replied : It will be easy for commanders to follow the approach of the enemy by means of balloons from permanent points of view and from portable observation points, which will be set up by every detachment intending to occupy a position. Therefore with the long range, precision and striking power of modern artillery, which make it possible to scatter fragments and bullets to immense distances, it will be possible to shell an enemy out of woods and from behind bushes and inequalities of the ground. There is no foundation for supposing that the enemy will select precisely those positions which will not give him the possibility of taking advantage of long-distance rifles and artillery. In addition to this, and to trenches and earthworks, he may prepare other obstacles for the overcoming of which the attackers from a short distance, in more or less dense masses, and under a constant fire will require no little time.

To this is replied that at short range the losses, not-withstanding the unquestioned improvement of the ballistic qualities of modern arms, will not be great. When the enemy is within close range the soldiers will be nervous, they will aim badly or not at all, and modern perfected small-arms will be little better than bows and pitchforks in the hands of barbarians.

But the soldier under cover will be subjected to very little danger. Resting his rifle upon the trench, he will fire without aiming, holding his rifle horizontally, and the bullet will bring death to whatever lies in its path for a space of 660 yards, while even if fired at too great an elevation it will fall among the reserves. The experience of the Chilian war demonstrates that at a range of from 1100 to 1320 yards the losses from random shots may be very considerable.

All this is well known to the advocates of war, yet they continue to maintain that soldiers will shoot badly, and that the perfected rifles now in their hands will be no more effective than the weapons they bore in the past. But is there any reason to suppose that with the favourable conditions for defence above indicated, soldiers acting on the defensive will aim badly ? Why, then, assume that the attackers will have sufficient courage to advance openly, exposing their whole bodies, when the defenders will be subjected to a danger eight times less ? In reality even this danger will not exist. At very short distances the fire of an enemy approaching at a running pace will be quite ineffective, while his rear ranks will be forced to cease fire.

Even if we were to admit that the defending army will always be of inferior quality, in such case his fire will be so heavy that it must work immense destruction among the attackers. To this also a reply is found. We are told that the stronger the fire the farther the contending armies will remain from one another ; they will rarely see one another ; rivers, woods, and hills will sometimes separate them ; there will no longer be direct clashes of troops, making of man a bloodthirsty beast, and ending in the ruin of one of the combatants. And since battles will take place at immense distances it will not be difficult in case of need to retreat from the field. But in such event more or less mutual extermination will have taken place without definite result.

Other writers admit the probability of terrible bloodshed and immense losses, but maintain that not this but the gaining of victory is the important point, whatever the losses may be. The war of 1870 showed that infantry is capable of enduring immense losses. Other specialists regard this opinion with suspicion in view of the fact that modern infantry is very different from that which fought in 1870. For many causes they admit that the losses will be incomparably greater.

Modern arms not only increase the direct danger but paralyse the medical service, since it will be impossible to organise ambulance stations in positions exposed even to the random shots of the enemy, and equally difficult to carry off the wounded. Modern rifles kill at two miles, artillery is effective at more than three and a half miles. And armies no longer consist of professional soldiers, but of peace-loving citizens who have no desire to expose themselves to danger. The propaganda against war may turn their minds in another direction. It is impossible to rely upon modern armies submitting to sacrifice and deprivation to such an extent as is desired by military theorists who lose sight of the tendencies which obtain in western European society.

Such contradictions of opinions are met not only by questions of a general nature, but even by matters of detail. Some declare that the improvement in firearms, and the adoption and application to military purposes of all the latest inventions, have cast into the background mere muscular strength, replacing it by military technique. With immense armies and high mental training of leaders, it will be possible by means of the strategical concentration of marching columns at a certain point to outflank and surround the enemy—all the more possible because the defence will be weakened in consequence of the greater distance of reserves.

To this the reply is : In order to carry out such an operation it will be necessary to know all the movements of the enemy, while against smokeless powder, long-range firearms, and against the precautions taken for guarding the centre of an army, the obtaining of information and the examination of the inhabitants will be more difficult ; the quick construction of light trenches will render vain attempts at turning flanks and surrounding an enemy ; while the constant arrival on the field of battle of fresh forces, which will be frequent owing to the distribution of armies over great areas, will endanger the position of an army which attempts a flanking movement.

Thus we find before us a whole series of hopeless contradictions. This it seems is inevitable and springs from the very nature of things. A war alone is capable of solving these questions.

In the future war, whatever the combinations may be, one side will stand primarily on the defensive; and if after the repulse of the enemy's attacks it in its turn resorts to attack for the purpose of finally overthrowing him, such operations can only be carried on for a short distance, as the newly attacking army will meet with similar insuperable obstacles. The contending armies in all probability will often exchange their parts.

French statisticians estimate that every attacking body, in order that it shall not be inferior to the defenders, when it has got within $35\frac{1}{2}$ yards (the distance at which it will be possible to rush upon the enemy), for each hundred men of the defenders it must have 637 men; while if it wishes to reach the actual positions of the defenders not numerically inferior, it must have eight times as many men.

By the statistics of General Skugarevski, a body of troops, double the strength of the defenders, beginning an attack from 800 paces, by the time they have advanced 300 paces will have less than half their strength available against the defence. With equal forces the defenders may allow the enemy to approach to within a distance of 220 yards, when they will only need to discharge the six cartridges in their magazines in order to annihilate the attacking force.

The celebrated Prussian authority, General Müller, declares that in order to avoid total extermination "soldiers will be compelled, in scattered formation, and as much as possible unobserved by the enemy, to creep forward, hiding behind irregularities in the field, and burying themselves in the earth as moles."

If this is so, is it possible to dream of taking an entrenched position? Let us suppose that, following the advice of General Müller, attacking troops will begin to form at 225 paces from the enemy, up to that time having suffered no loss. Let us also suppose that at that distance of 225 paces the attacking body numbers 400 men and the defenders in the trenches only 100 men. Now from the statistics of General Skugarevski, after the distance between the combatants has been traversed, only 74 men will be left to the offensive side for the actual attack with the bayonet. To suppose that the defending troops will have a clear field for aiming of less than 225 paces, or that 74 men will be able to wrest an entrenched position from 100 would be absurd.

All this leads to the conclusion that concerning methods of attack there can be no certain knowledge. To rely upon the assistance of artillery at the present day, when the quantity and quality of artillery will be on both sides the same, is impossible. To obtain a superiority of rifle fire over that of the defenders will be equally difficult, even with a considerable preponderance of strength ; so that the defending army in the very moment of attack may find itself in a position of complete security.

The Prussian General Janson expressed the view, to this time uncontroverted, that for attack it will first be necessary to employ artillery upon the enemy's position, and this of course can only be done by the concentration of a more powerful artillery than is at the disposal of the defence. If the rifle-pits and trenches of the defender's position are furnished with internal covering the assistance of siege artillery may be necessary for their destruction.

Only after such preliminary action may the actual attack by infantry begin. But to approach an adversary in a strongly fortified position, in the face of a fire over ground the distances of which have been ascertained beforehand, is a laborious task, and may even require two days to accomplish. In the first day the attacking body will advance to the limit of the line of fire of the enemy's artillery, and upon the approach of darkness must send into the belt of rifle fire small bodies, that is, companies taken from the assaulting army, always according to their order in the ranks. The advanced troops will proceed to the points selected, and immediately entrench themselves. These selected points of defence will form a line from which on the following day the storm of the position will be begun, after the opening of a strong rifle fire against the defence, and the advance of the rear echelons into the foremost line.

Now here comes in the chief difficulty in the execution of General Janson's plans. First of all the enemy will take such precautionary measures that it will seldom happen that the echelons advanced into the firing line before dawn will be able to find natural cover; on the contrary, the greater part of these echelons will remain without protection, and will stand exposed for a long time, while the attacking army, by means of fire, is preparing the position for attack.

General Janson himself is far from persuaded that the system of attack recommended by him will prove successful, even in the majority of cases. Indeed, as a condition precedent for the success of the attack, he assumes that the defenders will be disorganised and panic-stricken; at the same time adding that "we have no right to assume concerning the enemy what we would never admit about ourselves." Of course the system of attack he advocates could only prove successful after immense losses, and not always even after such losses.

To rely simply on the strength of the bayonet in face of modern intensity of fire would be to judge only by the tradition of those times when the bayonet was the last argument in battle. In the Russian army, faith in the bayonet is still sometimes expressed. Among foreign authorities it is no longer met with. The conditions have wholly changed. In former times the result of an infantry battle was thus decided: the combatants advanced upon one another without flinching, exchanged a volley or two, and then rushed upon one another. By such an assault the fate of the battle was quickly decided, the weaker side gave way, and escaped without difficulty if the enemy employed no cavalry. The victors sent two or three volleys after the vanquished, and the battle was over.

The conditions are very different now. Before an attack with the bayonet can be made a zone of murderous fire has first to be passed. Retreat after a repulsed attack upon a fortified position, will be accomplished only after the loss of more than half the attacking force. At such short ranges as will be found in bayonet attacks, almost every rifle bullet will disable one soldier, and often more than one. On a smokeless battlefield the results of such an overthrow will be visible to all. At such close ranges the present covered bullet will penetrate the cranium ; but in other parts of the body will have a shattering and tearing effect.

If we accept the opinions of the specialists cited that the defending troops by the force of their fire can stop the attack at some hundred yards distance, making further progress impossible, we are bound to admit that the defenders in their turn will not be able to undertake an assault, which would merely result in changing their positions with the enemy.

The attainment of success, as happened in the past, and especially in the war of 1870, by means of manœuvres and enveloping, will, in the war of the future, also be unlikely. In the first place such operations demand great superiority of force, whereas armies will be almost equal. Further, for the enveloping of an enemy's position reconnaissance under fire is necessary, and this is a very arduous task. A defending army driven from its positions, will begin to retreat by convenient roads, either finding new points of resistance prepared in advance, or again entrenching itself in suitable positions, continuing its opposition to the attacking army, and inflicting upon it new losses until reinforcements arrive.

In view of the conditions of modern war the question inevitably arises : Will leaders be found gifted with suffi-cient talent to decide the problems of war, and overcome difficulties which seem almost insuperable? Year by year the mechanism of war undergoes improvement, and it must continue to become more complex. The fortification of frontiers continues, the strength of armies grows. Would it not be madness to begin a war when the very methods of attack are the subject of dispute, and the only indisputable fact remains that every mistake, in consequence of the immense power of firearms, will be followed by ruinous results?

In enunciating the more important questions which arise from the new mechanism of war, we naturally meet the question: Is there not a strange contradiction in the preparation of powerful weapons of extermination, and the subjection to military service of almost the whole of the grown population in those states where the spirit of the time is so decidedly opposed to militarism? In order, however, to prepare a basis for a reply to this question we should be compelled to describe the entire action of that mechanism denominated an army of which the constituent parts are here marshalled.

General Count Caprivi declared in Parliament that the people was possessed by a madness for figures. And indeed all European states from the time of the introduction of universal military service have been in a position to call under the colours almost the whole of their able-bodied male population.

But these men are not soldiers. They are worthless save when they are properly armed and instructed. In addition they must be commanded, and without leadership the best army in the world would be an inert mob. Only men with commanders can be named soldiers.

Different authorities variously estimate the strength of armies which might be placed in the field on the outbreak of a war. To preserve impartiality we must introduce all such estimates.

But the following figures, which relate to the year 1896, appear to us the most probable.

The military strengths of the Powers are as follows:

Germany	.	.	.	.	.	2,550,000
Austria-Hungary	.	.	.	.	1,304,000
Italy	.	.	.	.	.	1,281,000
		Total		.	.	5,135,000
France	.	.	.	.	.	2,554,000
Russia	.	.	.	.	.	2,800,000
		Total		.	.	5,354,000

To arrive at this result the governments of these countries have lavished milliards. Yet it is a remarkable fact that the relative strength of armies has not changed, notwithstanding the efforts of every State to outdo its neighbours.

Conscription, as at present systematised, has one good side—it bears in itself the embryo of the abolition of war. On the mobilisation of the whole working population in the different countries difficulties may easily arise the consequences of which it would be difficult to foresee.

Within recent times immense sums have been laid out to ensure the rapid concentration of all possible forces as quickly as may be after the declaration of war, in positions near to the enemy, in order at once to begin a determined attack. Such arrangements in 1870 gave the Germans the most splendid results, and their necessity is now generally acknowledged. But since then the conditions have changed. The superiority which rapid concentration and mobilisation will give may be counterbalanced by the greater order which will result from less haste, and the less grave economic disorganisation which slower mobilisation will cause.

There can be no doubt that the immensity of modern armies and the weight of their equipment enormously increase the need for endurance among the rank and file. Infantry soldiers are compelled to carry a weight of from 25 to 35 kilogrammes, or from 70 to 87 pounds. To become inured gradually to this there will not be time ; long marches must be undertaken at once, and not a small proportion of the soldiers will break down from exhaustion.

The French medical authorities declare that after the first two weeks of marching the hospitals will contain 100,000 men, excluding those disabled by wounds.

To obtain quarters for an immense number of men will be impossible, and armies in the very beginning will be deprived of the most necessary conveniences. It will be difficult to guarantee large masses of men with provisions, with the same speed with which those men are mobilised. The local stores at the chief points of movement will be exhausted, and the transport of provisions from the central organisation will require time. Of the consequences of mobilisation we may judge, although imperfectly, by the experience of manœuvres. In France the manœuvres have already revealed imperfect training of officers, and unsatisfactory fulfilment by the reservists of their military duties. At every obstacle these men broke up into formless mobs ; they fired badly, so badly, indeed, that it was admitted that in the event of war three or four weeks' training would be required before they could be sent to the front, especially upon offensive operations.

It is improbable that in other countries similar inefficiency has not been observed ; and that this inefficiency is not spoken of so openly may be due to greater restraint or to insufficient means of publicity.

It may, indeed, be said that universal military service for short periods presents conditions in which lie concealed the germs of the impossibility of war itself. This impossibility lies mainly in the difficulty of providing for immense masses, as a consequence of the diminution in productiveness, the possibility of economic crises, and popular commotions, and, finally, in the extreme difficulty of directing armies consisting of millions of men.

With the growth of populations armies will continue to grow, and since even now the immensity of armies and the condition of armaments and tactics make the apparatus of war so complex that the directing, feeding, and forcing of armies into battle has become very difficult, in a not very distant future it will be more than questionable.

The more complex the apparatus the greater intelli-

gence will be required for its management, both in those
who command and those who obey. As the methods of
extermination grow more powerful the more essential will
it be to act at the psychical moment. In the network of
opinions, conditions, needs, and dangers which will arise
at almost every point of a struggle, in the opinion of
General Dragomiroff only a powerfully developed intelligence will be in a position to act. The immensity of
armies will cause great complexity in the whole apparatus
of war ; but, at the same time, side by side with the increase in the size of armies, grows the power of weapons
of destruction. The power of the rifle has been increased
fourteen times and that of artillery forty times.

In the past, success in war depended upon the ability
of the commander and the courage of his army. In the
future, success will depend more on the ability of the
commanders of individual bodies of troops, on the
initiative and energy of all officers, on the personal
example which they set to their men, and finally even on
the condition of the soldiers themselves.

For the just direction of all this gigantic mechanism
much experience will be required. But where will experienced commanders be found in the future, when experience
even of the present conditions is lacking ?

The conditions of modern war are such that of necessity
the directing power must pass from the hands of the older
commanders, not to speak of generals—from the hands of
colonels and even commanders of battalions—into the
hands of captains. Yet the French Professor Coumès,
in his work, " La Tactique de Demain," declares that for
the command of infantry on the field of battle such skill
will be required that in no army will there be found 100
officers out of every 500 fit to lead a company under fire.

If this can be said in time of peace concerning the
officers of standing armies, what will be the state of affairs
in war ? What will the chaos be when two-thirds of the
men in the ranks shall have been taken from the reserves,
who have forgotten their duties, who do not know their
officers, and to whom their men in turn are equally strangers?

The army will pass under the bâton of the Commander-in-Chief as it has been made by mobilisation. Consequently the dispositions for mobilisation have greater importance than before, and defects in mobilisation cannot be remedied in time of war. In view of the colossal size of modern armies their direction in time of war will be extremely difficult even for the most gifted leaders.

In addition to military skill, it will be necessary that a commander-in-chief shall be a good administrator. Everywhere it is recognised that the supply of an army will be a labour of Hercules, and attempts will continually be made by the enemy to destroy communications. To lead an immense modern army, to concentrate and deconcentrate it as necessity requires, is a labour in no way easy ; but to keep it in supplies will be an especially burdensome task.

Before the introduction of long-range firearms, battlefields were no larger than the exercise grounds of a modern brigade. The battlefields of the future will prove to be much greater in area than those of the past. The most powerful mind will not be able to embrace and combine all the details, requirements, and circumstances of an immense field. The receiving of information and the despatch of orders will be very difficult in the general uproar. The position will be all the more difficult since it will be seldom possible fully to concentrate the army for battle ; often many divisions will approach at their own time. Hence it will happen that the independence of commanders of divisions will play a considerable part. The wars of the eighteenth century required one commander. The present more mobile tactics necessitate as many commanders as there are independent sections of an army.

And yet Europe has no generals experienced in leading such masses, and none experienced in the keeping of armies supplied with provisions and ammunitions on a scale even approaching that which will be needed in the future. If dealing with such complex problems the commander-in-chief prove incapable, tremendous losses are bound to be sustained before he can be superseded.

Not only the question of supreme command, but the action of subordinate commanders, and of the officers generally, in view of the way in which troops will be scattered and of their loose relations to one another, and in view of the difficulty of taking advantage of cover as a consequence of smokeless or nearly smokeless powder, has become considerably more complex, and in future much more independent action will be required from officers. But in this necessary independence of action lies concealed another great danger.

Every meeting with an enemy will prove more threatening, and every mistake, every hesitation will have much more serious consequences than in the past, both in its material and its moral relations. A cloud of smoke will not cover the battlefield, concealing the horrors of the conflict. The soldier will not see the enemy, or hear the shot which may deprive him of life, but he will see around him his dead companions. As a consequence of such conditions, the nerves of all, in the battles of the future, will be subjected to a terrible and hitherto unexperienced strain.

The lack of officers trained in warfare is another notable fact. Since the Franco-German war twenty-nine years have passed, and since the last Russo-Turkish war twenty-two years. But even if these wars were less remote, conclusions drawn from them would be inapplicable to modern conditions, all the more so because each of these wars was characterised by exceptional circumstances. In the war of 1870–71 the strength and qualities of the two armies were too unequal, while the war of 1877–78, in European Turkey, presented itself chiefly in the form of the siege of a single fortress. Since then the introduction of smokeless powder, the general improvement of arms, and the growth of the importance of field fortifications, have completely changed the system of tactics.

Of officers who have studied military science, not on exercise grounds but on the field of battle, there are fewer than there were in former wars, and in a few years there will be none at all   The absence of experience must be

replaced by scientific instruction. But military science in
one important respect differs from other branches of knowledge, inasmuch as its theoretical teaching is not accompanied by the constant test of experiments, such as are
made for instance in chemistry, mechanics, and medicine.
Manœuvres give neither complete nor trustworthy information, as much that is allowed would prove impossible in war, and moreover they lack what Bismarck, at
the siege of Paris, called the "psychological moment."
It was not without reason that General Dragomiroff
observed that manœuvres would be much more instructive
if even one out of a thousand cartridges contained a
bullet.

Meantime a fundamental change has taken place in the
very elements of war from which depend, on the one hand,
its course, and on the other, its influence on all the departments of social order. On the field of battle, instead
of moderate, easily supervised armies and their reserves,
marching in deep and thick formation, elbow to elbow, there
will advance whole peoples up to fifty years of age, commanded for the most part (three-fourths) by officers from
the reserve, who will have almost forgotten the military
art.

These immense mobs will have at their disposal new
explosives of tremendous power, and arms with incomparably greater range and deadliness than before, but never
tested in a great war.

The immense extent of the theatre of war ; the vastness
of the field of battle ; the difficulties presented by attack
on entrenched positions and fortifications, and those
natural defences on the battlefield which soldiers are now
taught to utilise, and which inevitably will be utilised in
view of the deadliness of modern fire ; the impossibility of
massed attacks ; finally, the duration of battles, which may
be prolonged for several days, and which owing to the impossibility of pursuit may yield no decisive results—all
these are new circumstances.

In view of the increased importance of officers under
these conditions, systematic attempts will be made in all

European armies to kill off the officers of the enemy. Experience even of the last wars, when it had not been adopted as a principle to disable the officers of the enemy, showed how possible was the rapid diminution of the number of officers on the field of battle. At the end of the Franco-German war at the head of battalions and half battalions stood reserve officers of lower rank, and even sergeant-majors. In December 1870 in a Bavarian division there remained but one line captain.

As an illustration of what may happen in the future we may take the Chilian war, although only a part of the army of one of the combatants was armed with small-calibre rifles.

The losses in two battles were as follows :

Officers killed	.	.	.	.	23 per cent.
„ wounded	.	.	.	75	„
Men killed .	.	.	.	.	13 „
„ wounded	.	.	.	.	60 „

The high percentage of officers killed vividly illustrates the heavy cost of leading masses in war.

But the war of 1870 showed that if officers are lacking to give example the men will not attack. If this were so in 1870, what will be the case in the future, when for every hundred soldiers in the standing army it is proposed to draw from the reserves :

By Italy .	.	.	.	.	.	260 men.
„ Austria	.	.	.	.	.	350 „
„ Germany .	.	.	.	.	566 „
„ France	.	.	.	.	.	573 „
„ Russia	.	.	.	.	.	361 „

The majority of these reservists will have forgotten what they learnt during their period of service with the colours. Of the officers only a small proportion will be trained up to date. But it is in their hands that all leadership will rest. Yet the percentage of officers who possess a good preparatory training is :

In Russia	.	.	.	.	41 per cent.
„ Germany	.	.	.	.	100 „
„ France	.	.	.	.	38 „
„ Austria	.	.	.	.	20 „

Thus although experience has superseded science, we find that the officers who have been serving continuously will constitute less than half the staff, the other half will consist of officers of the reserve of all denominations, the majority of whom will have long forgotten the military art. Of this first half almost all will be taken for the formation of new staffs, &c., and the supply of line officers will be so exhausted that at the front there will remain in each battalion no more than eight of such officers—that is, no more than a fifth part, or 20 per cent., a deficiency of four-fifths remaining which must be supplied partly by retired officers, and partly by sergeant-majors and non-commissioned officers, for the greater part taken from those serving with the colours, but to some extent even from the reserve.

Thus every military undertaking owing to lack of leaders will present a terrible risk, and only daring advocates of a policy of adventure would now determine to solve international questions by war.

The frontiers of all states are sown with fortresses and fortified camps, and every road by which invasion might be made is prepared for defence beforehand. Even in times of peace immense forces stand at short distances from one another, and for the purpose of reinforcing them quickly strategical railroads have been built, so disposed that there can be no talk of the occupation of any country at once. A few days after mobilisation the opposing armies will almost directly confront one another.

In former times to hold great masses in hand, even in the case of failure, was comparatively easy. Long service and tactical exercises had turned soldiers into automata; in manœuvres as in war, great masses of men advanced, mighty by their own inert obedience.

In the present day armies almost always advance and act in loose formation, and with this the influence of the mass on the individual unit disappears. It is obvious that for the attainment of success the employment of a thin line of riflemen will not be sufficient. It will be necessary to prepare for an assault by artillery fire, and then by gradually strengthening the firing line with reserves, after which the position of the enemy will be finally attacked. Napoleon said that no decision in favour of battle should be taken where the chances of success were less than 70 out of 100; for when battle is once begun either victory or destruction must result. This rule of course remains applicable at the present day, but it must be noted that, with the immensity of modern armies and the vast spaces covered by the field of battle, if it be not impossible it will at least be much more difficult to estimate chances of success and to foretell the course of events.

Whatever technical improvements may exist, the first rule in battle is—obtain a superiority in numbers. The strategical problem (in the theatre of military operations) which lies in the union of forces exceeding the enemy's, corresponds in battle to the tactical problem, the acquirement of a preponderance at important points. Due defence, however, of the other points of one's position must be provided for, and the troops defending these latter points must sufficiently occupy the enemy's attention to prevent his forces from concentrating on the important point. A commander undertaking an assault must calculate the general consequences which will result from his initiative, and justly calculate as to his decisive blow, while providing in the execution of his plan for those contingencies which arise in the moment of battle.

Thanks to the system of furnishing troops with trenching instruments there will always be sufficient time for the construction of light earthworks, except of course on those occasions when the soil will prove frozen, marshy, or stony. A company by means of its own trenching tools may in the course of two and a quarter hours construct protection sufficient for a line of riflemen 250 paces in length. Small trenches, 100 paces long, for the protection of a whole company also require no more than two and a quarter hours, but larger earthworks and cover for artillery need from two and a half to eight hours' time. A battery is also provided with trenching tools, so that in the course of from two and a half to eight hours, according to the magnitude of the work, it may construct protection for its guns.

The chief difference between the tactics of modern and those of ancient times consists undoubtedly in the rare employment nowadays of direct attack. With modern arms and modern systems of defence generally, direct attack is accompanied by such immense losses that commanders, in all probability, will prefer flank attacks, especially if the enemy occupy a strongly fortified position.

But for this a considerable superiority of force will be required. In the words of Von der Goltz, the growing power of resistance of every military unit will enable a single division to accept battle with an army corps if it be confident of reinforcement within a brief time by another division. Even if the first division were exhausted by battle, yet so much time would be required for its decisive defeat that it might await the arrival of strong reinforcements, when the course of the battle might be entirely changed.

As an example we may cite the case of the army manœuvres in Eastern Prussia in the presence of the Emperor in 1894. Two divisions of the First Army Corps found themselves at the distance of a day's march from one another, yet the first of them succeeded in holding out against the assaults of the 17th Army Corps till the arrival of the second division, after which the defending divisions succeeded even in gaining some advantage over the enemy. In addition to this the flanking army cannot be certain that it will not meet with a fortified position on its road, and to count upon the negligence of the enemy would be foolhardy.

Formerly the conditions were much more favourable for attack. Napoleon, who, as the history of his campaign shows, always had a plan of battle ready, nevertheless allowed a considerable margin to accidents, to meet which he changed his plan in the very moment of action. "It is necessary," he said, "to strike at the enemy and then to think what further to do." This policy answered well at a time when, although armies were very large, the commander nevertheless held in his hand all the threads of the battle, thanks to the fact that with clouds of smoke, short range weapons and the closer order of the armies, he could himself follow the course of the battle, learn precisely all its events, and have ready close at hand considerable reserves. In the future such direct command will be incomparably more difficult, and, in consequence, in order to preserve unity of action it will be necessary to observe more rigorously the original plan.

Not only the question of supreme command, but also the action of the subordinate commanders and of officers generally, in consequence of the loose formation of armies and of the difficulty of taking advantage of the ground owing to smokeless powder, has become much more complex. In the war of 1870 one of the circumstances which helped the Germans to victory was that the German officers were much more independent and self-reliant than the French.

But what would the result have been if the French army had not been from the very beginning several times weaker than the German, and had been even in part well trained ?

The following is the judgment of the Prussian General Janson : " The characteristic features of the campaign of 1870–71 were, on the German side, a general advance and extraordinary liberty of the subordinate commanders— even down to captains. But this was accompanied by such dismemberment in the leadership that if the first attack had not succeeded there might have been the greatest danger for the attacking armies."

Let us examine a modern battle. As examples we will quote two sketches, the one borrowed from the celebrated work of Von der Goltz, the other from the French Captain Nigote. Both these sketches represent the course of a battle in its general features, and the second shows great skill also in depicting the battle of the future—that is, a probable picture of a battle under modern conditions.

Goltz describes an accidental battle, and then considers the differences between such a conflict and a battle which has formed part of the plans of the commanders-in-chief. It is obvious that in the accidental battle the chief part will be played by the eye of the commander-in-chief, his readiness in the appreciation of complex circumstances, and his resolution. " In such a state of affairs," he says, " the fortune of battle will lie with the commander who first comes to a clear decision, and who judges better the most distant events of the battle." On the other hand, in the "planned battle" all is arranged in advance, although plans may demand alteration owing to changed circumstances, contingencies requiring from the commander ability to take advantage rapidly of his position.

This picture gives no image of that which will happen.

The French Colonel B. in his composition " La Poudre sans Fumée," which awakened much interest, says : " Having no means of precisely judging our position, the enemy will be constrained to advance towards us in marching columns in order to deploy immediately on the discovery of our lines. But where shall he gain information ? He will be struck by artillery fire from a great distance, and the position of this artillery will be extremely difficult to determine precisely. . . . He will neither hear nor see enough for his purposes, and thus in a particular sense the words of Scripture may be applied : ' Eyes have they and they see not, ears have they and they hear not.' Reconnaissances and other means may be employed to determine the position of an enemy, but after these are made, changes in disposition may have taken place, and basing his operations on information thus obtained, an enemy may open fire on unoccupied points, and waste his ammunition, firing, as is said, ' at the sparrows.' "

Thus smokeless powder ensures long ignorance of positions and much search, and in consequence serious losses until the true position of things is ascertained. If the attacking troops be opposed by a capable and active foe, the period of uncertainty may cost them immense losses.

But the battle is now in full play.   We will quote here the picture of a modern battle drawn by Captain Nigote. This picture is, of course, only the fruit of imagination, as all the new instruments of extermination have not yet been employed in practice.   But imagination has worked upon a knowledge of the subject, and Captain Nigote's picture has as much claim on our attention as other theoretical sketches.

"The distance is 6600 yards from the enemy.   The artillery is in position, and the command has been passed along the batteries to 'give fire.'   The enemy's artillery replies.   Shells tear up the soil and burst ; in a short time the crew of every gun has ascertained the distance of the enemy.   Then every projectile discharged bursts in the air over the heads of the enemy, raining down hundreds of fragments and bullets on his position.   Men and horses are overwhelmed by this rain of lead and iron.   Guns destroy one another, batteries are mutually annihilated, ammunition cases are emptied.   Success will be with those whose fire does not slacken.   In the midst of this fire the battalions will advance.

"Now they are but 2200 yards away.   Already the rifle bullets whistle around and kill, each not only finding a victim, but penetrating files, ricochetting, and striking again.   Volley succeeds volley, bullets in great handfuls, constant as hail and swift as lightning deluge the field of battle.

"The artillery having silenced the enemy, is now free to deal with the enemy's battalions.   On his infantry, however loosely it may be formed, the guns direct thick iron rain, and soon in the positions of the enemy the earth is reddened with blood.

"The firing lines will advance one after the other, battalions will march after battalions ; finally, the reserves will follow.   Yet with all this movement in the two armies there will be a belt a thousand paces wide, separating them as if neutral territory, swept by the fire of both sides, a belt in which no living being can stand for a moment.

"The ammunition will be almost exhausted, millions of cartridges, thousands of shells will cover the soil. But the fire will continue until the empty ammunition cases are replaced with full.

"Melinite bombs will turn farmhouses, villages and hamlets to dust, destroying everything that might be used as cover, obstacle, or refuge.

"The moment will approach when half the combatants will be mowed down, dead and wounded will lie in parallel rows, separated one from the other by that belt of a thousand paces swept by a cross fire of shells which no living being can pass.

"The battle will continue with ferocity. But still those thousand paces unchangingly separate the foes.

"Which will have gained the victory? Neither."

This picture serves to illustrate a thought which, since the perfection of weapons, has occupied the minds of all thinking people. What will take place in a future war? Such are constrained to admit that between the combatants will always be an impassable zone of fire deadly in an equal degree to both the foes.

With such conditions, in its application to the battles of the future, the saying of Napoleon seems very questionable : "The fate of battle is the result of one minute, of one thought, the enemies approach with different plans, the battle becomes furious ; the decisive moment arrives, and a happy thought sudden as lightning decides the contest, the most insignificant reserve sometimes being the instrument of a splendid victory."

It is much more probable that in the future both sides will claim the victory. Examples of indecisive battles are found even in the war of 1870. Thus near Metz three battles took place which really constituted parts of one great battle. But which was decisively victorious at Metz? In reality neither. The German artillery proved its superiority ; the French infantry, armed with the Chasse-

D

pot, proved its.   Notwithstanding heroic efforts on both sides, neither one army nor the other gained a victory in the older and decisive sense of the word.

The shutting up of the French army in the fortress and its subsequent surrender were the consequence of the cutting off of supplies, the result of the numerical superiority of the Germans.   Theirs was not a victory of genius or military initiative—it was a victory of figures.

In a future war these conditions will be all the more important since the seal and sign of victory—the pursuit of the enemy—will be almost impossible.   The celebrated Liebert puts the matter in a few words : " In the past battles were ended thus : the field was ours, the enemy turned in flight ; the command to pursue was passed from flank to flank, and this crisis put strength into weary limbs ; instinctively horses were spurred, all thought only of drawing the greatest possible profit from victory, of causing the enemy even greater loss.   Now matters are very different."   Infantry having sustained modern destructive fire for a whole day, will be in a state of prostration, and so vast will be the space occupied by the army that even the reserves who are on the spot at the end of the battle will not be fresh.   As for cavalry, while rifle and artillery fire are powerful it must keep at a distance.   Napoleon's cavalry constantly went into attack at a trot, but Seidlitz at Zorndorf led his cavalry at a trot to within one hundred paces from the enemy, and at this distance raised it to a gallop.   In the face of modern fire, cavalry must exert all its strength to gallop across the zone of extermination.

In view of the difficulty of direct attack in the face of modern fire, the idea naturally occurs of attacking under cover of night.   Some military writers attribute immense importance to night attacks ; others, for a variety of reasons, find them inconvenient.   Concerning this question, it is useful to cite the opinion of Lieutenant-General Puzuirevski as the most impartial.   General Puzuirevski emphasises the laboriousness of movement by night after the work of the day, the difficulty of maintaining discipline, and the difficulty of looking after the soldiers. " Notwithstanding all this," says this authority, " movements by night are sometimes necessary in war, and therefore must be reckoned with."

Modern military history presents a remarkable example of a night attack—at Gorni Dubnak on October 12, 1877. After great losses the army was unable to continue the assault, but remained on the captured positions close to the enemy's trenches, and on the approach of night rushed upon the redoubts and captured them with trifling loss.

General Dragomiroff emphasises the following advantages of night attack : The attacking body may escape observation for some time ; it may find an unexpectant enemy, whose fire under such circumstances will be insignificant, and the bayonet may also be employed. General Dragomiroff finds that such operations as the storming of Kars and the battle of Kagaretch, where the Turks possessed an immense preponderance of forces, are possible only by night, and that generally in view of the destructiveness of modern fire, it will be necessary to accustom soldiers to operations by night. General Kuropatkin also declares himself in favour of night attacks, although he thinks they will succeed easier with small bodies of troops, and that picked men will be required.

On the other hand, the majority of foreign writers expect little profit out of night attacks. It is true that the French authority, Colonel B.,* thinks that having the advantage of smokeless powder the attacking body may approach very near to the enemy and create a panic in his ranks, but the author of an article in the *Neue Militärische Blätter*,† as an illustration of the danger of mistakes by night, quotes a case in the war of 1870 when the 101st Regiment of the French army, having come into conflict by night with a superior force of Germans, was defeated, and immediately fell under the fire of their comrades, who mistook them for the enemy. Hoenig‡ cites as example the battle at Le Mans in 1871, in which the Germans gained possession of all positions, but in another place he expresses himself decidedly against night attacks, on the ground that panics may easily occur in the attacking force.

* "La Poudre sans Fumée."   † Jahrgang 1890, p. 286.
‡ "Die Taktik der Zukunft," pp. 170 and 286.

However it may be, preparations are made in all armies for such contingencies. An illuminating bomb has been invented which burns from one to three minutes, according to calibre, and electrical projectors also which are capable of illuminating houses at a distance of 5500 yards, and by the aid of which the smallest movement on the part of the enemy may be observed.

It is unquestionable that the possibility of a night attack will cause great anxiety in every army. In former wars there were many cases of false alarms and panics. Assuredly they will be more common in future, as the dangers of war have increased, the nerves of modern soldiers are weaker, and owing to the system of short service, soldiers cannot be inured as were the veterans of the past. As far as nerves are concerned it may be assumed that the superiority will lie with the Russian soldier. The endurance shown by the Russian soldiers in the passage of the Balkans in the winter of 1877–78 awakened the astonishment of strangers. The Prussian General Von Kähler declared that the work which they accomplished surpassed the strength of men.

The following well-known saying of Napoleon is no longer applicable, " When the battle is over the vanquished in reality are little weaker than the victors, but the moral result constitutes such a great difference that the appearance of two or three squadrons is enough to cause great results." We have seen that such authoritative writers as the Prussian General Janson and the French Professor Langlois prophesy that battles will last several days, but a French Captain (formerly Professor) Nigote says plainly that battles may last for three or four days or even for a fortnight.* Other military specialists, and among them the well-known writer Fritz Hoenig,† think it not improbable that we are returning to the epoch of sieges. Belgrade, Mantua, and Plevna may be repeated. It is very possible that the attacking armies, finding decisive victory unattainable, will attempt to enclose the enemy in the position where they find him, and, after

* " La Bataille de Vesles," Capt. Nigote.
† *Op. cit. ante.*

entrenching themselves, begin to make raids in order to prevent the provisioning of the besieged. Such operations would be continued until the enemy are starved out.

It is hard to imagine it otherwise, when we remember that, with much inferior weapons, even the badly trained French mobiles of 1870 were rarely beaten at once, a second day having usually been necessary to drive them from newly occupied positions.

But the nature of the future war will be influenced by fortresses to an extent hitherto unknown. In the past, fortresses were situated in the more important strategical positions, but were only individual points equipped for passive defence. Nowadays, at all the most important thoroughfares are situated fortresses and fortified camps which contain such immense masses of troops that their turning is inconceivable. In addition to these, railways and roads are specially built to ensure the rapid concentration of troops immediately after war is declared; and, if the concentration of the enemy's troops should make it necessary, to provide for the quick transportation of troops from one spot to another.

Having constructed such works on their frontiers, States consider it more than probable that they will be able with inferior forces to oppose an enemy, thus counterbalancing all the advantages which he may draw from the more rapid accomplishment of mobilisation. But, however powerful modern systems of defence may be, science has yet contrived such destructive weapons that the question has already arisen : How many fortresses in a future war will accomplish that purpose for which they are destined ? This question has been the object of especial attention in military literature.

For us, the question whether modern fortresses will justify the hopes placed in them has an importance of the first degree. If an attacking army be held upon the frontier for a long time in conflict with an enemy defending himself in fortified positions prepared beforehand, the economic consequences of war will be very different from those which would follow if the invaders were to break at once through the lines of defences, and, having defeated the defenders in the interior of their own country, were within a short time to occupy the greater part of their territory.

All examples from the past, and even the history of the two last campaigns, throw little light on this question. Although fortress warfare in 1870–71 had an importance hardly dreamt of before, as the Germans captured fifteen French fortresses, still the methods taken from this campaign can hardly be applicable to the future. The objects of attack, with, to some extent, the exception of Paris, Metz, and Belfort, were fortresses of an obsolete type, and their defence was badly conducted.

On the other hand, the battles at Plevna, in the war of 1877–78, mainly proved the close bonds which exist between field and fortress warfare. But it has become clear to all that in a future war the example of the Turks will be followed as much as possible by an army acting on the defensive. At Plevna the besieged had but an insignificant quantity of artillery, yet the thought of taking Plevna by storm had to be abandoned ; it was hunger alone which compelled Osman to attempt to break out, and Plevna fell only after all the methods of siege warfare had been put in operation.

Since those days the science of fortress construction has made great advances, while, on the other hand, the means of attack have increased proportionately. The subject of fortress construction is very complicated, and its full elucidation would require detailed technical exposition, which would have too special a character.

Here we can quote only the general conclusions to which a study of the best authorities leads. The more important the fortress the more difficult will it be for the attacking army to pass it, since, if the fortress contained troops in a condition to attack, they would threaten the communications of the invaders. To seek a guarantee against such operations merely by placing against it posts of observation is impossible, since if the fortress contains a capable commander he will attack and defeat these detachments. The investment of great fortresses, from which vigorous sallies might be made, requires large armies and considerable time.

For the investment of a modern fortress, say, with thirteen forts, with intervening distances of $2\frac{1}{2}$ miles, and with fortified batteries between the forts, would require, according to a calculation made by Brialmont, an army of 122,000 men and a special siege corps of 50,000 men, in all 172,000 men. It may be mentioned here that the line of investment of Paris required 2·8 men for every $3\frac{1}{3}$ feet of fighting line. For the investment of the fortress postulated by Brialmont, according to this precedent, the investing army must be 246,400 strong, or together with a special siege corps, 296,400 men and not merely 172,000.

In order to give some idea of the time required for the siege of a modern fortress we will cite the approximate estimate, taken from a French publication on the attack and defence of fortresses : *

Period of investment, and arrival of sieging weapons, &c.	Defeat of the enemy's advanced lines . 8 days		30 days.
	Occupation of positions for close investment of the fortress . . . 10 ,,		
	Setting in position and construction of parks . . 12 ,,		
Attack on forts of the first line.	Construction and equipment of batteries of the first position . . . 12 ,,		45 ,,
	Artillery duels and bombardment . 8 ,,		
	Occupation of positions for batteries of second position, &c. . . . 25 ,,		
Successive capture of contiguous forts and attack on interlying defensive lines			20 ,,
Attack and capture of the fortress itself . . .			25 ,,
		Total . . .	120 days

* " Attaque et defense des places fortes ou Guerre de siège." Publiée avec le concours d'officiers de toutes armes et tout le patronage de la Réunion des officiers, Bruxelles 1886.

At the present day there is a conviction widely spread among military engineers and artillerists that, in view of the perfection of modern artillery, fortresses will not be subjected to siege, but will be attacked with open force. The downward firing of shrapnel out of short guns and mortars will deprive the fortification of defence ; direct fire from heavy artillery will batter the walls and open a free path for the storm of the fortress ; the introduction of shells containing five and a half hundred-weight of powerful explosives, will so increase the destructive power even of individual shots that all the older constructions will prove worthless, and even the new fortifications defended with armour will prove little better. Even a comparatively short bombardment with such projectiles will be sufficient to make the fortifications useless to the defence.

The chief upholder of such opinions is General Von Sauer, who proposes a system of shortened attack. The difference between systematic and accelerated attack in the exposition of General Sauer consists in the following : "Systematic or regular attack is directed mainly on one side of the fortress, while accelerated attack threatens all accessible sides. And since on the employment of the first method the besieged may devote all their strength to the defence of one side and even of one threatened point, accelerated attack is calculated to prevent such concentration, thus making it easier to overcome the scattered strength of the defence."

Against systematic attack the measures of defence consist firstly in this. The front or fronts which, according to the position of the roads are the nearest to materials which might serve for the construction of batteries and which by the configuration of the country will be most threatened, will be strongly fortified in advance. Against accelerated attack, which will be founded on considerations rather tactical than technical, it will be necessary to fortify strongly all fronts, for which resources will not always be found. But it is relying precisely on this circumstance, on the mobility of modern artillery, and on the difficulty of complete protection from projectiles, that the "tactical" attack is founded—the attack, as will easily be conceived, being directed not on the strong but on the weak parts of the defence.

But the defenders of a fortress will oppose the enemy with four consecutive lines of obstacles, that is, a first line of opposition, a chief defensive line, an intermediate line or line of reserves, and finally, a fortified unbroken rampart or central citadel. The capture of even the first line will require considerable effort, since this will consist of a series of field defences. The field will be strewn with numerous but small earthworks in the form of pits which the enemy cannot see from afar, and upon which artillery will have little effect, while, on the other hand, the skilful marksmen concealed in these pits may cause considerable loss.

In the attack on the chief defensive line it must be remembered that the improvements made in small arms and in artillery will prove as much in favour of the defence as of the attack.

The North American war of 1861–64, the Franco-Prussian war of 1870–71, and the Russo Turkish war of 1877–78 offer sufficient examples of the immense efforts and sacrifices which will be required in order finally to overcome an antagonist who has turned his circumstances to advantage in advance. What will happen in the war of the future when the defenders will have the support of a whole system of defensive works ready at hand ?

Milliards have been expended in Germany and France since 1870, in Russia since 1882, and in Italy, Austria, Belgium, and Switzerland in more recent times, in attempts to render frontiers impregnable, and, to provide for the contingency of the frontier defences failing to stop the enemy, on other defensive points at a greater distance from the frontiers.

Not only are the frontiers of all states studded with fortresses, but even in time of peace great forces stand at short distances from one another, and for the conveyance to them of reinforcements a system of railways exists so complete, that from the very outbreak of war armies will

almost immediately confront one another, and the space
free for movement will be very small.   With these conditions, in the war of the future an operation hitherto unknown must be undertaken—namely, to break through
frontier defences.   In view of the hundreds of thousands
of soldiers who will immediately be concentrated, the
breaking of a frontier line without a whole series of battles
is inconceivable.

The defenders, says General Leval, will know in advance the approximate position of the field of battle. They
know the chief points of the enemy's concentration, indicated by the position of his roads and military stores.
Mass attracts mass, such is the law of gravitation in war.
The enemy will advance upon our main forces, and even
the points of conflict may be approximately prophesied.
And so those "great uncertainties," of which we hear so
much, from the very beginning of war will not exist, and
both sides will have full possibility to fortify themselves
in corresponding positions.

The present armaments of all European armies may be
taken as equal in effectiveness, and the preparation of the
soldiers, both as concerns training and courage is the
same.   Therefore, if we set aside the capacity of the
commander-in-chief, as something which cannot be foreseen, we shall be obliged to conclude that the only element
of inequality is the number of soldiers in the ranks.
Supposing equality in the numerical relation, there would
be complete balance between the opposing forces, and equal
probability of success on both sides.   From this the
question naturally springs—With the equality of strength
which France and Russia have as against the Triple
Alliance, will it be possible for the armies of the attacking
powers in the present state of fortified frontiers to attain
any immediate and decisive success ?

Comparison with the past gives us little information
in this respect.   We find ourselves confronted with
an awful phenomenon.   In all armies a theory is pro-
claimed as to the superiority of offensive action.   But
meantime such strong positions have been created for

defence that their existence cannot be without influence on the course of events. The war of the future, whatever may be said, will be a struggle for fortified positions, and for that reason it must be prolonged.

If, in addition to the advance towards perfected mechanism, another fundamental change had not taken place, then it might have been possible out of the past to draw conclusions as to the future. But to-day whole nations will be under arms, the flower of every race —millions of men, just taken from the ranks of the workers, the producers of the substance of the people. The places they forsake will remain unoccupied, and their absence will be felt every day. The news of their fate will be waited with anxiety by the remaining millions; the destruction of whole divisions will call forth the groans and it may be the protests of hundreds of millions of people.

But the majority of those military writers who pay attention to the technical conditions of the matter, look on the question of the future war so objectively that they fail to see its relations with psychological and sociological questions—to express it in a word, they disregard the human side of the question. For this reason investigation of the conditions of a future war cannot be limited to the comparative military efficiency of the different States. Armies at present are the products of nations themselves. But the people, as Taine observed, judge not with the head but with the heart. It is therefore in the sentiments of the people that we must seek an indication of the frame of mind with which armies will enter upon war, and some guide as to the consequences among them of the first successes or failures. The temper of armies is a product of enlightenment, national character, culture, preponderance of civil or agricultural population, and those political and social ideals which in certain times influence the various countries.

Such were the considerations which impelled us to examine the data bearing on the condition and spirit of armies; to consider, for instance, those impressions which will be caused on the field of battle by the absence of a thick cloud of smoke obscuring the riflemen. Speaking generally, we attempted to determine the military spirit of the various European peoples according to the character peculiar to each. We attempted to bring under consideration all that might be drawn from the study of former wars, in order to form an idea as to the qualities of the chief European armies. But conclusions drawn from former wars have but very conditional significance. The spirit of armies in different countries does not always remain at the same level; after great height sometimes follow sudden fall and changes. And such changes take place in periods no greater than that which separates us from the last great European war.

A remarkable feature of our time is the rapidity with which changes occur both in the material and intellectual spheres. In the course of a few years greater changes take place in social life than formerly took place in decades. In this there is no ground for surprise. This great movement in life is ensured by the spread of education, the activity of parliaments, associations, the press, and means of communication. Under the influence of these conditions the intellect of the West finds itself under constant movement.

Another characteristic feature of our time is thus emphasised by Gervinus : " Movements in our century proceed from the instinct of the masses, and it is a very remarkable fact that in modern history are rarely found examples of the strong influence of individual personalities, rulers, or private workers. In our time as in the sixteenth century peoples move in masses."

The list of great gifts decreases, while the number of moderate talents have grown to an extraordinary extent. Few great and exalted personalities are produced, but in the whole a great revolution in social life has taken place.

It is for these reasons that the study of the spirit of armies in the future has such immense bearing upon the present work.

It was necessary to ask ourselves the questions: What will be the temper of modern armies in the event of defeat, or even of victory, if war should be prolonged? What will be the effect of the news from the field of battle on the civil population? What convulsions must we expect after the conclusion of peace when millions of excited soldiers return to their destroyed and desolated homes?

We attempted to collect data for the consideration of these questions, and with this object classified them in their constituent elements, resting upon precedent modified by the changes which have taken place in the constitution of armies, in armaments, and in tactics. But in order to draw from these data conclusions on all the different points, it would be necessary to make a tiresome repetition of the degrees of different qualities in armies, and, in addition, it would be difficult to represent in words with any precision the total of military qualities in the different armies in their twofold relationship—that is, their applicability to attack and defence. It would be necessary to cite the statistics of morals, culture, and sanitary condition of the various European armies. Only after such a laborious process could the system upon which we have estimated the respective values in attack and defence of the various European armies be followed. It is enough to give here the categories under which we have classified the elements which together constitute the general efficiency of armies:

(1) Susceptibility of application to the new conditions of war.
(2) Composition and completeness of the corps of officers.
(3) Capacity for initiative.
(4) Endurance under difficulty and privation.
(5) Discipline.
(6) Absence of egoism, dangerous for the general welfare.
(7) Faith in leaders and in companions-in-arms.
(8) Supplies and sanitary conditions.
(9) Age, disposition, and method for supplementing the lower ranks.

(10) Conviction in the merit of armaments.
(11) Courage.

As the final result we have obtained the following figures, showing the comparative military efficiency of the chief European armies in attack and in defence :

	In Attack.		In Defence.	
—	1st Summons.	2nd Summons.	1st Summons.	2nd Summons.
Germany . . .	95	80	98	86
Austria	80	68	86	76
Italy	65	51	74	59
France	72	59	85	72
Russia	88	80	94	86

Of all the details in the above chapter we find most clearly in relief the threatening features which a future war must present, both as regards the sacrifices of the population, and as regards the risks which must be run by the states participating. But both these factors are explained more fully in the chapter devoted to " Plans of Military Operations."

CHAPTER II

PLANS OF CAMPAIGN : POSSIBLE AND IMPOSSIBLE

THE first consideration to be taken into account in
estimating the chances of the next great war is the change
which has been brought about by the improvement in firearms and in the constitution of modern armies. These
changes have all tended to the advantage of the defensive and against the attacking force. Previous wars
under the old conditions had led to a conviction of the
superiority of attack. The new conditions which will
prevail in the future have reversed this opinion. Alike in
the equipment of troops and in the system of fortifications,
the changes have operated in favour of the defence.

The total numbers of fighting men effective for war in
1896 with their artillery were as follows :

	Thousands of men.		Artillery.
In Germany . .	2550	...	4552
„ Austria-Hungary .	1304	...	2696
„ Italy . . .	1281	...	1764
Together	5135	...	9012
„ France . . .	2554	...	7320
„ Russia . . .	2800	...	4952
Together	5354	...	12,272

Detailed calculations lead to the following estimate of
the probable distribution of the armies which might be
placed in both theatres of war, after deducting those forces
which would be employed on garrison duty in the interior

of each country, and for the defence of the frontier against
sudden intervention by any neutral State.

	In Thousands.						
—	Ger-many.	Austria.	Italy.	Total.	Russia.	France.	Total.
In the Russo-Austro-German theatre of war . .	690	979	—	1669	2539	—	2539
In the Franco-German theatre of war .	2035	—	—	2035	—	2126	2126
In the Franco-Italian theatre of war .	—	—	700	700	—	500	500
Total . .	2725	979	700	4404	2539	2626	5165

It is obvious that all these troops could not at once be
employed. The campaigns of the past were often begun
with from one quarter to one-eighth part of the armies
appointed for war. In the future the conditions in this
relation will have entirely changed. Speed in mobilisation,
as a consequence of the railways constructed specially for
strategical purposes, will ensure the rapid concentration
of armies at the very frontiers of States, reinforcing the
large armed forces maintained there even in times of
peace. All this makes it possible for immense armies to
meet face to face. And as in every case the attacking side
must exceed the defending in numbers, the question as to
the disposition of armies near the frontier, and the means
of transport of frontier forces to the positions which they
must occupy in war, is one of the first importance. But
it does not enter into the subject at present under discussion. It will be sufficient here to quote the opinion of
one of the first of modern military authorities, the Belgian

General Brialmont. Brialmont estimates that France is in a position to mobilise immediately nineteen army corps, and Germany twenty, each army corps counting forty-five to fifty thousand men. These will constitute the first line of the operating armies. The armies of the second line, according to General Brialmont, will on both sides be formed of more than half a million men.

Estimating thus, General Brialmont concludes that on the theatre of the future Franco-German war the forces of both sides will be almost equal, consisting, roughly speaking, of about 1,500,000 men on each side. In view of the fact that four years have passed since the time of General Brialmont's estimate and that two-years' service has been introduced into Germany, we may take the strength of the army of the second line at a million men. And since owing to the numerical equality of the opposing armies, and to the existence of the present fortifications, the advantage lies with the defending side, serious offensive action by Germany against France could be begun only after sending to the French frontier a great part of the German army. Under such conditions, Germany, of course, could not even think of contemporaneous assault upon Russia. She would be constrained, after allotting portion of her forces for strengthening Austria, to limit her remaining free forces to defensive operations. It is for this reason that we accept the strength of the Austro-Hungarian army against Russia as 1,669,000 as against 2,539,000 on the side of Russia.

An examination of the views of all authorities leads to the conclusion that Germany, having possibilities for more rapid mobilisation and concentration, will aim at successes in the first operations, while France will organise all her obtainable resources with the aim of retrieving the first failures. In order to consider the possibilities arising from this position we found it necessary to consider the conditions under which a new attack by Germany on France or by France on Germany must be begun, and first of all to study the fortifications of the

E

Franco-German frontier, and the probable paths of attack in Germany and France.

From a consideration of these conditions it clearly appears that to pass the newly constructed frontier lines of fortresses is impossible ; and there exists no means of direct invasion of France by Germany except by the attack of fortified positions or the forcing of a path through narrow passages purposely left.   These will be defended by forces which, within a short time after mobilisation, if they do not exceed the German armies, will at least equal them.

It is true that the German army will be better than the French, but the estimate we have made shows the difference to be insignificant.   The effectiveness of the German army in attack and the French in defence may be thus expressed :

	1st Summons.		2nd Summons.
German . . .	95	...	80
French . . .	85	...	72

Let us suppose that the German army will succeed in breaking through the frontier zone of operations and advancing on Paris by the routes indicated by General Brialmont. Having calculated the result of such operations, we come to the conclusion that at that time the French will have available 1,160,000 men, while for the siege of Paris the Germans wi.. have but 520,000 men.

The former German Chancellor, Count Caprivi, a man unquestionably competent in military affairs, on the discussion of the new military law in Parliament, said :

Supposing the French army were beaten, and retreated behind the walls of fortresses, then in order to enclose the present fortifications of Paris we must have at our disposal eighteen army corps, in addition to corresponding reserves.   It is very probable that the seige of Paris could now be carried on from one point only, but the example of Sevastopol shows that for this a whole year might be required.

Meanwhile our examination of the conditions in which the besieging army would find itself led us to the conclusion that if the military strength of Germany proved sufficient for the investment of Paris and the protection of its own rear, even then social and economic conditions would not permit of such operations being carried to an end.

Considering the possibility of an invasion of Germany by the French, it may be concluded that, with the present conditions of mobilisation and concentration of armies, such an invasion is probable only on the supposition that Germany in the beginning of the war limited herself in the west to defensive action, relying on the strength of Metz, Strasbourg, Thionville, and the Rhine fortresses, and sending her offensive resources to the east, calculating on the less rapid mobilisation of the Russian army.

In the opinion of specialists the only possible path by which France can attack Germany lies between Blamont and Longwy, with a movement thence on Mayence. But what tremendous obstacles would have to be overcome at the very first! The French would be obliged to cross, in the face of the German army relying upon the fortresses of Metz and Thionville, the Moselle and the Seille, and, defeating this army, blockade Metz and Strasbourg, take by assault the fortified positions on the Saar and the still stronger positions in the Hartz Mountains, and finally force a passage across the Rhine, about Mayence, Worms, Mannheim, or Speyers. And all this would have to be undertaken by armies which for attack are less efficient than the German.

After considering, from all points of view, the possible invasion of Germany by a French army a million and a half strong, against which Germany would place in the field 600,000 field troops and 600,000 Landsturm, it appears that the investment of Mayence and the forcing of a passage across the Rhine would be impossible. After deducting the losses in battle and on the march, the troops allotted for the investment of fortresses and the guarding of communications, France would have available 350,000 of the field army, whose quality may be expressed by the figure 72, and Germany 350,000 of the field army, whose effectiveness in defence may be expressed by the figure 98, and in addition a Landsturm whose effectiveness for defence is expressed by the figure 86.

But we assumed that Germany for defence would call up 600,000 Landsturm ; the same supposition applies to France. To complete her forces she would call up 600,000 men of the territorial army, which would be employed in secondary operations. Even with such conditions, which may be taken as very favourable to the French, it is hard to believe that the Rhine could be crossed. But even if the French army succeeded in forcing a passage across that river, after the losses sustained in the passage, and after the investment of Mayence, the French army would contain no more than 590,000 men, who would be opposed by 595,000 Germans, so that the numerical superiority would already be on the side of the Germans.

In addition, Germany would have the Landsturm reserves, in number not less than 1,200 000 men. A part of this force might also be moved to the Rhine, and in such an event the French armies would find themselves in a hopeless position.

In any case, we may safely prophesy a difficult and slow course of military operations, involving great losses, in consequence of the delay of immense forces by the defensive lines and fortifications of the enemy. And with the immensity of armies, and their prolonged stoppages on one spot, the difficulty of provisioning appears insuperable.

The losses from wounds, hunger, ordinary ailments, epidemics, and, it may be, even desertion, will cause all the more disorganisation in armies, because the war will disturb the internal life both of Germany and France. To decide whether Germany or France would prove itself stronger and more stable in its economic and social relations is difficult. The statistics of France and Germany show that both these states possess in an almost equal degree elements of endurability against the destructive influences of war. With such conditions, it is difficult to conceive that the statesmen of France or Germany would undertake a war.

Let us turn to the other possible theatre of a great European war and consider the operations of Germany, Austria and Russia. In this theatre also the most notable fact is the great chain of fortresses and defensive lines. As in Russia, so in Germany the attacking army will meet on its path great groups of fortresses and fortified positions, in mutual inter-relationship, and serving as a support for the operations of defensive armies. To invest such fortresses without sanguinary battles would be impossible, to force a passage in spite of them is difficult, while to evade them could only be done after leaving considerable forces behind for the protection of communications.

The alliances concluded between Germany, Austria and Italy on the one hand, and Russia and France on the other, in view of the great differences which exist between the strength and endurance of these states, render possible a great variety of combinations in actual war. In considering a struggle between France, Germany and Italy, plans of military operations are comparatively easy to define. In the case of an Austro-German-Russian war the conditions are much more complex. Here present themselves a greater number of combinations resulting from the vast extent of the theatre of war, and a greater room for initiative, owing to great differences in the period of mobilisation and concentration, but chiefly owing to the totally different social, political, and economic conditions.

The majority of writers assume that Germany would decide at the beginning to strike with all her force at one of her enemies, and having broken down his opposition, would attempt by means of railroads to move her main forces to the other theatre of war.

From this the question arises, to which frontier would she first direct her forces ? In order to form a clear idea on this subject it is necessary to take into consideration certain circumstances.

We have given reasons for assuming that the mobilisation and concentration of the German army would be carried through more speedily than that of the French or Russian armies. From this it follows that so far as Russia is concerned the initiative of action will belong to Germany. The German government, when demanding from the Reichstag credit for the increase of the army—and the Emperor William himself, on every convenient occasion—declared that the reason for demanding from the people such great sacrifices lay in the fact that Germany would be compelled to carry on offensive operations on two frontiers, and that if any other course were adopted German territory might be subjected to an invasion inevitably accompanied by the most terrible disasters for the people. But as it turned out, all the European powers immediately followed in the footsteps of Germany, and the relationship of strength remained unchanged, so that the German-Austro-Italian alliance has not now sufficient preponderance of strength for Germany to carry on serious offensive operations on both frontiers ; and, considering the defensive strength of the French and Russian frontiers and also the defensive strength of the German frontier itself, such an attempt would hardly seem rational.

With a division of forces the war would be still more prolonged, yet the immediate interest of Germany is to overthrow as quickly as possible one of its opponents, since Austria and Italy are less capable than she is of enduring the financial and social influences which would be aroused by a prolonged war. In the event of a lengthened campaign one or both of the allies of Germany might be compelled to cease military operations before the objects of the allies were attained. In addition to this, Germany must count upon the fact that her adversaries occupy a strong position for defence, so that the occupation of their defensive lines would demand immense sacrifices.

For such reasons it appears most probable that Germany would direct the greatest number and the best of her troops against one of her adversaries, placing on the other frontiers only such forces as would be required to support Austria against Russia or Italy against France. Other forms of operations on the part of Germany are hard to conceive. Some suppose that the chief strength of Germany will first be turned against France as more sensitive and less powerful than Russia, and not until she has broken down the opposition of France will she turn on her more dangerous enemy, Russia. Others assume that Germany will take the opposite course, striking first at Russia, the frontiers of which may not be so stubbornly defended as the frontiers of France, in consequence of the greater spaces, the absence of mountains, deep rivers and other obstacles, and also because of the slower mobilisation and concentration of the Russian forces. But what is more important, out of fear that Austria might be crushed at once, Germany may be forced to begin operations first of all against Russia, for the defence of her Western frontier relying upon Metz and the Rhine fortifications and on the diversion created by the Italians. The probability of such initiative is indicated also by the concentration of Germany's greatest forces on the Russian frontier. For Germany would have no need of such a concentration of troops on a frontier in time of peace if she did not intend to act offensively.

In a work published some years ago by Colonel Zolotaref, of the General Staff, devoted to an investigation of the Russian theatre of military operations, the following view is expressed :

Our adversaries will not fail to take advantage of the only superiority which they have over us, that is to say, their more rapid mobilisation and concentration, in order at once to cut off from Russia the western part of the theatre of war, to prevent reinforcement, and in a short time to make themselves masters of that territory. But this object could not be attained until they had succeeded in taking Brest-Litovsk, that important meeting-place of internal communications situated at the entrance to a difficult country. Thus, on the roads leading to Brest-Litovsk we must pay attention, as the most probable lines of operation of an enemy.

We have seen that the armed forces of the Triple and the Dual Alliances may be taken as almost equal, although as far as numbers are concerned some preponderance remains on the side of Russia and France. Adopting the supposition that Germany decides in the beginning of the war to stand on the defensive against Russia, we must ask ourselves on which of its defensive lines the German army will stand, on its eastern frontier or on the territory of Russia ? Major Scheibert,* of the German General Staff, supposes that the war will be begun against Russia as against France by strategical attack, but that after this, offensive operations must be discontinued on one theatre of war, in order, with concentrated forces, to strike a decisive blow at the other enemy. But when attack is discontinued it will be necessary to guarantee the successes gained by extensive fortifications. If this stoppage is made in the Western Provinces of Russia, Major Scheibert thinks that without great trouble the junction-points of roads and railways may be fortified by means of armoured gun carriages which can be speedily furnished from the German depôts. He further proposes to fortify the occupied Russian territory by crowding the rivers with steamers of small size (*die Flussnetze mit kleinen Dampfern zu bevölkern*), thus protecting the territory occupied by the Germans, helping the study of the locality, and facilitating the manœuvres of troops. He advises the organisation of communications between the different fortified points by lines of railways and steamers. In other words, Major Scheibert advocates the occupation of the kingdom of Poland.

Let us criticise these proposals more closely.

The kingdom of Poland forms a wedge between Prussia and Austria to such a distance that the Russian armies on the frontier may threaten Berlin, and what is more may take in flank Prussian forces sent into Eastern Prussia. But for precisely the same reason, Eastern Prussia forms a wedge between the Baltic Sea and Russian territory, bending round Poland and piercing to the Niemen, which makes it possible for the Germans to threaten the Russian forces in Poland by an advance on Brest and farther in the direction of Moscow, and also to operate directly against the second Russian defensive line of Kovno-

* " Aus der militärischen gesellschaft," Berlin, 1893.

Vilna, evading the first Russian position. In the opinion of the great majority of writers the defensive system of Russian Poland has been brought to perfection. (See map on next page of Russian Defensive System.)

In view of the strength which the Russian armies would present for the defence of the territories between the rivers Vistula, Bug, and Narev, supported by fortified positions on the Narev at Pultusk, Rozhan, Ostrolenka, and Lomza, and the fortresses of Warsaw, Novogeorgievski, and Zegrze, the military writers, Generals Brialmont, Pierron, and other foreign students, and Colonel Zolotaref assume that Germany, if she were to decide at first to turn her chief forces against Russia, would undertake an energetic offensive movement into the depths of Russia through Byelostok, to Brest from the direction of Warsaw, occupying the enemy with fictitious operations in order to cut off the main Russian forces from the other parts of the empire.

In other words, this means to pass the fortifications of the defensive line of the Vistula - Bug - Narev district. Such an undertaking might, of course, be very advantageous for the attacking Austro-German armies, but its execution would be attended with extraordinary dangers. If Germany and Austria could be assured that the Russian armies in this theatre of war were not in a fit state in their turn to make an attack upon vital points in the interior of Germany and Austria, or to cut the lines of communication of the invading armies, then such an attempt might have equal chances of success, and the Russian armies would be compelled to attack the invaders or to retire into the interior of the country. But the threat alone that the Russian armies might invade Silesia and the rich territories lying near the frontier would cause great alarm, acting all the more powerfully on public opinion in Germany since it would be in direct opposition to the declarations of the government and of the Emperor.

The opinion expressed by German writers that their armies would occupy the undefended territory on the left bank of the Vistula, which is at considerable distance from

Map of Russian Defensive System.

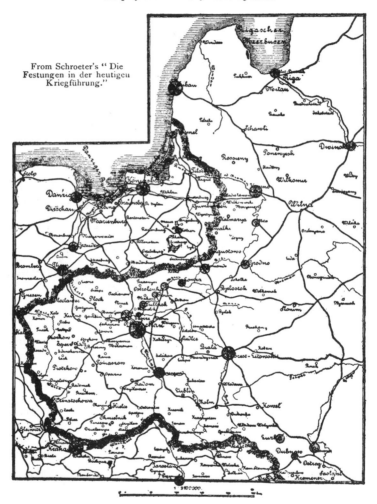

From Schroeter's " Die
Festungen in der heutigen
Kriegführung."

the fortresses, is therefore much more probable. In such event the losses which are demanded by attack would fall upon Russia. Further, in the case of the breaking of this line the Russian armies on the German frontier would be met by another defensive line.

Between the German and Austrian armies a junction might be effected by means of the railway leading from the Vistula on the Austrian frontier through Ostrobetz to the Vistula on Prussian territory. On this railway are situated many important towns—among them Lodz with more than 300,000 inhabitants—which might furnish large resources.

In view of convenience for the disposition of their armies, the Germans might usefully employ for the occupation of this line part of their older reserves, consisting of men who would be entirely unfit for field warfare and bivouac life. Nevertheless, in view of the risk of such an undertaking, it is necessary to suppose that the Austro-German armies would attempt primarily to direct their resources on the Vistula-Bug-Narev district, taking only defensive action against France.

After investigating the resources which Germany and Austria would have at their disposal for attack on Russia, the result appears that these powers, after allotting the forces needed for garrisons and for guarantee against France, would dispose of 2,100,000 men. Russia would have available not less than 2,380,000 men.

But of course neither Austria, nor Germany, nor Russia will be in a position to employ such forces at once. From the statistics of foreign authorities it appears that Germany and Austria for immediate attack would have available 900,000 men, Russia at first having available no more than 500,000 men.

But these figures seem to us untrustworthy. Before the Austro-German armies could penetrate to the Petersburg-Warsaw, the Moscow-Brest, and other railways by which Russian troops might be brought to the front, almost all will have been done to bring the Russian army of the first line up to its full strength.

The German army cannot attack before the Austrians, and therefore as a basis we must take the greatest distance and the longest period needed for mobilisation. In Austria mobilisation and concentration will take place much more slowly than in Germany, and the distances to be traversed will be longer by at least ten days' march. Meantime the Warsaw district includes reserves of 200,000 men, the Vilna district 270,000, and the Kief district 427,000 men. Thus it will be impossible to prevent the strengthening of the Russian armies situated on the Vistula-Niemen theatre of war to a million of men.

Plans of attack by the allies on the territory watered by the rivers Niemen, Vistula, and Narev have been analysed by the French writer General Pierron, who mentions that in June 1888 he, together with French officers of the General Staff, by order of his government made a tour through the theatre of war above mentioned. From the data collected by General Pierron the probable routes of attack by the Austro-German armies from their points of concentration would appear to be those indicated by the plan opposite. The probable paths of attack by Germany and Austria have also been considered by the Belgian engineer, General Brialmont. By combining the data of Generals Pierron and Brialmont the disposition of the allied armies in their concentric movement on Warsaw and Novogeorgievsk may be presented in the plan on page 78, in which we take as points of departure, not those positions which serve as bases, but those railway stations near which, in all probability, the concentration of the armies will take place. For convenience the routes of the attacking armies are indicated by straight lines, each straight line also representing an army corps of 50,000 men.

There is no doubt that in the Russian territories the attacking Germans and their allies will meet with strong defensive lines, which, if they are inferior in anything to the iron ring of defences constructed in France, nevertheless may be defended even against an enemy twice as strong. These Russian lines of defence include ten

Paths of Advance of the Austro-German Armies from Points of Concentration to the Vistula-Bug-Narev Theatre of War.

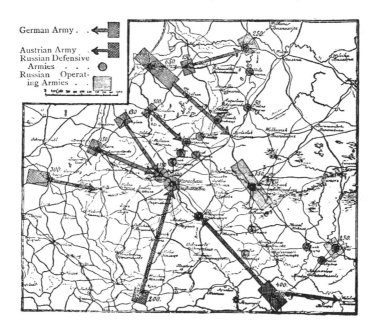

*Paths of Advance of the German and Austrian Armies on the Vistula-
Bug-Narev Theatre of War, from Pierron and Brialmont.*

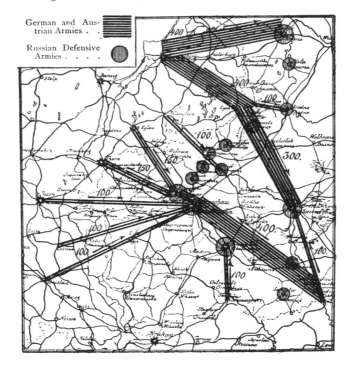

fortresses with fortified camps, situated on rivers, and making the passage of rivers and marshes extremely difficult.

With such conditions the Russian armies supported by internal lines of defence will, with energetic leadership and the known endurance of the Russian soldier, have full possibility of moving to every threatened point preponderating forces, before the junction in superior force of the Austrian and German armies can take place.

The greatest numerical superiority which can be admitted as possible on the Austrian and German side would be at Kovno, 400,000 men, and at Brest, also 400,000 men, against 100,000 defending the first fortress, and 250,000 the second. But Kovno and Brest are both first-class fortresses, and the troops defending them will be in strong positions, of the speedy capture of which the enemy cannot even dream. To their aid will hasten the fresh forces which will be mobilised within Russia, and the besiegers may easily find themselves in a dangerous position.

If Plevna with its improvised fortifications was held for months against an enemy four times stronger, by a garrison deprived of hope of relief, how much longer may such regularly fortified camps as Kovno and Brest hold out when help must come within the fortnight which will be required for the mobilisation of 415,000 men, or, at the worst, of a considerable proportion of that number? When these 415,000 men shall have marched to the relief of Brest and Kovno, the forces of Russia will not only equal those of the allies, but will even find themselves to a certain extent superior.

In addition to this must be borne in mind the difficulty of provisioning an invading army, a million strong, far from its base, while the Russian armies defending their own territory would fight under much better conditions. Even from the point of view most favourable to the Germans—even if they succeeded in taking Ivangorod, Warsaw, and Novogeorgievsk, with all auxiliary fortifications — they would find a tremendous obstacle in Brest-Litovsk alone.

Situated in the midst of a marsh it would be almost impossible to invest it closely, and in no case could it be invested speedily. It is obvious that before Brest could be taken the Russian army garrisoned there would be reinforced by more than 250,000 men. Even supposing, what is still more improbable, that the allies in operations against fortresses and first lines of defence were always victorious, yet such victories would cost them so dear that the stoppage of further operations would seem inevitable.

Estimates as to the probable loss of attacking and defending troops in battle and from disease show that by the time the allies were in a position to undertake operations against the second defensive line—that is, Brest-Litovsk and Kovno — the Russian forces would amount to 440,000 in fortresses, and 375,000 auxiliary forces acting in combination with these garrisons, a total of 815,000 men, to which must be added an army of 1,264,000, newly formed, approaching the scene of operations. The allied powers would dispose of 1,588,000 men. In such event the numerical superiority of the allies over the operating Russian armies would amount to only 773,000 men.

In the face of the Russian armies operating on internal lines and able to change front at discretion, and in face of the reinforcements daily increasing until on the arrival on the scene of action of the whole 1,264,000 of their reserved armies, the Russians would have a numerical superiority of 491,000 men, an advance into the interior of Russia would be an undertaking attended with too great risk. It is, therefore, more probable that the enemy would first invest the fortresses, and only afterwards attempt to defeat the armies of reserves.

In assuming this, we again allow the most favourable supposition for the allies, for this reason, that the losses in battle and in the investment of the fortresses of the second line of defence will be as follows : The 375,000 men of the Russian operating army, acting in combination with the garrisons of the fortresses, will lose a third of their strength, or 125,000 men ; the losses of the attacking armies will be twice as great, that is, 250,000 men. Further, we assume that only 10 per cent., or, 25,000 men of the Russian army would be able to take refuge in the fortress of Brest-Litovsk, the other 90 per cent., that is, 225,000, being taken prisoners. But even under such circumstances the German-Austrian armies would not have freedom for activity.

From the estimate of General Brialmont we find that for the investment of armies shut up in fortresses, an army of double the strength of the besieged is necessary—that is to say, the position of the Russian and Austro-German armies after the defeat of the operating Russian army, and the investment of the fortresses, would be as follows :

RUSSIAN ARMIES.

Approaching Reserves . . .	1,264,000
In fortresses	465,000

AUSTRO-GERMAN.

Besieging armies	926,000
Free for attack	412,000

These figures show that before the fall of the fortresses there could be no thought of any extensive advance of the allied armies into the interior of Russia. Let us admit, however, the extreme hypothesis that immediate attacks on the fortresses will prove completely successful, and that the Russian armies besieged will be compelled to surrender. Such a success apparently would in no way resemble the surrenders of the French in 1870-71. The capture of the Russian fortresses by assault could only be accomplished after terrible conflicts attended with tremendous losses in the ranks of the attacking armies.

We will suppose—a supposition again the most favourable to the invaders—that the losses of the allies under these circumstances were only half as great as the losses of the Russian armies in battle, that is 232,000 men, with a loss of no more than 10 per cent. from disease. In such

F

event there would remain only 1,013,000 men in the ranks of the allies against 1,264,000 in the armies of the Russian reserve.

Having gone so far, there are two questions which may well be asked. Having maintained her main forces for such a prolonged time on the Russian theatre of war, would Germany be in a position to defend herself against attack from France, and would the 70,000 men left by the allies for the guarding of Ivangorod, and the 200,000 Austrians left in Galicia be able to withstand the attack of the Russian reserves ?

From the foregoing figures and arguments we must conclude that the plans of attack by Austria and Germany in Russia proposed by foreign military authorities, taking into consideration the immense strength of the fortresses of the Vistula-Bug-Narev theatre of war, and afterwards of the second Russian line of defence, would be impossible to carry into effect.

It is true that another opinion has been expressed as to the possibility of outflanking the Vistula-Bug-Narev positions and even also that of Brest. But such an undertaking would be attended with such extraordinary and obvious dangers that it is unnecessary to consider it here.

Generally, the consequences which would ensue if the German-Austrian armies were to adopt the daring plan of direct movement on Brest-Litovsk in order to cut off the Russian forces in Poland, belong to the category of vexed questions. Plans, of course, are kept scrupulously secret, but some indications nevertheless may be drawn from the opinions current in military circles. First of all it is noteworthy that German officers no longer speak of the project of immediately occupying Warsaw and the whole of Poland, and of fortifying themselves there. But ten years ago, when war with Russia seemed near, this view was so widespread in Prussian military circles that certain officers invited Polish ladies to a dance in Warsaw at the next carnival. The well-known military writer, Scheibert,* expressing the opinion that the Germans must limit them-

* *Op. cit. ante.*

selves to the occupation of Poland, and fortifying themselves there, added that in the West Germany should afterwards confine herself to defensive operations, while her "Eastern neighbour, incited by the independent, premature initiative peculiar to its leaders, would try to gain successes by means of reckless enterprises."

Nowadays, of talk of the occupation of Warsaw there remains not a trace. But it is known that in Königsberg are collected immense stores of sections of bridges and materials for the construction and repair of railways. Apparently, the Germans have realised the delusiveness of an undertaking having as its aim to cut off the Russian armies in Poland, and place them between two fires. Such thoughts correspond to the spirit of self-confidence fostered in German military circles since the great successes of 1870–71, successes which awakened profound faith in the excellence of the German army, and a disposition to depreciate the value of other armies.

Thus the opinion of Scheibert that the Russian commanders will attempt to attain successes by means of daring, ill-considered enterprises, is repeated in Germany to the present day. And, indeed, if the German headquarters staff is convinced that it is capable always, at the right moment, to concentrate its forces, and that the Russian armies will not find themselves in such favourable conditions, it may easily set itself the task of defeating the Russian armies one after another, calculating by such operations to hasten the course of the war, and diminish the economic difficulties from which Germany would suffer. But such an undertaking would be so risky that its initiation would be desired by the most competent authorities in Russia. In war nothing can be calculated upon absolutely, and the strategical development of operations may result in no way so favourably as is relied upon in Berlin and Vienna. In such event the allies would be subjected to defeat.

Without analysing closely the opinions we have quoted, we must ask the question whether with such plans of operations the final objects of war could be accomplished.

All authorities on the war of the future are agreed that in order to force Russia to conclude peace on terms unfavourable to herself, the occupation of Petersburg and Moscow would be required. It is plain that in face of the immense, almost insuperable obstacles which separate both these capitals from the Austro-German base, the allies would not have the resources to advance at once upon Petersburg and Moscow as long as the chief fortified points remained uncaptured and the Russian armies unbeaten, since until these objects were accomplished, too great forces would be needed for the protection of communications.

Thus the allies would be compelled to choose between plans of attack either on Petersburg or on Moscow. To wait for an opportunity, in view of the intact Russian armies, would be impossible for the allies, because the Russian armies in the Vistula-Bug-Narev district would preserve open communications with the southern governments, and the Russian army might undertake a movement against Austria which would destroy the plans of the enemy. The opinions expressed on this subject in military literature lead to the conclusion that if the German government decided on a march into the interior of Russia the aim of the allies would, in all probability, be Moscow and not Petersburg, while the consequences of any such attempt would recall the fate of Napoleon's army, that is to say, it would result in absolute starvation.

For the Germans to limit themselves to the conquest of Poland, as certain authorities advise, and confine themselves to defensive operations is impossible, as such action would give no speedy and final result, and a prolonged war could not be sustained by Germany's allies. In addition, such a decision would expose Germany to great risk. The armies on the Vistula-Bug-Narev theatre of war would be directed against Prussia. It is true that the German frontier is very strongly fortified, and presents topographical conditions very favourable for defence. But the very attempt of the Russian armies to enter upon German territory would undoubtedly cause intense alarm among the German population.

The strength in that district of the Russian army which would be in a position to undertake operations against Germany we have already estimated at 650,000 men. The operations of this army would be directed against Eastern Prussia, in order to cut the communications between Berlin and the bases of attack of the German army in Russia—that is, Königsberg. The invasion of Prussian territory would be facilitated by the nearness of the lines of the Narev and Bug to the Prussian frontier. But it is evident that the Russian armies situated in that district would not be strong enough to strike a decisive blow at Prussia by operations against Berlin itself.

The occupation by the Germans of the left undefended bank of the Vistula in Poland would require separate armies at least as strong as the acting Russian forces. Therefore, at the disposal of the German headquarters staff would be 1,175,000 men ready for further advance into the interior of Russia.

If the fortresses of the Bug did not require investment, then Kovno, Ossovetz, Olita, and Grodno must undoubtedly be invested, for which purpose at least 375,000 men would be required. Thus for advance into the interior of Russia the Germans would only dispose of 800,000 men, a number obviously insufficient for such an undertaking. From this it follows that the Germans will be compelled to await the approach of the Austrians, and to continue their operations in combination with them.

We must bear in mind that the defences of Austria in Galicia are very weak. It is probable that this consideration will not exercise a commanding influence in the choice of plans of operations, for the decisive word will undoubtedly belong to Germany. But for that reason it will be difficult to compel Austria to advance her forces rapidly, she finding herself threatened by an invasion from Russia of her Slavonic provinces. Thus the German staff in all probability will not decide upon invasion of the interior of Russia, but will first of all occupy itself with operations against Olita, Ossovetz, Grodna, and Kovno. Detailed calculations show that after deducting the forces necessary to restrain Russia from active operations against Austria, the latter power would only have 600,000 men free for offensive action against Russia; thus the attacking forces of the allies may be estimated at 1,400,000 men.

Russia would dispose of armies 2,380,000 strong, which would be distributed as follows :

In the Vistula-Bug-Narev positions .	650,000
,, Kovno, Grodno, Ossobitz, Olita . .	250,000
,, Dubno, Kovno, Dutzke . . .	200,000
Total . .	1,100,000

Thus for active operations Russia would possess 1,280,000 men. Of course when the Austro-German armies began operations this force of 1,280,000 might not be concentrated. But as we already explained, long before the enemy could reach Moscow not only this army, but millions more, although with little training, would be ready to oppose the invaders, whose armies, every fifty miles they marched into the interior, would thaw as snow in spring.

In this connection the history of 1812 may perhaps be instructive. In the beginning of action the operating armies consisted of

	400,000 French	...	180,000 Russians
At Smolensk .	. 183,000	,,	...	120,000	,,
,, Moscow .	. 134,000	,,	...	130,000	,,

As the final result of investigation we must conclude that an advance on Moscow would require at least a two years' campaign, while the more prolonged the war, the better it would prove for Russia. Her immense resources gradually organised would every day be better prepared, and the numerical preponderance would finally pass to Russia, while the allies, weakened by immense losses in battle, and from illness caused by insufficient food, would be forced to close the war without attaining their objects, in consequence of the absence in the markets of Transoceanic and Russian grain, and probably also as a result of internal difficulties caused by the stoppage of work, and by famine.

Some military writers advise that operations against Russia should begin in winter, as the frozen ground would increase the difficulty of constructing earthworks, while the invaders would find greater facilities for transport, both in the sledge paths which replace in winter the bad marshy roads, and in the freezing of the rivers. This last circumstance, in their opinion, almost totally deprives rivers of their immense defensive value.

But the danger of advance into Russia by winter would be still greater for the German army (consisting, as it will, of four-fifths of reserves) than it was for the army of Napoleon, which was, for the most part, composed of veterans.

Such a decision on the part of the German Government is all the less probable because the roads in the frontier districts of Russia are often spoiled by thaws, as was experienced in the wars of 1806–7, and in the Polish campaign of 1831.

Thus after considering all possible combinations it is more than probable that an invasion of Russia would not lead to such results as would accomplish the ends of war. And modern conditions are such that even Russia, in the event of victory, could not attain the best results.

The carrying on by Russia of an offensive war against Germany and Austria after driving the armies of those powers out of her territories, or in the event of those states from the beginning restricting themselves to defence, or limiting their offensive operations to the occupation of certain Russian territories, would be accompanied by great, it may be insuperable difficulties.

Following on the heels of the armies which she had defeated, the Russian armies would be compelled to traverse vast territories entirely exhausted, and to draw all their provisions from an immense distance. The victories already gained would, of course, have cost them dear, and reserves of necessity would predominate both in the ranks and among the officers. With armies thus constituted success in an offensive war would be much less probable than with armies only completed from the reserve.

In addition to this, in advancing on German territory the Russian armies would meet with still numerous forces formed, it is true, mainly from the remnants of the attacking armies and from the Landsturm with its reserves, worthless for attack, but fully reliable for defence. As relates to commissariat, transport from the interior of Russia to Prussian territory—not to speak of possible failure of the administration—would require much time and immense outlay. In the war of 1870 the Germans lived at the expense of the enemy. But such favourable circumstances will not be repeated. Rapid advances and the possibility of making requisitions demanding contributions in the face of the present fortified frontiers, smokeless powder, and improved armaments, are inconceivable.

For the invasion, by Russia, of Prussian territory military literature offers several projects. The plan opposite illustrates the scheme of operations which military writers consider most probable.

But whatever the direction selected for attack on Prussia, it must be borne in mind that the invaders will be met by a scientific and long-prepared system of defence. Great rivers and fortresses constitute for the Germans a strong defence, while behind them a network of railways, satisfying all the requirements of modern strategy, guarantees the communications of the defending armies with the interior of the country. There will be no difficulty in completing the ranks of the Prussian army, for in addition to the remnants of the invading army the Landsturm with its reserves will be ready.

Thus, to conquer Prussia on her own territory will be no easy task, and the danger she will be subjected to by the occupation by an enemy's forces will be far less serious than the danger which will threaten her from famine. As relates to internal revolutionary movements it can hardly be supposed that the irruption of an enemy on Prussian

Plan of invasion, by Russia, of Prussian territory.

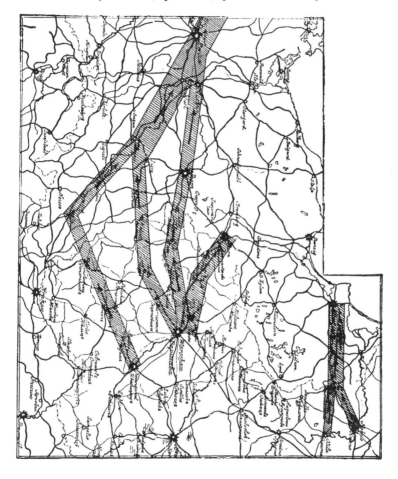

territory would strengthen such a movement. Invasion from Russia would in all probability have entirely different results.

It is necessary to consider one more combination—namely, that Russia, in view of the weakness of the Austrian defence in Galicia, as compared with the defences which exist in the Eastern provinces of Prussia, would restrict herself to defence against Germany, employing her remaining forces for the invasion of Eastern Galicia. But such a combination is improbable. The chief political question lies in the crushing of Germany. Having wasted her strength in a struggle with Austria, Russia would be still less able to force Germany to lay down her arms.

According to General Brialmont two Russian armies might at the same time operate against Austria, one having as its goal Vienna, and the other Buda-Pesth. The consideration of plans of operation in these directions leads to the conclusion that the Russian army would have to overcome immense obstacles, and to march through a country already more or less exhausted.

But even in the event of Russian victory the results obtained would hardly compensate for the war.

For in assuming that Russia were to carry the war into the territory of one of the allies, we must consider the possibility that Germany would return Alsace-Lorraine to France, and that the Government of France might not be in a state to oppose the popular movement in favour of the conclusion of peace. If this were to happen the whole plan of attack, based upon the diversion by France of half the forces of the Triple Alliance, would have to be abandoned.

Thus in all possible combinations a European war in which Russia took part would result in complete exhaustion of both combatants. Nevertheless, estimates of the strength and distribution of armies, the resources for keeping them up to strength, and economic endurance, prove that Russia will be in a condition to sustain a war indefinitely. Even the occupation of one of the Russian

capitals, perhaps of both, would not force her to unconditional surrender. On the other hand, the advance of the
Russian armies into Prussia or Austria would not result
in any certain success.

Generally, it is difficult to foresee what actual strategical
results would issue from this immense struggle, or how it
would end. Russia, even with the failure of her arms in
some directions, relying upon the immensity of her territories and the approach of an inclement winter, would not
be inclined to the conclusion of peace. As for western
countries, with the complexity of their economic and social
polity, with the mutual interdependence of all the wheels
of the internal mechanism, it is difficult to form any idea
how a great and prolonged war would react on the
economic and social order. It is unquestionable that the
fear of those internal agitations which would be awakened
by a crisis will have great influence in dissuading governments against undertaking a war.

On the other hand, once war has broken out the conclusion of peace will present great difficulties to any
government, either after failure or success. At first it
will seem that the results obtained in no way compensate
for the sacrifices made, and grave difficulties may present
themselves even in the disarmament of masses of men.
In the second case—that is, of failure—the stoppage of
military operations without attaining the results expected
might easily give rise to revolutionary movements. Even
in Russia, with all its political fortresses, the war of
1877–78 resulted in a temporary strengthening of the
revolutionary propaganda, although that propaganda
was carried on by an insignificant proportion of the
people.

General plans of operation against possible enemies
are elaborated by the General Staffs of all armies. In
these plans are unquestionably indicated the resources
and time that will be required for the attainment of certain
objects. But we may doubt whether in any of such plans
the economic conditions have been considered. On more
than one occasion we have spoken to M. Burdeau, the

French Minister of Marine, a man of the highest capacity, who frankly admitted that when M. Freycinet was Minister of War it was proposed to undertake an inquiry into the economic conditions which would accompany war, but this project had to be abandoned in consequence of the opposition met with in military circles.

CHAPTER III

THE FUTURE OF NAVAL WARFARE

SINCE the time of the Franco-German war certain principles have been advocated in relation to maritime warfare which, if practised, involve a return to the conditions of barbarism. The advance which has taken place in that period in naval affairs is interesting not only in itself, but also because of the influence which it must exert on the character of war on land. The possibility of the destruction of maritime towns, the interruption of oversea supplies, and the severing of certain states from communication with the rest of the world may awaken dangerous movements and cause the stoppage of a war on land earlier than the results expected have been attained. But a naval war between two European powers with equal fleets is improbable, since it would result in mutual destruction.

With the wars of the past, again, no comparison could be drawn. In view of the immense influence which a naval war may exert on the economic and social conditions of peoples, it might be expected that all questions connected with the building of warships and their operations had already been submitted to careful study and consideration. But it cannot be said that this has been done. In France, still dreaming of vengeance, every investigation which would emphasise the ruinous consequences of maritime war in its new conditions is unpopular, since such investigation would unquestionably lead to the conclusion that it will be almost impossible to carry on a war on dry land so as to realise the first hopes. In Germany, maritime war is treated of only by specialists, who restrain themselves in the expression of views as to the ruinous results which war might involve. Exceptions to this rule are few. Among their number may be found the economist Rudolf Meyer and Admiral Werner. In Italy, the Government is generally condemned for the intolerable burdens to which the people are subjected for the maintenance of armed forces generally, and in particular for the maintenance of the fleet; and it is the interest of the Government to prevent the circulation of pessimistic views. Russia and Austria concern themselves little with maritime warfare, since for them these questions are of secondary importance. England is an exception, and much interest is taken there; and this is natural, both on account of her geographical position and because her population depends directly upon oversea supplies.

But even in England no clear idea of the recent revolution in methods, and of the consequences of a naval war, has yet penetrated to the masses, and the assurance of specialists is accepted that between the naval warfare of the present and the past no fundamental difference which would exclude comparison exists.

In order to establish a contrary proposition, a searching study of the methods which have been prepared for naval warfare would be necessary. Without this it is impossible to estimate the significance of the change. But a popular description of systems of attack and defence at sea presents even greater difficulties than the description of war on land.

To give an idea to laymen of the mechanism prepared for maritime war to-day, and to facilitate comparison with the mechanism employed in the past, it is necessary to compare the growth and perfection of fleets, and the methods adopted for their utilisation by different states. In such a comparison we find a peculiar circumstance which greatly increases the complexity of the subject. In the comparison of armies we deal with a quantity of similar units—soldiers, artillery, and horses. But for the comparison of the fleets of the different powers at different times, we have to deal with varying units, since not only the armaments of ships have changed, but the very type. Many suppose that a single modern ironclad, a single swift cruiser with long-range weapons, supplied with explosive shells, will be able to accomplish work for which a squadron would formerly have been needed.

With the adoption of steamers for naval warfare, sailing ships gradually disappeared from the composition of navies. Yet as late as the beginning of the Crimean war the Black Sea fleet counted only 7 steam-frigates, of 1960 steam-power, armed with 49 guns, the remainder of the fleet being composed of sailing ships. The allied fleets contained the following number of steamers : England 24, of 5859 steam-power ; the French 12, of 4960 steam-power. The number of guns on the Russian fleet was about 2000, and on the allies 2449. The impossibility of sailing ships accepting battle with freely manœuvring steamers was then fully demonstrated, for the greater part of the Black Sea fleet was destroyed. It is not to be wondered at that the Baltic fleet, composed of weakly constructed vessels, made even a less successful show against the allies.

After the close of the Crimean war the Ministry of Marine actively undertook the construction of a steam fleet for the Baltic, as in accordance with the Treaty of Paris the destroyed Black Sea fleet was not to be rebuilt. This work was carried on in the spirit which generally characterises an epoch of reform. But, owing to want of experience, the new vessels did not answer requirements, especially in respect to long distance steaming. The programme of construction had not been fully executed when armour began to play such an important part in the building of warships that the wooden ships then building lost their value as fighting units.

At the end of 1870, when Paris was besieged by the Germans, the Russian Government, in view of the political changes taking place in Europe, declared that it no longer regarded as binding the articles in the Treaty of Paris relating to the keeping of warships in the Black Sea. But the new Black Sea fleet had hardly been built before the war of 1877 broke out, and the fleet had no influence on the course of operations, although the Russian sailors distinguished themselves by exploits, and destroyed several Turkish vessels.

The first appearance of armoured ships dates back to the time of the Crimean war.   The bombardment of Sevastopol by the combined Anglo-French fleets showed the allies that their wooden vessels might easily be set on fire and destroyed, in a battle with fortresses.   The consequence of this discovery was an attempt to protect vessels with iron plates, and in 1854 France began the construction of three armoured floating batteries destined for attack upon the Russian coast fortifications in the Black Sea.   The English, with the intention of attacking Cronstadt in 1856, constructed seven floating batteries.   The Russian shells directed against these batteries only occasioned damage when they accidentally fell into the embrasures.   From this the conclusion was drawn that if vessels were built well protected with armour, and able to manœuvre freely in the open sea, they would be indestructible.

In 1858, by order of the Emperor Napoleon III., the building of the first armoured frigate *Gloire* was begun on the plan of the celebrated engineer Dupuy de Lome. This frigate, in the words of its builder, was to be " a lion in a flock of sheep."   The cost of construction reached £280,000—that is, almost three times the cost of the greatest line-of-battle ships, but in view of the immense results that were expected, this outlay was not considered extravagant.

The initiative of France was quickly imitated both by England and America.   The deciding circumstance, however, which led to the final supersession of wooden ships was the American Civil War, when the exploit of the *Merrimac*, and the subsequent battle between the *Monitor* and *Merrimac* showed the ineffectiveness of wooden ships, and the immense power of resistance of armour.

This change acted most disadvantageously for Russia; the new steam fleet had only just been completed, and the need for re-building came when, as a consequence of the

Crimean war, the finances of the country were in a desperate state. But to delay was impossible, and fresh events emphasised the necessity for proceeding with the new construction without delay.

As is well known, Russia in the sixties was threatened with a rupture with the Western powers over the Polish question. In 1863 a committee was formed under the presidency of General-Adjutant Kruizhanovski to consider the measures necessary for placing Cronstadt in a position of defence. The general opinion of that committee was, that with the resources possessed by the enemies of Russia in 1863, Cronstadt could not be defended, and considering the skill and persistence of the enemy even the capital could not be considered safe. The committee found that by means of coast fortifications alone, without mobile defences consisting of forty floating batteries, monitors, and gunboats, the defence of Cronstadt would be impossible.

While vessels of war were constructed of wood, the materials and the capacity to work them were found in Russia. The case was otherwise when iron vessels had to be built and equipped with costly machinery and weapons. Nevertheless, considering the financial difficulties, energetic measures were taken to construct an armoured fleet.

Meantime the other maritime powers, recognising that they were almost defenceless without increase of their fleets of armoured vessels, began with feverish activity to attempt to attain what is apparently unattainable—that is, to build armoured vessels which would resist the action of the strongest artillery.

Not one of the details of naval affairs, not even the construction of ships, presents such amazing results in the way of novelty and improvement as have been attained since 1860 in naval ordnance. The best idea of this may be given by a contrast of the armaments of the Russian fleet of to-day with its predecessors. We will take the old 84 *Prokhor* and the modern *Piotr Veliki* which carries only four 12-inch rifled guns. With one discharge of its

G

guns the *Piotr Veliki* develops three times the power of a
similar discharge from the guns of the *Prokhor*.   The
whole 84 guns of the *Prokhor* if they could be directed at
once in one direction would not cause the slightest damage
to the armour of the weakest of modern armoured vessels,
while every shot fired from a distance of 7000 feet from
the modern 12-inch rifles against the strongest of modern
ironclads, will penetrate the side 3 feet thick and protected
by a 13-inch plate.   In addition to this, all four weapons
of the *Piotr Veliki* might be directed against a comparatively small space of the ship's side.   But even these guns
will be powerless against some of the ironclads now under
construction, which are protected by 20-inch and even
24-inch steel armour, and, in consequence, by the side of
these armour-clads will be invented even more powerful
guns.   The more perfect the guns the stronger the armour
which has been produced for protection against them. This
struggle continues even at the present day.

For employment against armour, steel projectiles were
made, and the force of the impact increased ; thus in turn
calling for stronger armour, against which still more
powerful projectiles are employed.   A rivalry in invention
began.   Sometimes armour was uppermost, sometimes
projectiles.   But no one listened to the voice of the economists who foretold the consequence of this rivalry.   To
illustrate this we may cite some figures as to the cost of
modern vessels of war.   The cost of a first-class line-of-
battle ship, impelled by sails, did not exceed £115,000.
The building of the first English ironclad *Warrior* in
1860 entailed an outlay of £350,000.   But this was but
the beginning in the growth in the cost of warships.   The
German ironclad *Koenig Wilhelm*, built in 1868, cost
£500,000, the Italian *Duilio*, in 1876, £700,000, the *Italia*,
1886, £1,000,000.   Thus in twenty years the cost of ironclads increased three times.   A great part of this outlay
is swallowed up by armour.   Of £840,000 spent on one
of the latest ironclads, *Magenta*, £600,000, that is, 71 per
cent., was spent upon armour.

Let us examine the instruments of destruction of these

maritime giants. A battleship of the old type of the first rank was armed with 120 guns, weighing 480 tons. The first ironclad carried only 32 guns, but these weighed 690 tons. On the ironclad *Italia*, built in 1886, were carried only 4 large and 8 small guns, yet they weighed nearly double as much as the 32 guns of the first ironclad, namely, 1150 tons. Thus since the days of sailing ships the weight of guns has increased more than 150 times. The size and weight of ammunition has, of course, correspondingly increased, and also the destructive force of explosive shells. The diameter of the shells of the ironclad *Warrior* was approximately 6⅓ inches, its weight 70 pounds ; on the armour-clad *Italia* the diameter is increased to 17 inches, and the weight to 2000 pounds. In the course of twenty years the power of a shell, taking only its weight into account, has increased 30 times.

It must not be supposed that this is the limit. England continues to stand at the head of the states who seek for improvements in weapons of destruction at sea. Some years ago English ships were armed with guns of a calibre of 12 inches, and armour nearly 12 inches thick. At a later time they carried guns with a calibre of 16 inches, weighing 80 tons, and throwing a shell weighing 1760 pounds. But in view of the fact that Italy had armed her ironclads *Duilio* and *Dandolo* with guns weighing 100 tons, the English consider a project of building 200-ton guns which will throw a shell of nearly three tons weight, and pierce armour 35½ inches thick.

What is the outlay on the use of such weapons ? *Le Progrès Militaire*, on the basis of statistics taken from the French naval budget, makes the following estimate. The firing of a shell from a 110-ton gun costs £166, which corresponds to a capital of £4160. This sum is thus apportioned : £36 for 990 pounds of powder, £130 for the projectile, total, £166. But this is not all. A 110-gun will stand only 93 shots, after which it becomes useless for further employment. As the cost of such a weapon amounts to £16,480 it appears that with every shot fired the value of the arm diminishes by £174, from which we find that every shot fired will cost £340. Thus with every shot is thrown away the yearly interest on a capital of £8500. A thousand of such shots would represent a capital of £8,500,000.

Passing to arms of smaller calibre it is shown that a shot fired from a 77-ton gun (the cost of which is £10,000, and which will stand 127 shots) costs £184, a shot from a 45-ton gun (which costs £6300, and is useless after 150 shots have been fired) amounts to £98. Only the lives of the sailors on fleets are considered as valueless.

General Pestitch draws a very interesting contrast. He says : "Six Russian ships taking part in the battle of Sinope were armed with about 600 guns, out of which the 300 guns employed destroyed all that was in Sinope, yet the cost of these 300 guns, in the values of that time, did not exceed the cost of a single modern 100-ton gun. What results are to be expected from one weapon which in an hour may be fired no more than five times ?" An answer to this question it seems can be given only by a future war. The guns on modern battleships will be able to bombard ports, fortresses and towns, as many specialists declare, from a distance of nearly seven miles.

But this increase of power has not been restricted to battleships alone. Many specialists consider it more advisable to build light and swift cruisers with powerful armaments, and torpedo boats which move almost unnoticed through the water with the speed of a mail train. As soon as the construction of ships was perfected to such an extent that England was able to place on the sea a considerable number of ironclads, armed with powerful guns, and protected by thick steel armour, the question naturally arose : Would it not be possible to direct mines underneath these immense ships, and destroy them by means of powerful explosions in the vicinity of weakly defended parts ? For a long time the application of this idea was unsuccessful, many obstacles had to be overcome, and only in recent times has the question been successfully resolved. Then began the construction of vessels specially designed for the purpose of discharging torpedoes. Ex-

perience showed that vessels discharging the torpedo ran
no risk in employing a mine of 55 to 66 pounds of powder,
13 to 15 pounds of dynamite, or 22 to 27 pounds of peroxylene, if it be not less than 19½ feet distant from the
place of explosion, the mine being at a depth of 7 feet. Since
from 19½ feet distance there is little difficulty in directing a
torpedo against an enemy's ship by the use of a pole, the
problem became simply how best to build vessels which
would be unnoticed on approach. In the Russo-Turkish
war of 1877, out of nine cases of attack by Russian torpedo
boats the Turks lost one ironclad and two steamers, while
three ironclads were injured. The loss in men is unknown.
On the Russian side three torpedo boats were injured, also
three steam sloops, while one torpedo boat was sunken.
Two sailors were killed and ten wounded.

Similar results were obtained in the time of the French-
Tonkin war of 1885. Two ordinary steam cutters, not more
than 46 feet in length, armed with torpedoes, on the
night of the 14–15 February, 1885, attacked a Chinese
frigate of 3500 tons and sank it. This frigate was hidden
in the harbour of Shein under the cover of fortifications,
but the French Admiral Courbet was at a distance of
several knots from this harbour. Hidden in the darkness
the French cutters covered the distance unnoticed, and
after destroying the Chinese ship returned uninjured to
the admiral's flagship.

The history of the Chilian war presents a similar case,
when, after an attack lasting no more than seven minutes,
the Congressionalist ironclad *Blanco Encalada* was sent to
the bottom.

From this is evident the immense danger with which
armour-clads are threatened by torpedo-boats armed with
Whitehead and other torpedoes of recent design. It must
be remembered that not only torpedo-boats, but almost all
ships of war are armed with such weapons of destruction
to-day.

It is natural that the complement of these inventions
was a new system of defence against the action of torpedo-
boats. A new type of war vessel, the torpedo-catcher, was

evolved, specially adapted for dealing with torpedo-boats, powerfully armed, and steaming at a speed of 32 knots an hour.

Admiral Werner declares that as soon as the price of aluminium falls so low that it may be employed for the construction of ships, the sides of ships will be so powerfully protected, in consequence of the lightness of the material, that the strongest explosive shell will not penetrate them, and a battle against torpedo-boats will become mere child's play. Now the price of aluminium has lately fallen to such an extent that it is already being employed for many articles of domestic use, such as keys. If this prophecy be fulfilled the European powers will be compelled to disburse fresh millions on aluminium ships. This could have but one consequence. Invention, even now stimulated in most countries by manufacturers and their patrons, would seek to discover even more powerful explosive combinations. The last act in this rivalry it is impossible to foresee.

For the purpose of protection against mines, the more important parts of warships, the boilers and engines, are now being protected even under water by especial armour, and surrounded with layers of coal. In addition water-tight compartments have been adopted to ensure the unsinkability of the ships, and torpedo-nets are carried. The value of such defences will be proved in the future. But experiments carried on in England have tended to show that the protection of torpedo-nets is ineffective. On experiment being made to ascertain whether a torpedo-boat might pass through an obstacle constructed of strong beams, it was shown that the torpedo-boat, striking the obstacle when at a speed of 20 knots, broke it and returned to harbour undamaged.

A commission appointed by the United States Government for the purpose of considering the question of attack by and defence against torpedo-boats, came to the almost unanimous conclusion that torpedo-boats will certainly destroy an armour-clad if they escape destruction during the two minutes in the course of which the vessel attacked will be able to employ its quick-firing guns. But the effectiveness of defence is weakened by the fact that in all navies the number of torpedo-boats is from three to seven times greater than the number of armour-clads, and the loss of several torpedo-boats cannot be compared in gravity with the loss of a single armour-clad carrying an incomparably larger crew, and costing an incomparably greater sum.

It is true that the smallness of torpedo-boats and the insignificant quantity of stores they carry prevent them from seeking an enemy in the open sea. But these obstacles are overcome by the building of special vessels for the transport of torpedo-boats. In addition, all torpedo-boats built to-day are seagoing, develop great speed, and steam a considerable distance with their own supply of coal, while their size is being increased on all sides.

In any event, it is not reckless to predict in the near future the invention of subterranean torpedo-boats, which will carry torpedoes of such power that even aluminium armour will not avail to save the vessel attacked.

A future war on sea might be considered under the following heads : Operations on the littoral, operations against ports and merchant ships, and battles between separate ships, squadrons, and fleets. With long-range modern guns and powerful projectiles, maritime towns may be threatened with a destruction from which they will not recover for a long time. Of the smooth-bore 12-inch mortar of the old type, the greatest range was 2500 yards ; the modern $12\frac{1}{2}$-inch guns of the Canet system throw a shell weighing 986 pounds, and filled with 275 pounds of explosives, to a distance of $13\frac{1}{8}$ miles, so that towns may now be bombarded from a considerable distance. It must be remembered that, as is shown by the practice at manœuvres, the principle that undefended towns are not to be subjected to bombardment is not acknowledged, and in a future war no town will be spared. As evidence of this the following case may be cited. On August 24, 1889, the following letter was addressed by the commander of the *Collingwood* to the Mayor of Peterhead :

By order of the Vice-Admiral commanding the 11th division of the fleet : I have to demand from your town a contribution of £150,000 sterling. I require you to deliver to the bearer of this letter a guarantee of the immediate fulfilment of this condition. I regret the necessity of demanding such a large sum from the peace-loving and industrious population of the town, but I cannot act otherwise in view of the immense contributions exacted by your warships from the prosperous city of Belfast. I must add that in case the officers who deliver this letter do not return within the course of two hours the town will be burnt, the shipping destroyed, and factories ruined.

This letter was printed in all the newspapers, and called forth no protest. On a question being raised on the subject in the House of Commons, the First Lord of the Admiralty answered evasively. It is evident then that England will not refrain from such action when convenient, and as her voice is the most important in naval matters, the other powers will certainly follow her example.

To avoid such dangers, all powers have occupied themselves with the defence of their coasts by means of fortifications, and the building of railways for the transport of artillery from one point to another as the exigencies of defence demand. But the firing from coast batteries, notwithstanding ingenious methods of measuring the distance of moving and hardly visible objects, would be only waste of powder and shell. A steamer moving with a speed of 13 miles an hour will in 30 seconds traverse 175 yards while a shot from coast artillery requires about five minutes. By skilful artillerymen this time might be shortened to from two to three minutes. On the other hand, in the bombardment of the immense spaces covered by coast towns almost every shell will find its sacrifice, and each upon explosion will cause ruin over an immense space.

The blockade of ports in a future war is also likely to have immense importance, since each of the combatants will consider as a main object the interruption of the maritime communications of the other, and the causing of all possible damage to trade by blockading his ships in ports and harbours.

But history teaches that even in a time when sails were the only method of sailing, single vessels and even whole squadrons succeeded in escaping into the open sea. It would seem that nowadays, what with the speed of vessels, and the strength of coast defences which compel blockading ships to remain at a considerable distance, no state can rely absolutely upon closing the ports of even a weaker enemy, whose cruisers may therefore keep the sea, and injure and interrupt the trade of the stronger power.

In contrast with that which is the case on land, the field of battle at sea is in no way limited, and both sides have a free choice of movement. Here we find not a certain number of human beings, but a limited number of floating fortresses equipped with complex machinery, and armed with guns and torpedoes of almost miraculous power, cruisers which for rapidity of movement may be likened to the fabled giant with the seven-league boots, and finally torpedo-boats equipped with forces capable of sending the greatest battleship to the bottom. In open sea battle will take place only at the will of the swifter fleet. The commander will also find himself in a position different from that of a general on land. At sea the commander is first in the battle, he stands in the midst of all, he is the first object of the enemy's fire, his decision must be immediate. In the opinion of the majority of specialists, vessels which take part in great battles will issue from them damaged to such an extent, that for the rest of the period for which the war will last they need not be taken into account.

In the first half of the present century the effect of shore batteries on ships, and the results of battles between ships themselves, were not very terrible. The heavy shot discharged by smooth-bore guns carried for a very short distance, often missed its target, and the greater part of the damage it caused could be repaired by means at hand.

The adaptation of rifled guns, and of shells charged with high explosives, have entirely changed the conditions of war.   The destruction now caused by a single well-aimed shell is so great that in comparison the effect of red-hot shot is but a trifle.   Modern shells will not merely penetrate vessels, causing a puncture their own diameter in size, but will destroy whole sections of the ship, annihilating everything around them.   Yet on modern vessels are found machinery of every kind, marine engines, dynamo-electric engines, pumping, steering, hauling, and ventilating apparatus.   Every gun, every steam pinnace has its own complex machinery.   Add to this miles of electric wire, and a wilderness of constructions of every kind concentrated in the machinery departments, in which men by artificial light, and in artificially induced atmosphere, in isolated groups, and cut off from their commanders, must with full control of their business, execute immediately and coolly orders proceeding from an unseen leader by telegraph. Such, in brief, is the modern man-of-war.

To give some idea of the *rôle* played by machinery in modern ships we may cite a comparison made by Admiral Makarof between a wooden frigate of the old type and the modern cruiser *Rurik:* " The engines and boilers of the cruiser *Rurik* occupy 192 feet length in the widest part of the ship.   In order to understand what this means we may say that if we were to take out of the ship the engines and boilers, also the coal bunkers, and fill the vacant space with water, a frigate of the old type might easily be moored inside, with all its equipment and all its guns.   Around the frigate there would be sufficient space to steer a pinnace.   Within this space of 192 feet all is compressed to a seemingly impossible extent. . . . The engineer must be an acrobat, and the stoker, who with forced draught must make the boiler give twice the steam pressure that corresponds to its dimensions, must in endurance and energy give way in little to Satan himself."

With growing complexity of the mechanism the need for intelligence has also grown.   In former times when wind was the only motive power of vessels the result of battles depended much from skilful seamanship, and in the end of ends was decided by boarding. Steam power has entirely changed these conditions. The course of the battle will be determined by steam alone, whatever may be the direction of the wind, and it will be decided by torpedoes, by artillery, or by the ram. In the time of sailing ships a movement once determined upon could not be concealed; with steam it need not be revealed until the last movement. Thus the need for leadership and decision has grown to a remarkable degree. The German authority Henning justly remarks: " As far as technique is concerned, it may be said that everywhere, in England, France, Germany, Russia, and Italy, it will give similar results. Here the whole question lies in the training and firmness of the commander and of the crew, and afterwards in the successful employment of technical factors. Of course he will have an advantage who commands a crew formed of born sailors, but in battle this advantage may be counterbalanced by individual qualities of command."

After making a study of the conclusions which are drawn from the battle of Lissa, the wars of 1870 and 1877, the Chilian war of 1879, the Tonkin Expedition of 1885, the naval operations in the Chilian war of 1891, and, finally, the war between China and Japan, and having in view the opinions of the best authorities, such as White, Brassey, and Werner, it is impossible not to conclude that a battle between fleets equal in speed and armament will lead very quickly to the destruction by shell-fire and conflagration of the upper decks in which are concentrated the chief directing elements, while a considerable part of the crew will be killed, and in the number every officer who successively occupies the post of commander. In one word, in the first battle a considerable proportion of the ships will be destroyed, and the remainder will be forced to go into port to refit. Therefore in war the strongest will prove to be the nation which possesses the greatest number of arsenals and ready stores of ammunition and coal at points selected in times of peace ; and in addition to that a fleet in reserve, even a fleet of old type, but equipped with modern artillery ; with such a fleet it will be possible to strike deadly blows at the enemy when the fleets of the first line shall have been forced to leave the seas in consequence of damage sustained in battle.

In all probability future naval battles will present this difference from those of the past—even from recent battles—that solitary vessels will not take part, but whole squadrons consisting, as armies, of their own sort of cavalry, artillery, and infantry, that is, their swift cruisers, their battleships, and, finally, of their torpedo-boats and torpedo-catchers.   With this the element of accident will play such an important *rôle* that naval battles will almost resemble a game of dice in which the stakes will be millions of money and thousands of lives.

It is certain that all that is not defended by armour will be swept from the decks by the shell-fire of quick-firing guns, and it remains an open question if even that portion of the crew which is in protected positions will be able to stand the concussion produced by the explosion of shells. Attention must be called to the ease with which shells produce conflagrations of decks, masts, bridges and everything inflammable.   All that is near the region of explosion of a shell will be totally destroyed, a thousand steel fragments will fly about with inconceivable rapidity, penetrating decks and corridors.   Some of the shells which fall in an ironclad will immediately make a part of its guns useless, and the employment of the larger guns will be impeded, since the turning of the turrets will be impeded by torn plates.   Shells containing heavy charges will cause immense destruction.   If a shell loaded with 22 pounds of melinite were to fall between the two decks of an ironclad its explosion would destroy the balks supporting the deck, rend the iron sheets, pierce the deck, stretch the electric wires until they broke, damage the steam pipes and boilers—in one word, disable all the vital organs of the ship for a space of several yards around the region of explosion, and in addition produce suffocating fumes which would prevent approach for a quarter of an hour, however perfect might be the ventilation.

. It needs no evidence to prove that it is extremely

doubtful that any one state can obtain a decided preponderance above the others in the quality of its ships or their armament. In the present state of technical science every improvement adopted by one power is immediately adopted by all the others. The number of vessels of an obsolete type is great, but these less effective ships are divided among the different powers in proportion. The fate of future battles will therefore depend primarily on accidents which cannot be foreseen, and secondly on the possession at a given moment of preponderating strength. But in this respect we find that in spite of all efforts the relative strength of fleets has changed but little, and the comparison made by Admiral Werner therefore seems entirely true. " A naval battle," he says, " if both adversaries are determined and energetic, will resemble a conflict between two stags which in a moment of fury rush upon one another, entangling their antlers, and in the end of ends destroying one another. Or if the enemies are less determined a naval battle will resemble a contest of athletes, the combatants moving backwards and forwards in serpentine lines ; both will keep up fire from a great distance until neither has enough ammunition left to strike a decisive blow."

To cruisers and torpedo-boats will be allotted a duty not less ferocious—a duty which, in the Middle Ages, was fulfilled by pirates and privateers—to pursue merchant ships, fall on them by night and sink them, with passengers, crews and cargoes, with the object of cutting the communications and paralysing the trade of the enemy. The following passage, which we find in " Les Guerres Navales de Demain," is an interesting illustration of this : " A war on commerce will have its regulations, precise, constant, and unconditional ; the weak will be attacked without mercy, the strong will be evaded by flight without any false shame. Our torpedo-boats and cruisers as soon as they discover an English squadron from afar, or even a single battleship, it may be not exceeding them in fighting strength, but capable of offering even slight opposition, will be bound to disappear."

From such passages, and from the declarations of unquestioned authorities, it is impossible not to conclude that the effect of future naval wars on future trade will be incomparably more disastrous than before. A future war on sea will also draw after itself economic and political consequences quite different from those of the past, when every state found its needs supplied within the limits of its own dominions. The general use of shells loaded with explosives which may be thrown a distance of some miles, shells, one of which falling into a town or settled locality may cause the most terrible destruction; and the speed with which vessels may be moved from one point of a coast to another, independently of weather and wind, must affect the minds of peoples, and even give rise to agitations. And such agitations, in view of the present general socialistic tendencies, may not be limited to temporary disorder. On preparations for naval war immense sums are yearly expended by the powers, but shipbuilding so constantly and so rapidly advances towards perfection, that a large proportion of modern fleets is obsolete, and incapable of meeting in battle vessels of the newer types, some being unfit for employment even after the destruction of the latter.

All this was more or less clearly foreseen ten years ago on the appearance of smokeless powder. And in the present time, in view of the speed attained by cruisers armed with strong artillery, and also by torpedo-boats of the latest type; in view of the improvements in the propulsion of torpedoes, and in view of the progress made in the building of submarine boats, it may be affirmed that even vessels of the latest types, however they may be divided among the different nations, cannot guarantee the attainment of the ends of war.

Meantime, for the improvement and increase of fleets new credits are required every day. We may well inquire what degree the discontent of peoples may attain when they learn that even the newest types of ships and the last inventions in artillery have been adopted everywhere, while requirements still continue to grow. In view of those elements which in Western Europe to-day contend with all political and social order, even more absurd appears the rivalry of states in the increase of their fleets, while the relation of fighting force remains the same, and immense sums are yearly squandered which might have been devoted to the satisfaction of social needs.

A comparison of the growth of expenditure on armies and fleets is presented by the following table (counting the rouble as equal to three shillings) :

	EXPENDITURE.			
	On Armies.		On Fleets.	
	Millions of Roubles.	£	Millions of Roubles.	£
1874 .	. 615.4	92,325,000	... 158.2	23,730,000
1884 .	. 688.1	103,215,000	... 218.6	32,790,000
1891 .	. 885.1	132,765,000	... 247.2	37,080,000
1896 .	. 893.6	134,040,000	... 299.6	44,940,000

To express more clearly the comparative growth of outlay on armed forces, we take the outlay of 1874 at 100, and find the following percentage increase :

				Armies.		Fleets.
1874 .	.	.	.	100	...	100
1884 .	.	.	.	112	...	138
1891 .	.	.	.	144	...	156
1896 .	.	.	.	145	...	189

The comparison which we have made as to the naval resources of the different states shows that these millions can have no practical result, even if we admit that war is as unavoidable in the future as it has been in the past.

Calculations made by us show that England alone in a prolonged war could obtain the mastery of the sea, forcing the other naval powers to give way everywhere. But on the other hand, the interruption of communications at sea would cause the English such great losses as to eliminate the possibility of a prolonged war, even although they were absolutely certain of victory. The cessation of the import of provisions would not allow of England continuing a prolonged war. Of wheat, barley, and rye England lacks supplies for 274 days and of oats for 76 days in the year.

Even if we agree with the baseless opinion of optimists and assume that the transport of supplies to England might be carried on under convoy, still we must bear in mind the terrible rise in prices in consequence of the risk. And side by side with this rise in prices would proceed the interruption of industry.

Thus, in continuing to increase their fleets and to perfect their armaments at immense cost the European powers are striving at aims undefined and unattainable. But the financial and social difficulties which yearly increase may result in such dangers that governments must be compelled after immense sacrifices to do what it would be wiser to do to-day, namely, to abandon a fruitless competition.

Such is a brief picture of what Europe may expect from a future war. But over and above the direct sacrifices and material losses, by slaughter, fire, hunger, and disease, a war will cause to humanity a great moral evil in consequence of the peculiar forms which a struggle on sea will assume and of the examples of savagery which it will present at a moment when the civil order will be threatened by new theories of social revolution.

What wearisome and ungrateful labour will be needed to repair the losses, to cure the wounds which a war of a single year will cause ! How many flourishing countries will be turned into wildernesses and rich cities into ruins ! How many tears will be shed, how many will be left in beggary ! How long will it be before the voices of the best men, after such a terrible example, will preach to humanity a higher principle than " might is right " ?

CHAPTER IV

DOES RUSSIA NEED A NAVY?

A CHARACTERISTIC feature of our time is the technical improvement of all military apparatus. Hardly has a new rifle or a new gun been adopted before it is necessary to replace it by fresh weapons. Within a short time we may expect new improvements in powder, and this in its turn will require changes in all war material. In recent times these changes, consequent on new inventions, have taken place more and more swiftly. Of this, perhaps the building of fortresses is the best example. After fabulous sums had been lavished on the building of fortresses on a new system with all the latest technical improvements, the opinion has gained ground that modern strategy requires fortresses only to a limited extent, a view, the probability of which is increased by the fact that every army will be equipped with instruments for the construction of its own defensive works.

A similar process of change may be observed in the building of fleets. In the past one and the same type was employed in the course of three hundred years without essential change. After this began the building of ironclads, and in the course of thirty years the various types of ships may be counted by tens. In the present time opinions change so rapidly that no sooner is a vessel launched than it is found not to come up to the newest requirements. Meantime, every new ship costs more than the last. Even the richest nations have begun to groan under the burden.

In this relation Russia especially finds herself in a

H

difficult position.   At a time when in Western countries
a powerful social initiative heaped up wealth, when towns
sprang up, not as centres of local authority, but as trading
and industrial centres, and when in the country free labour,
full ownership of land, and the accumulation of savings
ensured the erection of good and durable buildings for
man and beast, the construction of good roads, the regulation of water communications, and the building of factories, in that time in Russia the economic life of the
people, their social initiative, and even the satisfaction
of their necessities were paralysed by the existence of
serfage.

The Crimean war resulted in disorder in the finances
and in the money system which had only just been brought
into order, and in addition to this, shook the faith of men
in the old system of government.   The reform of the
administrative apparatus was all the more essential owing
to the subsequent emancipation of the serfs.   The necessity
for building roads was recognised.   The peasants received
their freedom and occupied themselves with the working
of their fields.   Savings they could not have.   They
lived in poverty and the conditions of their lives were
most primitive.   Landowners had not the capital to carry
on agriculture, and were forced to let their land to the
peasantry for labour or on lease.   The work of the
peasantry, both on their own lands and on that of the
landowners, continued to be most primitive.   Meeting no
support from industry in the utilisation of their products,
agriculturists were compelled to export them in a raw
form.   Russia exported grain, cattle, and phosphates to
improve the soil of foreigners, while Russian soil itself
constantly deteriorated.   Such, briefly, was the condition
of the chief part of the Russian population at a time
when Western Europe was advancing in industry and
prosperity by bounds.

Meantime, the population rapidly grew.   In a time
when the population of the Empire was estimated at some
hundred and ten and odd millions, the census of last
year gave the figure at more than one hundred and

twenty-nine million souls.   This yearly growth of the population, estimated approximately at two millions, undoubtedly constitutes an increase of wealth, but only in the event of there being sufficient resources for the feeding and training of the growing population.   Otherwise it must only result in an increase of the proletariat.

In comparison with its revenue the Empire has an immense debt.   Interest on the Imperial Debt occupies the second place in the Budget, and is only a little less than the expenditure of the Ministry of War (£40,800,000 and £43,200,000 in 1898).   The finances showed a deficit even before the Crimean war.   After the Crimean war the position was worse, and every attempt to diminish the extraordinary expenditure proved fruitless in consequence of the war of 1877–78.   Meantime, fresh expenditure was entailed by re-armament, the construction of fortresses and strategical railways.   Independently of these it was necessary for the development of industry to return to the construction of railways which had been suspended in 1875, although a great part of the railways promised only to pay, or even cover their expenses, in the future. It is natural that this increase in indebtedness had as inevitable consequence an increase in the burden of taxation.

To contend with such a position was very difficult, but thanks to twenty years of peace and the energetic efforts of the Ministry of Finances, the deficits vanished from the ordinary Budget, and it seemed that money could even be found for productive purposes.   But in all circumstances the finances of a country depend on the economic condition of the people.   We have already briefly pointed out, and shall hereafter show in greater detail, how badly Russia compares in this respect with the countries of Western Europe.   The severity of the climate prevents agricultural work during a considerable part of the year, and involves greater demand for clothing, dwelling, food, heat, and light.   The great number of holidays still further shortens production, even in the working season. With such conditions it is inevitable that savings for a rainy day among the Russian people should be insignificant, and such they are shown to be in reality. Every famine, even a local failure of harvest, is the cause of a veritable disaster.

With such a state of affairs it is needless to point out the absolute necessity for great caution in the expenditure of money on military purposes. It is quite true that in this respect Russia cannot fall behind the other powers, but she must not follow blindly after them, and, above all, she must not attempt to outstrip them, for such a course might lead to the most disastrous consequences. In the struggle for money the rivalry is unequal. Russia is weaker for two reasons—first, she has less reserves; secondly, she gives orders abroad, pays more than other powers, and sends her money out of the country. While England, Germany, and France themselves construct and prepare all that they need at the lowest possible cost, keeping their money at home, Russia is compelled to take a less advantageous course. Thus, for instance, in ordering ships of war in England, or building them at home to a large extent with imported materials and machinery, Russia pays at least 25 per cent. more than the building of warships costs the English Government, and sends into that country money which England afterwards uses for the strengthening of her own fleet. By her orders Russia helps to keep up English shipbuilding yards, which in time of war would make it easy for England to repair quickly the losses she sustained.

Every effort put forth by Russia in the strengthening of her fleet calls forth corresponding activity in foreign countries. The recent assignation of £13,500,000 (ninety millions of roubles) to strengthen the fleet may serve as an example. As the direct consequence of this the project of the German Government to allot several millions of marks to increasing the fleet during a period of seven years, a project which had met with strong opposition in the Reichsrath, was agreed to without any further difficulty. As a natural consequence the French and Austrian Governments already demand from their parliaments extraordinary credits for the same purpose. Thus, as the final result of this rivalry, the relationship of the naval powers will remain what it was before.

All this only confirms the necessity for greater caution and concentration of resources in the satisfying of those requirements which in a given time are most insistent. Precisely as climatic conditions in every country demand a suitable distribution of agricultural labour, in military affairs a definitive plan also is essential corresponding with needs and resources. The first question which would be asked after the adoption of such a system is : Must Russia be equally ready to carry on war on land and on sea ?

In order to define the importance of naval power in a naval war two propositions must be made—first, that a war impends with the Triple Alliance, in the event of which Russia has the support of France ; and secondly, that a war is probable with England. It is necessary, first of all, to observe the immense preponderance of armies and of operations on land over naval forces and possible operations at sea. The armies which would enter upon war on the Continent are numbered by millions of men. The armies of the first line of both alliances number more than six and a half millions. The armies of the second line would number almost six millions.

What *rôle* will be played by the fleet during the conflict of such masses ? To this question we get the best answer by reverting to the war of 1870. Germany then possessed a fleet in no way fit to oppose the fleet of France. Yet the French fleet was compelled to abandon all plans of a landing upon the German coast, and did not even make an attempt to accomplish them. From the first, Moltke was so convinced of the impossibility of such a diversion that in his plan of military operations in 1870, relying upon the numerical superiority of the German army, he declared : " The superiority of our forces at the point where the decisive blow will be struck will be all the greater if the French undertake an expedition against the northern coast of Germany." This is the best evidence of the disregard he paid to all projects of invasion.

From that time the organisation of the armies of the great powers has gone still further, so that, even if the whole of an army and its reserves were engaged in operations on the frontier or in the territory of the enemy, it would nevertheless not be difficult to oppose a superior force to any that could be landed on the coast.

From estimates made in Italy, the transport of an army corps fully equipped with provisions for a month, and corresponding train, would require a fleet with a displacement of 116,000 tons. Professor Deguis says that, in the first 15–20 days from the beginning of operations, France could despatch an expedition of not more than 30,000 men. But in the face of modern artillery, small arms, and coast defences, a landing could only be accomplished with great difficulty.

Only a change of wind, a sudden storm or a thick fog is needed to interrupt the operation of landing, and to place the forces already on shore in a critical position.

It is true that we hear talk of the possibility of warships holding the coast-line under their guns and keeping it entirely clear of the defenders' troops. In reality, it happens that warships of deep draught, in order to keep clear of rocks and shoals, are compelled to stand at a distance of 1100 to 1600 yards from the shore, and, incommoded in movement by their transports, they regulate their fire with difficulty. But the enemy, relying upon long-range artillery, does not show himself at all upon the open shore, but shelters himself behind dunes and eminences or keeps even farther in the interior. The fire from warships may be powerful, but it is scattered and for this reason cannot be effective. During the bombardment of the insurgents' camp in Crete the allied squadron fired seventy shells, with a resulting loss to the insurgents of three killed and fifteen wounded.

We will not speak of the possibility of a Russian descent upon the coast of Germany. But let us suppose that the Germans were to land troops, of course without cavalry, on the Baltic coast, what could they effect? We have heard of course of the possibility of the Germans landing near Riga in order to cut the communications of the Russian army situated in Lithuania, or descending near Narva in order to operate against St. Petersburg. But this is almost a phantasy. Wherever they might be landed, an enemy's forces moving into the interior would be gradually weakened by the allotment of a considerable proportion for the purpose of preserving communications. Meantime the strength of the defence would continuously grow. With the aid of the telegraph and the railway, troops might be brought to the threatened locality in a very short time. Nor could their arrival at the scene of operations be interfered with by the destruction of the railways, for the invading army will be without cavalry.

The success of the allied armies in the Crimea may be adduced against this argument. Such an objection has been answered by Von der Goltz in his work "Das Volk in Waffen." He says : "If the armies landed in the Crimea were victorious over the local forces the cause of this was that, however difficult communication by sea was for the allies, these conditions were more favourable than the land communications used by the defenders in their own country. If in 1854 Russia had had her present network of railways, the French, the English and the Turks, at first landing in the Crimea to the number of 120,000 men, would not have remained there long."

The undertaking of a descent in considerable force is improbable, if only for the reason that it weakens the strength of the army which must defend the frontier where superiority of forces is aimed at by both sides. In certain events Germany would be compelled to carry on war on two frontiers. Her enemies would only desire that she should make the mistake which Moltke expected from France.

Thus for the protection of her coasts, Russia has no need whatever to increase her fleet, for the descent of an enemy would place her in no danger whatever, even if she did not dispose of her present fleet.   This opinion is held even in Germany.

The bombardment of a coast town, however important it may be as a political, industrial, or trading centre, can only cause material losses to private individuals and to the state.   But such operations can have no effect on the resources which a country possesses for the purpose of carrying on war.   The destruction caused can have no influence whatever on the course of the war on land, and even if all the seaports of a country were bombarded it could in no way change the course of events.   The essential fact is this, that a continental war will not be carried on merely with the object of causing losses to the enemy and beginning negotiations for peace on the basis of the losses caused.   A future war will be a struggle between whole peoples, and each side will have as its object the total overthrow of the enemy.   Therefore such bombardments of coast towns, however wealthy and important these latter may be, would only represent so much destruction with little influence on the issue of the struggle.

Even in this respect Russia is in a better position than Germany ; the Russian coast being less thickly populated, the losses from bombardment would be less, and consequently a numerous fleet is less necessary for Russia than for Germany.   With the exception of Riga, Revel, and Helsingfors, strongly fortified, there are no important towns on the Russian coast.   And the Russian fleet, even as constituted now, represents a very considerable force.

Even the complete destruction of a fleet could have little influence upon a continental war.   In commenting upon the experience gained from the last wars in Europe, we may point first to the destruction of the Italian fleet by the Austrians at Lissa in 1866.   What benefit did this naval victory bring to Austria, beaten at Sadova?   In 1870 a German fleet scarcely existed, while the French fleet had full freedom to act, yet Germany sustained no damage and her naval inferiority in no way influenced the course of the war. The French sailors were far more needed for the defence of Paris. It is true that the maritime trade of Germany was arrested. But whatever the number of warships may be, communications by sea will be cut. Nowadays every power has sufficient cruisers, and merchant ships which might be turned into cruisers, in order to stop all trade by sea.

Battleships against this will be of little use. In speed they must give way to cruisers which will evade them and simply laugh at their unwieldy adversaries. Battleships will be valuable only for battle between themselves and for attack upon coasts.

But let us postulate that the Russian navy had a decided preponderance over that of the enemy, sending to the bottom many more of his ships than she lost herself. Even in such case the Russian fleet would at best be in the position of the French fleet in 1870, which not only gained no victories, but found no foe. The victorious fleet would steam along the coast and threaten certain localities. Suppose that the Russian fleet were to act more energetically than the French fleet in 1870 and bombard mercilessly a great number of the smaller coast towns of Germany. The great German cities, Bremen, Hamburg, Stettin, Kiel, Dantzig, and Königsberg would remain inaccessible, standing too far from the coast.

But to attain results, even in the case of the less important towns, would be no easy task for a fleet of ironclads. On approaching the coast they must meet with the torpedo-boats, submarine mines, and submarine boats of the enemy, and run very great risks. Modern science has contrived a very different system of coast defence from that which obtained in 1870. But we will suppose that the Russian fleet were uninjured. Yet if the fleet does not dispose of swift cruisers, hundreds of merchant vessels will escape from harbour and the blockade will be ineffective. In this respect one cruiser may do more than a whole fleet of unwieldy battleships, which consume immense quantities of coal, a material which the Russian fleet could obtain only with difficulty. Thus, if

the battleships cannot be devoted to the interruption of
trade, their operations must be confined to the destruction
of peaceful settlements, the slaughter of unarmed men,
women and children, leading to an increase of savagery in
the relations of the contending peoples.

Suppose that victory should remain on the side of
Germany, acting, it might be, in co-operation with England, the results would be even less considerable, for the
Russian coast is much more thinly peopled.   We will
even go farther and suppose that the German fleet proved
victorious over the French.   What influence could such a
result have on the events of the war on land between the
two states ?   In all probability no more than the superiority
of the French fleet in 1870, for Germany would certainly
not make the mistake of attempting a descent upon the
French coast.

Prince Bismarck, in one of his speeches, drew the
following comparison of the importance of successes on
sea and land in a war between continental powers : " It
must not be forgotten that the capture of every village
represents a real success, the importance of which is
immediately felt, while the capture of an enemy's vessel
only goes into the general account, which must be settled
at the conclusion of the war.   The capture of a fortress
ensures the possession of territory, while the capture even
of a whole fleet at best represents only means for undertaking fresh conquests."   But Russia, even if she aimed
at conquests in Germany and Austria, would not need a
fleet, for the land frontiers of both these countries are
conterminous with hers for an immense distance.

Let us consider two hypotheses : (1) That the armies of
Russia were defeated, while her fleet gained a complete
victory : in the final result of course Russia would be
beaten.   (2) That the Russian army gained complete
victory while her fleet was annihilated ; the result would
be that Russia would gain all the fruits of her victory on
land.   The conquered on land would be forced to pay
contributions, and even their fleets might pass into the
hands of Russia.

To this it may be replied that since France, Germany, and England increase their fleets we must do the same. Whether France is acting wisely in increasing her fleet we will not stop to consider, since France must bear in mind the possibility of a conflict with Italy, protect her interests in the Mediterranean and her colonial possessions, and, we may observe, the greater her naval forces increase the greater will be the security of Russia, although it must be noted that in France every expedition to distant countries gives cause for complaints as to unreadiness, disorder and defects in the *personnel*. It is enough to read the work of M. Lockroy, former Minister of Marine, to be convinced that the French fleet is far from being on a level with the English, and that the incessant attempts made to overtake England have only resulted in hindering the French fleet in its efforts to be fully ready for war. Even if we allow that there is much exaggeration in the complaints which have been made, it is impossible not to conclude that as France cannot rival England in the number of her ships, the French Government would do better to devote all its attention to preparing the fleet in its present composition for war.

For Germany an increase in the navy is not demanded by any interests in Europe, and if it had not been for the example of Japan, in all probability, the Emperor William would not have set himself so passionately to the increase of his fleet.

In a very different position is England. Her fundamental interests demand that she shall remain mistress of the seas, everywhere and against every possible enemy, preserving from all danger not only the British Islands, but her maritime trade, her immense colonies in all quarters of the globe, and those communications by which the riches of the Old and New Worlds are exchanged to her advantage, and from which depend the ebb and flow of her social life. Mistress of the seas, England can be at rest, both as concerns herself and as concerns her colonies. For her the mastery of the seas is no empty word, and she has every good reason to devote all her resources to the strengthening of her fleet.

In its turn this example of England may be instructive for other countries.   England does not rely on the strength of her armies.   A country composed of islands, having a commanding fleet is secure, and consequently it may wisely sacrifice all to the increase of its fleet.   Russia is in a very different position, and her fleet can in no way guarantee her safety.   A decisive blow can be struck only on land, and for Russia a navy has only an auxiliary importance, in proportion as it influences operations on land.   If a naval war be carried on independently of these operations, and without influence upon them, it represents a mere waste of strength and money.   Even in relation to England it is more important for Russia to be strong on land than to increase her fleet, which never can be made to rival the navy of Great Britain.

Not only is an increased fleet not essential for the safety of Russia, but an increase would produce very little moral effect on her possible enemies.   Germany, as we have already pointed out, has no fear of a landing on her coast, and her fleet will always have the Northern Canal available as a means of refuge.   In England an increase in the number of Russian battleships would produce no impression.   There remains only Japan.   But there is not one of Russia's vital interests which Japan could damage.   The Siberian railway is important only as a means of transport, and neither Japan nor China has any interest in opposing transit across Siberia.

For England the competition of the Siberian railway is insignificant.   The freight rate from Hankow to Odessa or to London is only about twopence per pound, and the great proportion of Asiatic trade will continue to prefer this cheaper route.   It is true that transport by railway will be shorter in time, but this has little importance.   The use of the Siberian railway for purposes of trade cannot assume large measures for many years.   For this an immense development in China would be required, and China is above all things a country of stagnation.

In recent times Russia has made no small efforts to strengthen her fleet.   In the course of the twenty years period, 1876–96, the expenditure of the Russian Ministry of Marine grew at a much greater rate than other branches of expenditure—that is, from £4,050,000 to £9,000,000 (in 1896, £10,050,000), or 122 per cent. In the same period the expenditure on the army increased only 50 per cent. Now the maritime trade of Russia for one inhabitant only amounts to fourteen shillings and three-pence—that is, the trading interests of the Russian population are twenty-two times less than those of the population of the United Kingdom, and seven times less than those of France, Germany, and the United States. Thus maritime trade has for Russia less importance than for other countries, not only from its smaller value but owing to her geographical position ; the land frontiers of Russia being immense, while her limited coast is icebound for a great part of the year.

A more important consideration lies in the fact that those very powers which could place obstacles in the way of Russian maritime trade are those which are most dependent upon it, for neither Germany nor England could manage without Russian products. The stoppage of Russian trade would cause great injury to both these countries. From this it results that the maritime trade of Russia will be defended by the very nature of things, and not by the number of her warships. Yet Russia spends for every ton displacement of her own ships more than any other European state : that is to say, £5 4s., while France spends £4 1s. 8d., Italy £2 13s., Austria £1 8s., Germany £1, and England only 12s. 9d.

Naval expenditure amounts to 7 per cent. of the total value of her maritime trade, while that of France is 6 per cent., that of England 3½ per cent., and that of Germany less than 2 per cent. From this we see how insignificant are the trading interests of Russia. In the East they are quite inconsiderable.

First of all it is necessary to consider what is the extent of that trade in China and Japan which so captivates the imaginations of Europeans. China imports goods of average value of £41,050,000, and exports her own products to the average value of £23,850,000. The imports of Japan are valued at £6,750,000, and her exports at £8,700,000. These figures refer to a time before the war between China and Japan, since which those countries have permitted themselves such expenditure that they have undoubtedly impoverished themselves, and will not quickly recover from the consequences.

In this trade the share of Russia is quite inconsiderable. Of five hundred mercantile firms trading in China ten only are Russian. In the general export and import trade of China the share of Russia is as small as 4 per cent. The number of vessels entering Chinese ports in the year 1889 was 19,100, with a displacement of 15,800,000 tons. Of these vessels but 44, with a displacement of 55,000 tons, were Russian, or less than $\frac{1}{2}$ per cent. of the total.

True, we may expect that the construction of the Siberian railway will lead to the increase of Russian trade with China. But it will be safer not to have any illusions in this respect. A comparison of the present freight from Hankow to Odessa with the railway freight from Odessa to Moscow, will show what transport by the Siberian railway even with the lowest possible freights will cost.

The political influence of a great fleet in the Far East may be of course adduced. We hear talk, for instance, of the acquisition of Corea. The possession of Corea could be of no possible advantage to Russia. Corea has a population of twelve millions, and the whole value of her trade, import and export, amounts to no more than £780,000. With the conquest of Corea, Russia would have another distant point for the defence of which she would have to provide, and the greater the number of such weak places in the state the more its power is weakened. The immense defensive strength of Russia lies in the fact that she is a compact continent with a short coast line on which attack could be made.

While Russia could draw no possible profit from the acquisition of Corea, she would suffer from the fact that the Coreans, becoming Russian subjects, would begin to immigrate into Siberia, leading the Chinese after them. When we recall the case of the United States, compelled to prohibit the immigration of Chinese coolies, it will appear plain that Russia would be compelled to take limitary measures against her Corean subjects, measures which would not exactly tend towards the reconciliation of the Coreans with their new position. It is not to be supposed that Russia is spending half a milliard roubles on the Siberian railway in order to facilitate the competition of Coreans and Chinese with the Russian settlers in Siberia. The settlement of Eastern Siberia with Coreans would also give rise to difficulties from the political point of view. For all such reasons the acquisition by Russia of Corea is not to be desired.

In addition to this, from the direction of Japan there can be no serious danger. In her excessive armaments Japan is making efforts to follow in the footsteps of Europe, like the frog in the fable which, seeking to rival the size of the ox, blew himself out until he burst. Something of this nature must happen with Japan. The Amur territory of Russia is a wilderness which Japan cannot threaten. It is inconceivable that she would enter upon a war with Russia even though she were possessed of a preponderance in battleships.

CHAPTER V

WHAT WARS HAVE COST IN THE NINETEENTH CENTURY

IN considering the expenditure on past wars it would be necessary to add to the direct expenditure of Treasuries the losses sustained by populations through destruction of property, shortening of production, loss of trade, and generally from economic perturbations. The total of such losses would unquestionably exceed the total of the sums directly devoted by governments to the carrying on of war. But this total, of course, can only be estimated approximately. According to M. Leroy Beaulieu the expenditure by England in consequence of the French wars of the Revolution and of the First Empire, amounted to £840,000,000; and the losses of men in Europe amounted to 2,100,000. Some authorities estimate this loss of men at a much higher figure; Sir Francis Duvernois finds that France alone, up to the year 1799, had lost 1½ millions of men.

The cost of the war with France from 1812 to 1815, according to the accounts presented by Prince Barclay de Tolly to the Emperor, amounted to £23,325,000. It is interesting to note some of the larger items in this account. Thus we find that £10,650,000 were devoted to pay, £1,800,000 to provisions, £1,050,000 to the purchase of horses, and £1,200,000 to rations.

In reality the expenditure caused by this war was very much greater. The issue of assignats amounted to £43,850,000, and debts in consequence of loans, &c., to £22,950,000. In addition to this, Russia expended the subsidies received from England, and large sums, both in money and in kind, contributed by private individuals.

The Crimean is the first of great wars the expenditure of which can be defined with accuracy. The extraordinary expenditure caused by this war amounted to:

England	£74,200,000	or	1,855,000,000	francs.
France	66,400,000		1,660,000,000	,,
Russia	160,000,000		4,000,000,000	,,
Austria	13,720,000		343,000,000	,,
Turkey and Sardinia	25,680,000		642,000,000	,,
Total	£340,000,000	or	8,500,000,000	francs.

Let us present these totals graphically:

Expenditure on the Crimean War in Millions of Francs.

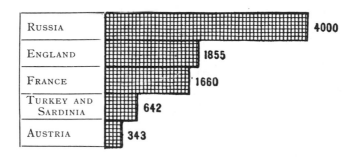

Thus the Crimean war laid on Europe an additional burden of £340,000,000. The total of the indirect losses caused by this war it is quite impossible to estimate.

The expenditure on the war of 1859 is thus estimated by Leroy Beaulieu:

I

France	.	.	£15,000,000	or	375,000,000	francs.
Austria	.	.	25,400,000		635,000,000	,,
Sardinia	.	.	10,200,000		255,000,000	,,
Total	.		£50,600,000	or	1,265,000,000	francs.

Expenditure on the War of 1859 in Millions of Francs.

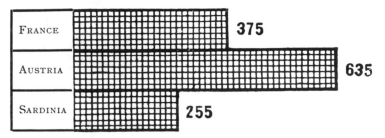

After this we come to the North American Civil War. In the course of four years the Northern States put in the field 2,656,000 volunteers, and the Southern States 1,100,000. The North expended in this struggle £560,000,000, and the Southern States about the same sum. In a word, this conflict cost the United States £1,000,000,000 direct outlay, and probably double that sum from destruction of property and decline in production. Estimating the average value of a slave at £40, we find that an expenditure of £160,000,000 would have been sufficient for the peaceful decision of this question.

In the Danish war of 1864 the expenditure was much less. It amounted to about £7,200,000 for Denmark, and about the same for Prussia and Austria together. The Prussian-Austrian war of 1866 involved an expenditure of about £66,000,000. In the war of 1870 the expenditure of Germany was covered by the French indemnity. As relates to France, the following are the statistics of her losses in the war of 1870 : From August 1, 1870, to April 1, 1871, France lost 3864 men through desertion, 310,449 taken prisoners, 4756 dis-

charged from the service for inefficiency, &c., 21,430
falling on the battlefield, 14,398 dying from wounds, and
223,410 discharged for different reasons, including sickness. The money expenditure and losses of France
amounted to : Military indemnity and payment for outlay
on occupation, £225,118,554 2s. 6d. ; contributions from
Paris and other towns, £10,040,000. The total expenditure, indemnity and contributions caused by the war
with Germany amounted to £506,680,000. To this must
be added losses from interruption of communications
and work, so that the general total of losses caused by
a war over the candidature of a Hohenzollern prince
amounted to about one thousand millions of pounds
sterling.

The extraordinary expenditure of Russia caused by the
war of 1877–78 was as follows :

					£	s.
1876	.	.	.	.	7,649,717	2
1877	.	.	.	.	64,399,213	7
1878	.	.	.	.	61,221,445	10
1879	.	.	.	.	19,816,397	8
1880	.	.	.	.	8,222,724	9
Total	.				161,309,497	16

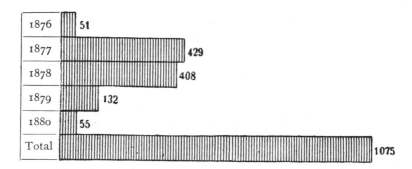

The figures in the diagram stand for millions of roubles (a
rouble being taken as equivalent to 3s.)

Of the losses and expenditure of Turkey statistics are not available.   But taking the losses of Turkey at half of those sustained by Russia—that is, at no more than £80,700,000, we get an expenditure on both sides of £241,950,000.

Thus we find that from 1853 to 1878, a period of twenty-five years, the expenditure on the great wars of Europe, that is, the Crimean war, the war of 1859, the Austro-Prussian war of 1866, the Franco-Prussian war of 1870, and the war with Turkey of 1877–78, reaches the immense sum of £1,221,360,000.

Expenditure of Europe on War in the second half of the Nineteenth Century.

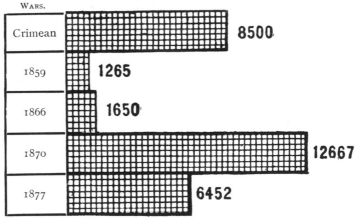

The figures in heavy type stand for millions of francs, the total of which amount to £1,221,360,000.

But heavy as is the cost of actual warfare, the burdens entailed by militarism in time of peace are no less crushing, and no easier to estimate precisely.   The need of preparation for unforeseen events entails a growth of expenditure not only in the military and naval departments, but in other departments of government.   In 1883 the military expenditure of Russia is defined as

£30,234,693 3s., but this in no way formed the limit to the military outlays of Russia; for pensions, and outlays by the Ministries of Internal Affairs and Ministry of Finances arising directly out of military necessities, increased this outlay by £3,000,000. The building and exploitation of railways further complicates such estimates. In 1893 the Ministry of War expended £33,829,681 7s. But to these figures it would strictly be necessary to add the following expenditure. Ministry of Finances, pensions over £900,000; assistance to lower ranks, £675,000; recruiting, £93,750, and extraordinary expenditure by the Ministry of War in re-armament over £4,050,000. This extra expenditure, with other smaller items which we omit, show that the military budget of 1893 must be increased by nearly £6,000,000.

But it is by no means sufficient to take into account direct expenses alone; the diminution of the revenue in consequence of a strained economic condition is no less grave. In addition to this the interest paid by states on loans concluded to satisfy military needs must be taken into account as one of the consequences of the permanent armaments of Europe. An attempt to present in figures these losses and expenditures would lead too far. We must confine ourselves to a short comparison of military expenditure as expressed in the budgets of different countries.

First of all it is interesting to see the amounts which the Great Powers, that is, Prussia, Austria, Italy, Russia, France, and England, spent and spend yearly for the maintenance of their land and sea forces, the outlay of every thousand inhabitants, and the percentage of increase in twenty-two years.

Year.	Maintenance of Armies and Navies.	Burden on 1000 Inhabitants.		Increase per cent. taking 1874 as 100 per cent.
	£	£	s.	
1874 . .	116 040,000	432	3	100
1884 . .	136,005,000	458	11	117
1891 . .	169,845,000	530	11	146
1896 . .	178,995,000	586	4	154

The above table shows that military and naval expenditure develops ceaselessly, and since 1884 more rapidly than in preceding years. Thus war budgets grow not only proportionately with the increase of the population, but in a degree much greater. In 1874 every inhabitant of these countries paid eight shillings and eightpence ; in 1891 this figure had grown to ten shillings and sixpence, in 1896 almost to twelve shillings.

The table opposite shows the increase in the expenditure on the creation and maintenance of armaments of each state separately.

Increase per Cent. of Military Expenditure between 1874 and 1896.

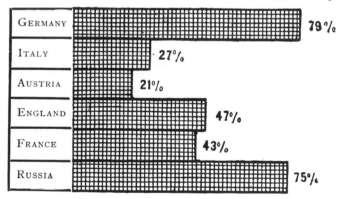

From the above diagram we see that the greatest increase in the war budget in this period took place in Germany, after which Russia follows, then England, France, Italy and Austria. If we take the period 1874–91 we will see that Germany most of all increased her armaments in the latter year, expending twice as much as seventeen years before. After her follows Italy, and then Russia. If we take the period 1874–84 we find Italy at the head, after her follow France, Germany, England and Austria. Russia in this period not only did not increase her war budget, but even diminished it by 4 per cent. It is

Increase per Cent. of Military Expenditure in 1896 in comparison with 1874.

	1874.	1884.		1891.			1896.			
	War Budget in millions of pounds sterling.	War Budget in millions of pounds sterling.	Per cent. increase in comparison with 1874.	Military Budget in millions of pounds sterling.	Per cent. increase in comparison with 1874.	Per cent. increase in comparison with 1884.	War Budget in millions of pounds sterling.	Per cent. increase in comparison with 1874.	Per cent. increase in comparison with 1884.	Per cent. increase in comparison with 1891.
Germany	17.76	22.125	25	40.61	100	61	31.89	79	44	—10
Italy	9.6	12.665	31	14.445	50	15	12.195	27	—3	—16
Austria	11.19	12.51	12	14.19	27	13	13.515	21	8	—5
England	23.595	29.385	24	29.55	25	0.6	33.77	47	18	18
Russia	29.625	28.395	—4	42.855	46	51	51.975	7	83	21
France	24.27	30.975	28	33.195	37	7	34.635	43	12	4
Total	116.04	136.055	17	174.845	46	25	177.98	54	32	5

interesting and characteristic that in the very time when
Russia's armaments were being decreased, Prince Bismarck and his supporters attempted to spread throughout
Germany and all Europe the idea that Russia was arming
against Germany. It was this policy which induced the
Reichsrath to consent to increased outlays on armaments,
thus dragging all Europe deeper into the gulf of militarism.
If we compare the two rival states of Central Europe,
Germany and France, we will see that in 1874 France
expended £6,450,000 more than Germany, in 1884,
£8,850,000 more, in 1891, £2,400,000 less, and in 1896,
£2,700,000 more than Germany. But general figures
such as these give no clear idea of the increase of the
burden on the population.

It is necessary here to call attention to one circumstance.
The expenditure cost of maintenance of soldiers constantly
increases, in consequence of perfected technique, the
greater knowledge required, and, at the same time, improvement in food and quarters. From statistics showing
the strength and cost of armies we have drawn up the
following table showing the yearly cost of the maintenance of a single soldier.

	1874	1884	1891	1896
	£ s.	£ s.	£ s.	£ s.
Russia . . .	33 15	26 5	36 12	56 8
France . . .	37 10	43 19	43 19	44 11
Germany . .	39 0	44 8	67 19	51 9
Austria . . .	34 1	39 15	45 18	39 0
Italy . . .	36 0	33 0	41 11	35 17
England . . .	60 0	88 19	81 3	77 5
Average .	40 1	49 1	52 17	50 15

Attempts have been made to estimate the comparative
cost of maintenance of a cavalry soldier, an infantryman,
and an artilleryman. From these calculations it appears

that the cost of armament constitutes only a small percentage of the general expenditure of maintenance. As the military value of every soldier depends largely upon the greater or less degree of perfection of his firearms, a natural consequence appears in the ceaseless endeavours of every state to improve upon the weapons of its rivals. From this rivalry springs one of the most important items of expenditure on armies. Naval forces demand even greater changes in armament. Old vessels have scarcely any fighting value, and can only be employed when the conflict of newer types has resulted in mutual extermination.

In order to give some idea of the vastness of the sums expended on fleets we quote some statistics as to the cost of the creation of the French fleet. The cost of the modern fleet of France, according to figures given in *Engineering* amounted to £29,172,000; its actual modern value is £18,538,000, to which must be added expenditure on artillery to a sum of £2,113,666 13s. 4d. Consequently we see that two-sevenths of the value of the French fleet is irrecoverably lost.

The following table (p. 138) from the *Rasvedtchik* gives a detailed analysis of the expenditure of the Great Powers on armies and fleets in 1893.

From this table may be seen the immense sums swallowed up in military preparations. But in addition to the ordinary expenditure on armies and fleets, the sum of which rises from £12,000,000 in Austria-Hungary to £45,000,000 in Russia, every state makes extraordinary expenditure on the increase of its army and fleet. In 1893 such outlay in Russia and France reached the sum of £6,840,000 for the army, and in the Triple Alliance £10,066,000. As concerns extraordinary outlay on fleets we have statistics only for Austria-Hungary and Germany; in 1893 these states expended £2,254,000. These sums increase year by year. And they are by no means confined to the Great Powers.

At the same time, and as an inevitable consequence, the essential requirements of the people remain unsatisfied. In Austria in 1896, £13,500,000 were devoted to the army

ARMY.

Ordinary Outlay during 1893.

	Austria-Hungary.	Germany.	Italy.	Russia.	France.	Great Britain.
	£	£	£	£	£	£
Administration	128,280	149,200	87,960	1,646,360	153,640	291,200
Technical Department	304,360	65,920	87,000	—	55,360	—
General Staff	196,000	329,760	161,200	—	500,720	43,960
Intendancy	149,880	109,840	127,600	—	573,800	124,000
Instruction	168,040	300,160	190,640	1,182,120	515,080	111,800
Pay, &c.	4,118,160	5,922,120	4,535,640	9,013,680	8,865,600	6,800,000
Provisions }	3,200,000	5,928,400	1,380,560	6,071,040	3,951,000	1,686,480
Forage			708,440	2,567,840	2,807,720	524,000
Medical Department	330,520	326,720	95,440	576,920	373,280	283,360
Transport	—	326,400	719,440	1,101,600	555,800	581,440
Uniforms	1,880,000	1,056,160	196,280	3,181,960	2,579,680	1,219,560
Remount	306,760	475,720	207,000	—	700,680	78,800
Artillery establishments	8,800	1,366,000	239,920	1,418,480	549,120	1,613,760
Engineering establishments	240,000	171,160	847,920	—	636,360	185,880
Various	16,280	4,921,080		10,509,880	466,960	3,896,960
Total	11,047,080	21,448,640	9,585,040	37,269,880	23,285,400	17,441,200
Extraordinary expenditure.	2,014,360	7,856,240	196,000	4,737,120	2,098,960	—
Total expenditure on Army	13,061,440	29,304,880	9,781,040	42,007,000	25,384,360	17,441,200

FLEET.

	Austria-Hungary.	Germany.	Italy.	Russia.	France.	Great Britain.
Ordinary expenditure.	1,111,280	2,444,800	3,989,560	7,982,840	10,224,000	14,240,080
Extraordinary expenditure.	256,480	1,997,880	—	—	—	—
Total expenditure on Fleet.	1,367,760	4,442,680	3,989,560	7,982,840	10,224,000	14,240,080

and fleet, while only £2,850,000, or 4½ times less was devoted to popular education. In Italy in the same year the expenditure on armaments was £12,650,000, while £1,500,000, or eight times less, was spent upon education. In France £32,400,000 are spent upon the army, and £6,600,000, or a fifth part, on education generally. In Russia the army devours £41,520,000, while education receives but £3,540,000, that is, a little more than a twelfth.

These figures speak for themselves; and give a plain indication of the degree of intellectual and moral culture we may expect from mankind when all its labour and strength are swallowed up in the creation and maintenance of armed forces. The United States in this respect have an infinitely better record. There all, from the children of the millionaire Vanderbilt down to the poorest peasant, attend the public schools, and receive elementary education. There knowledge for all is free and obligatory. The state makes it a duty to guard and maintain the popular schools.

But expenditure on past wars, and on armaments in peace have but a secondary importance in determining the significance of modern armaments. It is more important to estimate the expenditure which may be expected in a future war.

CHAPTER VI

WHAT THEY WILL COST IN THE FUTURE

THE expenditure which the actual carrying on of war will demand can only be estimated approximately. But some consideration of this question is indispensable for the purposes of this work.

It is useful to indicate some of those new conditions of modern warfare which will be the cause of immense expenditure. First of all, military stores must be drawn by every country from its own resources. This in itself is a circumstance which will tend greatly to increase the cost of war for individual states. The quick-firing rifle is a costly weapon, and the quantity of ammunition it will require cannot even be estimated. The same may be said concerning modern artillery and artillery ammunition. The vastness of armies, and the deadliness of modern weapons, will immensely increase the requirements of the sick and wounded. The preparations for sudden irruption upon an enemy's territory and destruction of his communications, having in view the fact that local resources must quickly be exhausted, constitutes another factor which must be borne in mind. The demand for provisions must grow to an immense extent, corresponding, as it will, to the increase of armies ; and this will be followed by a great rise in prices. In the supply of these provisions each country must provide for itself. That an immense army cannot exist on the resources of an enemy's territory is plain, especially when the slowness of advance, in a struggle for fortified positions, is taken into account. A future war will not only involve the question of victory in the field, but also the problem of forcing the enemy into such a position as to render military operations on his part impossible, in consequence of the failure of supplies. As we have already explained, communications by sea will be interrupted at the very outbreak of war. In consequence of this those countries which do not grow sufficient corn for the support of their populations will be compelled to expend immense sums in obtaining food. In this respect, as we shall hereafter point out in detail, England is in incomparably the worst position.

The increased demand for corn in time of war will, of course, cause an immense rise in prices. At a time when armies had but one-fifth of their present strength, and when there was no thought of the interruption of sea communications, the authority Stein estimated that the expenditure on provisioning an army would be three times greater in time of war than in time of peace. Another authority, S. N. Kotié, considers that even in Austria, which grows a superfluity of corn, the rise in prices consequent on war would amount to from 60 per cent. to 100 per cent. But if war were to prove as prolonged as military authorities declare—that is, if it were to last for two years—the disorganisation of agriculture caused by the withdrawal from work of the majority of agriculturists, would raise the price of bread to an inconceivable height.

There are serious reasons for doubting the proposition that a future war would be short. Thanks to railways, the period of preparatory operations would be considerably shortened, but in marches, manœuvres, and battles, railways can be employed only in very rare cases, and as lines of operation they cannot serve.

General Jung estimates that the mobilisation of the French army would require £12,000,000, and that the daily expenditure would grow from £60,000 in time of peace to £360,000 in time of war.

The *L'Avenir Militaire* estimates the daily expenditure in time of war at the following totals :

France	.	.	.	.	.	£396,880
Germany	.	.	.	.	.	388,920
Italy	.	.	.	.	.	248,040

From detailed calculations, made on the basis of past wars, it appears that a war breaking out in 1896 would have cost daily :

Germany (for an army of 2,550,000)	.	£1,020,000
Austria (,, ,, 1,304,000)	.	521,600
Italy (,, ,, 1,281,000)	.	512,400
		—————
Total for Triple Alliance . .	.	£2,054,000
France (for an army of 2,554,000)	.	£1,021,600
Russia (,, ,, 2,800,000) .	.	1,120,000
		—————
		2,141,600

The following diagram represents this more clearly :

Probable Daily Expenditure on a Future War in Millions of Francs.

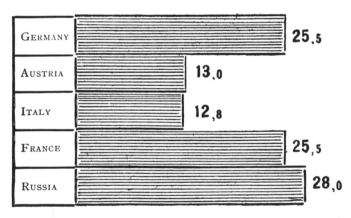

GERMANY	25.5
AUSTRIA	13.0
ITALY	12.8
FRANCE	25.5
RUSSIA	28.0

Thus it may be said that for five of the chief European states the daily expenditure in a future war would amount approximately to £4,200,000. In reality, however, this sum would probably be much higher. The provisioning of armies would be carried out not only with stores obtained from the central commissariat, but also from local products. The extent to which such a circumstance raises local prices may be shown by the history of the Crimean war. In the Crimean peninsula the price of victuals during war rose 10, 15, 16, and even 25 times, hay 16¾ times, and grain, milk, and wood from 5 to 9 times ; the price of manufactured articles increased 2 and 3 times, and transport from 5 to 7½ times. In the neighbouring southern governments prices were two and three times greater than in time of peace, and even in governments distant from the seat of war they doubled themselves. To-day the employment of railways would somewhat relieve this condition, but it would be a mistake to assume that the whole provisioning of an army, and especially the supply of forage, could be carried on by means of railways.

The extraordinary expenditure caused by war will by no means be limited by these items. The following table, which is based on detailed calculations, shows the extent to which governments would be compelled to come to the assistance of families left without resources on the outbreak of war :

	Daily.
Germany (783,000 families) . .	£78,300
Austria (351,000 ,,) . .	21,060
Italy (341,000 ,,) . .	20,460
Total for Triple Alliance .	£119,820
France (659,000 families) . .	£52,720
Russia (531,000 ,,) . .	25,488
Total for Dual Alliance .	£78,208

The following diagram illustrates this more plainly :

Probable Daily Expenditure of Governments on the Assistance of the Families of Soldiers in Thousands of Francs.

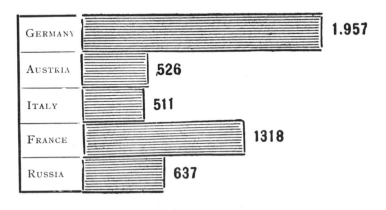

GERMANY	1.957
AUSTRIA	526
ITALY	511
FRANCE	1318
RUSSIA	637

Probable Yearly Expenditure on War in Millions of Francs.

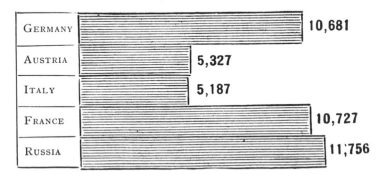

GERMANY	10,681
AUSTRIA	5,327
ITALY	5,187
FRANCE	10,727
RUSSIA	11;756

For these five states the daily expenditure in assisting the resourceless part of the population would amount to

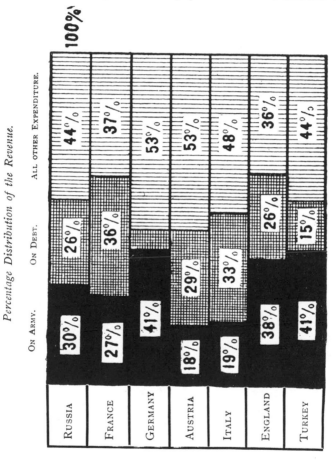

£198,028. This sum cannot be considered exaggerated, considering the immense increase in the price of the necessaries of life. This rise in prices, independently of the

general economic crisis caused by war and interruption of communications, will tend towards the depreciation of paper money, to the increased issue of which governments will be compelled to resort in order to meet growing expenditure.

The amount which will be required by the Great Powers of the continent to carry on war for a year may be seen from the diagram at the bottom of page 144.

We may well ask the question—where will such resources be found ? Already militarism and public debts swallow up the greater part of the revenue of most European states, as the diagram on page 145 shows.

An examination of the foregoing statistics naturally raises the question, Will it be possible to raise resources so vastly exceeding the normal revenues of states ? And what results must we expect from such extraordinary tension ?

CHAPTER VII

THE CARE OF THE WOUNDED

I.—Effect of the Improvement in Firearms upon the Character of Wounds.

The adoption of long-range artillery and quick-firing, small-calibre rifles with four times the energy of those employed in former wars, gives reason for fearing that not only the losses in battle will be incomparably greater than in the past, but also that the assistance of the wounded will be much more difficult. It is true that many authorities do not share these pessimistic views ; in their opinion the difference in the wounds caused by the old and the new weapons being in favour of the latter. The wounds inflicted by modern weapons, they say, will be more easily cured ; even when the wounded are left a long time without assistance the loss of blood will be small. The number of wounded will not be so great. According to this view the losses in future battles will be determined not alone by the power of arms, but also by those tactical methods which have been adopted as a consequence of the improvements in arms. As the result of perfected weapons, armies will seek or construct cover, and will attack in loose formation, while battles will be carried on at greater distances, all of which factors must tend to the decrease in the number of wounded. In addition to this, every soldier will be supplied with materials for dressing wounds, while blood-poisoning will be almost wholly eliminated, and the medical staffs of armies will be much stronger than before. Such are the opinions of optimists.

It is interesting to consider the proportions and nature of wounds in past wars in comparison with those inflicted by the weapons now in use.

Injuries from Cold Steel.—Fisher estimates the proportion of wounds inflicted by cold steel in the war of 1866 in the Austrian army at 4 per cent., and in the Prussian army at 5 per cent., of all wounds. In the war of 1870–71 the proportion of wounds caused by cold steel in the German army was 1 per cent. In the Russo-Turkish war the percentage of wounds inflicted by cold steel was 2.5 per cent. in the Russian army of the Danube. The percentage of deaths caused by cold steel is also very inconsiderable. In the last Russo-Turkish war, of the number killed in the army of the Danube only 5.3 per cent. of deaths were caused by cold steel, and in the army of the Caucasus barely 1 per cent.

Injuries from Bullets and Shells.—The mutual relations of injuries by rifle and artillery fire, both as to quantity and nature, present different results in previous wars. In a future war the differences will be still greater. In the past the wounds from shell-fire were many times more dangerous than those caused by rifle bullets ; in the present day this would appear to have changed. The bullet of a modern rifle, weighing several grammes, has such force that it may strike five or six men, and cause even greater destruction than is caused by fragments of shells. The mutual relations of injuries from bullets and shells in a future war will depend from the manner in which the war is conducted—that is, whether it be determined chiefly by open battles or take the character of sieges.

Since the adoption of rifled weapons we find that casualties have been caused mainly by bullets. Thus at the battle of Inkermann 91 per cent. of all wounds were inflicted by rifle fire. At the battle of the Tchernaya the proportion of wounds from rifle fire reached 75 per cent. Similar rusults took place in the Italian war, at Düppel and at Königgrätz. In the war of 1859, 80 per cent. of all wounds were caused by rifle fire, while at the storm of Düppel the proportion of bullet wounds among the

Prussians was 80.6 per cent. The statistics given by Weygand concerning the Franco-Prussian war are as follows : Artillery fire was the cause of 25 per cent. of the losses of the French and 5 per cent. of the losses of the Germans, while rifle fire caused 70 per cent. of French and 94 per cent. of German losses.

Thanks to the introduction of smokeless powder, diminution of calibres, and the covering of bullets with steel, the infantry rifle, of all arms the most important, has been so perfected that grave questioning has arisen concerning the losses in future war. Especial alarm has been caused by the increased penetrative power of the new composite bullet over that of the old.

The following diagram illustrates the result of firing experiments from an 11-mil. rifle. The shots were fired against fifteen folds of cowhide, 3.6 inches of hard beechwood, and finally pine planks 1 inch thick, at a distance of $32\frac{1}{2}$ feet from one another.

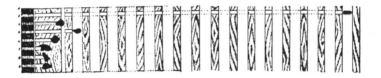

3. Compound.   4, 5, 6. Hard leaden bullets.
         7, 8, 9. Soft bullets.

From this we see that the penetrative force of the compound bullet is many times greater. It is generally accepted that a bullet which will penetrate an inch of pine has sufficient force to kill or wound a man or horse.

But even here invention has not stopped. The sketch on page 150 shows the action of a 5.5-mil. bullet fired with an initial velocity of about 2600 feet against a 14-mil. steel plate. The force of this bullet was sufficient, from a distance of $81\frac{1}{4}$ feet, to penetrate the plate, the bullet, on issuing from the plate taking the form of a mushroom.

In view of the small diameter of bullets and the force
with which they penetrate the body, the German surgeons
Reger and Beck, and, to some extent, Bruns, consider that
wounds from the new bullets will be less terrible than those
caused by the old, in consequence of which they have given
to these bullets the title " humane."   In an address read
in 1885 by Reger to the Berlin Military Medical Society,

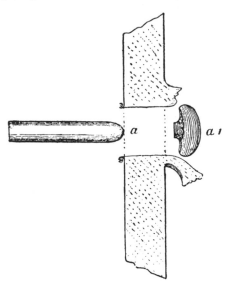

we find the following expression of opinion : " I welcome
the new bullet with great joy and believe that if it were
generally adopted by international consent, all humanity
would have cause to rejoice."   Similar views have been
expressed by Bruns, who considers that the new bullet is
not only the most effective, but also the most humane, tending to decrease the horrors of war.

But it must not be supposed that these views were
unanimously held.   As far back as the Franco-German war
we find that both combatants reproached one another with
the employment of explosive bullets.   The foundation for

these accusations was the fact that ordinary bullet wounds often took the character of wounds caused by explosive bullets. A closer acquaintance with facts would have prevented these accusations. Numerous experiments which have been made show that bullets fired at great initial velocity (not less than $812\frac{1}{2}$–975 feet) cause injuries similar to those caused by explosive bullets. Various attempts have been made to explain this circumstance. The opinion most widely accepted is that an explosive effect is produced when the bullet falls in some organ rich in liquids, the liquids being cast on all sides with destructive action on the neighbouring tissues similar to that of an explosion. This theory is elaborated by Reger in particular.

As modern rifles are immensely superior to those of former times, both in range, accuracy and power, it would seem natural to expect a greater proportion of mortal wounds than before. If this be so, it is difficult to see how they deserve the title "humane." It must first of all be stated that against the immense force with which modern bullets move, the opposition of the human body has little power to arrest their movement. The experiments of Bruns, in which a bullet fired from a distance of 2600–3900 feet penetrated 2–3 human corpses one behind the other, and fired from a distance of 400 metres penetrated 4–5 bodies, even the strongest bones of the human body being shattered, have not only been confirmed but strengthened by later investigations, which showed that at any distance up to 6500 feet the penetrating force of a composite bullet was sufficient to pierce several bones.

The absolute number of wounded in war, even with an equal number of combatants, must be incomparably greater than before. The causes of this are obvious : the increased quantity of ammunition expended per man, rapidity of fire, increased range, greater accuracy, smokeless powder, and greater penetrative force, thanks to which many forms of cover, formerly effectually protecting the soldier will be of no value.

Professor Bardeleben draws a melancholy picture of the

action of the new weapons. He agrees that the number of wounded in the course of a given time will increase, not only because the magazine rifle allows the discharge of many more bullets than formerly, but because one bullet will strike three or four men, one behind the other, it may be even more. On the other hand, he finds that the proportion of killed on the field of battle will increase in consequence of the increased force of the blow. Fired from a distance at which the old bullet was stopped by the skull or the ribs, the modern bullet will penetrate to the brain and heart.

The sketches of Bircher (opposite page) give some idea of the effect of fire at long range. These experiments were carried on in Switzerland with the 7.5-mil. bullet at a distance of 9750 feet and 11,375 feet.

Such shattering of the bones at a distance of 9750 feet and 11,375 feet will be comparatively rare. In the zone of actual fire cases of shattered bones will be more frequent and more serious ; and the mortality will be greater in consequence of greater loss of blood resulting from direct injury to the blood-vessels.

As relates to the wounds caused by artillery fire, as a great part of these wounds will be caused by the fragments and bullets of shrapnel, it may be assumed that the injuries they inflict will differ little from those inflicted in past wars.

II.—HELP TO THE WOUNDED.

Not only may we expect that the quantity of wounds and sickness will increase in future wars, but the assistance of the wounded and sick will be much more difficult than in the past. It must be noted that this side of the question has received little attention. The whole attention of specialists has been bent upon the increase of the deadliness of weapons of extermination, and upon the strengthening of armies. The chief physician of the Bavarian army, Porth, calls attention to this fact, and declares that the German strategists in the race after

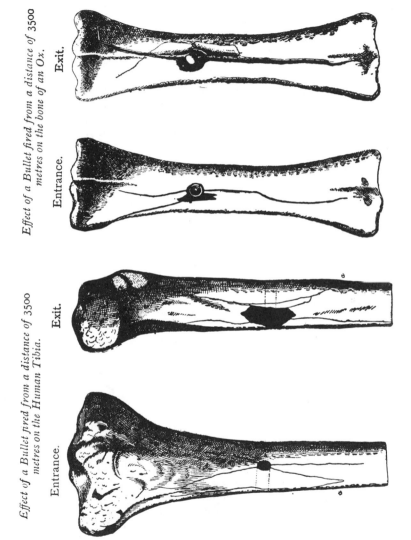

Effect of a Bullet fired from a distance of 3500 metres on the bone of an Ox.

Exit.

Entrance.

Effect of a Bullet fired from a distance of 3500 metres on the Human Tibia.

Exit.

Entrance.

perfection of weapons of extermination, have left behind them all plans for the amelioration of the lot of the wounded in war. Indeed, they go even further, and refuse to grant resources for the perfection of the medical organisation, thinking that such a course would hinder military operations. Meantime, the modern weapons will cause wounds requiring, if anything, more rapid aid to the wounded than those inflicted by the old type.

In recent wars provision for the wounded generally proved inadequate. Even in the war of 1870 it was impossible to make arrangements for ambulances as easily as formerly. "Bullets and shells," says Pigorof, "carried much farther than before ; it was difficult to find a safe spot in the vicinity of the field of battle, and such a position once found was quickly rendered untenable by the rapid movements of the armies. Another element of difficulty lies in the fact that all stations for dressing wounds in modern wars are quickly overcrowded owing to the rapidity of fire, whole files being stricken down at the same time ; in consequence there is no possibility of avoiding terrible overcrowding in the ambulances if the wounded are not sent off the field at once.

" After the battle of Weissenburg the wounded French lay two days upon the field. In the village of Remilie lay some thousands of men wounded at Gravelotte, brought thither in two days and two nights in peasants' carts, and, to attend to these thousands of wounded (nearly 10,000) during the first few days only four doctors were available." Similar was the experience after other battles of this war. Pigorof continues : " The wounded remaining after battle were named by our old servant 'garbage and bits,' and there they all lay, garbage and bits, scattered over the battlefield till some one lifted them up and bore them away. The rapidity and accuracy of modern fire are such that whole files fall together, and the accumulation of wounded in a very short time is immense."

No better was the state of affairs in the war of 1877–78. Professor Botkin says that the wounded remained not only without medical aid, but even without water for days, and all this thanks to the fact that no one had thought of this matter in time. The position of the wounded in hospital was also unsatisfactory. In a memorandum of the Chief Controller we find it plainly stated that the military hospitals, both in the Caucasus and in Bulgaria, were characterised by great defects, especially when compared with the institutions opened by the Red Cross Society, and at the expense of private individuals. The temporary military hospitals were supplied by the commissariat with inferior stores, and the medicine-chests were lacking in some of the most necessary remedies. The supply of the hospitals was carried on unpunctually, and sometimes resulted in a lack of medical attendance. These deficiencies were especially felt in the time of the outbreak of typhus at the close of the war.

The chief representative of the Red Cross Society, Mr. P. A. Richter, writes in his report as follows : " Of what were the military hospitals in need ? It would be easier to answer this question if it were reversed, and it were necessary to enumerate not those things which they wanted, but those with which they were fully supplied." Again he says : " The shortsightedness and inactivity of the military administration in this case cannot be placed to the account of the hospitals themselves." Among other things, Richter complains bitterly of the absence of clothing.

All society is anxious to know that such events should not be repeated in a future war. It is interesting to see what improvements have been made in this department of military administration.

Let us take France as an example. In 1870 France committed the unpardonable sin of considering herself ready for war. In the present day we also hear complaint as to the possible failure of arrangements to fulfil in practice what has been claimed for them. When in 1881 General Farre was questioned as to the sending of dressing materials for the Algiers and Tunis armies he replied : " Our ambulances will in no respect show deficiencies." In reality it was shown that in this

respect nothing was ready.   Notwithstanding the fact that
all the necessary material was bought with a liberal hand,
it did not reach its destination.   It even appears that in
Kef (May 1881) after numberless vain applications
the officers were obliged to raise a subscription among
themselves for the purchase of sugar, wine, and coffee
for the sick in the improvised ambulances.   In Grardimay in May 1891 the wounded and sick of General
Lozhero's column awaited for twenty days the arrival of
material from the regular ambulance.   In Gulletta in May
and June 1881 the sick officers were compelled to live at
their own expense in the wretched coffee-houses of the
town ; and on the whole extent of coast from Gulletta to
Philippeville the ambulances and hospitals were overcrowded to such an extent that by August no more could
be admitted, and the sick from Gulletta had to be sent
down to the coast and set on board ship, until finally they
were again brought to Philippeville.   At Pont de Fahs in
October 1881, 4000 sick men of Filbert's brigade, finding
themselves left to the care of a single doctor, were compelled, owing to the absence of transport, to await the
arrival of the wretched waggons hired from the natives in
order to bring them to Tunis.

The state of affairs in the Italian army in the Abys-
sinian war was no better.

There is reason for turning attention to the aid of the
wounded and sick, the more so since the new weapons have
made the position of affairs infinitely worse ; increase in
the number of wounded will increase proportionately the
difficulties of the ambulance corps ; the time for its operations is diminished, thanks to the greater accuracy,
rapidity, and range of fire which sometimes must make it
impossible to carry off the wounded and grant them first
aid ; while there is an inevitable loss of working force
caused by greater distance of the dressing stations from
the fighting line which the immense range of modern
fire-arms must involve.

One of the most celebrated surgeons of the century,
Professor Bilroth, declared that in order to give full assist-

THE CARE OF THE WOUNDED 157

ance to the wounded, the sanitary corps must be equal in strength to the combatants. This is in no way an exaggeration, but merely expresses the fact that with the modern conditions of war, and the probable great length of battles, it will be almost impossible fully, immediately, and satisfactorily to give medical assistance to the wounded. The very work of removing the wounded must be carried on under fire, and will be extremely difficult. The ambulance servant must pick his way with his burden, bending down to avoid the shots if both he and the wounded man he bears are not to be killed. The work of collecting the wounded will be made even more difficult by the fact that they must be sought for in the covered positions where they lie. And delay in the carrying off of the wounded means an increased percentage of deaths, not only from loss of blood but even from hunger.

In a time when rifle and artillery fire were beyond comparison weaker than they are now, those who were left unhelped on the battlefield might hope for safety. But now, when the whole field of battle is covered with an uninterrupted hail of bullets and fragments of shells, there is little place for such hope. But even here the list of terrors of a future war does not cease.

The Bavarian Chief Military Physician Porth calls attention to yet another danger which may threaten the wounded. After the battle of Worth he set out with his assistants to aid the wounded, and came across a great number of Turcos who needed assistance. After this, on entering a wood he came across great walls of corpses lying across the road. The lower parts of these walls of corpses were constructed regularly, while the upper parts were formed of corpses lying in disorder. These last, apparently, were corpses of soldiers struck by bullets after the wall had been built. Porth examined the corpses carefully in order to see if any living men were among them, but found that all were dead. "This will easily be understood," observes Dr. Porth, "as the weight of those on top and fresh bullets had finally killed off any who had been placed there alive." Porth supposes that such walls of corpses will also be raised in a future war. Trenches constructed in haste have not any connecting passages behind, so that the reinforcements sent to the front will have to pass an exposed space, and hastily jumping into the trenches may cause injuries to the wounded already lying there. When the trenches shall have become encumbered with dead or those considered as dead, it will be necessary to throw these out ; they cannot be thrown out behind, since such a course would result in impeding the path of reinforcements ; they will be placed of necessity, in front of the trench, that is, on the side of the enemy, thus forming a breastwork. "To be cast there alive," adds Dr. Porth, "will be the best of fates, for a new bullet will shortly end all sufferings, while those wounded who are left lying in the trenches will suffer long."

It is plain that the introduction of long-range rifles, the improvement of artillery, the immense increase in the strength of armies, and finally, changes in the rules of war, demand the introduction of radical reforms in the methods of assisting the wounded on the field of battle. For the benefit of the ambulance service, it would be absolutely necessary to give independence to the authority to which is subject both official and voluntary organisations for aiding the wounded.

Without voluntary co-operation, without public participation in time of war, it would be impossible to manage, but this participation must be regulated in good time. In Russia it is especially necessary to constitute committees with authority : (1) Over the hospitals ; (2) over the supply of medical stores ; (3) over the transport of the sick and wounded ; (4) over the equipment of the hospitals with domestic necessaries. The rational organisation of such a committee would result in immense benefit.

We will quote here some more evidence as to the necessity for improvement. Writing of the Russo-Turkish war, Pigorof says : "In the end of September, on our inspection of the hospitals we came across hundreds of cases of frost-bitten feet, and in answer to our inquiries found that almost all ascribed their sufferings to wet boots, which for a long time had been worn without taking off. If *valenki* (felt over-boots) had been given only to half the men in a company it would have saved many from frost-bites, as it would have been possible for the soldiers to take off their boots and dry them."

Those who control the lot of soldiers must remember that although a large increase in the ambulance service would result apparently in a loss of fighting strength, in reality it would directly result in strengthening the fighting forces by increasing the percentage of sick and wounded who would return to the front, by diminishing the mortality and by, raising the spirits of soldiers in consequence of the conviction that care would be taken of the victims.

And in the present time, when in a battle between the armed forces of Europe, the mechanism of destruction is so perfect that shells may be thrown with unexampled rapidity to unheard-of distances, creating on every field a vast area of absolute destruction ; when owing to power of fire attacks can only be made in loose formation, and every soldier may shirk the battle—the spirit of armies has a much greater importance than before.

END OF PART I.

PART II

ECONOMIC DIFFICULTIES IN TIME OF WAR

CHAPTER I

IN RUSSIA

In order to understand the economic and social consequences which would follow a war in which Russia was
engaged, it is necessary to consider the degree of well-
being of the population, and the amount of its income ;
and to explain how war will shorten the demand for certain
products and increase the demand for others ; lessen the
exports, and deprive a considerable portion of the population of their means of livelihood. In considering " Plans
of Military Operations " in a struggle between the two
great continental alliances we attempted to make some
comparison of the endurability of the states engaged
against the destructive influences of war. The conclusions
which sprang from a general consideration of military
plans were in accord with the following proposition of
General Brialmont, that "the state to which war is least
dangerous is Russia, guaranteed as she is by the immensity of her territories, the character of her soil and climate,
and still more, by the social condition of her people, occupied for the greater part by agriculture." Rich in men, in
horses, and in food, having many industrial and trading
centres, accustomed for a century to the circulation of
paper money, Russia is in a state to keep up a defensive
war for some years, which the Western and Southern
powers, standing on a high degree of culture, but producing
insufficient food for their populations, could not do. These
rather would be threatened with ruin and even disintegration. The strategical superiority of Russia lies in the fact
that the occupation by an enemy of all her frontier terri-

tories would not produce a decisive result.   Even the taking of both her capitals, and the defeat of all her ready forces, would not deprive her of the means of resistance, whereas any Western state in such circumstances would be decisively crushed.   Such are the general conclusions to which a consideration of the plans of attack on Russia, formulated by foreign authorities, have led.

But in considering the effect of war on the condition of the people in Russia, we are compelled to glance more closely than will be necessary in the case of other states, if only for the reason that the enormous extent of Russia, and the immense reserve of men for the formation of new armies—that is, the two unquestioned elements of Russian superiority—are likely to inspire far too optimistic hopes. In the opinion of foreigners, military specialists in Russia in this respect are liable to exaggeration, forgetting that in Russia as elsewhere war would be felt intensely, and, in certain respects, even more disastrously, on the finances and on the general economic condition of the country.

It would be a mistake to think that these exaggerated views are current in all military circles in Russia.   But it must be admitted that the very strength of Russia, her richness in territory and in men, affords a basis to certain minds for very natural exaggeration.   That such exaggerations have their dangerous side is unquestioned by every impartial student of history, from which we learn that exaggeration has led, if not directly to military enterprises, at least to more decisive actions which easily awaken the dangers of war.

Unfortunately, the difficulty of a detailed investigation of the present condition of Russia and the future consequences which a war would entail for her, is very great, owing to the absence of those exhaustive statistics which are everywhere available in Western Europe, in America, and especially in England.   In Russia the compiling of statistics began only in the reign of Nicholas I.   But that reign, based solely on military-bureaucratic principles, did not look with favourable eyes on the publication of official statistics. Co-operation or advice from the side of society in general was not only not looked for, but not even admitted, and the need for communicating to the public statistics on which judgment might be based was consequently ignored. Figures were a secret of state, concealed sometimes even from the Council of State itself. It was only in later years that statistics became available to the student.

I.—FALL IN THE FUNDS AND INFLUENCE OF WAR ON THE FINANCES.

In order to determine the economic durability of Russia against the influences of war, we are compelled to consider two contingencies, that is, a war carried on with the aim of invasion of an enemy's territory, and a war carried on with the object of repulsing attack, and, in the latter case also, to consider what forces Russia would dispose of if, after the repulse of the attack, she decided to undertake a counter-invasion of the territories of the enemy. First of all, of course, it is necessary to consider the perturbations which must be produced immediately after the declaration of war. Whatever might be the causes of war, it may be assumed, that mobilisation would be accepted as something inevitable, and the possibilities of difficulty which might arise in Western states if war were declared in defiance of popular feeling, in Russia need not be considered.

The immense majority of the soldiers mobilised will consist of peasant-agriculturists, men of simple minds, uninterested in political questions. The educated soldiers will be mainly officers, who will also, without question, obey orders, and easily assimilate official declarations as to the unavoidability of war. The number of soldiers taken from trade and industry in Russia will be comparatively small. But it is unquestioned that among the Russian soldiers belonging to this category, perturbations may be called forth even more serious than those which will arise in Western states. The systems of agriculture, industry, and of trade in Russia are less elaborate than in Western countries. Owing to the absence of educational institutions the knowledge and *morale* in trade and industry are low ; the women of Russia, whom, of course, mobilisation will not directly affect, are little engaged in business; and therefore it will be more difficult to replace the directing forces summoned under the flag than it would be in the West.

Of the difficulty of satisfying demands for money for the mobilisation of the army we have already spoken. Here it is only necessary, in view of the possible occupation by an enemy of Russian territory, to set out the distribution of the revenue, &c., over the different parts of the Empire—in one word, to present a financial physiological picture of Russia in the present day.

It needs no evidence to show that the perturbations which a future war will cause in the sphere of finance will be incomparably more serious than those caused by the war of 1877. The finances of Russia are distinguished by the fact that even in times of peace the course of Government securities and paper money is most variable. In a memorandum presented to the Emperor Alexander III. in 1882, M. N. H. Bunge thus defined the causes of these fluctuations (in addition to the main reason— unlimited issue). (1) The internal political position of the State, the danger of risings, anarchy, the absence of settled political programmes. (2) The internal economic condition of the country, famines, crises in industrial, commercial, and banking circles, caused by dishonesty, speculation, and failures, and so forth. (3) The general financial position, disproportion between revenue and expenditure, financial extravagance, deficits, and so forth. Independently of these internal elements are others—for instance, the danger that the state may be drawn into a great European war, and the risk of military failure.

Such is a judgment formulated in 1882. Since then fifteen years have passed, and in that period the position has improved in many ways, but not enough to guarantee, in the event of war, that the description quoted above would not again apply in full force.

We have seen that in 1870 the Prussian state and municipal loans were depreciated 25 per cent., and banking, industrial, and railway shares 35 per cent. In 1877 the value of the Russian credit rouble (100 kopecks) fell to 56½ kopecks metal.

Thanks to the arrangements of the present Ministry of Finances, statistics are yearly printed as to the value of the Government securities and the manner in which they are distributed. From these statistics it appears that on January 1, 1896, there existed of such securities:

Metallic	.	.	2249 millions of roubles*	(£337,350,000)
Credit .	.	.	3330 „	„	(£449,500,000)
	In all .	5579 „	„	(£786,850,000)

Of these in cash, in treasuries, and in banking institutions the amount of such securities was:

Metallic	.	.	210 millions of roubles	(£31,500,000)
Credit .	.	.	2293 „	„	(£343,950,000)

Thus it appears that there were in circulation, partly among private individuals in Russia, but for the greater part abroad:

Metallic Loans	.	2039 millions of roubles	(£305,850,000)
Credit Loans	.	1037 „	„	(£155,550,000)

Now if we take the depreciation in time of war of securities guaranteed by the Government at 25 per cent., and of other securities at 35 per cent., which depreciation has already been experienced in the wars of 1870 and 1877, the immense economic perturbation which would be caused by war will be at once made plain. A depreciation of 25 per cent. of the nominal value of Government securities would amount to 52,000,000 of metallic and 573,000,000 credit roubles (£7,800,000 and £85,950,000); a depreciation of 35 per cent. on the nominal value of securities unguaranteed by the Government would amount to 48,000,000 metallic roubles, and 404,000,000 credit roubles (£7,200,000 and £60,600,000). Thus war would

* The rouble is taken as equivalent to its face value of 3s.

at once cause a depreciation of securities held within the
country of 1,100,000,000 roubles (£165,000,000).

*Depreciation of Securities circulating in Russia at the Outbreak
of War in Millions of Roubles.*

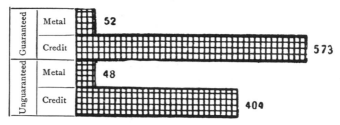

All this leads to the conclusion that in the beginning of
war there cannot even be thought of the issue of new
loans, and therefore war can only be carried on by the
immense issue of credit notes, the unavoidable consequence of which will be to shake to its foundations the
financial condition of the country.

The position in which Russia found herself in the war
of 1812–1815 is so different from modern conditions that
to draw practical lessons from the experiences of that
time is impossible. The extraordinary outlays caused by
the Crimean war amounted to about $1\frac{1}{2}$ milliard of
roubles (£225,000,000), which led to an immense increase
of indebtedness and to a fall in the value of the credit
rouble, although war was carried on only at one extremity
of the country, and the whole of the western frontier
remained open to trade.

In the Turkish war of 1877–78 the extraordinary outlay
amounted to

In 1876	. .	50,998,114 roubles	(£7,649,717 2s.)
„ 1877	. .	429,328,089 „	(£64,399,213 7s.)
„ 1878	. .	408,142,970 „	(£61,221,445 10s.)
„ 1879	. .	132,100,316 „	(£19,815,047 8s.)
„ 1880	. .	54,818,163 „	(£8,222,724 9s.)
Total	.	1,075,396,652 „	(£161,308,167 16s.)

What may be expected from a future war ? First of all
it must be noted that the new military organisation of
Russia, founded on conscription and short service, not
only has not diminished, but on the contrary has increased
the ordinary military expenditure. The expenditure of
the Ministry of War in the course of the twenty years
period, 1875 to 1894, increased from 175,000,000 roubles
(£26,250,000) to 239,000,000 roubles (£35,850,000). The
cause of this increase lies partly in the increased number
of the army, and partly in the better treatment of the
soldiers, as is seen from the following figures indicating
the cost of maintenance of a single soldier :

1874	225 roubles	(£33 15s.)
1884	175 „	(£26 5s.)
1891	244 „	(£36 12s.)
1896	376 „	(£56 8s.)

Of the proportion of expenditure by one inhabitant on
army and fleet, estimated according to geographical position,
the chart on page 170 gives a clear idea. A glance at this
chart will show that the satisfaction out of the ordinary
revenues of the requirements of the budget in time of war
will be all the more difficult since the revenue will be
diminished, while the expenditure on popular needs is so
small that its diminution in time of war will be almost
impossible.

Russia, with a mobilised army of 2,800,000 men, will
daily need for their maintenance and equipment 7,000,000
roubles (£1,050,000). In addition to this, considerable
sums will be needed for the maintenance of families of
soldiers on service. The greater the number of married
soldiers the greater will be the need for aid. But, as is
hereafter shown, the number of married persons and
children in proportion to the general population is greater
in Russia than elsewhere, from which it appears that the
expenditure in this respect must be greater.

It is true that Russia will find an advantage in the fact
that the proportion of soldiers withdrawn from industry is
insignificant when compared with the proportion in other
countries, for in Russia about 86 per cent. of the number

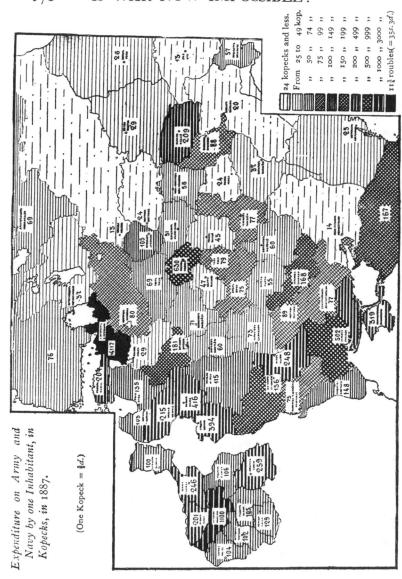

Expenditure on Army and Navy by one Inhabitant, in Kopecks, in 1887.

(One Kopeck = ¾d.)

24 kopecks and less.
From 25 to 49 kop.
„ 50 „ 74 „
„ 75 „ 99 „
„ 100 „ 149 „
„ 150 „ 199 „
„ 200 „ 499 „
„ 500 „ 999 „
„ 1000 „ 3000 „
11¾ roubles(= 35s. 3d.)

summoned to the colours will belong to the agricultural class. This circumstance is particularly favourable for Russia, as the agriculturist will leave behind him members of his family who can continue his labour, and such families will not be threatened by a complete cessation of work. But on the other hand, the Russian agricultural population, which even in times of peace lives in extreme poverty, will soon exhaust its resources, and the Government will be compelled to come to its aid. By exhaustive examination of the comparative degrees of well-being of the persons engaged in different occupations, it would be shown that Government will be compelled to assist the families of not less than one quarter of the soldiers engaged in agriculture, of less than half of the small traders and clerks, and of 10 per cent. of the free professions. Detailed calculations show that these number 531,000 families in all. All of which shows that the expenditure in time of war will be immense and immediate, while to cover it by new taxation or by the increase of old taxes will be impossible. Popular savings, which might be taken advantage of for loans, are in Russia extremely small, and it is very probable that in order to cover the ordinary expenditure in time of war, not to speak of extraordinary expenditure, the chief resource must inevitably be the issue of credit notes. In the time of the wars of 1812, 1857 and 1877, although financial crises occurred owing to the increased issue of assignat and credit notes, these crises were not of such a nature as to influence the continuance of military operations. In all probability a future war will resemble the past in this respect.

During the last war with Turkey the value of the rouble credit note was depreciated to $55\frac{1}{2}$ kopecks, and that this depreciation was not greater must be ascribed to exceptionally favourable circumstances. On the one hand, Russia possessed a large reserve of corn, and on the other, in consequence of scarcity abroad, the prices of corn, the chief article of export from Russia, and many other articles of food, rose considerably, thus increasing the export of Russian products.

In the second chapter of this work we attempted to show the advantages which a defensive war promised to Russia, a defence which, after exhaustion and disorganisation of the enemy's resources, might transform itself into attack.   But in the economic relation such a war would have the disadvantage that the country would be compelled to support the armies of the invader in addition to its own.   We showed that it is impossible to avoid the conclusion that a defensive war would result in victory for Russia.   But this cannot alter the fact that the sacrifices which the people must sustain would be incalculably great.

In order to be persuaded of this, it is not enough to consider only those perturbations the immediate consequence of war, but to examine also, although briefly, the economic and moral condition of the country.

II.—Economic Upheaval in consequence of the Interruption of Trade.

On the declaration of war, the external European trade of Russia will immediately cease.   The losses which this will cause must be considered.   The average Russian export and import for the six years 1889–94 are shown thus in millions of credit roubles :

	Russian Statistics.		Foreign Statistics.
Export	585 (£87,750,000)	...	783 (£117,450,000)
Import	399 (£59,850,000)	...	237 (£35,550,000)

Let us present this graphically :

Average Export and Import, 1889–1894, in Millions of Credit Roubles.

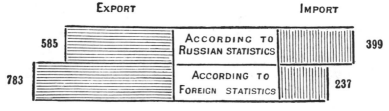

If these totals are distributed among the population we will find the following export and import for one inhabitant :

Years.	Roubles.		Per cent. relation of Export to Import.
	Export.	Import.	
1885–1893 . .	3.52 (10s. 6¾d.)	2.31 (6s. 11d.)	1.52
1894–1895 . .	3.89 (11s. 8d)	2.87 (8s. 7¼d.)	1.26

Of the four great groups under which the foreign trade of Russia may be classified, in export trade provisions predominate (57 per cent.), after which follow raw and half-dressed materials ($37\frac{1}{4}$ per cent.), manufactures ($3\frac{1}{4}$ per cent.), and animals ($2\frac{1}{2}$ per cent.). In imports predominate raw and half-dressed materials ($58\frac{1}{4}$ per cent.), after which follow manufactures ($21\frac{1}{2}$ per cent.), provisions (20 per cent.), and animals ($\frac{1}{2}$ per cent.).

In the number of Russian exported provisions the first place, of course, is taken by grain, the export of which, although with fluctuations, constantly increases, and in 1894 had risen to 640,000,000 poods * (205,714,295 cwts.), or $5\frac{1}{3}$ poods (192 lbs.) per inhabitant. The following table illustrates with more detail the nature of this export :

	Millions of Poods (English Equivalent in millions of lbs.)				
	Wheat.	Rye.	Oats.	Barley.	Maize.
1893–94 . .	200 (7200)	22.6 (803.6)	104 (3744)	149 (5364)	33 (1188)
1894–95 . .	224 (8064)	82.7 (2977.2)	96 (3456)	109 (3924)	24 (864)
1895–96 . .	201 (7,236)	—	56 (2016)	74 (2664)	9 (324)

* A pood is really equal to 36.1127 lbs., but for purposes of our equivalents we take it as equal to 36 lbs.

We find that the average harvest of corn for the whole world, taking a twelve years period, was 3,294,000,000 poods (1,058,800,000 cwts.), while the harvest of

```
1893 was 3,427,000,000 poods (1,101,535,715 cwts.)
1894  „   3,503,000,000   „   (1,126,000,000  „ )
1895  „   3,385,000,000   „   (1,088,035,715  „ )
```

By investigations lately made it has been shown that in twelve years the yearly quantity of grain harvested in Russia increased by 150,000,000 poods (48,214,300 cwts.), and the area of sowing by 5 per cent., while the population in that period increased by 11 per cent. This may be expressed in another form : the yearly increase of demand in consequence of the growth of the population amounts to 40,000,000 poods (13,000,000 cwts.), ten years 400,000,000 poods (130,000,000 cwts.), while in that period the production of grain increased by 150,000,000 poods (48,214,300 cwts.).

But the export from Russia is composed only of that part of the harvest which remains free after the satisfaction of the minimum requirements of the population :

	English Equivalent in Millions of lbs.		Percentage of Export to Average Harvest.
—	Average Yearly Harvest in Millions of Poods, 1890-94.	Average Export.	
Rye . . .	1059 (38,124)	32 (1152)	3.0
Wheat . .	455 (16,380)	156 (5616)	34.3
Oats . .	552 (19,872)	56 (2016)	10.1
Barley . .	286 (10,296)	111 (3996)	30.0
	2352 (84,672)	355 (12,780)	15.1

Let us present these figures graphically :

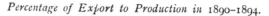

Percentage of Export to Production in 1890–1894.

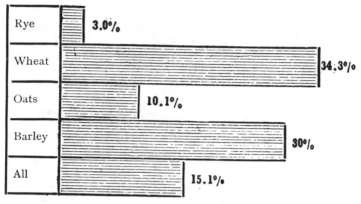

Rye	3.0%
Wheat	34.3%
Oats	10.1%
Barley	30%
All	15.1%

In the chart on page 176 we give some figures as to the production of all grains. But these figures give no sufficient material for determining the influence which war would produce on the trade in corn. This influence will depend upon in whose hands the superfluity of corn rests, whether in the hands of private proprietors or in the hands of the peasants. Among the immense majority of larger agriculturists the superfluity is very considerable, while the products of the peasants serve mainly to satisfy their own needs.

It is obvious that private proprietors may bear the strain better than the peasants. If the export of grain be only shortened the first will be able to dispose of their grain by such routes as remain open. But if the export of grain entirely cease and prices in the internal market considerably fall, certain landowners will sustain the crisis by means of their reserve of capital, while those whose estates are mortgaged would in case of war take advantage of the inevitable postponement of payments into bank, and in addition to that of the loans of the Imperial Bank. The peasants will have no auxiliary resources ; and in the

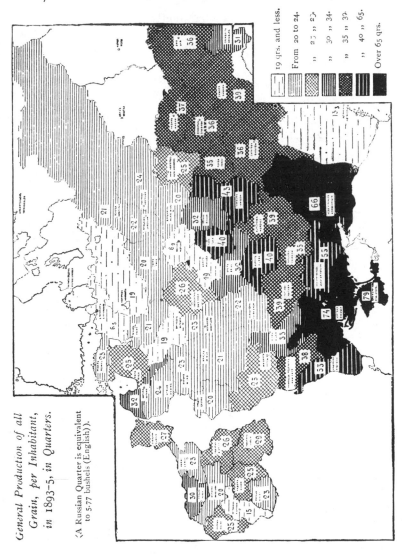

General Production of all Grain, per Inhabitant, in 1893–5, in Quarters.

(A Russian Quarter is equivalent to 5.77 bushels (English)).

19 qrs. and less.
From 20 to 24.
  ,,   25 ,, 29.
  ,,   30 ,, 34.
  ,,   35 ,, 39.
  ,,   40 ,, 65.
Over 65 qrs.

majority of cases the corn they raise is insufficient for their needs, for the payment of taxes, rent on leasehold land, the purchase of implements, salt, and clothing. The income of the peasantry arises partly from the sale of corn, and partly from auxiliary work, of which some—for instance, temporary work in factories—in time of war, must undergo diminution. This last circumstance will react in terrible form on the condition of the country population.

With the cessation of export, too, the demand for corn will decrease, with a consequent fall in prices, and diminution in the income both of landowners and peasants. Fluctuations in prices will arise, since the standard is determined by the export, which will be interrupted. Increased purchases for the army may to some extent compensate for the stoppage of export. But the supplying of the army with bread will be extremely difficult when the rolling-stock of the railways is occupied with the transport of troops and munitions of war.

The remaining articles of export from Russia mainly belong to the category of raw or half-dressed materials— seeds, flax, hemp, timber, bristles, wool ; these products, together with grain, constitute 80 per cent. of the whole export. The cessation of the export of these goods will result in confusion similar to that caused by the cessation of the export of grain.

The imports of Russia are of a nature much more varied than the exports. Russia buys abroad not only finished products, such as machinery and metallic wares, but also raw materials, cotton, wool, silk, pig-iron, iron, steel, coal, and paper. But the most considerable part of her imports consists of tea, coffee, and colonial products, wine, and other drinks. In the " Review of the External Trade of Russia," exports and imports are classified in four groups : (1) provisions ; (2) raw and half-worked materials ; (3) animals ; (4) manufactured articles.

M

	Export.		Import.	
—	1891–94.	1895.	1891–94.	1895.
	°/₀	°/₀	°/₀	°/₀
Provisions . . .	57.08	56.90	19.70	18.40
Raw and half-worked materials . .	37.24	37.70	58.32	54.40
Animals . . .	˙2.41	2.30	0.56	0.90
Manufactured articles	3.27	3.10	21.42	26.30

But such a classification gives no clear idea of the influences which would reveal themselves on the interruption of foreign trade. The following classification under provisions, clothing, agricultural implements, building materials, manufactured products, intellectual, various, gives a better idea :

Imports into Russia in Millions of Roubles in 1889.

Provisions	56.6	(£8,490,000)
Clothing	150.2	(£22,530,000)
Instruments of husbandry . .	13.2	(£1,980,000)
Building materials . . .	72.1	(£10,815,000)
Manufactured products . .	71.3	(£10,695,000)
Intellectual	6.2	(£930,000)
Various	1·9	(£285,000)

Classification of Imports—Raw, Half-worked, and Manufactured.

The first consequence of the interruption of external communications will be a considerable fall in the price of corn and other chief articles of export, and a rise in the price of articles of import, more particularly of those of which large stores are not in the hands of traders.

From the interruption of export will result a considerable decrease in the railway traffic, and in consequence, as the majority of railways belong to the crown or are guaranteed by it, the state will sustain a loss of revenue ; while, on the other hand, the railways, especially those going westward, at the outbreak of the war will be entirely, and afterwards to a considerable extent, occupied in the transport of troops and munitions of war. Great difficulties would arise from this circumstance were it not for the fact that transport by water has been so developed that upon the stoppage of export it will be able to satisfy almost all internal needs. The interruption of export abroad, the fall of prices, irregular supply, and great local fluctuations—such are the factors which will strongly influence the course of trade. It is difficult even to foresee what form they will take, and by what influences prices will be determined. When internal competition remains the only factor in determining prices, those districts will be in the best position where competition is most highly developed, as is the case in the western, southern, and metropolitan governments, and in the worst position those districts where monopoly obtains. As relates to the number of traders, it will be found that Russia is in a less advantageous position than the western states. Thus we find that while out of 10,000 inhabitants in Belgium 437 are engaged in trade, in France 429, in Germany 347, and in Austria 164, in Russia only 67 are thus occupied.

From the following statistics (pp. 180–181) it will be seen that at a time when the interruption of communications by a great war would cause famine and even social convulsions in all western states with the exception of Austria, in Russia the danger will be much less, but

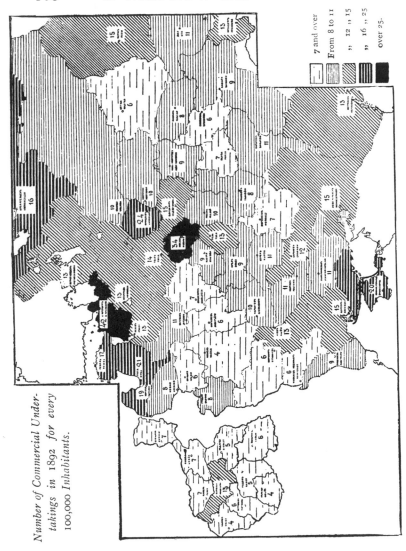

Number of Commercial Undertakings in 1892 for every
100,000 Inhabitants.

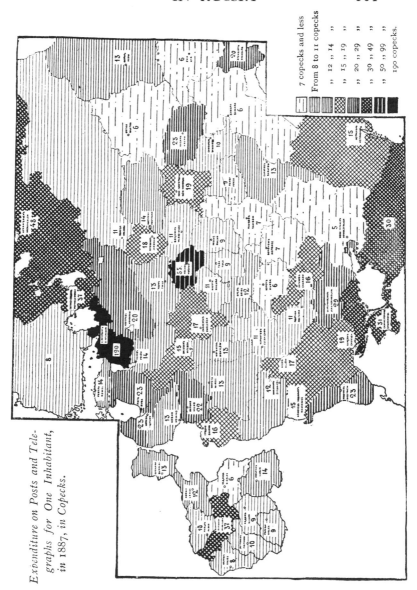

Expenditure on Posts and Telegraphs for One Inhabitant, in 1887, in Copecks.

7 copecks and less
From 8 to 11 copecks
,, 12 ,, 14 ,,
,, 15 ,, 19 ,,
,, 20 ,, 29 ,,
,, 30 ,, 49 ,,
,, 50 ,, 99 ,,
190 copecks.

nevertheless will be expressed in a considerable decrease in the income of the population, and in a difficult position of trade.

III.—Manufacturing Crisis in Time of War.

On the manufactures and industries of Russia a great European war cannot fail to react seriously in many respects. The interruption of communications with the West will mean a cessation of the supply of raw materials. Thus the supply of American, Egyptian, and Indian cotton will be stopped. The withdrawal from work of mechanics and experienced workmen will be a factor of great difficulty. The sale of manufactured articles will decrease, firstly, in consequence of the difficulty of transport on railways already occupied for military purposes, and, secondly, in consequence of a decreased demand resulting from diminished incomes and from the dislike of the moneyed classes to unnecessary outlay in a critical time. As a result of these unfavourable conditions production in certain manufactures must be decreased considerably, and in others entirely stopped.

In the time of the last war with Turkey (1877–78), the entire yearly industrial production of Russia barely attained 893 million roubles (£133,950,000); at the present day it has risen to 1828 million roubles (£274,200,000), as is shown by the following table :

Year.	In Millions of Credit Roubles. (English Equivalents, in Parentheses, in Millions of Pounds Sterling.)			
	Industrial Products not subject to Excise.	Yearly Production of Excised Articles, &c.	Mines and Metal Working.	Total.
1878	588 (88.2)	185 (27.75)	120 (18)	893 (133.95)
1892	1266 (189.9)	367 (55.05)	195 (29.25)	1828 (274.2)

The distribution of this production is shown in millions of roubles in the plan on the next page :

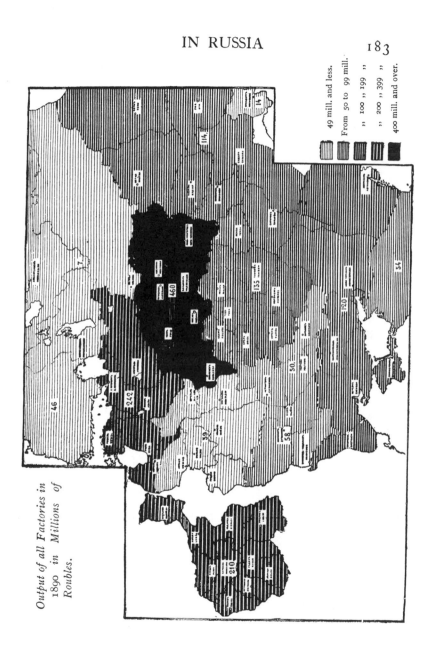

Output of all Factories in
1890 in Millions of
Roubles.

49 mill. and less.
From 50 to 99 mill.
,, 100 ,, 199 ,,
,, 200 ,, 399 ,,
400 mill. and over.

In order clearly to judge of the crisis which would be caused by war we must bear in mind the relations existing between imports and home production. The following table shows the percentage relation of import to production of some of the chief imported articles in 1876 and in 1892 :

	1876.		1892.
Steel	90.4	...	3.1
Iron	36.5	...	9.6
Copper	64.7	...	65.6
Stone Coal . . .	44.1	...	29.4
Machinery . . .	40.3	...	30.8
Glass articles . . .	40.5	...	10.3
Chemicals and paints .	79.2	...	55.1
Paper	24.0	...	14.1
Leather manufactures .	12.8	...	4.9
Cotton	24.9	...	3.0
Wool	77.3	...	12.1
Sugar	4.0	...	—

These statistics show the greatest development in the following industries : cotton, wool, paper, machinery, chemicals and paints, leather, glass, and sugar refining. In the same period the working of coal and of naphtha increased considerably, while iron smelting and the working of iron and steel also made considerable advances.

From the statistics above set forth it is obvious that the crisis which wars would cause in industrial and manufacturing circles of Russia is incomparably less than would be produced in the Western States. While in the other great European States with the exception of Italy, industry occupies a considerable part—in England the greater part —of the population, in Russia the number of workers in all industries does not exceed 1½ million men, out of a population of 120 millions. Further, from comparison of the average total of industrial productiveness with the number of men engaged, it appears that in Russia the turnover for every workman engaged is only about 1000 roubles (£150), and that the average factory has a yearly turnover of 50,000 roubles (£7500), and employs about 45 hands. It is obvious that very small industrial undertakings are not included in this calculation. But such being the statistics for large and moderate-sized undertakings, taken together, it is plain that in Russian industry the mechanical apparatus is much less complex and engages much less capital than in those countries where industry predominates. From this it follows that, upon the decrease and partial interruption of Russian industry, the capital invested will sustain much less loss from the interruption of work than capital similarly invested in the West. But if we suppose that war is to be carried on within the limits of Russia itself, we must bear in mind the difficulties in communication, and the decreased demand in localities occupied by the combatants. The district where military operations were carried on might be considered as lost from the industrial point of view.

Russian industry is based on internal demand, a fact which constitutes an advantage in case of war, as Russian manufactures will not, as those of England, Germany, and France, be threatened with the loss of foreign markets in consequence of interrupted communications. But this superiority will decrease proportionately with the increase in the area embraced by the war. And, although stoppage of work would take place in Russia on a smaller scale than in the West, it would nevertheless place in a difficult position a great number of workers. There is a general opinion that Russian factory hands, being peasants, are guaranteed by their land, and take to industry only temporarily, always reserving the possibility of returning to their farms. In recent years this opinion has been shaken by statistical investigation which undoubtedly proved the existence in Russia of a working, landless proletariat. For such workers the stoppage of production will have precisely the same consequences as in the West.

Mr. E. M. Dementyeff in a recent work, on the foundation of a series of statistics, comes to the conclusion that the current belief as to the absence in Russia of an industrial class is unfounded. There is indeed no doubt that this class is still small. But the question is not one of number, but of the conditions rapidly creating this class, and of the consequences indissolubly bound up with it.

The wages of workmen in Russia in comparison with those which obtain in other European states is very low, and it may safely be assumed that the savings they possess are insignificant. After a detailed calculation M. Dementyeff declares that wages in England, and particularly in America, are greater than in Russia by two, three, and even five times. The following table and diagram show the percentage difference in wages in these countries :

			Men.		Women.
Russia	.	.	100	...	100
England	.	.	283	...	114
America	.	.	404	...	254

Percentage Comparison of Wages in Russia, Great Britain, and Northern America.

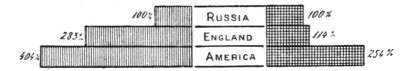

" But comparison of wages alone," says M. Dementyeff, " conveys no meaning, and even may lead to false conclusions, if the purchasing power of money in the different countries is not taken into account. Only by considering this we can form an idea as to the extent to which wages guarantee the existence of the worker." The author, after making a calculation as to the quantity of the first necessaries of life which a rouble will command in England and in Massachusetts, comes to the conclusion that " the incomparably lower wages in Russia can in no way be explained by the greater cheapness of necessaries ; such an explanation could only to a certain extent be admitted even in comparison with England."

A characteristic feature of the condition of the Russian factory workers is that they do not live in their own lodgings. Of the general mass of cases examined in this respect by M. Dementyeff, 57.8 per cent. lived at their factories, either in the workshops where they work, or in barracks specially built for them, while the workers having their own lodgings constituted only 18.1 per cent.

The lodgings of factory workers, in the majority of cases, are such that of the " conditions " of their lives, there cannot even be speech. " Workers from distant localities for the most part have a sack or box with personal property, such as changes of linen, and sometimes even bedding; while those who are regarded as not living at the factory—that is, workers from the neighbouring country who go home on Sundays and on holidays—have literally nothing. In no case has either one or the other class any vestige of bed."

The food is no better. In the majority of cases the supply of the workmen is carried on on the *artel* principle, and as far as quantity is concerned no complaint can be made, but the food is of the lowest quality—coarse, monotonous, and with a deficiency of animal substance. It consists of black bread, *stchi* of sour cabbage, porridge of wheat or buckwheat, with beef fat, potatoes, sour cabbage with hemp-oil, or *kvas* with cucumbers—such is the food of the workers from day to day, without the slightest variety throughout the year; only on fast days, of which there are 190 in the year, the beef or salt beef in the *stchi* is replaced by herrings, &c., and the beef fat by hemp-oil. The food of the workers who occupy hired quarters is still worse, both as to quantity and quality.

It is obvious that with such conditions there cannot even be thought of savings for a rainy day, and the crisis caused by war will be reflected on the life of workers in a fatal form. In view of this, common sense will demand that at the outbreak of war organised help of the workers should be begun. But this is a question which ought to be decided in time of peace.

IV.—Economic Endurability of the Population in
Time of and after War.

We have referred more than once to the tremendous
effect which war must produce in those countries which
possess a highly developed industrial system, and where
the economic and social order is more complex than in
Russia. It will easily be understood that the sudden
summons to the colours of a great number of masters and
experienced workmen will be felt especially severely in
those countries where a highly developed industry absorbs
large capital, and gives work to half the population. This
crisis will be less severe in those states which still preserve a character generally agricultural, which have less
complex organisation and less mutual dependence between
the different forms of social and private enterprise.

But from this, of course, does not follow that the
poorer the country the better will it bear the strain of
war. It is plain that war breaking out after several years
of good harvest would have less effect than if it were to
appear after a series of unfruitful years. There is a
certain minimum of well-being, not only material but also
moral, which will enable peoples and districts to bear
the strain of war and to recover from its consequences.
If we take as example a country standing on a low level
of economic development, or a semi-barbarous country,
we will see that there war cannot stop the turning of
millions of wheels, and will not ruin great undertakings.
But the economic consequences of war in such a country
will be extremely sensible; a considerable part of the
population will die of hunger, and whole districts will be
turned into wildernesses. In Central Asia are districts
which formerly were flourishing oases, but which, in consequence of a series of wars among a poor population,
were simply covered with sand and turned into deserts.

Thus, in considering the relative endurability of the
Russian population in time of war and afterwards, we are
bound to pay attention to the moral and material level of

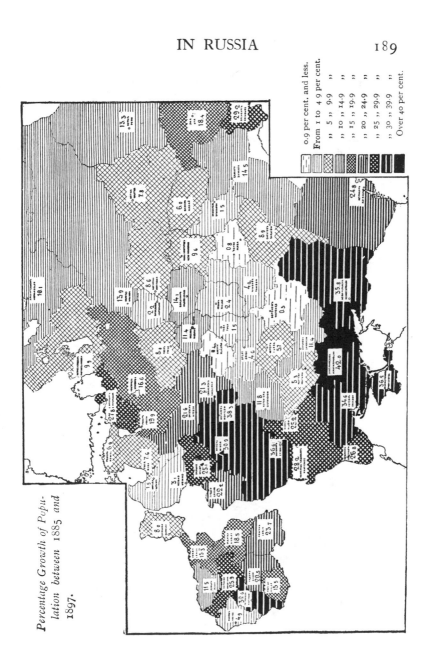

Percentage Growth of Population between 1885 and 1897.

0.9 per cent. and less.
From 1 to 4.9 per cent.
,, 5 ,, 9.9   ,,
,, 10 ,, 14.9   ,,
,, 15 ,, 19.9   ,,
,, 20 ,, 24.9   ,,
,, 25 ,, 29.9   ,,
,, 30 ,, 39.9   ,,
Over 40 per cent.

the population, and to define the differences in this level in various parts of the country in order to estimate the economic endurability not only of the whole country but of its different parts.

Growth of the Population.—Modern economic science, following the statistics of biology, acknowledges that every limit placed on the production of resources necessary for the nourishment, education, and moral well-being of the people, is at the same time a principle inimical to its very life—that is, to its increase. Thus, when considering prolonged periods, one of the first standards must be the natural growth of the population in the different parts of the kingdom. In Russia nine-tenths of the population is composed of peasants, and the general statistics of growth relate mainly to them.

Following the system of M. A. Malshinski in his work on " Popular Well-Being," we adopt the following classification for determining the degree of well-being in the different governments of Russia :

(1) Condition excellent, where the yearly growth of the population amounts to 20 and more in every thousand of the general population.

(2) Condition very good, with an increase of from 15 to 20 in the thousand.

(3) Condition fair, with a growth of from 10 to 15 per thousand.

(4) Condition unsatisfactory, with a growth of not less than 8 per thousand.

(5) Condition bad, with a growth of less than 8 per thousand.

As relates to the general growth of the population in the various governments it is impossible to distinguish the natural growth from the growth which has resulted from immigration. But the chart on the preceding page illustrates the comparative growth of the population in 1885 and 1897.

Distribution of the Population.—But statistics as to growth of population are in themselves insufficient to

Average Number of Houses in a Settlement.

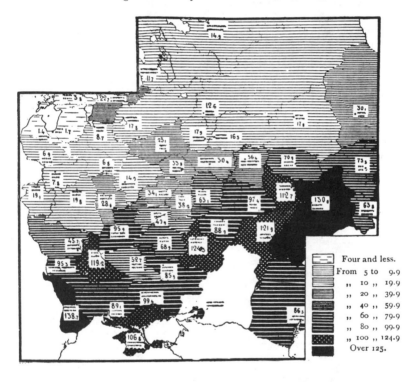

enable a judgment to be formed as to the level of well-being.   It is therefore necessary to complete them with other information.   The distribution of the population in villages is another factor from which conclusions may be drawn.   The chart on the previous page shows the average number of houses in a settlement.

Fires.—Of the comparative condition of the country population in different parts of the empire we may judge by the number of fires, and also by the losses caused.   It is generally taken as proven that the poorer the population the greater the number of fires, while the losses from fires, falling in general on a single householder, are relatively smaller.   In the two charts (pp. 194–195) we show the average value of a single burned property in the villages in the period 1860 and 1887 in roubles, and the average total of losses from fires in villages by every 100 inhabitants.   From these charts it appears that wealth is greater in those governments which may be considered as the theatre of war, as the value of burnt properties is greater ; while on the other hand the general loss is less owing to the smaller number of cases of fire.   In foreign states the yearly losses from fire per hundred inhabitants are shown in the following table in metallic roubles :

Great Britain	.	.	.	.	160 (£24)
France .	.	.	.	.	50 (£7 10s.)
Germany	.	.	.	.	81 (£12 3s.)
Austria .	.	.	.	.	63 (£9 9s.)
Belgium .	.	.	.	.	55 (£8 5s.)
Holland .	.	.	.	.	63 (£9 9s.)
Sweden and Norway	.	.	.	99 (£14 17s.)
United States	.	.	.	.	220 (£33)
Canada .	.	.	.	.	288 (£43 4s.)

In Russia the losses from fire in the period 1860–1887 amounted to 116 roubles (£17 8s.) per hundred inhabitants of the towns, and 52 roubles (£7 16s.) per hundred inhabitants in the country, in all about 62 roubles (£9 6s.) From this we see that of all the European states only in France and Belgium do fires cause less damage than in Russia, notwithstanding the fact that the Western states, as far as wealth is concerned, generally stand much higher than Russia.

It is useful here to note the relation of values insured to losses in different countries :

	Per Cent.			Per Cent.
France . . .	75	Canada . .		44
Germany . .	74	Belgium . .		43
United States .	55	Russia . . .		9
Great Britain .	46			

From this it will be seen that in Russia guarantee against fire by insurance is from 6 to 8 times less than in other countries.

Towns.—Through insufficiency of statistics it is difficult to speak of the towns in Russia. One thing, however, stands out in relief—that is, that they grow more slowly than in Western countries, while the population of the country increases quickly. In Western Europe the agricultural population increases slowly, and even inclines to diminution, as may be seen from the following table :

Percentage Growth of Town and Country Populations to 1885, taking the Population in 1863 as 100.

	Country.		Towns.
European Russia . .	+ 31	...	+ 64
Poland	+ 65	...	+ 75
Austria	+ 2.5	...	+117.9
Germany . . .	− 4.6	...	+ 61
Prussia	− 5.3	...	+ 80.1
Saxony	+ 1.4	...	+ 76.9
France	− 3.6	...	+ 26.6

Savings.—The level of deposits in the savings banks is one of the best bases for judging of the degree of well-being of a population. But in Russia this factor cannot wholly be relied upon, as, although since the foundation of savings banks the agricultural population has begun to entrust to them its savings, still this practice has not yet become as general in Russia as abroad. Compared

N

Average Value of one Property destroyed by Fire, between 1860–87, in Roubles.

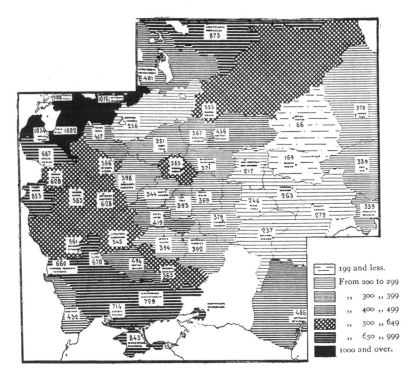

Average Losses from Fires in the Country, in Roubles, per 100 Inhabitants, between 1860–68.

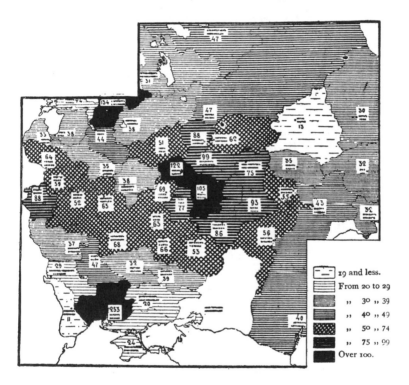

with the other European states Russia in this respect
occupies the last place.

Condition of Agriculture.—The emancipation of the
serfs thirty-five years ago could not fail to react upon the
condition of agriculture. Both large and small agriculture,
with the abolition of free labour, had to be reformed
radically on the principles of hired labour and intense
cultivation. Resources for floating capital were realised
through ransom. But the suddenness of the transfer to
the new conditions operated in such a way that the
majority of private landowners could not or would not
undertake the new work. Some proprietors abandoned
personal participation in agriculture, and went into the
services ; others continued to work, as far as was possible,
on the old basis, with the difference that they no longer
had the advantage of free labour. It may be said that
agriculture in Russia presents a compromise between the
conditions of serfage culture and the requirements of a
rational system. To a considerable extent it is still
carried on without working capital, labour being paid for
with a proportion of the harvest ; and agriculture remains
almost in the same position as in the days of free labour.

To introduce variety in cultivated products in peasant
agriculture is very difficult. The peasants specialising
ever more and more in one kind of corn, in consequence of the fall of prices, cannot draw from agriculture,
even in the event of superfluous crops, sufficient money
for redemption payments, taxes, and for the purchase
of necessary articles. To all these requirements for
ready money, owing to the growth of the population
is added the necessity for leasing land from private
proprietors and from the Crown ; for even in the case
of lease from private proprietors payment is made not
only in kind—that is, by ploughing, harvesting, and
threshing—but partly also in money. Thus the growing
need of the peasantry for money has led them into debt,
and encouraged in the country the growth of a burdensome usury.

The increased tendency of the peasantry in many localities towards emigration shows that peasant agriculture has been played out in consequence of the exhaustion of the land and of the impossibility of obtaining money. Together with this, the decrease in the number of cattle, the absence of improvements in tillage, and the poverty of domestic life, show the wretched condition in which the remaining peasants find themselves. And, indeed, in some governments the greater part of the peasants, in order to satisfy their needs, are compelled to seek additional support in labour away from home.

With such extremely unsatisfactory conditions the consequence of a great war could only be to increase the difficulties of peasant agriculture, all the more so since a war would interrupt for a long time many auxiliary employments.

In relation to indebtedness, large and especially moderate landowners are in no better position than the peasantry. Compelled to seek floating capital for the carrying on of industry, landowners had recourse to mortgage. True, the advances they received were made on terms incomparably lighter than those made to the peasants, but their total indebtedness is unquestionably greater than the indebtedness of the peasantry. On the 1st January, 1896, the value of mortgages issued by thirty-six lending institutions was 1,618,079,807 credit roubles (£242,711,971 1s.), 2,689,775 roubles metal (£403,466 5s.), and 7,101,900 German marks (£355,095).

Although before the emancipation of the serfs a considerable proportion of Russian estates was mortgaged, yet the percentage charged by the Imperial Loan Bank was lower than that since charged by joint-stock banks ; and as the loans were made upon the number of souls, the very growth of the population, by remitting auxiliary loans, facilitated the payment of part of the first loan. The institution of the Nobility Bank, and the consequent diminution of yearly payments, constituted indeed a considerable relief; but, without dwelling upon the fact that credit in the Nobility Bank is not accessible to all landowners, borrowing generally lays upon agriculture a heavy burden, and can only result in advantage when the money raised is devoted to increased production, and even this depends upon satisfactory harvests. But there is reason to believe that the greater part of these loans was employed in unproductive objects, and also in provision for inheritances, so that the growth of the population acted injuriously.

To such influences were added the fall in the price of corn in Europe, in consequence of trans-oceanic competition, and in Russia by special local circumstances. In addition, it must be remembered that local purchasers of corn are less numerous in Russia than in other European states, owing to the relatively smaller urban and industrial population. If the production of corn did not decrease, it is due to the opening up of new lands, and increased attention to tillage in the south and east of the country. For further extension of tillage, room remains now only in the east and in the north. In the course of time, if the present primitive methods for working the land are not improved—and for this are required those financial and intellectual forces which are now devoted to the strengthening of the military power of Russia—the production of corn will not only cease to increase, but will begin to diminish. Even now the breeding of sheep and cattle is declining.

Number of Domestic Animals.—The quantity of cattle raised is a chief sign of the well-being of the agriculturist, not only because cattle represent capital, but because the very feeding of the population can be guaranteed only by the aid of the products of cattle raising. In this respect large horned cattle take the most important place, and the quantity of these in different parts of the Empire differs and submits to fluctuations. Up to the time of the building of railways, the raising of cattle was generally looked upon as a necessary evil, for the price of such products was very low. Nevertheless as the outlay caused by the distance of the markets from the place of production, owing to primitive methods of transport, was great, proprietors of necessity had recourse to cattle

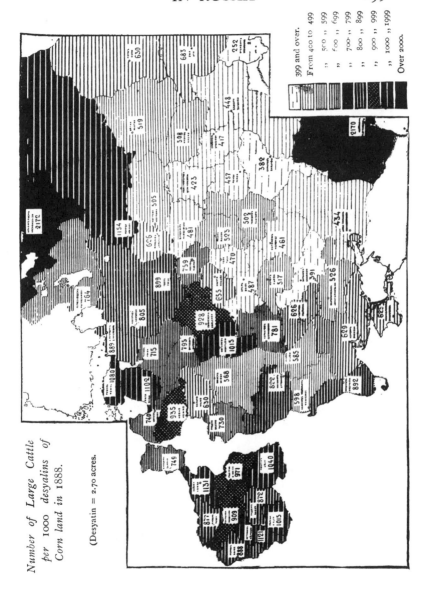

Number of Large Cattle
per 1000 desyalins of
Corn land in 1888.

(Desyatin = 2.70 acres.)

breeding in order to draw some revenue from their estates. It is very natural that after the building of railways cattle breeding in those districts where improvement was not valued began to decay, at the same time the production of corn giving much worse results. In the chart on the preceding page will be found the distribution of stock in the different governments, taking as unity a head of large cattle, or 10 sheep, 12 goats, 4 pigs, and $\frac{2}{3}$ horse.

Comparative Merit of Agriculture.—It is well known that by the number of domestic animals we may judge of the merit of agriculture in a given locality. The more persistently agriculture is carried on, the more, with normal conditions, it requires improvement of the soil, and in consequence the quantity of domestic animals must be greater. Now the productiveness of land in Russia is much lower than in other states, as will be seen in the annexed chart.

Yield per Desyatin (= 2.70 acres) in Quarters.

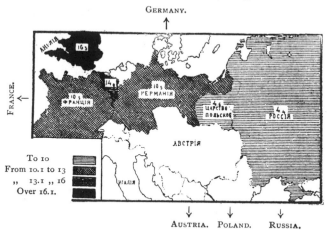

To 10
From 10.1 to 13
„   13.1 „ 16
Over 16.1.

The circumstance is not without significance that in case of war a certain area of land gives a small reserve of corn. By comparing harvests with the number of domestic animals, the condition of Russia is also shown to be very bad, as will be seen from the following chart :

Number of Large Cattle per 100 Quarters yield.

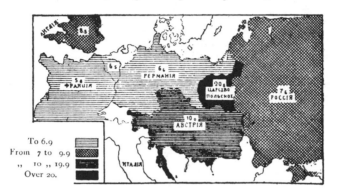

To 6.9
From 7 to 9.9
„ 10 „ 19.9
Over 20.

The following table is even more instructive :

	On 100 Desyatins of Land under Seed Russia has Less Cattle than		The Harvest from a Desyatin of Land in Russia is Less by	
England . . .	75 per cent.	...	73 per cent.	
Belgium . . .	63 ,,	...	69 ,,	
Austria . . .	53 ,,	...	38 ,,	
Germany . .	51 ,,	...	58 ,,	
France . . .	43 ,,	...	58 ,,	
Average . .	62 ,,	...	59 ,,	

From which we see that in Russia 100 *desyatins* (270 acres) of corn land have 62 per cent. less domestic animals, and yet produce a harvest only 59 per cent. less than in other states. Such a comparatively favourable result proceeds from the fact that in recent times much land formerly lying idle has been devoted to agriculture, and partly from the abundance of land; for Russia in comparison with other states has the smallest proportion of her land under seed—precisely 26 per cent. of her area—while the other states have 43 per cent.

The time in the course of which the population of each government of Russia might feed itself from its own harvests is shown in the chart on the next page, from which it is seen that the most unfavourable conditions in this respect would be found by an invading enemy in the governments of Vilna, Grodno, Minsk, Vitebsk, Moghilef, and Tchernigov. This conclusion is founded on statistics as to the relations of population to harvest—that is, on the extent of the superfluity of the general harvest. To give a clearer idea of this matter it is necessary to show separately the harvests on the lands of private proprietors and on the lands held by the peasantry. Private proprietors of course utilise a very insignificant proportion of the grain they raise, while the peasants chiefly live on their own corn, and sell only a small surplus, sometimes even being forced to buy. In view of the importance of this question, we show in the two diagrams on page 205 the harvest of the chief grains on the lands of proprietors and peasants in millions of quarters in 1893, in fifty provinces of European Russia, and ten governments of Poland.

The tillage of land by proprietors might be considered a favourable factor if it were a sign that proprietors occupy themselves with agriculture, and exploit the land in regular form. But, unhappily, facts are entirely opposed to this. In the majority of cases proprietors have no interest, under present circumstances, in working the land with their own resources, and lease it to the tenants by the *desyatin*,* at a rent, for a proportion of the harvest, or for labour. To improve the methods of agriculturists is extremely difficult. The conditions under which the emancipation of the peasantry took place, the consequent agricultural crisis, and those measures which were taken in foreign countries for its avoidance, placed Russian agriculturists in an extremely difficult if not hopeless position. And there is no need to be a prophet

* A desyatin is equivalent to 2.70 acres.

to foretell that the economic condition of Russia will become every year worse and worse if the present state of affairs continues. Russia is a country which exports agricultural products, yet by that very action she exports also the native virtues of her soil. From an estimate of the quantity of wheat, oats and barley—that is, the chief grains—and the number of domestic animals and bones exported, it appears that Russia sends out of the country every year more than 80 million roubles (£12,000,000) worth of the value of the soil. These figures are in no way surprising. By calculations made by Komers it is shown that in order to retain the fruitfulness of the soil it is necessary to devote to that purpose from 20 to 33 per cent. of the income which it yields.

A more intense system of culture is therefore for Russia a first necessity; but for this is required a certain tension of intellectual and material resources of which a deficiency is now experienced. In the "Agricultural Reviews," published by the Russian Department of Agriculture, we constantly meet the statement that the unsatisfactory harvests of Russia depend less upon climatic and natural conditions than upon unsatisfactory methods of culture. Especially loud, in this respect, are the complaints made against the methods of the peasantry.

It is necessary to repeat that the emancipation of the serfs left landed proprietors, as concerns resources, in the most lamentable position. More than three-quarters of the total number of estates were mortgaged to the old Credit Associations, scarcely one proprietor possessed savings, and agriculture was carried on only because free labour enabled proprietors to do without ready money. Even agriculture carried on on a large scale in pre-emancipation times required the most inconsiderable capital. But agriculture as lately carried on, without floating capital and without productive outlay, can only lead to the exhaustion of the soil.

Indebtedness of the Peasantry.—As concerns the

peasantry emancipation shook the country out of
torpitude, and introduced new conditions of life, freedom
of activity, and immediate responsibility for payments to
the state. The possibility was created of buying and leasing
land, but, at the same time, arose also the need of acquiring bread and seed, and other objects formerly received

Harvest in Millions of Quarters in 1893.

Proprietors.

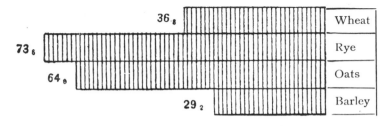

Peasants.

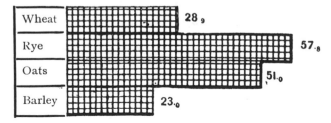

from the proprietor, or gained by work at home. The
peasants disposed of more time for work among themselves, but, at the same time, a need arose for money
payments instead of service. Natural agriculture was
replaced by agriculture on a money basis. It was plain
that money was to serve as the chief factor in the new
conditions.

It was from such a circumstance that the indebtedness of
the peasantry arose. It is obvious that if extreme need

for money were only experienced by the peasants on special occasions, they might either take advantage of their own savings or borrow money from their neighbours. But with the absence among the people of any considerable savings, and the non-existence of popular credit, the peasants were obliged to have recourse to the so-named *miroyeds* and usurers, on the most burdensome terms.

A systematic and comprehensive investigation of the debts of the Russian peasantry has not yet been made. For this purpose it would be necessary to collect precise information in all governments, as has been done by the Zemstva in those governments where statistical bureaux exist. At the present time we have only fragmentary statistics.

From the statistics collected by the Zemstva it is shown that private credit costs the peasants of Great Russia from 40 to 60 roubles (£6 to £9) yearly on a loan of 100 roubles (£15), and this only for common loans, individuals paying at a higher rate, even as much as 150 per cent. "Owing to the difficulty of obtaining money on any conditions," writes M. Sokolovski in his work on the subject, "the peasants have recourse to the most ruinous means—to the sale of their summer labour in advance, to the sale of corn necessary for their families, even to the sale of corn immediately after harvest. It may be imagined that in such conditions the very lowest prices are obtained ; thus soon appears the necessity for new loans, and a veritable system of slavery results.

"Such slavery in the Great Russia is exploited by the *miroyed* on a lawful basis. . . . Thus, for instance, the winter price of summer field labour is but a half or a third of the summer price, so that the *kulak* having made a loan on this basis receives from 100 to 300 per cent. on his advance. . . . There exists a veritable trade in slave labour. Travelling from village to village these usurers furnish the peasantry with money, binding the borrower to repay the debt by summer work ; and having thus acquired a working force, sell it at a price two to three times

higher to those who require summer labour.   This system
obtains as generally in the south as it does in the north.
In winter time when some unfortunate peasant is threatened
with an execution for non-payment of taxes, or in spring
when he is threatened with starvation, the usurer buys
for a trifle his summer labour, giving him in advance from
15 to 30 roubles (£2 5s. to £4 10s.).   In spring the usurers
drive whole *artels* of labourers to field labour and to factories, having sold their labour at double the price they
paid.

"Traders of another sort travel through the country
engaged exclusively in the traffic in children.   Many
poor parents for a trifling sum sell their children for a
certain number of years, in the course of which the
children are to be left with tradesmen or artisans in
the capacity of apprentices.   Having bought in this
manner a score of children, the trader sends them in
carts to St. Petersburg, precisely as traders of another
kind send calves.   In St. Petersburg these children are
sold to shops and factories at a profit of from 200 to
300 per cent.   Such a trade in children and in adults is
generally prevalent in the Moscow, Ryazan and other
governments."

Marriages, Births, and Deaths in Russia.—We have
already considered the growth of the population in Russia,
in its association with other conditions of the population.
In the following table will be found a comparison of the
growth of the Orthodox population of Russia with the
growth of the general population of other European
countries :

Increase in a Thousand Inhabitants.

	1881–85.		1867–73.
Russia	15.0	...	12.6
Prussia . .	12.0	...	9.1
Austria . . .	7.1	...	8.8
England . . .	14.1	...	12.2
Italy	9.5	...	8.5
France . . .	2.5	...	2.7
Belgium . . .	9.7	...	6.9

Let us present this comparison graphically :

*Growth of the Orthodox Population in Russia, and the General
Population of other Countries, per Thousand.*

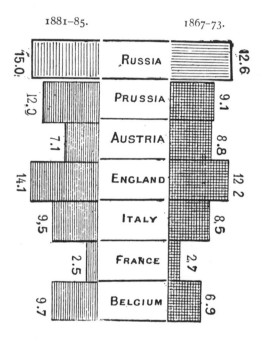

In Russia the proportion of marriages, as will be seen
from the diagram at the top of the next page, immensely
exceeds the proportion of other states.

In the number of births a similar preponderance is
shown in the case of Russia, the rate being twice as great
as that of France, and one and a half times greater than
that of England.

The number of births in Russia in the period 1881–
1885 in 1000 inhabitants is expressed by the figure 56.0,
while among the other European states the greatest birth-

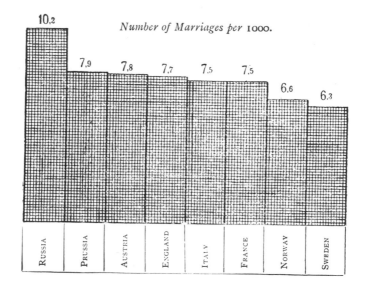

Number of Marriages per 1000.

10.2   7.9   7.8   7.7   7.5   7.5   6.6   6.3

RUSSIA   PRUSSIA   AUSTRIA   ENGLAND   ITALY   FRANCE   NORWAY   SWEDEN

Number of Births per Thousand.

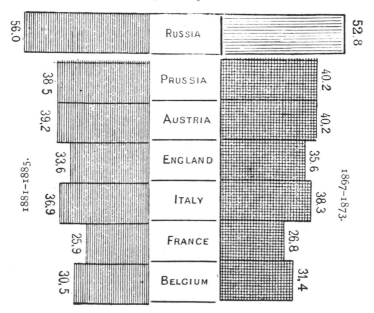

	1881–1885.			RUSSIA			1867–1873.	
56.0				RUSSIA				52.8
38.5				PRUSSIA				40.2
39.2				AUSTRIA				40.2
33.6				ENGLAND				35.6
36.9				ITALY				38.3
25.9				FRANCE				26.8
30.5				BELGIUM				31.4

rate was only 39.2 (Austria). But at the same time the mortality in Russia is greater than elsewhere in Europe ; in the above-mentioned period it amounted to 41 in the thousand, while in other countries the greatest mortality, that of Austria, was only 31.4 in the thousand.

Mortality per 1000.

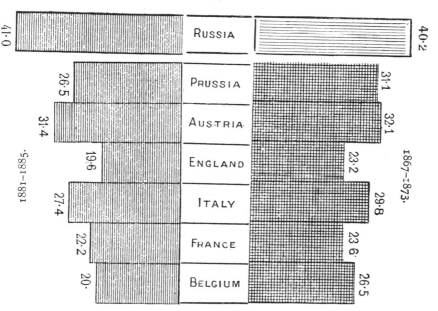

In Russia the death-rate of children is especially high. In the period 1865–1878, out of 100 deaths the number of children under 11 years old in Russia was 36.2, in Prussia 32.2, and in France only 18.7.

Still more characteristic is the mortality among infants under one year old ; in Russia it amounts to 29.5 per cent. of the number born, and in certain governments, for instance Pskov and Smolensk, to 31.4 per cent. ; in foreign

o

countries, as is shown by the following diagram, the mortality of infants of under one year is higher only in Bavaria and in Wurtemburg.

Percentage Mortality of Children under One Year.

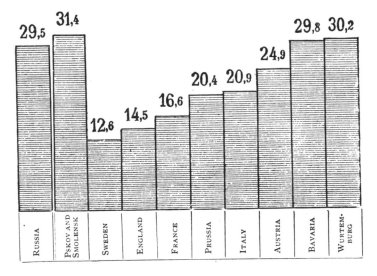

The mortality of infants of this age is an important factor in judging of the degree of culture of a people and of its moral condition. There can be no doubt that economic well-being and intellectual development constitute factors opposed to a heavy infant mortality. It is obvious that in the interests of a state it is less important that children should be born than that those born should live, the consequence of which is the preservation of a greater quantity of working forces and money resources, not only in individual families, but in the whole country. Infant mortality depends mainly upon nourishment, or in other words on the degree of prosperity of the people. The investigations of Pfeiffer show that of the total number of infants dying within a year of birth, from 40 per cent. to 70 per cent. die from bad or insufficient food.

Deficiency of suitable food, that is, plainly, hunger, is the cause of the high mortality among the infant population of Russia. The Protoierei Gilyarovski, in his valuable work, " A Sanitary Investigation of the Government of Novgorod," mentions the following circumstance as an illustration of the condition of the agricultural population. The labourers on going to work leave the unweaned infants behind, and in order to prevent their death by hunger, owing to want of milk, "employ a system which for simplicity and horror might be the method of savages. Having made dumplings out of masticated black bread, they bind them to the hands and feet of the children, in the belief that the child when rolling on the floor will lift its hands and feet to its mouth and suck the nourishment from the bread."

Mortality is also found to depend upon a number of other conditions—geographical, climatic, and racial, from the occupations of a people and from its medical organisation. But the chief factor determining mortality remains nevertheless the degree of economic well-being ; and thus from the mortality statistics we may fairly judge of the condition of a population.

We have already quoted statistics showing that in 1867–73 the mortality of the Orthodox population of Russia amounted to 40.2 in the thousand, and in the period 1881–85 to 41. The growth of the population, representing the preponderance of births over deaths among the orthodox population in the period 1867–73 was 12.6, and in the period 1881–85, 15.

It is not surprising that the statistics of births, mortality, the composition of the population, age, &c., in Russia, are extremely unsatisfactory in comparison with those of other states. It is enough to emphasise the fact, illustrated by the chart on the next page, that of 1000 persons of both sexes born in Norway, 717 attain the age of 25 years, in Prussia 581, while in Russia only 508 attain that age.

Number of Survivors out of 1000 *Children Born, at all Ages up to* 75.

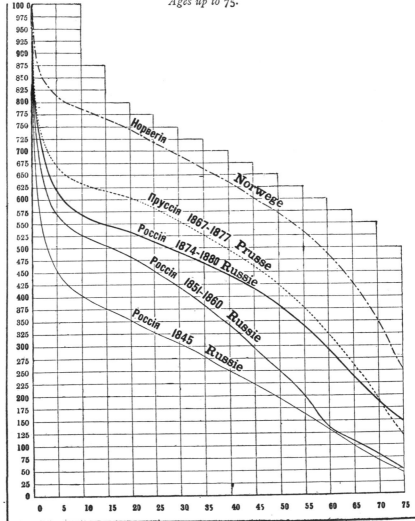

The life of every individual represents a certain quantity of potential energy necessary for the fulfilment of his appointed work ; in other words, the life of every man has a definite value to the state. The value of life on the basis of potential energy is estimated in England in the following form :

		£
A new-born child of the farming class has a value of		5
At 5 years of age has a value of	. . .	. 56
,, 10 ,, ,, ,,	. .	. 117
,, 15 ,, ,, ,,	. .	. 192
,, 20 ,, ,, ,,	. .	. 234

It is necessary to observe that up to the age of 17 years the average value of the labour of a man is lower than the cost of his maintenance. The value of human life in Prussia, estimated in five-yearly periods, separately for manual and for intellectual work, is given by Professor Wittstein, as in the diagram on the following page.

But in addition to the loss of capital, the death of every man causes special outlay for medical treatment and burial, and constitutes a direct loss to the state. The figures given in the following table, taking 1000 births, show that the number of individuals living to a working age of 15 years, and also to 60 years, is less favourable to Russia than to other states :

	To 15 years.		To 60 years.
Russia . . .	452	...	213
Sweden . . .	727	...	440
England . . .	695	...	365
Switzerland . .	694	...	362
France . . .	680	...	383
Germany . . .	609	...	311
Italy	576	...	320

Having examined these statistics of mortality, it is impossible not to come to the conclusion that the cause of the greater mortality in Russia is the poverty of its population and the lower degree of its culture.

Value of Human Life in Thousands of Thalers.

V.—Moral Condition of the Population.

We have already cited a number of facts indicating the condition of poverty of the mass of the population of Russia. This question especially required enlightenment in view of the gravity of the consequences which war might call forth and which might follow in its wake. General conclusions here can only be drawn from the impartial evidence of figures, and it was this consideration

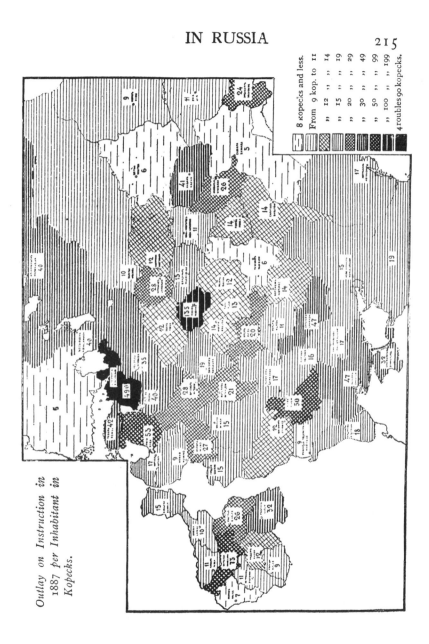

Outlay on Instruction in 1887 per Inhabitant in Kopecks.

8 kopecks and less.

From 9 kop. to 11
  ,, 12 ,, ,, 14
  ,, 15 ,, ,, 19
  ,, 20 ,, ,, 29
  ,, 30 ,, ,, 49
  ,, 50 ,, ,, 99
  ,, 100 ,, ,, 199
4 roubles 90 kopecks.

which impelled us in treating partly of the economic and
partly of the moral condition of the country to treat also of
matters which it may appear have no direct immediate
bearing upon the contentions of this work.   But this incon-
sequence is only apparent.   The significance of war for
Russia, as for all other countries, cannot be estimated
merely by the number of armies which may be put in the
field, the number of shells which may be discharged in a
given time, and the extent of ground which would be
covered by their fragments.   Many factors in the policies
of peoples which in times of peace stand little in relief,
in that revolution of all conditions which war may cause
will acquire a special significance, and it is in the consideration of these factors that we find it necessary to
delay.

Popular Education.—In Russia popular education stands,
unhappily, on a very different foundation from that which
would be desired.   Devoting all its resources to the satisfaction of military requirements and the payment of loans,
the Government has had little left to devote to education.
From the chart on the preceding page, which shows the
yearly outlay on education for one inhabitant, it will be
seen that the expenditure on education is distributed over
the country very unequally, fluctuating between 3 kopecks
and 4 roubles 90 kopecks (from $\frac{3}{8}d.$ to 14s. $8\frac{2}{5}d.$)

The low level of education in Russia is shown most
clearly of all by the number of illiterates accepted for
military service.   It will be seen from the diagrams on the
opposite page that the number in Russia is 50 times greater
than in Germany, 6 times greater than in France, and
50 per cent. greater than in Italy.

If we examine the distribution of illiteracy by governments we shall see that in the Baltic provinces the number
of illiterates, compared with the total population, is less
than 5 per cent., whereas in Great Russia it is as high as
94 per cent.   In the government of Moscow it is 47 per cent.,
and in the six contiguous governments it fluctuates between
58 per cent. in Vladimir and 76 per cent. in Smolensk.   In
Kishenef and Ufa the number of illiterate recruits in the

period 1874–83 was 92 per cent. and 94 per cent. respectively.

Such a lamentable condition of things is not confined

Percentage of Illiterates accepted for Military Service.

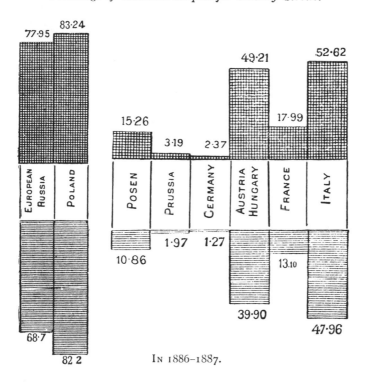

In 1886–1887.

to the lower levels of education only. In intermediate and higher education we find a state of things relatively similar. The diagrams on pp. 218–219 give some illustration of this statement.

As an illustration of the deficiency of special training

*Number of Students in Higher and Intermediate Educational
Institutions, per 100,000 of the Population, Classified according to Social Condition.*

IN UNIVERSITIES.

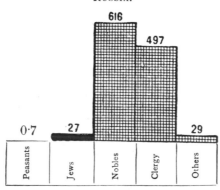

RUSSIA.

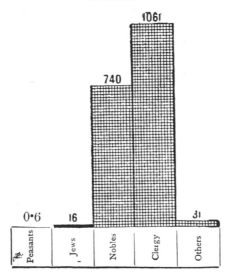

POLAND.

Number entering Universities per 1000 *trained in Intermediate Schools.*

RUSSIA.   POLAND.

66		PEASANTS		20
114		NOBILITY		97
70		CLERGY		251
69		JEWS		73
80		OTHERS		42

Numbers Receiving Special Training per 100,000 *of the Population.*

RUSSIA.

Jews.   O.her Religions.

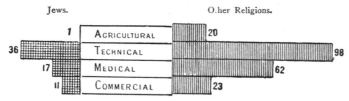

1	AGRICULTURAL	20
36	TECHNICAL	98
17	MEDICAL	62
11	COMMERCIAL	23

POLAND.

Jews.   Oth:r Religions.

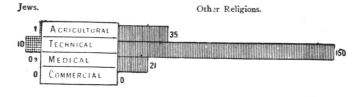

1	AGRICULTURAL	35
10	TECHNICAL	150
0 9	MEDICAL	21
0	COMMERCIAL	0

in Russia we have constructed the following diagram showing the number of doctors in Russia and in other states :

Number of Doctors in European States per 100,000 Inhabitants

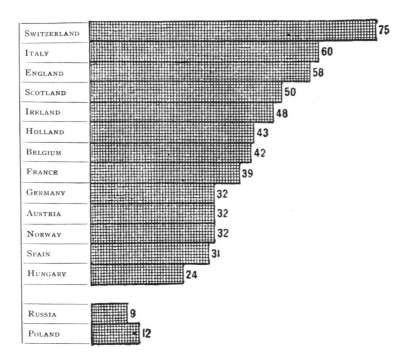

From the above diagram it will be seen that the number of doctors in Russia is quite insignificant, being from 3 to 8 times less in proportion than in other European states. In the first place stand the metropolitan governments ; in the government of St. Petersburg the number of doctors for every million of the population is 557, and in the Moscow government 420. The minimum is found in the government of Vologda, with 37 to the million, in Ufa with 35, in Orenburg with 31 and in Vyatka with 30. Still more striking are the facts illustrated by the following diagram :

Number of Quadratic Kilometres for every Doctor.

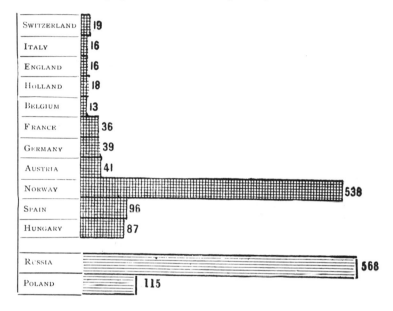

Thus considered in relation to area we find in Russia 44 less number of doctors than in Belgium, 35 less than in Italy and in England, 16 times less than in France, and 14 times less than in Germany and Austria. Norway alone approaches Russia in this respect. Statistics as to the outlay on medicine are also interesting, as showing the immense disproportion of means of relief attainable in various parts of the Empire. The chart on the next page illustrates this subject :

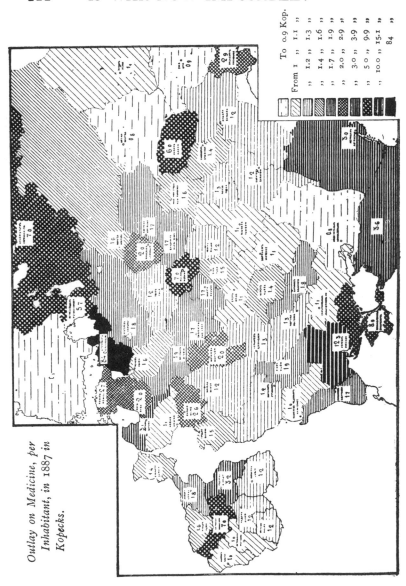

Outlay on Medicine, per Inhabitant, in 1887 in Kopecks.

Sickness.—As a natural consequence of poverty, ignorance, and the absence of medical aid, we find a correspondingly unsatisfactory state in the health of the population. In the number of serious illnesses typhus takes
the first place. Although in recent times it is acknowledged that typhus is caused by a peculiar infectious
micro-organism, still the proportion of cases of sickness to
cases of death must be acknowledged as a symptom of more
or less culture. In this respect Russia also finds herself
in an unfavourable condition. From the statistics for the
period 1887–91 (see next page) it is shown that the number of cases of typhus fluctuated in various governments
from 57 per 100,000 in the Astrahkan government to 914
per 100,000 in the government of Tula, and that the proportionate mortality from this illness was immense in
certain places, amounting to as much as 21 per cent. in
the government of Siedlicz.

In other respects, as regards health, it will be found
that Russia is in an equally unfavourable condition. And
if unfavourable material conditions increase the liability to
sickness and death of a population, these same conditions
similarly react on its moral condition. It is obvious that
where the general level of material prosperity is high
there will appear less tendency to crime, greater softness
of manners, and a stronger tendency towards education.
It is interesting therefore to consider some phenomena
illustrating the moral condition of the country.

Illegitimacy.—Although it must be admitted that certain
of the causes increasing the figures of illegitimacy must be
sought outside the domain of ethics, nevertheless statistics
on this subject may be considered as proving much as to
the moral condition of a people. In relation to illegitimacy Russia finds herself in a favourable position, the
percentage of illegitimate births being less than in any
other European state, as is shown by the diagram on
page 225.

This circumstance is explained by the comparative earli-
ness of marriage among the peasantry. The percentage of
married soldiers accepted for military service in the period

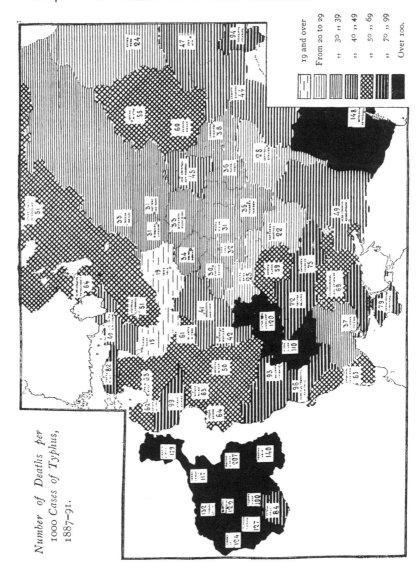

Number of Deaths per 1000 Cases of Typhus, 1887–91.

1874–83 reached in four governments over   per cent., and in the greater part of Russia was between 30 per cent. and 60 per cent., though in the Northern and North-Western provinces it fluctuates between 2 per cent. and 18 per cent.

Suicide.—Professor Oettingen in his work on "Moral-statistik," declares that suicide " is the consequence of

Number of Illegitimates in 1000 Births.

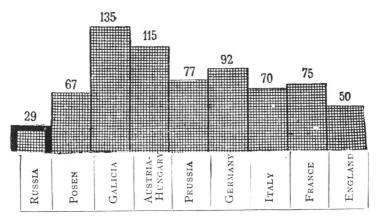

that despair which results from social evils and from immoral social relations." The new school of Italian physiologists and psycho-criminologists, at the head of which stand Lombroso and Morselli, on the other hand, find the cause of suicide in the struggle for existence. Professor Gvozdeff, at the beginning of his remarkable work on suicide, sets down the following words : " In proportion as the requirements from life increase increases also the number of suicides." Thus suicide is one of the gravest questions of the nineteenth century, and statistics as to its prevalence may serve as an indication of the condition of a people.

From general statistics we find that the increase of

P

drunkenness corresponds to the increase in the number of suicides.   Mulhall finds that approximately 15 per cent. of suicides in Europe result from drunkenness.   From 20 per cent. to 30 per cent. of suicides are caused by dis-

Number of Suicides per 100,000 Inhabitants.

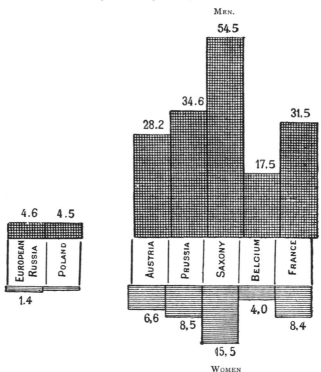

satisfaction with material conditions ; from which we must conclude that unfavourable economic conditions are an important factor in determining the number of suicides.   The proportion of suicides in Russia is much smaller than in other states, as may be seen from the above diagram, showing the number of suicides among men and women in Europe.

It is impossible not to notice the characteristic fact that the proportion of female to male suicides is greater in Russia than in other states, a fact which may be explained by the lamentable position of women in Russia.

Drunkenness.—It is well known that in Russia drunkenness is a widespread social evil, eating away the lives of whole generations, ruining the organisms not only of men but of women and even children. Without taking into consideration those dying directly from drunkenness, drink is the cause of serious illnesses, with all their unfortunate consequences. The victims of alcoholism, as those deprived of reason, lose all power of resisting their passions. Their actions are carried on under the influence of immediate animal impulses, in no way regulated by reason. The poisoning of the brain of alcoholics does not at once react upon the physical strength, but their conduct shows no trace of a rational will. In such form they become insane or criminal, and in any case dangerous members of society both in the present and in the future. In Germany, Herr Baer, chief physician of the Plötzensee Central Prison, showed on the basis of statistics, the relations between drunkenness and crime. He found that out of 32,837 criminals confined in 120 German prisons, 13,706, or 42 per cent., were drunkards. Investigation as to the causes of insanity in England, France, Denmark, and in the United States showed that approximately 14 per cent. of cases were caused by drunkenness. In France insanity caused by the excessive employment of spirituous liquors grows continually. In 1836, 7 per cent. of cases of insanity were found to be caused by drunkenness. From the last available statistics we find that this percentage had increased to 21 per cent., or three times. In Holland in 1882, 12 per cent. of the cases of insanity were traced to excessive drinking. Similar figures are found for other European countries. In the United States the proportion of insanity caused by alcoholism amounts to 26 per cent.

In Russia the use of alcohol per unit of the population is less than in other countries. But this depends upon

the irregular use of vodka, and in no way affects the fact
that in that country drunkenness is very common.   Rarely
does the peasant or workman in Russia consume alcohol
in small innocuous quantities.   Usually Russians either
do not drink at all or drink to stupefaction, and often to
unconsciousness.   In addition to this, in the opinion of
many investigators, the use of alcohol in Russia is especially injurious in consequence of climatic conditions.

Nevertheless, the opinion which attributes the eagerness
of the peasantry for spirituous liquors to an immoral
impulse is narrow and unfounded.   That eagerness is the
consequence of many elements—the lamentable conditions
of life, the absence of recreation, and the very nature of the
food of the people, consisting as it does almost exclusively
of vegetable substances.   It is a well-known fact that the
whole aboriginal vegetarian populations of islands discovered by Europeans were exterminated by the rapid
spread of drunkenness.

But whatever its causes may be, drink is undoubtedly one
of the causes of crime and of impotence in the improvement of social conditions.   In general it may be said that
as long as the causes of drunkenness are not removed, no
restrictive or punitive measures will be effective in out-
rooting the evil.   Measures for raising the economic level
of the people and the wide development of popular education are necessary first.

The consumption of spirituous liquors in Russia in
comparison with other countries is shown in the diagram
on the opposite page.

The number of sacrifices to drink is shown in the diagram on page 230.

Crime.—The criminal statistics of every country may be
taken as a factor in determining the level of material and
moral well-being of its population.   A comparison of the
criminal statistics of Russia with those of other countries
is made extremely difficult owing to the irregular classification of offences, and the irregular jurisdiction of the
lower courts.   In consequence of this the statistics found
in the Abstracts published by the Ministry of Justice have

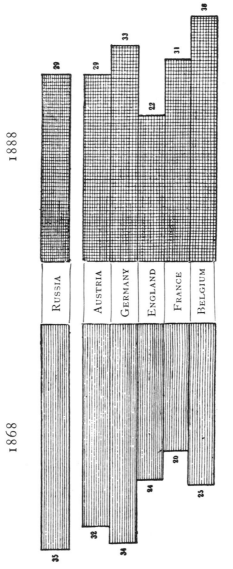

Consumption of Spirits in Vedra* by 100 Inhabitants in 1868 and 1888.

1888

1868

* The Vedra = 2·70 gallons.

little value as a basis for comparison, and indeed comparison of these statistics with those of Western European countries gives results far too optimistic and quite untrustworthy, as a great part of the offences of the greater part of the population, which fall under the jurisdiction of the Volost courts, are omitted.   An arithmetical comparison even of serious crimes cannot be safely made ; for the

Number of Deaths from Drunkenness in 1,000,000 of the Population.

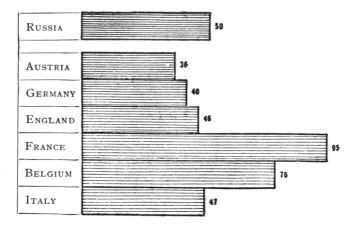

Volost courts, through ignorance of the law and incapacity to distinguish in a single case different forms of lawbreaking, very often determine criminal cases which by law are outside their competence.

Information collected in three governments, Podolsk, Moghilef, and Voluinsk, has served as a basis for estimating the total number of persons convicted by the Volost courts.   Adding the number of such convictions to the figures in the ordinary criminal statistics we have constructed the following diagram, showing the proportions of crime in Russia and Poland :

Average Number of Convictions in 200,000 of the Population
(100,000 men and 100,000 women) in 1878–1885.

Assize and
Civil Courts.

| POLAND | ОКРУЖНЫМИ МИРОВЫМИ 182 |
| RUSSIA | 97 ВОЛОСТНЫМИ 194 201 492 |

Volost Courts.

АРЕСТЪ И РОЗГИ   ПРОЧIЯ НАКАЗАНIЯ

Arrest and Whipping.   Other Punishments.

The attempt to draw a comparison between the amount of
crime in Russia and in foreign countries is made extremely
difficult by the differences in criminal codes. To add to
this difficulty the criminal statistics in some countries
relate to the number of accused, in some others to the
number of crimes, and in others only to the number of
convicted.   But even an approximate comparison cannot
be without value.   The most useful information would be
given by the distribution of convicts according to religious
faiths, but unfortunately through the lack of statistics as
to the religious profession of the peasants of the Empire,
such a classification was impossible.   We have therefore
been compelled to divide the convicts in the Empire
into three groups—peasants, Jews, and others. (See diagrams on pages 232, 233, 234, 235.)

It is not without interest to consider the number of
those convicted according to sex.   The table at top of
page 236 gives the percentage relations of the sexes in the
number of convicts.

To complete this picture it is only necessary to show
the increase or diminution of crime in Russia in comparison
with that of other states.   In this case, irregular registra-
tion does not play so serious a part, as we are not dealing
with the quantity of crime, but with its increase and
diminution in a certain period.   For Russia we take the
periods 1878–82 and 1888–89.   After examining the

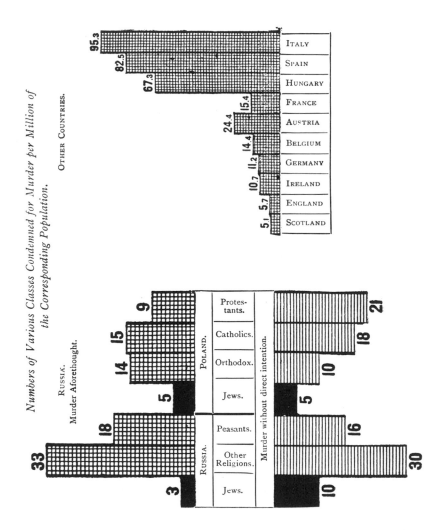

Numbers of Various Classes Condemned for Murder per Million of the Corresponding Population.

OTHER COUNTRIES.

95.3	ITALY
82.5	SPAIN
67.3	HUNGARY
15.4	FRANCE
24.4	AUSTRIA
14.4	BELGIUM
11.2	GERMANY
10.7	IRELAND
5.7	ENGLAND
5.1	SCOTLAND

RUSSIA.
Murder Aforethought.

Murder without direct intention.

POLAND.

Protestants.	9	21
Catholics.	15	18
Orthodox.	14	10
Jews.	5	5

RUSSIA.

Peasants.	18	16
Other Religions.	33	30
Jews.	3	10

Numbers Condemned for Theft per Million of the Corresponding Population.

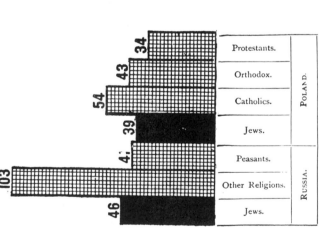

Numbers Convicted of Highway Robbery and other forms of Robbery with Violence per Million of the Corresponding Population.

AUSTRIA AND GERMANY.

19	Greek Orthodox.
7	Catholics
5	Protestants.
3	Jews.
11	Catholics.
7	Protestants.
1	Jews.
14	Catholics.
8	Protestant-.
0.5	Jews.
18	Catholics.
8	Protestants.
0	Jews.

AUSTRIA.   GERMANY.   PRUSSIA.   POSEN.

RUSSIA.

34	Protestants.
43	Orthodox.
54	Catholics.
39	Jews.
41	Peasants.
103	Other Religions.
46	Jews.

POLAND.   RUSSIA.

*Numbers Condemned for Swindling per Million of the
Corresponding Population.*

RUSSIA.

SWINDLING.

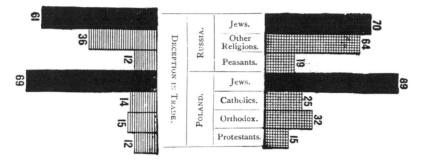

PRUSSIA AND GERMANY.

DIFFERENT FORMS OF SWINDLING.

AUSTRIA.

Percentage Relations of Men and Women Convicted.

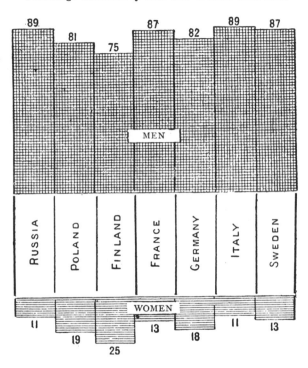

Percentage Increase in the Fifecen Chief Forms of Crime.

THE EMPIRE.   POLAND.

statistics of fifteen of the chief forms of crime we find an increase in crime in the second period in Russia of 14 per cent., and in Poland of 46 per cent. The diagram at the bottom of the preceding page presents these relations more effectively.

For comparison with foreign states we will take Great Britain, France, Austria, and Germany. In this respect Great Britain is in the most favourable position of all, as the following diagrams show :

Number of Convictions in Great Britain per 100,000 Inhabitants.

1860—1869.	*92*
1870—1879	*69*
1880—1889.	*55*
1894.	*44*

Thus we find that since the year 1860 the number of convicted persons in Great Britain has fallen by 109 per cent.

Among countries where the increase of crime has been inconsiderable may be named France and Austria :

Number of Convictions in Thousands.

FRANCE.   AUSTRIA.

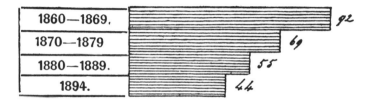

FRANCE		AUSTRIA
675	*1887*	*519*
660	*1888*	*569*
651	*1889*	*60*
679	*1890*	*60.*
684	*1891*	

In Germany, on the other hand, we find the same phenomenon as in Russia.

Number of Convictions in Germany per 100,000 Inhabitants.

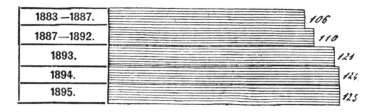

1883 —1887.	106
1887—1892.	110
1893.	121
1894.	124
1895.	125

It is interesting in the case of Russia to see the distribution of crime among the population in its relation to education.

	Empire. Per Cent.		Poland. Per Cent.
Higher education	1.2	...	.08
Educated .	25.3	...	13.4
Illiterate .	73.5	...	85.8

The chart on the opposite page shows the outlay on justice of all kinds and on prisons in 1887 per inhabitant.

To fill in this brief outline of the moral condition of Russia we will cite some statistics relating to recidivism, pointing out, however, that these statistics are not quite complete.   Nevertheless they may give a very fair idea of the amount of social evil caused by reversion to crime :

—	Number of Recidivists.		Percentage Growth of Recidivists.
	1878.	1889.	
Empire . . .	10,168	18,993	180
Kingdom of Poland	1,543	3,545	233

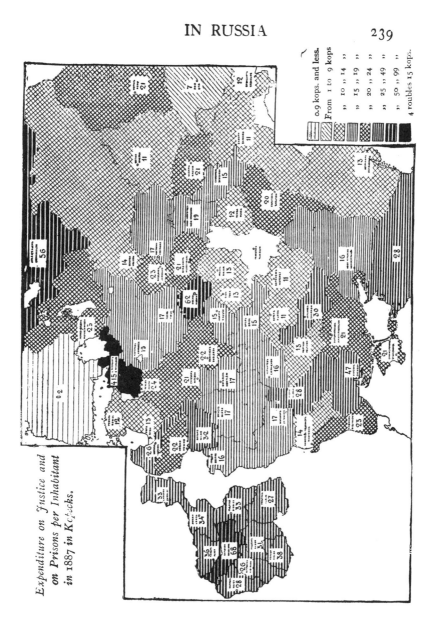

Expenditure on Justice and
on Prisons per Inhabitant
in 1887 in Kopecks.

Those who understand the gravity of criminal recidivism for the state will be able to judge of the significance of these figures in arriving at an estimate of the moral condition of the people.

VI.—ELEMENTS FOR THE RENEWAL OF THE ARMY.

The greater the probability of a prolonged European war, the more serious becomes the question of means and methods for the reinforcing of armies. The general conclusion, formed from an examination of Russia's resources, was that Russia, having an almost inexhaustible reserve of men and horses, might sustain a prolonged war incomparably better than the other states of Europe. But in this consideration we took into account only the average statistics for the whole of Russia. The question is made more complex by the fact that, in view of the immensity of Russia, the conditions for the renewal of armed forces in various districts must be very different, while in the event of a defensive war a certain portion of Russia's territory might be occupied by an enemy. In addition, with interrupted communications, all material for renewing armed forces must be obtained within the country itself. The question therefore naturally arises : Are they sufficient ?

It is evident that no deficiency can arise in men. Means of provisioning are also so abundant as to constitute in the very beginning of war a great advantage for Russia. In an earlier part of our work we have given figures to show the advantage which Russia also possesses in the matter of horses. The percentage of these which might be used in war is more important in the present connection. To form some idea of this, the chart on the next page, showing the percentage and distribution of grown horses over the country, will be useful.

Since 1864 an immense increase has taken place in the number of horses in the country, an inconsiderable decrease showing itself only in ten provinces, while all over the rest of the country a large increase took place, in certain provinces amounting to nearly 300 per cent.

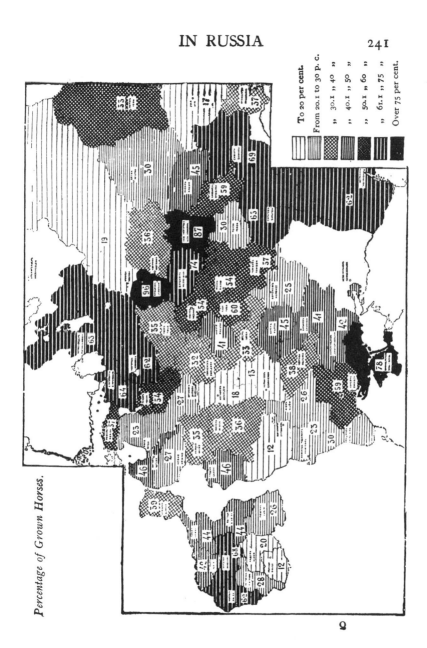

Percentage of Grown Horses.

To 20 per cent.
From 20.1 to 30 p. c.
" 30.1 " 40 "
" 40.1 " 50 "
" 50.1 " 60 "
" 61.1 " 75 "
Over 75 per cent.

It may be said, therefore, that no Western state will find itself in so good a position as relates to the supply of horses; and that however great may be the area occupied by an enemy's forces, deficiency in horses fit for military purposes cannot arise.

As relates to the supply of arms it may be assumed that no difficulty will arise in obtaining workers, owing to the stagnation caused in other industries. The working and application of iron has grown so rapidly that no difficulty can arise in this respect. In 1890 the pig-iron worked amounted to 55½ million poods (892,000 tons), manufactured iron to 25⅔ million poods (412,500 tons), while in 1895 the working of pig-iron amounted to 87 million poods (1,400,000 tons) (an increase of 57.5 per cent.), and manufactured iron to 27 million poods (434,000 tons) (an increase of 5 per cent.).

On the chart given on the next page is shown the distribution of the production of iron and steel. From this it may be seen that the chief resources of this material are situated in the East, and far away from those districts which might be occupied by an enemy's forces.

VII.—CONCLUSIONS.

From the above statistics the conclusion naturally springs that, while the interruption of communication will threaten with famine and social perturbations the states of Western Europe, the danger to Russia is less, although still very serious, meaning, as it would, decrease in the incomes of the population and the most lamentable results for trade and industry.

The incommensurate widening of the area of production at the expense of the area of nourishment, the replacing of horned cattle by horses, and the decrease of stock-raising generally, are factors against which must be placed the systematic efforts at improvement. Otherwise, in view of the yearly export of the products of the land and of the rapid growth of the population, Russia would go farther and farther on the path to the exhaustion of her natural

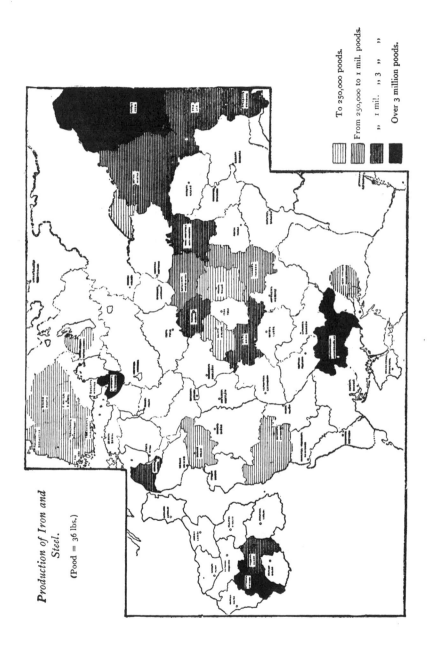

Production of Iron and Steel.

(Pood = 36 lbs.)

To 250,000 poods.

From 250,000 to 1 mil. poods.

„ 1 mil.   „ 3 „   „

Over 3 million poods.

resources and the multiplication of an agricultural proletariat.

And thus Russia, although so far as the products of
agriculture are concerned she is in a position to carry on a
serious and prolonged struggle—such a struggle as could
not even be dreamt of by the states of Western Europe—
nevertheless is as interested as are those countries in
the preservation of peace.

In comparison with the income derived from agriculture
the total of the income received from industries is insignificant.   But in the event of a great war even this
income must diminish to a considerable extent.   In such
industries as directly or indirectly relate to the supply and
armament of the army there will, of course, be no stagnation.   But the interruption of the supply of trans-oceanic
cotton and various other materials, and difficulties in the
supply of coal, will shorten the output of many articles.
It is true that Russian industry, relying upon an internal
sale, will not lose its market in consequence of interrupted
communications, as English, German, and French industry
will.   But in time of war the demand on the internal
market would undoubtedly fall, proportionately with the
fall in incomes derived from agriculture and the general
disruption in agricultural life.   Russian industry relies
mainly on the demands of the peasantry.   Thus, even in
times of peace every serious failure of crops causes
stagnation.   It is obvious that the diminution in the
resources of the peasantry caused by war would react on
industry and shorten production considerably.   As a
result of this, workers who live in poverty and absolutely
without provision for the future will find themselves in a
position no less terrible than that of the workers of
Western Europe.

Only traders, in consequence of their comparative few-
ness, and usurers who take advantage of the backwardness
of the agricultural population of Russia, will find that war
creates favourable conditions, opening a wider path for
exploitation of the popular needs.

All this leads to the conclusion that, in consequence of a

generally unsettled agriculture, of the primitive and already insufficient systems of working land, of absence of savings, and of indebtedness both of proprietors and of peasants, the economic perturbations caused by war might assume immense gravity. We have pointed out some of the conditions which in Western Europe would make a prolonged war impossible. But there immense capital representing the savings of the people, high development of technique, force of social activity, and at the same time of private enterprise, would tend towards quicker healing of the wounds caused by war in the popular organism. That this might be is shown by the history of France since the war of 1870–71. We may suppose that a future war would result even more disastrously, but it is unquestionable that a strong economic organism might rapidly recover. It is for this reason that Western states have less to fear from the economic consequences which might arise from war than from the growth of socialism and the possibility of revolution.

It is not so in Russia. The weaker the economic activity is, the less are its dangers from war. Where accumulated riches are small and economic life simple, the direct losses will not be so acutely felt. But for a country mainly agricultural, in which both peasants and proprietors can hardly make both ends meet even in times of peace; a country burdened with indebtedness and in consequence cursed with forced labour ; a country where the finances have only lately been reduced to order, and would again be disorganised by a great issue of paper money—for such a country the consequences of war would be especially disastrous, and would result in an economic crisis and a loss of productive forces from which it would need a long time to recover. And thus, although Russia is not threatened with those revolutions which might be feared in Western Europe after a great war, yet the consequences for her of such a war would be in the highest degree serious.

The necessity for Russia not to fall below the other states in expenditure on armaments entails on her a heavier burden than France and Germany and even Austria have to bear. In those countries the war budget, however immense it may be, constitutes only a small part of the expenditure of the state, of the municipalities, of private associations and of village communities, on productive works, on improvements in agriculture and in sanitation, on the development of communications, trade and industry, and finally (although this is by no means the least important item) on the spread of education. In Russia, the expenditure on land and sea forces constitutes a third of the whole budget ; and, if we deduct the sums devoted to interest on the Imperial debt, we find that all expenditures which might in any way be productive taken together are less than the expenditure on armaments alone.

In view of all these circumstances it is impossible not to conclude that a great European war would move Russia still further back in economic relations, it may be, even for a prolonged time. And, bearing this in mind, it may well be asked whether even the most successful war could result in sufficient compensation for such sacrifices.

True, facts and figures demonstrate that, thanks to her immensity and to the nature of her soil and climate, Russia is less vulnerable than other countries. There can be no doubt that with her vast population, her abundant production of food and horses, and with industries guaranteeing the equipment of her army, Russia might carry on a defensive war for a long time. Even financial conditions would not operate disadvantageously at first, for Russia has for a long time been accustomed to the circulation of paper money. All these are plainly advantages for Russia in a defensive war against countries enjoying a higher degree of culture, possessed of great industries and trade, but which, through deficient production of corn for the feeding of their populations, could not carry on war for years, as would certainly be possible for Russia.

But in an offensive war these factors, which constitute an advantage for Russia in defence, would be turned into disadvantages.

From detailed investigation of the economic condition of different districts of Russia, we came to the conclusion that however sensibly she were to feel the occupation by an enemy of her frontier provinces, such occupation could not produce any decided result. The opposition of Russia could not be broken at once, even by the irruption of innumerable forces. In the extreme case of the Russian armies experiencing such defeats as to expose the capitals, the vastness of the country and the immensity of its population would supply the means for continuing the struggle. The fragments of her defeated forces, retreating to distant centres of population, would form the nuclei of new armies, and the struggle would burst out again with fresh fierceness—and that in the very moment when the weakened and exhausted invaders were compelled to retreat.

But it must not be assumed from this that victory, by means of pursuing the invaders and carrying the war into their own country, would be an easy task. Pursuit would have to be carried on through the ruined districts of Russia into the exhausted territory of the enemy; while for the successful carrying on of an offensive war new armaments, war material generally, would be required, and, above all, armies would have to be supplied exclusively from purchased provisions.

To this would have to be added financial difficulties almost impossible to be overcome, for the economic perturbations produced by war would be of such gravity as to prevent the further straining of the national resources.

Russia has now within the country, in circulation and on deposit, Government securities to a sum of two and a half milliard roubles (£375,000,000), and other securities to a sum of 1200 million roubles (£180,000,000). On the declaration of war the depreciation of these securities would entail a loss of 1100 millions of roubles (£165,000,000). It is obvious that the issue of new Government loans to provide for the immediate necessities of war would be impossible. From this would inevitably result the issue of paper money in immense quantities.

The history of past wars of Russia can give no idea of

the economic perturbations which would be caused by war to-day, in view of the vastness of the army and the complexity and costliness of all military apparatus. The occupation by an enemy of the Western and Southern provinces, now in the most satisfactory economic condition, and the interruption of internal communications, would have a tremendous effect on the receipt of the ordinary Imperial revenues. Even the war of 1812 cannot be compared with the irruption into Russia of armies counted by millions, while the need for money in the present composition of the army would be unprecedented. It is enough to repeat that for the satisfaction of military requirements in a state of war, under present conditions, Russia would be compelled to spend daily about seven millions of roubles (£1,050,000).

As we have pointed out (in the section devoted to " Plans of Military Activity "), it is almost impossible to admit that a war with Russia could be decided in less than two years. For such a war lasting two years five milliards would be required (£750,000,000). The late N. K. Bunge, as we have already mentioned, declared that if credit notes were issued for 300 million roubles (£45,000,000) their value would fall 25 kopecks the rouble (that is, one-fourth). With the issue of paper money in a quantity seventeen times greater it is quite impossible to see the extent of depreciation. It is very probable, however, that depreciation would reach the same level as at the beginning of the present century—that is, that paper money issued for the carrying on of war would be depreciated by three-fourths of its nominal value. Under such circumstances even the estimated five milliards might prove insufficient.

The prices of all things would rise, and the Treasury, receiving taxes in depreciated credit notes, would pay a higher price for everything ; the maintenance of the army and of the fleet would require immense outlays. A considerable part of the population of towns and all serving in the army and in the civil service would suffer from extreme privation.

At the moment of the declaration of war the whole export of agricultural products will cease. A sudden fall of prices will ensue, with a proportionate diminution in the incomes both of landowners and of peasants. These phenomena will be accompanied by fluctuations in prices, for the standard of prices has always been determined by export, which will cease. When the only regulator of prices will be internal competition those districts will be in the best position where competition in trade is most highly developed, as is the case in the Metropolitan, Northern, Southern and South-Western provinces and also in the Southern provinces, and in the worst position those where trade is to a great extent a monopoly.

In addition to the economic shock, recovery from which will take years, many material and moral factors which we have examined in detail, which have little visible effect in times of peace, will in the revolution which war causes have grave significance.

All of which leads to the conclusion that war for Russia, whatever might be its issue, could not be less ruinous, although from other causes, than for her enemies.

But this conclusion is not enough. A consideration from all points of view of the influences which war might exert on the economic condition of the country, leads to a conviction not less important—that is, that a decrease of expenditure on preparations for war is no less, and it may be even more, unavoidable in Russia than in other European states.

The conversion to productive purposes of a part of the outlay now fruitlessly devoted to armaments—since there is not even a probability of war breaking out—is the first interest of the people, and is essential for the development of the vital forces of the country. These forces are needed by Russia for the carrying on of a successful struggle, not on the field of battle, but with her economic backwardness and the poverty and ignorance of her people. Progress in her internal life, and the development of productive forces are far more necessary for Russia, which, even in the case of war, would, in all probability, at first have to content herself with defensive operations, than the increase of armed hordes and the accumulation of implements and munitions of destruction.

But if, even in times of peace, we find all possible preparations made, so that the country in time of war shall in no respect be behind its enemies, how much more necessary is it to prepare to meet those perturbations and difficulties of every kind which will be caused by war in the economic position of the country.

CHAPTER II

THE ECONOMIC DIFFICULTIES OF GREAT BRITAIN IN TIME OF WAR

A GREAT European war must react disastrously on the economic condition of Great Britain even in the event of her taking no part in that war. The interruption of maritime communications will affect disastrously, it may be even fatally, the industries of the country and the feeding of her population. The immense development of British industry is calculated upon access to the markets of the whole world, and relies upon the uninterrupted export of products. In England every cessation of export means a stoppage of work, involving the withdrawal of the means of subsistence from the greater part of her population. The production of wheat in that country, notwithstanding the increase in the population, has steadily diminished, diminished to such an extent that the stoppage of the import of wheat into England would threaten the whole population with famine.

I.—DEFICIENCY OF PRODUCTION.

The diminution in the area devoted to the raising of grain in England may be illustrated by the following figures:

Year.	In Thousands of Hectares. (English Equivalents, in Parentheses, in Thousands of Acres.)		
	Area devoted to Raising Grain.	Under Meadow.	Total.
1875 . . .	7330 (18,325)	5389 (13,473)	12,719 (31,798)
1880 . . .	7156 (17,890)	5841 (14,603)	12,997 (32,493)
1885 . . .	6964 (17,410)	6211 (15,528)	13,175 (32,938)
1890 . . .	6782 (16,955)	6485 (16,213)	13,267 (33,168)
1895 . . .	6464 (16,160)	6725 (16,813)	13,189 (32,973)

Thus the area of land devoted to agriculture in twenty years increased to the insignificant amount of 1175 thousands of acres. And not only does all this increase come under meadow, but under meadow we also find 2250 thousands of acres, that is, almost one-eighth part of the land formerly devoted to tillage.

The average harvests of the United Kingdom in recent years are shown in thousands of quarters in the following table :

Crop.	1893.	1894.	1895.	Average 1893-95.
Oats . . .	21,074	23,858	21,810	22,247
Barley . . .	8,218	9,825	9,378	9,140
Wheat . . .	6,364	7,588	4,786	6,246
Beans . . .	608	900	703	737
Peas . . .	594	779	591	655

The average yearly harvest, expressed in kilogrammes is shown by the following figures :

Oats .	.	.	282,537 thousand kilos.
Barley	.	.	116,078 ,,
Wheat	.	.	79,324 ,,
Beans	.	.	9,360 ,,
Peas .	.	.	8,319 ,,

The import into England of bread stuffs is shown in thousands of kilogrammes in the following table:

	1890.	1893.	1894.	Average.
Grain—				
Wheat .	768,020	831,367	890,600	829,996
Barley .	211,811	290,119	396,761	299,563
Oats .	161,633	177,228	190,233	176,365
Maize .	551,662	417,855	449,136	472,884
Others .	74,511	89,954	110,198	91,554
Flour—				
Wheaten	200,317	259,182	243,014	234,171
Others .	8,420	8,395	9,830	8,882
Total .	1,976,374	2,074,100	2,289,772	2,113,415

This table, in thousands of English quarters (reckoning 1 kilogramme as equal to 22 lbs.), would be as follows:

	1890.	1893.	1894.	Average.
Grain—				
Wheat .	60,344.4	65,321.70	69,976	65,214
Barley .	16,642.2	22,795.07	31,174.1	23,537.13
Oats .	12,699.7	13,925.06	14,946.9	13,857.22
Maize .	43,345.1	32,831.50	35,289.3	37,155.3
Others .	5,854.6	7,067.90	8,658.4	7,193.7
Flour—				
Wheaten .	15,739.2	20,364.30	19,094	18,399.2
Others .	662.0	659.00	772.3	697.8
Total .	155,287.2	162,964.53	179,911	166,054.35

From this table it is seen that the import of bread stuffs to satisfy the requirements of the population continually grows. The import of wheat is more than ten times greater than the home growth : of oats alone the home production exceeds the import in the proportion of three to two. If we calculate the number of days on which bread would be lacking in England if she were forced to rely alone upon her own harvests, it will appear that England would be without wheat for 333 days, without barley for 263 days, and without oats for 140 days.

A more favourable result is obtained by a comparison of the growth and import of potatoes. The growth approximately expressed in thousands of tons amounts to

1893	.	.	.	.	.	6541
1894	.	.	.	.	.	4662
1895	.	.	.	.	.	7065
	Average	.	.	.		6089

The import of potatoes is shown by the following figures :

In 1893	.	.	.	.	. 142 thousand tons.
In 1894	.	.	.	.	. 135 ,, ,,

As concerns meat, England is still less dependent on products from abroad. The number of head of cattle and sheep imported into England is shown by the following table :

			Cattle.		Sheep.
1880 .	.	.	. 389,724	...	941,121
1885 .	.	.	. 373,078	...	750,886
1890 .	.	.	. 642,596	...	358,458
1893 .	.	.	. 340,045	...	62,682
1894 .	.	.	. 475,440	...	484,597

In addition to this, England imports a quantity of carcases here set out in thousands of hundredweights :

	1891.	1893.	1894.	Average.
Bacon	5000	4187	4819	4669
Beef	2129	2008	2346	2161
Salt, and other sorts of fresh meat . .	1760	2149	2484	2131
Meat dried and in preserve . . .	735	561	554	627
Fresh pork . . .	300	369	405	358

In order to illustrate the relation between the import and production of meat in England, we give the following totals, it being understood that, following the general principle, ten sheep or pigs or fifteen hundredweight of meat are considered as a head of cattle.

The number of cattle held in England are presented by the following tables:

	In Thousands.	Horned Cattle. In Thousands.
Cows	2,486	
Horned cattle of two years and over	1,432	
,, ,, from one to two years . . .	1,190	
,, ,, less than one year	1,247	
	6,355	= 6,355
Sheep and rams one year old and over	15,997	
Lambs	9,795	
	25,792	= 2,579
Pigs	2,884	= 288
		9,222

By this process of reducing all stock to units we find that England possessed in 1895, 9222 thousand head of native cattle. The import into England in 1894 was 523 thousand head of living cattle, and 10,608 thousand hundredweight of meat of different sorts, representing

707 thousand head of cattle.   That is to say, the import
into England amounted to 1230 thousand head of cattle,
or 13 per cent. of the number in the country.

*Number of Native and Imported Cattle in England in Thousands
of Heads.*

NATIVE.   IMPORTED.

9222   1894   1230

From this it appears that as far as the supply of meat
is concerned England would be guaranteed, even in the
event of import being interrupted ; but prices would rise
immensely, as English cattle is very valuable, and meat in
that country is dear even at the present day.

Of other products for which the raising of cattle is
necessary, England requires yearly :

| | In Thousands of Hundredweights. | | | Average. |
	1890.	1893.	1894.	
Butter	2028	2327	2595	2310
Margarine . . .	1080	1300	1109	1163
Cheese	2144	2077	2266	2162
Tallow	1273	1118	1401	1264

With such an immense demand it will be no easy task
to supply the interrupted import by increased internal
output.   In these respects there would undoubtedly arise
great difficulty in the supply of the population.   A similar
deficiency would exist in the supply of various colonial
products.   England imports :

	1890.	1893.	1894.	Average.
Rice, in 1000's of cwts.	5,957	5,449	5,194	5,523
Cocoa ,, lbs.	28,112	32,982	39,116	33,403
Coffee ,, cwts.	864	827	731	807
Tea ,, lbs.	223,494	249,546	244,311	239,117
Sugar ,, cwts.	9,977	11,550	13,945	11,824
Raw silk ,, ,,	15,717	16,032	14,306	15,352
Molasses,, ,,	563	585	853	667
Glucose ,, ,,	737	1,236	1,062	1,012
Rum ,, gals.	6,238	5,942	6,123	6,101
Cognac ,, ,,	3,100	2,739	3,402	3,080
Other spirituous drinks (colonial and foreign), in thousands of gals.	3,375	2,182	2,495	2,684
Wine (in ditto) .	16,194	14,675	14,369	15,079

A clearer picture is presented by the following table, which shows the average consumption per inhabitant of the United Kingdom of imported articles of food and drink :

Imported Products.	1892.	1893.	1894.
Bacon . . . (in lbs.)	14.10	11.73	13.29
Beef, fresh and salted ,,	6.70	5.68	6.59
Smoked and preserved meat ,,	2.10	1.55	1.49
Mutton, fresh . . ,,	4.99	5.74	6.62
Pork, fresh and salt . ,,	0.98	1.03	1.12
Butter and margarine . ,,	6.23	6.59	7.27
Margarine . . . ,,	3.80	3.75	3.17
Cheese . . . . ,,	6.39	5.87	6.38
Cocoa . . . . ,,	0.55	0.54	0.58
Coffee . . . . ,,	0.74	0.69	0.69
Wheat in grain . . ,,	180.40	188.82	201.48
Wheaten flour . . ,,	64.36	58.83	54.71
Currants and raisins . ,,	4.58	5.02	4.90
Eggs . . . (number)	35.03	34.39	36.68
Potatoes . . . (in lbs.)	8.71	8.14	7.68
Rice . . . . ,,	8.91	8.54	7.26
Sugar, raw . . . ,,	47.22	45.68	40.17

R

Imported Products.	1892.	1893.	1894.
Sugar, refined . . (in lbs.)	30.62	33.17	39.89
Tea . . . . ,,	5.43	5.41	5.52
Tobacco . . . ,,	1.64	1.63	1.66
Wine . . . (in gallons)	0.38	0·37	0.36
Spirituous liquors . ,,	0.21	0.20	0.20
Wine and strong drinks together (imported) . ,,	1.04	0.98	0.97

II.—FALL OF WAGES AND INCOMES.

In England the cost of the first necessaries of life is high, and the means for obtaining them constantly diminish.

The population of the United Kingdom is engaged in the following occupations, per thousand of the population of all ages:

—	England and Wales.	Scotland.	Ireland.	United Kingdom.
Liberal professions .	32	28	44	33
Domestic service . .	66	50	51	62
Trade	48	45	20	44
Agriculture and fisheries	46	62	200	67
Industry . . .	253	256	140	239
Without settled occupation . . .	555	559	545	555
	1000	1000	1000	1000

In view of the importance of the question we will present these figures graphically.

Classification by Occupation of 1000 of the Population of Great Britain.

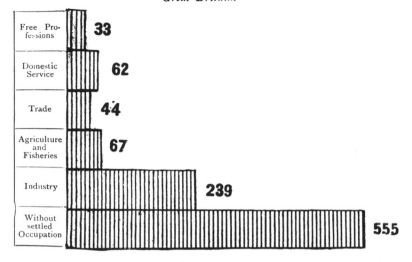

The existence of an income tax in England has resulted in the compiling of precise statistics which give some idea of the perturbation which war would cause. We quote here some of the more apposite figures. The yearly value of the real estate, capital and earnings subject to this tax is shown in pounds sterling in the following table :

England	.	.	.	.	£602,388,699
Scotland	.	.	.	.	65,188,840
Ireland .	.	.	.	.	38,553,336
United Kingdom .		.	.	£706,130,875

Out of this total of 706 millions sterling, 263 millions arise from the possession or lease of land and immovable property, 91 millions from pensions and salaries, and the remaining 352 millions from industrial and professional occupations.

Distribution of the Income of the Population of England in Millions of Pounds Sterling.

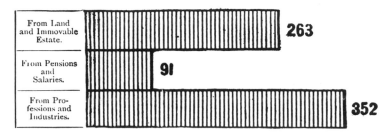

From Land and Immovable Estate.	263
From Pensions and Salaries.	91
From Professions and Industries.	352

These figures bear eloquent testimony to the tremendous economic earthquake which war and the resulting decrease and even stoppage of industrial activity would create in England. On the other hand it must be borne in mind that the reserves of money are greater in England than anywhere else ; the whole public debt is placed inside the country, and an immense total of foreign values is held.

But a very grave circumstance presents itself in the fact that these resources are in the hands of a very small number of persons. Precise statistics as to the distribution of the public debt of Great Britain are available only up to 1880. But these statistics show that the number of persons who receive interest on the public debt are :

£			In 1855.		In 1880.
Up to	5	· ·	83,877	...	71,756
,,	10	· ·	38,129	...	32,662
,,	50	· ·	82,426	...	67,068
,,	100	· ·	21,978	...	17,456
,,	200	· ·	12,418	...	9,439
,,	300	· ·	3,501	...	2,655
,,	500	· ·	2,342	...	1,966
,,	1000	· ·	1,051	...	990
,,	2000	· ·	299	...	356
Over 2000		· ·	145	...	217
			246,166	...	204,575

Thus we find that the number of proprietors of consols

has increased only in the two highest categories, and in all the lower has decreased. It may be assumed that this phenomenon continues the same to-day.

The sums deposited in the Post Office Savings Bank amounted to . .	£89,266,066
In Savings Banks	43,474,904
Total . .	£132,740,904

The number of depositors is:

In the Post Office Savings Bank .	6,108,763
In Savings Banks	1,470,946
Total . .	7,579,709

State of Savings in Great Britain in 1895.

DEPOSITORS IN MILLIONS.   DEPOSITS IN MILLIONS OF POUNDS STERLING.

7.6 **1894.** 132.7

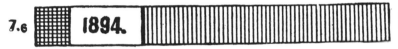

However it may be, the distribution of riches in England is more unequal than in any other country. Even in time of peace, with normal conditions, the state, various philanthropic institutions and societies are forced to give monetary assistance to a considerable part of the population to an extent unheard of among the peoples of the Continent. The following figures relating to January 1895 show the number of poor receiving help (with the exception of tramps) from the Boards of Guardians:

England and Wales . . .	817,431
Scotland	126,918
Ireland	101,071
Total . .	1,045,420

The danger in the event of a great economic upheaval is all the greater since the unquiet elements crowd into the cities, and the population of the towns in Great Britain exceeds the population of the country, at the expense of which they constantly grow, as is shown by the statistics relating to Scotland, where in the decade 1881–91 the urban population increased by 324,446, and the village population by 17,952, while the country population decreased by 52,324.

It is impossible owing to the absence of statistics to show in similar form the change in the distribution of the population of the entire United Kingdom. But there is sufficient indication that the position there is similar to that of Scotland. In England and Wales in 1891 the country population consisted of 8,198,248 souls, that is to say, only 28.3 per cent. of the whole, while the urban population consisted of 71 7 per cent. Thus two-thirds of the population of Great Britain resides within towns. In addition to that it must be noted that the proportion of women to men in towns is 7 per cent. greater than in the country, and it is well known that in times of crises women constitute the least tranquil element.

Statistics show that in the towns of England is crowded an immense number who do not wish to work, and a still greater number who cannot find work. To this idle crowd will join the workers discharged from factories and workshops on the shortening of work. An approximate idea may be formed of their number by the fact that in the weaving industry alone 1,084,000 persons are employed, in the number being 428,000 men and 656,000 women.

The majority of this working class is engaged in factories, of which the largest group constitutes cotton-spinning, weaving, and printing. It is this work which must cease in the event of the interruption of the import of material by sea. Bankruptcy in industrial circles will inevitably appear, as such factories are not guaranteed by sufficient reserves of capital.

The system of joint-stock companies in recent times has made possible an immense development of trade and industry. In the report of the Commission appointed by the Board of Trade the number of joint-stock companies on the 1st of April, 1894, is given as 18,361, with a total capital of £1,035,029,835, while in France the total capital of such companies is £420,000,000 only, and in Germany from £200,000,000 to £300,000,000.

III.—CONCLUSIONS.

If the waters which wash the British Isles ensure a greater security than the frontiers of the Continent, nevertheless they place the country in direct dependence from uninterrupted and regular maritime communication. The immense fleet of Great Britain, although guarding her against the attacks of an enemy, cannot guarantee the security of her merchant vessels in all the waters of the world. A few swift cruisers would be enough to interrupt the maritime trade of Great Britain. And with the immense development of English industry, and the insufficient local production of food stuffs, the stoppage of maritime communications would threaten England with stoppage of work, would involve a great rise in the price of provisions, and terminate in famine.

In such events attempts even at revolution are probable, all the more probable because the British army is small, recruited from the lowest ranks of the population and composed of hired soldiers. In the English army cases of general insubordination have been by no means rare.

In addition to this, a considerable agitation in England is carried on against the burdens enforced on the population by the army needed for the preservation of British power in subject countries, and more particularly by the gigantic fleet. Yet the expenditure on armaments continually grows, as the following table shows :

1864–5	.	.	.	.	£25,281,000
1874–5	.	.	.	.	25,779,000
1884–5	.	.	.	.	27,000,000
1894–5	.	.	.	.	35,449,000

Expenditure of England on Armed Forces in Millions of Pounds Sterling.

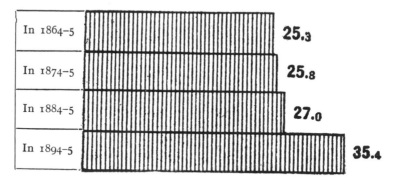

In 1864–5	25.3
In 1874–5	25.8
In 1884–5	27.0
In 1894–5	35.4

Thus in the ten years period 1884–1894 the expenditure on armaments has increased by £8,449,000 sterling. In addition to this a yearly expenditure of £18,000,000 represents the result of former wars, and agitators lose no opportunity of calling attention to it. In 1727, at the death of George I. the public debt, increased in consequence of the Spanish war, stood at £52,500,000, and the interest at £2,360,000. In 1775, before the war with the American colonies, the debt was £126,000,000 capital, and £4,650,000 interest. This vast increase was the consequence of another war with Spain over the right claimed by England of searching merchant ships, afterwards of a war with France over the Austrian legacy, and finally from the action she took during the Seven Years War. It is interesting to note that in the second of these wars England helped Maria Theresa against Frederick II., and in the last Frederick II. against Maria Theresa.

In 1792, before the beginning of the long war with France, the public debt of England amounted to £237,400,000, paying interest at £9,300,000, an increase mainly resulting from the war with her North American Colonies. And this war in reality was caused because the proprietorial classes in England, predominating in

Parliament, desired to shift the burden of increasing taxation upon the shoulders of others.

In 1816—that is, the year after the battle of Waterloo—the debt of England amounted to £846,000,000 in capital, with yearly interest of £32,100,000.

The war with France which cost such immense sums arose from the interference of England in the struggle against the French Revolution, in which the propertied classes who ruled England saw a danger to their privileges and to their exploitation of the whole country. The duty on imported corn set in time of war was kept in force by the landlord class even after the end of the war, mainly in order to sustain the high price of corn, and in consequence the high incomes from their property.

In 1854, at the beginning of the Crimean war, the debt of England had decreased to £794,713,000 capital, paying a yearly interest of £25,662,000. In 1856, on the conclusion of peace, it had risen to £826,000,000 capital, with £25,545,000 interest. This war also was waged in no way in the interests of the English people. Finally, in 1893 the debt of England (not including the value of her shares in the Suez Canal) amounted to £658,944,000 capital, paying an interest of £18,302,000.

From the above statistics it is shown that as long as the aristocracy carried on war itself, and bore the expenses, a public debt did not exist. Afterwards, thanks to its numerical preponderance in Parliament, it succeeded in managing so that, however great might be the expenditure of the state, the sum of tax from the land should not exceed two million pounds yearly; the debt began to rise, and war after war followed. These wars were directly advantageous to the aristocracy, as they increased employment in the army, and in addition resulted in raising the price of corn.

CHAPTER III

ECONOMIC DIFFICULTIES OF GERMANY IN TIME OF WAR

In order to explain the economic and social consequences which would result from war in Germany, it is necessary first to examine the distribution of the population according to occupation, the height of incomes, and probability of savings, and then to consider how a war would shorten demands, decrease the sale of products, and in consequence cause stagnation in industry.

We have already pointed out that the interruption of land and sea communications must cause an immense rise in the price of agricultural products, particularly in industrial districts. And as at the same time work will cease, the danger of disaster will be great. To a certain extent government aid may be relied upon. But whether this will be effective or not depends upon the gravity of the crisis produced by war.

The question as to satisfaction of the needs of life concerns only those classes which are imperfectly guaranteed —that is, to those with insufficient and moderate incomes ; the wealthy class will always be safe as regards the necessaries of life.

The following table represents the distribution of the population by occupation in 1882 :

		Percentage of the Population.
I.	{ Agriculture	40.75
	{ Arboriculture	0.65
		——
		41.40

		Percentage of the Population.	
	Mining	2.96	
	Building	6.08	
II.	Manufacture . . .	24.93	
	Communications . .	3.16	
	Transport	2.95	
			40.08
III.	Trade	5.27	5.27
	Engaged in medical, educational, and religious pursuits	1.65	
IV.	Administration . . .	1.45	
	Military	1.17	
			4.27
V.	In service	4.30	4.30
VI.	Without regular occupation .	4.67	4.67

Thus we have six main classes as follows :

	Per Cent.		Per Cent.
I. . . .	41.40	IV. . . .	4.27
II. . . .	40.08	V. . . .	4.30
III. . . .	5.27	VI. . . .	4.67

The effect on the first of these classes will be comparatively small. But owing to the bonds joining to a certain extent all classes of the population, the crisis called forth by war may in the course of time react even upon the agricultural population. The first consequence of the rise in prices will be an increase in the income of this class of the population. Part of the agricultural labourers will be taken from work, but these may be replaced by contingents of men engaged in industry, who will be deprived of work in consequence of the shortening of production.

The fifth class is also comparatively secure, since in consequence of mobilisation a deficiency of such will arise.

The third class, engaged in trade, may also be regarded as secured, since war, while lessening certain forms of activity, will give rise to others. But individually, members of this class will suffer greatly. As the crisis entailed by war approaches there will be lessened activity in trade, the prices of goods will fall, and only those traders who happen to have reserves of products required for the army, or products the import of which will be stopped, will draw advantage. Generally speaking, in consequence of sudden changes in prices immense difficulties will arise in trade.

The second class—that is, those engaged in industrial undertakings, either as masters or servants—will suffer the most. The greater part of this class is composed of persons occupied in factory work, and these will suffer immense losses. And the proportion of this group to the general population of Germany is very considerable, amounting to 40.08 per cent. It must be borne in mind that these figures relate to the whole of Germany, and that in various parts of the country the proportions are very different. Occupied in agriculture we find :

> In Saxony .   . 19.7 per cent. of the population.
> In Posen .   . 63.1   „   „   „

On the other hand, we find 16 per cent. of the population is occupied in industries in one province, and as much as 62 per cent. in others. The proportions occupied in trade in different parts of the country, excluding the great centres, fluctuate between 57 and 11 per cent.

It will be understood that the greater the proportion occupied in industry, the greater the crisis caused by war. In some of the great industrial localities the stoppage of work may cause serious disorders such as happened in June 1848, and March 1871 in Paris.

That stagnation and inevitable crisis in industry will be caused by war is inevitable, for certain reasons. The increase in the price of provisions in consequence of the interruption of communications will immediately diminish the purchasing resources of the population. On the declaration of war all state, commercial, and industrial securities will be depreciated, want of money will be seriously felt, and the rate of discount will be raised. The more highly developed the trade and industry, the greater will be the perturbations caused and the more numerous will be cases of failure. Generally speaking, not only will the credit of the state, but the credit of all private individuals in all classes of society, be impaired.

The following forms of industry will suffer most of all:

Working and manufacture of metals .	607,481
Machine building	94,807
Chemical manufacture	71,777
Spinning and weaving	910,089
Leather working and paper making .	221,688
Manufacture from wood	469,695
Building	533,511
Preparation of clothing	1,259,791

Does there exist among the German working classes such savings as would make the stoppage of work called forth by war unfelt? The accumulation of savings depends upon national and individual character, and also upon the level of work in normal times. The thrift of the Germans is unquestioned. But a considerable part of the population receives insignificant wages, which only satisfy their daily needs; and among this class there can hardly be any savings.

The existence in Prussia of an income tax, and the corresponding statistics, make it possible to judge of the distribution of income among the population, and conclusions drawn from Prussia may be applied approximately to the rest of Germany. The following figures relate to the year 1890:

	Proportion of the Population.		Average Income.
Incomes insufficient .	40.11 per cent.	...	197 m. (£9 17s.)
,, small .	. 54.05 ,,	...	276 ,, (£13 16s.)
,, moderate .	4.81 ,,	...	896 ,, (£44 16s.)
,, considerable	1.3 ,,	...	2781 ,, (£139 1s.)

Thus we see that 40 per cent. of the population belong to the necessitous class, while 54 per cent. have small

incomes, and are hardly in a position to save.   The
average income of an individual of the first class is only
197 marks (£9 17s.), and of the second class only 276 marks
(£13 16s.).

For the more precise exposition of this matter let us
take a province with developed industries.   The following
figures relate to the kingdom of Saxony.   In 1894 the
number of persons in Saxony receiving incomes was
estimated at 1,496,566.   The number of these

Who did not pay income tax was only   . 85,849   or   5.7 %
Having incomes under 600 m. (£30)   .   . 633,929   ,,   42.4 ,,
    ,,   from 600 to 2200 m. (£110) 675,862   ,,   45.2 ,,
    ,,   ,, 2200 to 6300 ,, (£315)   79,928   ,,   5.3 ,,

The incomes of the population of Saxony are thus
distributed :

From landed property . 287 mill. m. (£14,350,000) or 22.5 %
  ,,   capital   .   . 220   ,,   ,, (£11,000,000) ,,   17.2 ,,
  ,,   salary and wages 771   ,,   ,, (£38,550,000) ,,   60.3 ,,
                         1278   ,,   ,, (£63,900,000) ,,   100 ,,

From this it will be easily seen what convulsions
would be caused by the stoppage of work.   The following
are the figures relating to all Germany.   The general
income of the population estimated on the years 1893–94
amounted to 5,725,338,364 marks (£286,266,918 4s.).
This income was distributed as follows :

Urban population . 3878 million m. (£193,900,000) or 68 %
Country   ,,   . 1846   ,,   ,, (£92,300,000) ,, 32 ,,

In 1866 the total income amounted to 3,600,000,000
marks (£180,000,000) and was distributed thus :

Urban population . 1620 million m. (£81,000,000) or 45 %
Country   ,,   . 1980   ,,   ,, (£99,000,000) ,, 55 ,,

Thus, when in 1866 the incomes of the urban population of Germany amounted to 45 per cent. of the general

income, the crisis caused by war affected only £81,000,000 of the income of the people. To-day such a crisis would threaten an income of £193,900,000, for now not a half but two-thirds of the general income proceeds from industry and trade.

All this indicates a position by no means favourable. But it is improved by the fact that the amount of savings is considerable. Thus in Saxony in 1893 the number of pass books issued by the savings banks was 1,783,390. The average deposit was £18 9s. But though the existence of such savings is favourable as an economic phenomenon, it could hardly serve to stave off the crisis naturally resulting from war. The average deposit, £18 9s., is too small. In addition, it must be borne in mind that the savings banks would not be in a position to meet a general or even a very large withdrawal of deposits. The deposits in these savings banks amount to £32,900,000, of which over £25,000,000 is placed on mortgage, and £63,500,000 in the public funds. It is obvious that to realise these mortgages in a short time would be impossible, while state securities in a time of war could only be sold at an immense loss. The associations and individuals to whom the remainder of the money is lent would not be able in a moment of crisis to repay their loans, and only the cash in the offices of the savings banks—that is, but £350,000—would be at the disposal of the depositors.

It is very necessary to note that in those industrial localities where the stoppage of work would be felt most acutely, the Socialist teaching and propaganda are most widely spread.

With such a state of affairs, what could the government and society do to lessen the disaster ? A certain number of hands deprived of industrial work might be turned to agriculture, and replace the agricultural labourers summoned to the colours. But, in the first place, only the strongest of the manufacturing class could turn to labour in the field, and the vast majority is unfit for such work. In addition, such men would unwillingly

take to field labour, all the more so because the treatment
of agricultural labourers in Germany is inferior to that to
which factory hands have been accustomed.

To organise public works on a great scale is a difficult
task. And the very nature of such works by which the
state might undertake to help the unemployed is by no
means fit for all. Public works require either great physical
strength or special training. And workmen who have been
engaged in weaving, in spinning, or in the manufacture of
chemicals would, for the greater part, be incapable of
work with the crowbar, the pickaxe and the wheel-
barrow. The experience of Paris in 1848 in this respect
is instructive. When workmen formerly engaged in
trades which required only attention and some dexterity
were given pickaxes and spades, it was found they could
not stand the bent position of the body, and soon had
their hands raw from the friction of the tools. The
government may give aid to the families of soldiers on
service, but obviously cannot feed the whole of the
unemployed population.

It must be noted that in Germany, in the number of
persons receiving incomes, the proportion of women is
very considerable. Out of every thousand persons
occupied in industry, trade and manufacture respectively,
176, 190, and 312 are women. The number of women is
especially great in the lower and ill-paid forms of work.
The greater part of the women are engaged in the following industries :

	umber of men Engaged.		Percentage of Total Number of Workers.
Making, repairing, and cleaning of clothing	551,303	...	43.8
Spinning and weaving . .	362,138	...	39.8
Trade	184,537	...	22.0
Hotels and buffets . . .	141,407	...	45.0
Preparation of food products .	96,724	...	13.0
Paper making	31,256	...	31.2
Stone working	27,660	...	7.9
Wood „	27,372	...	5.8

In general in Germany the rate of wages is very low,

the yearly earnings of individuals engaged in industry
fluctuating between £30 6s. and £50 2s., which to the
large families of the German working classes means
poverty. Women workers in Germany receive much less
than men, generally less than a shilling a day, while no-
where except in Anhalt do the daily earnings of women
reach two shillings. If 24 shillings a week be considered
moderate payment, over 24 shillings high, and under
15 shillings low, the distribution of workers according
to these categories appears :

—	Low Wages	Moderate Wages.	High Wages.
	%	%	%
Men and women together . .	29.8	49.8	20.4
Men separately	20.9	56.2	22.9
Women separately . . .	99.2	0.7	0.1

In view of the importance of this question we present
the result graphically :

Classification of Workers in Germany according to Wages.

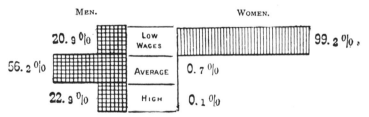

From this it will be seen that women receive much
lower wages than men. Less than a fifth part (19.76 out
of 99.2) receive more than 10 shillings a week, while 70
per cent. receive less than 10 shillings, and more than
half receive less than 8 shillings a week. To such
women, living independently, the cost of lodging and

s

food is not less than 5 shillings a week. It will be
seen how little remains out of weekly earnings of
6 to 8 shillings, for clothing, against sickness, and for
other unforeseen contingencies.

Thus it cannot be expected that on a stoppage of
work caused by war the workers of Germany could find
any considerable resource in their savings.   In particular
this will be the case with the women workers, and it must
be borne in mind that in times of disorder women always
appear as a dangerous element.   The assistance which
the government grants to the women whose fathers and
husbands have been called away to the army will be
insignificant, especially in view of the rise in the price of
food of which we have above spoken.

It is very probable that the condition of the working
classes in Germany will constantly deteriorate.   It is true
that emigration to America in recent years has fallen off, as
the following diagram shows.

Emigration from Germany to America in Thousands.

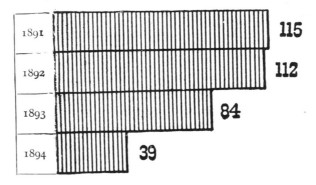

1891	115
1892	112
1893	84
1894	39

But such a decrease took place in consequence of the
difficulties with which emigration was attended.   In view
of the immense development of German industry, and
of the raising of protective duties in other countries,
Germany, in order to keep her place in the foreign

markets, has been forced to work and sell more cheaply. The lowering in the price of manufactured goods has had its natural consequence in a fall of wages. This in itself is a misfortune. But when we add the misfortunes of war, which will shorten work even at low wages, it is difficult to foresee the consequences.

It is necessary also to consider how war will react on the interests of the propertied classes in Germany. Their savings are very considerable, and the German debt is almost all held in Germany. War will produce a great panic on the money market, and the value of the securities in which are invested the savings of the propertied classes will be greatly depreciated. To carry on war it will be necessary to obtain a loan of fifty millions sterling, and, in the event of failure, it may be of several times this sum to pay contributions. And even in the event of a successful war those loans which will be issued for carrying on operations can be placed only at low prices. So early there can be no assurance of victory, while defeat might entail the disruption of the German Empire.

It need hardly be pointed out that shares in industrial undertakings will fall even more than government securities. But in addition to government funds and industrial securities, foreign securities are held in Germany to an immense amount. Since the introduction of a stamp duty on foreign securities, on their admission on the German Bourses, vast quantities of such securities have been acquired. Between 1882 and 1892 foreign papers were presented for stamping to the value of 20,731 million marks (£1,036,550,000), of which 5644 millions of marks (£282,200,000) were actually stamped, that is, admitted officially on the Bourse. In this number were admitted securities of countries which might take part in a war.

Russian	.	.	1003	million marks	(£50,150,000).
Italian .	.	.	968	,,	,,	(£48,400,000).
Austrian	.	.	660	,,	,,	(£33,000,000).
Turkish	.	.	266	,,	,,	(£13,300,000).
Servian .	.	.	57	,,	,,	(£2,850,000).

We will present this graphically :

Value of Foreign Securities stamped in Germany in Millions of Marks.

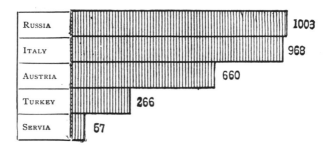

RUSSIA	1003
ITALY	968
AUSTRIA	660
TURKEY	266
SERVIA	67

Of course not all of the securities stamped in Germany remained there in circulation.   But if this be so, they have been replaced by others, since local capital still continues to seek advantageous investments.

The immense quantities of government and trading-industrial securities, both local and foreign, circulating in countries where the propertied classes are numerous and dispose of immense savings, increase the risk of war for such countries, and accentuate the crisis which it will cause.   Thus in Germany an unsuccessful war would result in immense losses in such securities, and in those which would be issued to meet military necessities.   But even in the event of a successful war, Germany would sustain great losses in the securities of those countries which had lost.

CHAPTER IV

THE ECONOMIC DIFFICULTIES OF FRANCE IN TIME OF WAR.

A CONSIDERATION of the economic convulsions which war would cause in France is not only very important in itself, but instructive in view of the fact that France has within recent times felt the whole burdens of a war. Judging by appearances, it might be supposed that a future war would have precisely those consequences which the war of 1870 produced. A detailed consideration of the results of the war of 1870, and of the degree of economic prosperity of France before and after that war, would show with what caution such a judgment must be received.

The change of rule in 1871 had a favourable influence on the economic life of the country. Although for a long time it was feared that the Germans would take advantage of the first pretext to declare war again and effectively restrain the military development of France, these fears in no way hindered the economic regeneration of the country. Disappearance of the dread of those political adventures so long carried on by Napoleon III. ; the general tendencies of the new government encouraging the spread of education and economic prosperity ; the keen struggles of political parties which prevented the unpunished violation of the law—all these in no small measure helped the development of France. The very loss of Alsace-Lorraine reacted favourably on her trade and industry. In those provinces industry was so highly developed that they furnished the rest of France with their products. With the foundation of the Republic began a great increase

in other localities in the production of goods formerly
obtained from Alsace and Lorraine.

In this time, also, when the prosperity of foreign and
especially of trans-oceanic countries increased rapidly,
there began an increased demand for French articles of
luxury and fashion.   The following diagram illustrates
the position of French trade since 1860 :

Imports and Exports of France in Millions of Francs.

IMPORTS.   EXPORTS.

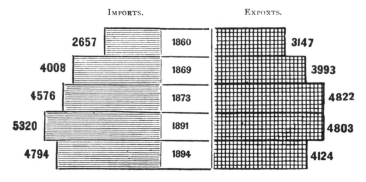

Thus statistics show us that the loss of Alsace-Lorraine
had no considerable influence.   The exports in the period
1869–73 increased at a greater rate than in the period
1860–69.   From that time the increase of exports continued uninterruptedly to 1891, after which we find a
decrease, caused by the protectionist policy of Europe.
These fluctuations became still more noticeable if we take
the average yearly increase of imports and exports in the
period 1860–69 at 100, and show the corresponding figures
for the following years :

		Absolute Figures of Increase or Decrease of Imports in Millions of Francs.		Absolute Figures of Increase or Decrease of Exports in Millions of Francs.	
In the period	1860–69	+ 150	+ 100	... + 94	+ 100
,,	1869–73	+ 142	+ 94.7	... + 207	+ 220.2
,,	1873–91	+ 41	+ 27.3	... − 1	− 1.1
,,	1891–94	− 175	− 116.7	... − 226	− 240.4

If instead of values which change we take the quantity of imports and exports, we receive results indicated by the following diagram :

Trade of France in Thousands of Tons.

4165	1860	4290
6773	1869	6847
7770	1873	7969
15.599	1891	16001
14.065	1894	14472

But these figures give no precise idea as to French trade. The following table is more detailed :

	Imports.			
	1863.	1869.	1873.	1894.
Cheese, butter, margarine (in thousands of tons)	7	14	15	20
Coal and coke ,, ,,	5388	7457	7461	10,266
Coffee ,, ,,	39	50	44	69
Cotton, raw ,, ,,	55	124	88	186
Cotton manufactures (in thousands of pounds sterling)	360	920	1880	1280
Flax ,, ,,	920	1760	2520	2440
Guano and manure (in thousands of tons)	82	118	137	181
Hides and fur ,, ,,	45	64	61	67
Cotton yarn (in thousands of pounds sterling)	280	480	840	720
Silk manufactures ,, ,,	180	1120	1200	1640
Woollen ,, ,, ,,	1320	2880	2360	1720

	Imports.			
	1863.	1869.	1873.	1894.
Meat (in thousands of tons)	8	6	23	24
Silk, raw „ „	7	8	9	11
Sugar „ „	236	201	154	166
Tallow, &c. „ „	40	37	36	32
Wool „ „	63	108	120	224

In comparing yearly statistics it is necessary to bear in mind that certain articles of import diminished owing to the development of industry within the country, and were partly replaced by other imports. Thus the diminished import of sugar is explained by the production of beet-sugar at home, which increased from 3833 million kilogrs. (3,833,000 tons) in 1873–74 to 5148 million kilogrs. (5,148,000 tons) in 1893–94.

The following two diagrams show the fluctuations in the external trade of France since 1883, in millions of francs :

French Trade in Millions of Francs.

IMPORT.

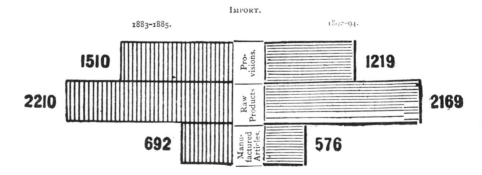

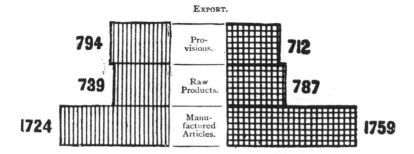

EXPORT.

794 Pro-visions. 712

739 Raw Products. 787

1724 Manufactured Articles. 1759

The revenue of France, which may be considered as a measure of the prosperity of the population, is shown in the following diagram :

Revenue and Expenditure of France in Millions of Francs.

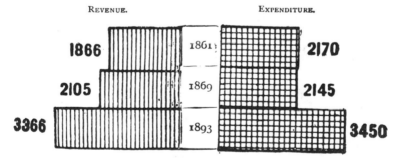

REVENUE. EXPENDITURE.

1866 1861 2170

2105 1869 2145

3366 1893 3450

A striking example of financial self-sufficiency is presented by France. The war, the Commune, the payment of five milliards (£200,000,000), the payment of the expenses of the war, the reorganisation of the army, the reform of the government in all its departments—all this required immense expenditure, yet France found all these resources within herself.

The debt of France has grown immensely, as is shown by the following diagram :

Debt of France in Millions of Francs.

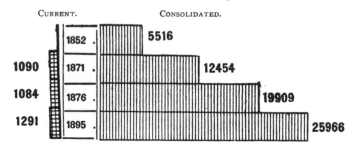

CURRENT.   CONSOLIDATED.

1090	1852 .	5516
1084	1871 .	12454
1291	1876 .	19909
	1895 .	25966

Thus since 1871 the debt of France has grown by almost 14 milliards of francs (£560,000,000). All this sum was found within the country, and in addition, immense sums were invested in industrial undertakings and in foreign loans.

As a measure of the increase of wealth in France we may take the statistics of the savings banks. The number of depositors and the amount of deposits are shown in the following table and diagram :

	Pass Books.		Deposits.
1869 .	2,130,000	...	711,000,000 fr. (£28,440,000)
1894–95	6,314,000	...	3,260,000,000 „ (£130,400,000)

Savings in France.

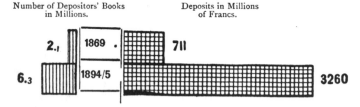

Number of Depositors' Books   Deposits in Millions
in Millions.   of Francs.

2.1	1869 .	711
6.3	1894/5	3260

Consideration of other statistics confirms the general belief as to the increase of wealth in France. In France the transfer of estates is subjected to a duty. The following diagram shows the value of estates passing by legacy and gift in France in millions of francs :

Average value of Properties passing by Legacy and Gift in Millions of Francs.

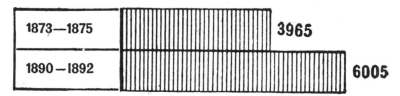

From these brief statistics it may be concluded that France has borne the heavy losses caused by the war of 1870 much more easily than any other state could have done.

The economic consequences of war would be much more easily borne in France than in other countries if it were not for a whole series of unfavourable circumstances, thanks to which the image of war appears not less threatening for her than for every other country. The interruption of communications will be alone sufficient to strike a deadly blow to industry. The moment export and import by sea have ceased the price of the necessaries of life will rise, the springs of income will be dried up, and many different industries will be unable to continue the production and sale of their goods. The theatre of war will become a closed market. In the country itself the demand for manufactured articles will decrease, not only owing to the fall in the income of the majority of the population, living from day to day, but also owing to the natural indisposition of the propertied classes to unnecessary expenditure in time of war. Factories, mines, and workshops, with the exception of those whose products are necessary for the equipment of armies, will be compelled to decrease their output. It must be remembered that in France a great number of foreigners are engaged

in industry.   The production of these in time of war would
also cease.   In certain industries the number of foreigners
rises as high as 22 per cent.   Another circumstance which
must have a serious influence and cause great difficulties,
is that a high percentage of the population will be summoned under the colours.

The following diagram illustrates the distribution by
occupations of the population of France in 1886:

*Distribution of the French Population according to Occupation
in 1886.*

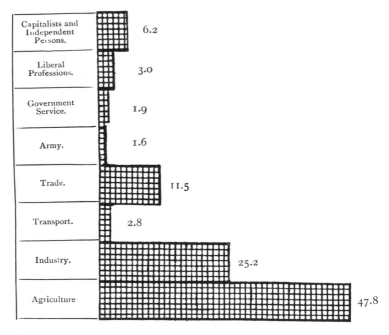

Capitalists and Independent Persons.	6.2
Liberal Professions.	3.0
Government Service.	1.9
Army.	1.6
Trade.	11.5
Transport.	2.8
Industry.	25.2
Agriculture	47.8

From this we see that nearly half the population of
France is engaged in agriculture.   The agricultural
class of the population is divided into the following

classes : Large and small proprietors, farmers and hired labourers. Of 17,698,000 persons belonging to this class, the labourers number about 2,772,000 men. In a country where landed property is distributed among a large number of families, peasant proprietors constitute the chief part of the population, and wages are comparatively low everywhere excepting in those departments where large farming prevails. The struggle for existence in this class of the population is much less serious than it was twenty years ago in many departments. Although agricultural labourers suffer less than factory hands from uncertainty as to regular work, their life on the whole is more difficult owing to the fact that they, while knowing the extent of their earnings, are deprived of all hope of improving their position. The peasant proprietor, the corner-stone of France, is bad material for agitation, but the hired labourer is in a very different position. It must not be thought, however, that in the event of war no danger for the state would arise from the agricultural class. The fact is that the agricultural population is not in a position to feed itself out of the land. Investigations made in 1882 showed that out of 5,672,007 registered agricultural properties 2,167,667 were of an area of less than a hectare (two and a half acres), and 1,865,878 were of an area of one to five hectares (from two and a half to twelve and a half acres). A detailed examination of these statistics would considerably reduce the number of small properties ; but it would still show that 1,700,000 persons of this class are little removed from the position of agricultural labourers.

Still the danger to the state from the agricultural population will be small. Of other classes of the population this cannot be said. In order to be convinced of this it is only necessary to consider the distribution of the incomes of the population.

I. Personal Earnings.

	Millions of Francs.
3,434,938 agricultural labourers . .	2,000 (£80,000,000)
3,834,580 workers engaged in industry, trade, and transport .	3,600 (£144,000,000)
1,132,076 serving for wages . .	1,000 (£40,000,000)
1,950,208 domestic servants . .	1,400 (£56,000,000)
3,700,000 small landowners, artisans, traders, porters, soldiers, sailors, lower officials, teachers, and others, whose earnings little exceed the earnings of labourers .	4,000 (£160,000,000)

II. Capitalists.

1,683,192 landed proprietors from 3½ to 4½ milliards .	
1,009,914 manufacturers, merchants, and others, from 3½ to 4½ milliards . . .	10,500 (£420,000,000)
1,053,025 of private property, rentiers, and free professions, from 2⅓ to 3 milliards . . .	

17,797,933	Total . .	22,500 (£900,000,000)

These figures, of course, are only approximately correct, but they may serve as a basis for determining different influences on the economic condition of the people. We see that the whole 10½ milliards (£420,000,000) when divided among 3,746,131 capitalists represents only 2800 francs (£112) the family. Leroy-Beaulieu supposes that in all France there are only 700 or 800 persons with incomes of 250,000 francs (£10,000) or over, and from 18,000 to 20,000 with incomes of from 50,000 to 250,000 (£2000 to £10,000).

From statistics relating to May 1886 in a population of 38.2 millions, the distribution by occupation was as follows :

	Women.		Men.
Agriculture and woods .	. 2,138,236	...	4,777,729
Independent persons .	. 937,539	...	3,108,625
Persons with higher duties	. 42,428	...	55,407
Labourers . . .	. 1,158,269	...	1,613,697
Hotels and restaurants .	. 164,964	...	325,318
Spinning and weaving .	. 376,602	...	414,695
Tailoring, &c. . . .	. 433,650	...	130,999

In addition to these France has many important fields of labour for women. In trade and in the banks served :

Women .	. 503,197	or	35.6 per cent.
Men .	. 909,058	„	64.4 „

In case of the interruption of the general economic life of the people the agricultural class will feel the crisis less acutely than others. On every farm exists some reserve of food, while that part of the population whose earnings come from industry and trade, and a considerable proportion of those living in service, will be in a desperate position—all the more desperate since in France women, as is seen by the above statistics, live by their own earnings. Taking such an active part in national work, the French woman has an extraordinarily beneficent influence on her country. It would be very interesting to consider what direction the activity of French women would take in a critical moment of the war. But here it is impossible to enter into the question.

France is generally considered to be a rich country, but even if we suppose that only 5 per cent. of the population lives in poverty, it appears that 2,000,000 persons require in times of peace either state or private assistance. In time of war the number of the needy population would, of course, increase. Indeed, the proportion of unemployed will be greater in France than in other countries in consequence of the fact that the most important section of her products are articles of fashion and luxury, the sale of which would, of course, decrease. The number of unemployed in France even in normal times is considerable.

If we may believe the French Radicals the proportion out of work in France amounts to one-fifth, or at the very least to one-sixth of the population. In Paris things are even worse. In favourable times one-fifth of the working classes are without employment for three to four months, while in years of crisis 45 per cent. of the working classes are without employment—that is to say, 300,000 families are without the means of subsistence. In ordinary times these unemployed draw little attention upon themselves, but in time of war their number would undoubtedly grow, and all would consider they had a right to government assistance. The following diagram shows approximately the amount of assistance given to the poor in France in 1889:

Assistance given to the Poor in France in 1889.

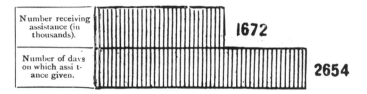

It is easy to foresee the consequences which must result from such a state of things in a country like France, where the socialistic movement bears unerring witness to the existence of general discontent with the existing order of things. If after the war of 1870 a Commune sprang up, what must we expect now when Socialism has raised its head and created a permanent organisation, while before the war the government of Napoleon III. crushed every attempt at socialist propaganda.

For another peculiar reason war would be more disastrous for France than for any other country. We have seen how rich is France in capital, how industrious and how economical is her people. But all these factors would not be so remarkable if it were not for a special circumstance which, while being itself of a negative character, has an immense influence on the growth of wealth.

As is well known, the birth-rate in France is considerably lower than in other states, while the death-rate is almost the same, so that the growth of the population is quite insignificant. There have even been years when the growth not only ceased, but a loss actually occurred. The following diagram shows the proportion of old men and children in percentage relation in the population in some of the chief European states.

Number of Old Men and Children in Percentage Relation to Population.

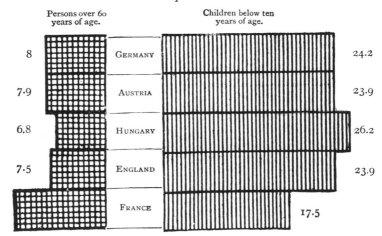

Thus in France the proportion of children under the age of ten years is only 17½ per cent. of the population, while in other countries it rises as high as 24 per cent. and 26 per cent. Persons of 60 years and over in France constitute 12.6 per cent., and in other countries 7–8 per cent. The relation of married and unmarried persons in France is also less favourable than in other countries, as is shown by the following sketches :

T

Number of Bachelors in Percentage Relation to Population.

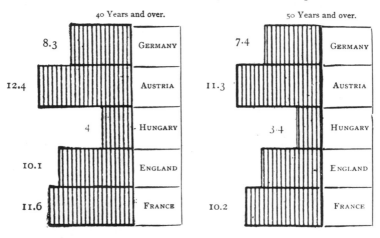

40 Years and over.

8.3   GERMANY

12.4   AUSTRIA

4   HUNGARY

10.1   ENGLAND

11.6   FRANCE

50 Years and over.

7.4   GERMANY

11.3   AUSTRIA

3.4   HUNGARY

ENGLAND

10.2   FRANCE

The diagram opposite shows the unfortunate position of France in all its blackness.

From this we see that in France the birth-rate is approximately equal to the death-rate, while in Germany the birth-rate exceeds the death-rate by 12 in every thousand. The diagram relates only to the last ten years. But the same phenomenon may be seen during the whole of the present century.

From the diagram on p. 292 it will be seen that 100 years ago the strength of Germany was 40 per cent. lower than that of France, while at the present day France is weaker than Germany by 20 per cent. From these statistics we must conclude that France will become weaker in comparison with other countries where the growth of the population is more normal. The artificial measures proposed for the increase of the birth-rate cannot be of much avail. Projects may be drawn up to increase the birth-rate, but to carry them out is shown to be impossible.

The decrease in the birth-rate has yet this inconvenience, that more care is taken of children, the death-rate among

Increase or *Decrease of the Population in France and Germany*
per Thousand.

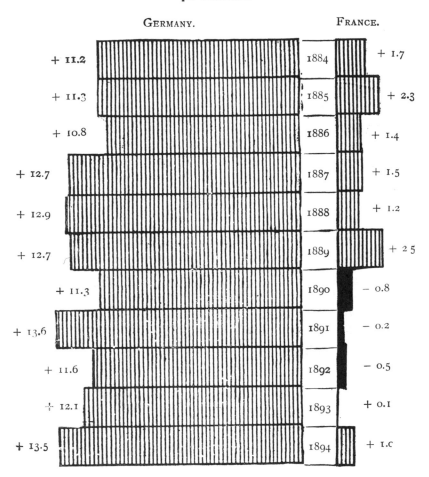

GERMANY.		FRANCE.
+ 11.2	1884	+ 1.7
+ 11.3	1885	+ 2.3
+ 10.8	1886	+ 1.4
+ 12.7	1887	+ 1.5
+ 12.9	1888	+ 1.2
+ 12.7	1889	+ 2 5
+ 11.3	1890	− 0.8
+ 13.6	1891	− 0.2
+ 11.6	1892	− 0.5
+ 12.1	1893	+ 0.1
+ 13.5	1894	+ 1.c

them is smaller, and the natural process of the elimination
of weak organisms is stopped, from which the general
physique of the people is bound to suffer.   In France even
at the present time the race is weaker than in England,
Germany, or Russia.

Number of Population in 1788 *and* 1888 *in Millions.*

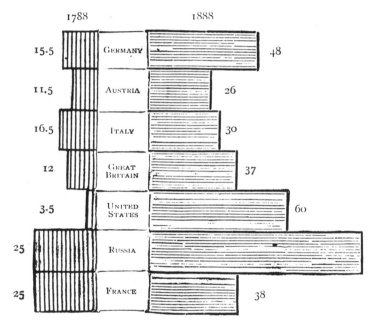

This unfortunate position of affairs has, however,
although only temporarily, good sides, since with an inconsiderable growth of the population France has more room
and a less serious struggle for the development of productive forces.   In addition, the people spend less money on
education and save all the more ; capital is not split up
as it is in more populous states, and in consequence
material prosperity increases.   But these considerations

do not alter the fact that every year the strength of France grows less and less in comparison with that of other states. But for the masses living to-day the future is hidden in the splendours of a temporary prosperity.

If we take the value of each inhabitant at 3000 francs (£120) and make an estimate of such wealth accumulated by France and Germany in the past century, we will get some interesting results, as shown on the following diagram :

Value of Growth of Population from 1788 to 1888 in Millions of Francs.

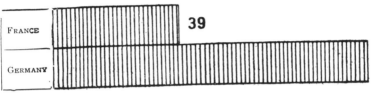

FRANCE **39**

GERMANY **97.5**

In the event of a war under modern conditions the losses, as we have already pointed out, would be immense for all states engaged. But France, above all, must avoid loss of men in consequence of her present position, as losses would be relatively greater for her than for other states. War could in no possible way change the position of France for the better. With the loss of the flower of her youth would follow not merely the "national danger" but absolute ruin.

France with so many milliards invested in foreign countries, and with the greater part of her savings invested in her own debt, is a country which, while admitting no offence against her honour or her interests, must at the same time aspire to peace, as in peace alone, and not in war with all its disasters and misfortunes, will she find the best path for a national genius to which all humanity is indebted.

CHAPTER V

EFFECT OF WAR ON THE VITAL NEEDS OF PEOPLES

DIFFICULTIES in the satisfaction of the vital needs of populations, interruption or stagnation in the employment of the productive forces of the population—these are the factors which will influence statesmen against undertaking war, or if war be undertaken, these are the factors which will at one moment or another decidedly veto its continuance. For certain states yet another danger appears (as one phantom hastens after the other in the vision of Macbeth), that is, the danger of revolutionary movements, not only political but also socialistic.

In considering the effect of a future war it is essential to examine the manner in which it will react on the needs and condition of the people. If famine is not to find states unprepared, some account of the dangers which follow on war must be taken. The consideration of this question may be useful in another way. By revealing with what a tremendous influence a great war may react on the conditions of peoples, it must result in a tranquillising conviction that in our time to decide on war without grave hesitation will be impossible.

I.

Those countries which in times of peace import large quantities of grain and other necessary products will stand in a particularly critical condition. Supply by means of railroad will be extremely difficult, and indeed there will be no country whence to import, since every European country will be compelled to shift for itself. Of the two countries which serve as the granaries of Europe, Hungary will be forced to place her superfluity at the disposal of Austria, while Russia will be deprived of the possibility of supplying her friends with grain, and will not wish to supply her enemies.

Transport by sea from America, India, and Australia

Home Production and Import of Wheat, Barley, and Rye.

—	Home Production in Thousands of Tons.	1888–91.			1894–95.		
		Import in Thousands of Tons.		Import in Percentage Relation to Home Production.	Import in Thousands of Tons		Import in Percentage Relation to Home Production.
		From Russia.	From other Countries.		From Russia.	From other Countries.	
Germany	10,151	1254	853	20.7	1773	1330	30.5
France .	9,852	295	656	9.6	448	635	11.0
England	3,672	721	2770	95.0	1885	3493	146.4
Italy . .	2,410	361	262	25.8	535	83	25.7
Austria .	6,016	—	28	0.5	47	62	1.8

will become impossible, as it is unquestionable that in the beginning of war privateering will be carried on, interrupting communication with trans-oceanic countries, or at the very best making transport so difficult that freight and insurance will rise very high, and thus the price of trans-oceanic supplies will rise prohibitively. It is enough to remember that in the time of the Crimean war, when import from Russia alone ceased, the price of wheat in England rose 80 per cent. In the American Civil War the operations of a single Southern cruiser, the *Alabama,* were enough to cause a perceptible rise in the price of wheat.

Thus it becomes necessary to determine the degrees of peril to which in the event of a great war the different states of Europe will be subjected in the feeding of their populations.

A calculation of the times in the course of which the population of each state may exist on the local production of wheat, barley, and rye can be made from the table given on the preceding page.*

If on the foundation of these figures we calculate the number of days on which food will be lacking after the exhaustion of local products we find the following results :

	1888–91.		1894–95.
In Germany . . .	69 days	...	102 days.
„ France . . .	32 „	...	36 „
„ England . . .	178 „	...	274 „
„ Italy . . .	76 „	...	75 „
„ Austria . . .	2 „	...	7 „

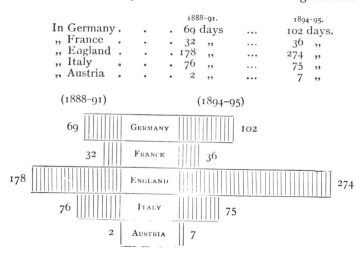

(1888–91)   (1894–95)

69 GERMANY 102

32 FRANCE 36

178 ENGLAND 274

76 ITALY 75

2 AUSTRIA 7

The greatest danger will consequently threaten England, which imports the largest quantity of grain, by far the greatest part from trans-oceanic countries.   Germany and

* Statistics from "Statistisches Jahrbuch für das Deutsche Reich," "Annuaire Statistique de la France," "Oesterreichisches Statistisches Handbuch," "Annuario Statistico Italiano," "Obzor Vneshni Torgovli," &c.

Italy will find themselves in a better, although still in a difficult position. Germany imports foreign grain, for the greater part Russian, for 2–3 months, and Italy for about 2½ months. France will suffer only from a month's deficiency, while Austria may be considered as fully supplied.

The most favourable position will be occupied by Russia, which with her export trade interrupted will not only not suffer from deficiency but will possess so much superfluous grain that her population can in no way suffer. The export from Russia of wheat, barley, and rye in the course of the periods considered shows a yearly average of 3,967,213 tons, or a superfluity after the satisfaction of local requirements of 21.6 per cent.

In addition to wheat, barley, and rye, we find a considerable deficiency in oats; for all the states of Central Europe mentioned, with the exception of Austria, produce less oats than is required for local needs.

Production and Import of Oats.

	Home Production in Thousands of Tons.	1888–91.			1894–95.		
—		Import in Thousands of Tons.		Import constitutes Percentage of Production.	Import in Thousands of Tons.		Import constitutes Percentage of Production.
		From Russia.	From other Countries.		From Russia.	From other Countries.	
Germany .	4759	183	4	3.9	263	63	6.8
France .	3279	131	82	6.5	227	187	12.6
England .	3065	426	262	22.4	625	163	25.7
Italy . .	213	13	11	11.5	—	5	2.3
Austria .	2792	—	—	—	66	48	4.1

From which appears the following deficiency of home production :

	1888-91.		1894 95.
In Germany . . .	18 days	...	31 days
„ France . . .	21 „	...	41 „
„ England . . .	66 „	...	76 „
„ Italy . . .	38 „	...	8 „
„ Austria . . .	— „	...	15 „

Number of Days on which Oats would be Lacking.

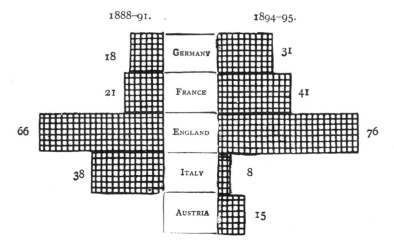

Russia, on the contrary, yearly exports 836,065 tons of oats, or a superfluity of 16.7 per cent. after the satisfaction of her own needs.

Such deficiencies of grain, of course, are not everywhere the same.   In each country there are localities which produce sufficient of these products.   In other localities, on the other hand, the need to import grain arises immediately after harvest.

The following table shows, for instance, the distribution of harvests in Germany :

District.	Superfluous Local Production, comparatively with the Requirements for One Inhabitant, in Hundredweights	Deficiency of Local Production, comparatively with the Requirements for One Inhabitant, in Hundredweights
Posen	1.78	—
Pr. Saxony . . .	1.63	—
Bavaria	0.84	—
E. and W. Prussia . .	0.57	—
Hesse-Cassel . . .	0.21	—
Average for all Prussia .	—	0.65
Silesia	—	0.624
Westphalia . . .	—	1.888
Brandenburg (and Berlin)	—	1.844
Hesse-Nassau . . .	—	2.06
K. Saxony	—	2.43
Wurtemburg . .	—	2.834
Pri. Rhine Provinces .	—	2.892
G. Duchy Baden . .	—	2.938
Other parts of the Empire	0.4	—

Thus the harvest appreciably exceeds the demand in Prussian Saxony, the kingdom of Bavaria, Eastern and Western Prussia—that is, in the Eastern territories of Germany near the Russian frontier. A considerable superfluity is also found in Hesse Cassel and in other parts of the Empire which for the sake of brevity are not set out separately. In all the other provinces the demand exceeds the supply, and in certain parts of the empire—as in Brandenburg, Baden, Wurtemburg, the Rhine provinces, and Saxony—by more than half.

And as in these parts of the empire agriculture occupies about 42 per cent. of the population, agriculturists through dread of famine will hold their stocks of provisions for themselves, and for the remainder of the population it will be necessary on the very day after harvest to draw grain from other localities.

In times of peace the industrial districts may import grain from America, Austria, Roumania, and Russia, and even from the eastern provinces of Prussia where a surplus exists. With the declaration of war, for the reasons we have indicated, this import must cease. To rely on supplies from Austria and Roumania is out of the question when we consider local needs and decreased efficiency of the railway system resulting from military operations. To avert famine, even temporarily, the eastern provinces might be drawn upon, but in consequence of its proximity to the theatre of war, grain there will be bought up for the use of the army.

Mr. V. I. Hedzvetski, in a remarkable article on " The Struggle with Famine in a Future War," comes to the conclusion that in the granaries of the future base of the German army near the Russian frontier there will be but a month's or a month and a half's provisions for 960,000 men and 220,000 horses. But on the figures of General Leer we find that the number of men to be fed will amount to 1,200,000. And as armies at the theatre of war will not be in a condition to supply their needs from local sources, it is plain that the above-mentioned stores must be constantly replenished, if not for the whole number of men mentioned, at least for the greater part.

Even if Posen and Eastern Prussia were in a condition after the satisfaction of military requirements to distribute part of their superfluity among the neighbouring provinces which require grain, which is very unlikely in view of the demands of the commissariat, still prices must so rise that among the poorer classes famine will be inevitable.

To form a general idea of the commotion which war would cause in Germany, we must take into account not only average figures of production, import and demand, but also the operation of undetermined forces, the influence of which may be disastrous. The very fear of need, owing to the impossibility of drawing supplies from the usual sources, may not only appreciably raise prices, but even call forth a panic. In the famine of 1891 we had a living example of the fact that, notwithstanding the full possibility of import of corn by sea and land, the dread of need may have immense influence on the rise of prices.

It is necessary also to take into account the fact that between the harvests of different years a considerable difference exists. If we take the average yearly harvest in the period 1885–1889 in different countries, in millions of bushels, at a hundred, then for separate years in each country we will find the following departure from the average:

	Average Harvest in 1885–89 in Millions of Bushels taken at 100.	Harvest 1885–89.			
		Maximum.		Minimum.	
—		Year.	Per Cent.	Year.	Per Cent.
Russia	1725.7	1887	114.7	1889	86.2
Germany	701.8	1886	106.2	1889	91.9
France	701.8	1886	102.6	1888	96.6
Austria-Hungary	692.9	1887	108.4	1889	87.1
Gt. Britain	312.8	1885	104.5	1887	95.4
Italy	221.2	1887	105.5	1888	91.9
Roumania	140.9	1887	135.5	1885–86	77.7
Servia	25.9	1888	131.9	1885 1886 1887 1889	91.5

From these statistics we see that the departure in Germany amounts to 6 per cent. above the average and to 8 per cent. below it. In other countries the difference is still more striking, as for instance in Russia and Austria, where in consequence of a lower culture, harvests are more unequal. In Russia this difference amounts on both sides to 14 per cent., while in Austria the difference amounts to 8 per cent. on the good side and 13 per cent. on the bad.

All these conditions: the small production in comparison with the demand, the cessation of import from abroad, the indispensable supply of millions of soldiers who consume much more than when fed at their own expense at home, and finally, the efforts of the prosperous part of the population tc guarantee themselves by storage against the danger of famine—all these conditions must inevitably give rise to vast speculations in wheat which will cause an unprecedented rise in prices.

The disasters which will take place in consequence of the want of bread in time of war have not failed to attract the attention of statesmen and economists.   Still this question, notwithstanding its gravity, has up till to-day remained an abstract one, and has never permeated to the minds of the people.

In the German parliament the problem was raised more than once, but was not considered publicly, and each time its solution was entrusted to the consideration of a secret committee.   The Government revealed to this committee its project for furnishing Germany with corn from Egypt through the Suez Canal, through Italy by the Swiss and Austrian railways, and partly from Hungary and Roumania. How vain these hopes would prove to be might easily be shown by an examination of the probable condition of maritime communications in time of war.   In any case, even if under the protection of the Italian and English fleets it were possible to import grain through the Suez Canal, the risk and costliness of such an undertaking would cause so great a rise in the price of bread that the difficulty would in no way be surmounted.

In view of this, other means for the solution of the question have been devised.   Thus the author of the brochure *Auf der Schwelle des Kriegs*, on the supposition that war may break out suddenly with France, comes to the conclusion that at present only three Great Powers may be considered independent as relates to the feeding of their population—the United States, Austria-Hungary, and Russia.   Germany after the stoppage of the export of bread from Russia would find herself in the position of a besieged fortress.   What would her position be in case of a prolonged war when home production would be diminished, and transport from oversea would be threatened by the powerful fleets of her enemies?

The author of this pamphlet proposes to found state granaries, not only for the supply of the army, but also as a guarantee against famine among the civil population. Such granaries would have the further advantage of serving as a corrective against exceptional rises in price.

But from the statistics given 'above as to the quantity of grain needed yearly, it is easy to see the difficulties which present themselves in the execution of this project. The quantity of provisions which it would be necessary to hold and renew would require such great yearly expenditure that the consent of parliaments would be extremely difficult to obtain.

II.

The deficiency of bread is but one of the difficulties with which nations will have to contend upon entering upon war. A similar deficiency will appear in many other necessaries of life. Of these meat is the chief, and it is necessary to consider the relations between the local supply and the quantity imported. The following table sets forth the relation :

	Trade in Meat in Tons (1000 Kilogrammes).			
	Import.	Export.	Superfluity.	Deficiency.
Austria . . .	328	8,820	8492	—
Russia . . .	20	1,623	1603	—
Italy . . .	123	1,443	1320	—
Germany . .	28,787	16,721	—	12,066
France . . .	20,262	2,016	—	18,246

From this it appears that Austria, Russia, and Italy produce more meat than they require, while Germany and France are compelled to supply their deficiencies by import. In Germany in 1890 the import exceeded the export by 12,066 tons, in France by 18,246 tons. Thus

those countries which produce sufficient grain are also
guaranteed against deficiency of meat.   In the event of a
prolonged war, Germany and France will suffer from a
deficiency in both the chief necessaries of life.

It is true that both in Germany and in France the stock
of cattle is so great that it seems possible by increasing
the number killed to compensate for the diminution in
import, but in view of the high value of the cattle raised

Superfluity or Deficiency of Meat in Thousands of Tons.

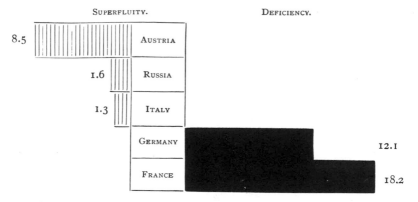

in those countries, the cost of meat will be raised to an
extreme height so as to compensate the producer.

In relation to salt Russia is in a less favourable position
than the Western Powers.

	Trade in Salt in Tons (1000 Kilogrammes).			
	Import.	Export.	Superfluity.	Deficiency.
Austria . .	—	10,098	10,098	—
Germany . .	20,967	199,607	178,640	—
Italy . . .	—	191,475	191,475	—
Russia . .	17,246	7,475	—	9771

Superfluity or Deficiency of Salt in Thousands of Tons.

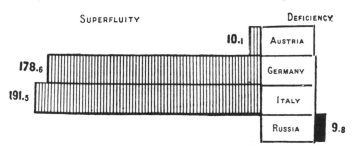

But the deficiency of salt in Russia of 9771 tons yearly may be supplied, with but an insignificant increase in price, by the increase of local production.

As relates to the supply of kerosene, which has now become a product of the first importance, Russia is in an enviable position :

	Trade in Kerosene in Tons (1000 Kilogrammes).			
	Import.	Export.	Superfluity.	Deficiency.
Russia	—	12,459	12,459	—
Austria .	252,459	6,230	—	246,229
Italy	70,000	—	—	70,000
France .	129,770	—	—	129,770
Germany	647,295	—	—	647,295

The known richness of the naphtha springs of the Caucasus makes it possible to export a considerable quantity of kerosene. Germany, Italy, and France all import kerosene from abroad. The import into Austria is also considerable, although local production (in Galicia) grows constantly, and in a short time Austria may be fully supplied by local production.

U

Superfluity or Deficiency of Kerosene in Thousands of Tons.

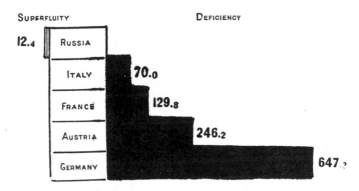

The question of stone coal presents itself as follows. The net import, after deducting the export, is, in France, 8049 thousand tons, in Austria 1623 thousand tons, and in Russia 1525 thousand tons. The export of coal from Germany exceeds the import by 4492 thousand tons.

Superfluity or Deficiency of Stone Coal in Thousands of Tons.

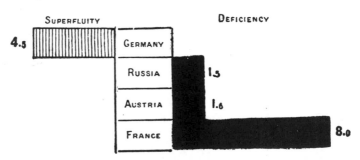

Thus in regard to coal Germany finds herself in the most favourable position, after her coming Austria, which may supply decreased import by increased local working, although, in consequence of the stoppage of many factories, this, in all probability, would not be required.

In Russia the supply of coal is thus obtained : From the Dombrovsk mines about 2475 thousand tons, from the remaining mines 3754 thousand tons. In time of war the supply from the Dombrovsk mines might cease, but, on the other hand, the demand would inevitably diminish owing to the stoppage of factories. A considerable part of the Russian population employs wood for heating purposes, and there will be no difficulty in this respect.

As regards cotton, Russia is to a considerable extent guaranteed by supply from Bokhara. Of wool, skins, and linen there will be no deficiency.

A grave question also arises whether all these countries will be in a position to renew their armaments and munitions of war. In this respect the majority of states are guaranteed. With the exception of Italy, Turkey, and Roumania, there exist everywhere immense factories for the production of arms and ammunition, so that in any case war will not be stopped through want of arms.

Thanks to the energetic measures taken by the government, the working and manufacture of iron and steel in Russia has grown uninterruptedly, as the following figures demonstrate :

	Production in Thousands of Tons.		
—	Pig-iron.	Iron.	Steel.
1881	460,000	286,071	287,678.6
1890	908,035.7	424,286	371,250

This quantity of material is, of course, more than sufficient for military purposes. In an Imperial decree of October 1866 we find the following directions : " To cease for the future to give government orders abroad . . . and all orders, both of the Ministry of War, the Ministry of Paths and Communications, and of the other departments of state to fulfil inside the country, notwithstanding the difficulties and inconveniences which may arise at first." As the result of this decision there arose a large number of factories furnished with the latest mechanism and machinery for the manufacture of articles of military equipment. It is enough to mention that even in 1880 out of 686 guns on the fleet, 498 were cast in the Obukovsk factory alone, and that these guns, as was demonstrated by test against armour, were in every way equal to the guns of Krupp. Thus the 12-inch gun, at a distance of 7000 feet, penetrated armour of a thickness of 12.6 inches, the 9-inch gun armour of a thickness of 6.59 inches, and the 6-inch gun armour of a thickness of 3.1 inches.

III.

It cannot be too often repeated that the disastrous consequences of war will be especially felt in countries with highly developed industries—that is, in Germany, France, and England. With the interruption of the ordinary communications, with the diminution in demand, and the approach of danger, factories, mines, and workshops, with the exception of those whose products are necessary for the equipment of armies, will be forced to discontinue working. The fathers of families, taken from their homes and sent to join the army at a few hours' notice, will leave their families, in the majority of cases, unprovided against the needs of the morrow.

The following statistics are interesting as giving an idea how far the population of Germany is guaranteed against hunger by the income it receives in time of peace:

	Millions of Pounds Sterling.		Per Cent.
Insufficient incomes amount to	. 16.3	*i.e.*	22.1
Small „ „	. 22.53	„	30.5
Limited „ „	. 13.345	„	18.1

	Millions of Pounds Sterling.		Per Cent.
Moderate incomes amount to	. 12.33	*i.e.*	16.7
Large ,, ,,	. 6.555	,,	8.9
Very large ,, ,,	. 2.69	,,	3.7

It is unquestionable that these incomes "insufficient" for supplying the first necessaries of life, and "small" and "limited" incomes represent the earnings on which an immense proportion of the population lives, and that the stoppage or even the diminution of income will place this proportion in a critical position. The earnings of those in these classes constitute more than 70 per cent. of the entire income of the people. The class which enjoys a "moderate" income can only to a small extent help those in need in the moment of danger. There remain the rich classes, and on them must fall the chief duty of helping the majority. But the income of this class, with "large" and "very large" incomes, forms only £9,250,000, or 12½ per cent. of the whole income of the people. In what way can the incomes of the rich class compensate the majority of the population for the decrease by a considerable extent, a decrease of a half or even a third, of the incomes of that majority which constitute £52,175,000?

Is it possible that 12½ per cent. of the total income, even though it went entirely to the aid of the needy classes, could appreciably compensate the latter for the losses to which they would be subjected (70 per cent. of the total income of the people)? And this, when we bear in mind that the incomes of the rich themselves will be reduced in time of war?

As relates to the provision which the working classes in a time of crisis would find in their own savings, we must bear in mind that these savings are very inconsiderable. Here is the picture drawn by Dr. Von Schulze-Gävernitz in his work, "Der Grossbetrieb" (Leipzig, 1892). "In the great majority of cases the earnings hardly cover expenses, and very often a deficiency appears which is supplied by recourse to charity, often to prostitution, while in many cases families are compelled to endure privation and even hunger."

In the investigations of Chief Factory Inspector Varischoffer, issued by the Bavarian Government, it is explained that even in large manufactures (for instance, in chemical factories) the workers receive barely enough to satisfy the " physiological minimum " of existence. In the great industries wages hardly suffice for necessary food, which consists chiefly of potatoes and rye bread. But these earnings are nevertheless higher than those yielded by handicrafts and work at home. Under the most favourable circumstances the wages of workers are sufficient only for food, nothing remaining over. It is plain, therefore, that in a critical time savings cannot be counted upon.

The unfortunate fact must be noted that need will appear with especial force in those very localities in which there is a deficiency of grain, and where the supply of grain will present the greatest difficulties. In the kingdom of Saxony, as we have already seen, there is an average deficiency for each inhabitant of 267.3 lbs. of grain, or about 50 per cent. of the demand, while in that kingdom only 22.6 per cent. of the population lives by agriculture, and 77.3 per cent. by trade.

In the Rhine provinces we find a deficiency of 278.1 lbs. kilos of grain per inhabitant, or about 60 per cent. of the demand, while 65 per cent. of the population lives on incomes derived from trade and industry.

In addition, it must be borne in mind that the proportion of the population living by industry grows rapidly. In an inconsiderable period of time the industrial population of Germany has been quadrupled. This increase has already gone too far. The working forces newly appearing, competing ceaselessly with the old, lower the wages of the older workmen to an extreme level. Statistics witness that even now a great part of the workmen in Prussia, though working twelve or fifteen hours a day, earn extremely little.

Industry.	Weekly Wages.
Glass and kerosene production	15s. 9d.
Iron foundries	14s. 8d.
Working of iron ore	14s. 10d.
Cotton factories	13s. 0d.
Chemical factories	10s. 8d.
Spinning	10s. 7d.
Cigar factories	9s. 6d.
Preparation of agricultural products	9s. 2d.
Milling of all kinds	9s. 10d.

Taking these circumstances into consideration, we must conclude that in certain portions of Germany the Government, especially in view of the propagandas and tendencies which now operate among the masses, will not be able to remain indifferent to the needs of the population.

A war with the terrible methods of destruction now employed and in view of the masses of people which will be sent to the front may, in spite of the predictions of military authorities who prophesy years of struggle, prove to be short and decisive. But even in that event the danger for the present social order cannot be considered small.

By a very natural coincidence the greatest deficiency of food will be experienced in those localities where trade and industry are most highly developed—that is, in districts thoroughly permeated by socialism. A glance at the chart on the next page, which illustrates the voting for Socialists and *Freisinnigen* at the elections of 1890, is sufficient to confirm this statement. In the districts marked in black were elected for parliament Socialists (Socialdemocraten, Socialistes - democrates), in those lined Freethinkers (Deutschfreisinnig, progressivists), those with black dots indicate that Socialist candidates stood but were not elected.

In 1890 were elected for parliament:

Conservatives	73	
Adherents of the Government	20	
Freisinnigen	108	
Members of the Centre	106	
Poles	16	
Socialists	35	

Popular Party	10	
Wollfites	11	
Alsatians	10	
Dane	1	
Anti-semites	5	
Others	2	

Chart showing the Comparative Development of Socialists and Freethinkers in Germany according to the Elections of 1891.

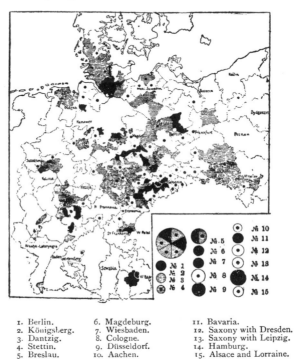

1. Berlin.
2. Königsberg.
3. Dantzig.
4. Stettin.
5. Breslau.

6. Magdeburg.
7. Wiesbaden.
8. Cologne.
9. Düsseldorf.
10. Aachen.

11. Bavaria.
12. Saxony with Dresden.
13. Saxony with Leipzig.
14. Hamburg.
15. Alsace and Lorraine.

*** In the localities marked in black, Socialists were elected ; in the shaded localities, Freethinkers ; the black dots indicate socialist candidatures which failed.

Even if it be assumed that the Socialists and their adherents in the ranks of the army will fulfil their duties as other citizens fulfil them, still the question remains : Will disarmament be carried out as easily as armament ? To answer this question definitely is impossible now. But before war is decided upon it is worth considering whether the most splendid successes can compensate for the dangers that hasten on the path of war.

In France the position will be somewhat better. Of 17,798,000 persons, whose incomes together constitute £900,000,000, almost five-sixths belong to the class of poor people whose incomes are quite inconsiderable :

	Persons.		Per Cent.
Working in industry, trade, and transport	3,835.000	*i.e.*	21.5
Serving for salaries	1,132,000	„	6.4
Domestic servants	1,950,000	„	11
Small producers, workers and subordinates whose incomes do not appreciably exceed the highest wages of workmen	3,700,000	„	20.8
Total . . .	10,617,000	„	59.7

The incomes of the above-mentioned categories amount to £400,000,000. Agricultural labourers number 3,435,000, *i.e.*, 19.3 per cent. Their incomes, amounting to £80,000,000, are also not guaranteed.

No better will be the position of England, where the question of the feeding of the people has recently awakened great interest. The *National Review* quotes a speech of Sir Samuel Baker, in which we find an argument which touches closely upon our subject. " To such a degree have we become accustomed to have everything necessary for the support of life and uninterrupted work arrive in our ports in due time, that we cannot even imagine a different position. Yet there is not the slightest doubt that in the event of war with a naval power the price of wheat would rise greatly in England, and, reacting immediately on all industries, produce an unprecedented catastrophe. In her present state of defence, England has not the strength to guarantee the transport of provisions." Lord Charles Beresford, with similar confidence, declared that in time of war England could not count upon the supply from oversea of the necessaries of life. Admiral Hornby,

presiding at a meeting with the object of presenting a
petition to the Government on the subject of the taking
of precautions against the stoppage of supplies, said
"that if England gained several victories at sea, and
the regular transport of provisions were still interrupted, it would be worse for the people than several
defeats."

In Russia, at first sight, the position of the people in
the case of war seems enviable ; 86 per cent. of the
population is engaged in agriculture.   But, as the price
of agricultural products is very low, the agricultural class
earns an income amounting only to 52 per cent. of the
general income, while in Germany an agricultural
population of 37 per cent. earns 35 per cent. of the
income, in France 42 per cent. of agriculturists earn 40
per cent. of the total income, and in Austria 49 per cent.
of agriculturists earn 45 per cent. of the income.

But worse than this is the fact that s⌐vings in Russia
are inconsiderable, and thus the consequences of war for
Russia might be not less terrible than for other countries.
Such a proposition is all the more probable since the
poverty arising from war springs not only from direct
losses, but from the disorganisation caused by the
destruction of ordinary relations, and by the fall of
values.   To cover the expenditure on war all states will
be compelled to take refuge in the raising of loans or the
issue of paper money.

The price of all the necessaries of life must grow,
and the purchasing power of the inconsiderable savings
possessed by the people will be greatly diminished.

All this leads to the conclusion that, *nolens volens*,
governments will be forced to take on themselves the care
of feeding the families of those serving with the army.
The results of such an undertaking cannot be foreseen.
If we suppose that governments will be forced to interfere
in the regulation of prices, and to support the population,
we must ask, will it be easy after the war to abandon this
practice and re-establish the old order ?   And will not this
moment of transition to the normal order of things be

characterised by events similar to those which took place in France after the war of 1870–71 ?

The destitute position of the population in time of war may be extremely dangerous to social order if war be prolonged, and in the opinion of very authoritative military writers this is more than probable. In connection with this subject we may quote the opinion of General Leer : " Even with small armies, the years 1812–13–14 present a continuous three years war. How much time will be needed to conquer (to employ the expression of Von der Goltz) the modern Antæus and tear him from the earth, sending against him army after army ? The impending struggle will not be decided by swift, heavy blows, but will be prolonged, it may be, even for years." Such is the opinion of the best German and French military specialists—war with Russia cannot be finished in one year, but will require several campaigns.

In the composition of the German army will be found the whole male population fit for service, from 17 to 45 inclusive. Considering that for agricultural labour the working age is between 15 and 65 years, it will be shown that 56 per cent. of the working class will be called under the flag. Even if we suppose that not all Germans liable to service will be employed in war, still if Germany proposes, as was announced by Caprivi, to carry on an offensive war on both frontiers, it will be necessary to withdraw from work such a quantity of working forces that the remaining population will not be able to accomplish a work which in times of peace occupies the whole working male population. For this reason alone production in time of war must be greatly diminished ; the need for the import of food will grow ; and the question of supply will become a hopeless one.

In addition to this insufficiency of workers, we may point also to the difficulty which will arise in the matter of horses. If we may believe the statistics given in *L'Année Militaire* in 1892 the demand for horses in the different states on mobilisation will be as shown in the following table :

—	In Thousands.			From each Hundred Horses will be required for War Purposes:
	In Time of Peace Army holds	In Time of War will be required	Number of Horses in the Country.	
Russia .	160	340	25,000	1.36
France .	142	308	3,000	10.26
England .	15	14	2,000	0.70
Italy . .	45	75	750	10.0
Austria .	77	173	4,000	4.32
Germany .	116	334	3,000	11.13

Percentage of Horses which would be taken for Military Purposes.

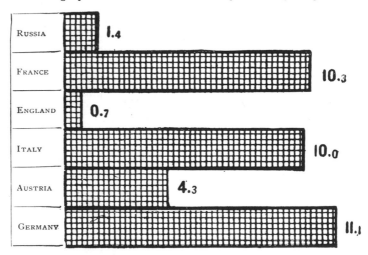

Of the 334,000 horses which will be required by Germany the majority will of course be taken from farmers. But this cannot fail to react injuriously on agriculture. It must not be forgotten that with the intense system of farming in Germany, fields never rest, one crop follows after another, and delay in working will undoubtedly cause difficulties unknown under the more primitive systems of farming. As is well known, a holiday is kept in Germany at the beginning of field labours, the so-named *Busstag* (day of prayer and penitence), and after this work is carried on through the whole summer without intermission on Sundays or holidays. In Germany, even under normal conditions, labour is so intensely utilised that to supply the labour of those serving with the army by working the remaining labourers on holidays is impossible.

In the German army will be found 38 per cent., in the French 42 per cent., and in the Austrian 49 per cent. of the total number of agriculturists. Even if we suppose that a certain proportion of factory labour will be diverted to agriculture, it is nevertheless unquestionable that the harvests in time of war will be sensibly diminished.

In Russia this question rests on an entirely different basis. There the absence of working agriculturists will be supplied more easily than elsewhere, for an important proportion of the peasants' land is held in common. It is easy to be an opponent of this system of agriculture and even to attribute to it the low condition of agriculture among the peasantry; but it must be acknowledged that the diversion to war of a great number of working hands will be borne much more easily under this system than under individual proprietorship. In general the land abandoned by the labourer who has been summoned under the flag will not remain wholly neglected. Without doubt it will be cultivated by the *Mir*, and the owner of the land on return will re-assume his former rights.

In addition to this, agriculture carried on on a low level will suffer less from the neglect and even from the absence of the owner than a more intense system. In the absence of a system of progressive improvement, the agriculturist on returning to his home may be assured that he will find his land in much the same state as he left it when summoned to the front. The workers in factories and in industries in Russia do not as a rule cease their connection with the village community.   On the stoppage of factory work at the outbreak of war they will return to their villages and devote themselves to agriculture.   In addition, it may be noted that in Russia the number of holidays is so great that, if in time of war the supreme ecclesiastical authority permitted work upon holidays, this alone would compensate for the loss of working forces through the exigencies of war.

It must not be forgotten that out of the whole population between 20 and 50 years of age, the army (considering only attacking forces) will take in Germany 31 per cent. (3,000,000 men), in Austria 28 per cent., in France 47 per cent., while in Russia (3,500,000) it will take only 15 per cent.   As Sundays constitute 15 per cent. of working time, then the lost contingent of working hands may be compensated for by Sunday labour alone, without trenching upon the immense number of holidays which are observed.

Upon survey of the facts and statistics above set forth it is impossible to avoid the following conclusions :

(1) The advantage rests on the side of those states who possess sufficient means of production and who in consequence will be in a condition to carry on a prolonged war without the danger of internal difficulties.

(2) In view of the prime importance of the feeding of the population, those states whose internal resources are deficient must see that crops have been got in before war breaks out, and only in extreme cases decide on war before harvests are over.

(3) It is most probable that war will break out when the harvest of the country which intends to take the initiative is above the average ; with a bad harvest peace may be considered as guaranteed.

(4) The most serious indication of approaching war will be the feverish acquisition of provisions by those states which would be endangered by their deficient internal production.

(5) In time of war, and especially after it, the gravest popular commotions may appear in Western Europe.

CHAPTER VI

PROBABLE LOSSES IN FUTURE WARS

I.—Statistics for Estimating Losses.

Cold Steel.—The use of the bayonet, the lance, and the sword have not changed. As we have shown in detail in another place the proportion of casualties caused by cold steel is insignificant.

Small Arms.—Since the last great wars the power of arms has grown immensely and every day witnesses fresh improvements.

Let us quote some facts as example. In Germany, Austria, France, Russia, England, and Turkey a rifle with a calibre of from 7.62 to 8 mil. is employed. The distinctive feature of these weapons is the force of the blow, depending from greater initial speed and rotation of the bullet. This initial speed varies from 680 to 700 yards a second, and the number of revolutions from 2475 to 2640 a second. In the Italian, Dutch and Roumanian armies rifles have been adopted with a calibre of 6.5 mil., with an initial speed of 750 yards, and rotation 3830 a second. In the United States a 6-mil. rifle has been adopted. In Germany and Austria experiments with a 5.0-mil. rifle gave remarkable results. The significance of these changes may be understood from the fact that the penetrative force of the 6.5-mil. rifle is 44 per cent. greater than that of the 8-mil. rifle.

The effect of a rifle shot depends first of all upon the energy preserved by the bullet on reaching its target and then upon the weight of the bullet in relation to its diameter

and upon the speed of its flight. The following diagram
illustrates the difference in power of the rifles of 1877
and 1890.

*Amount in Metro-Kilogrammes of Living Force of a Bullet on each
Quadratic Centimetre of its Transverse Area on Striking
Obstacles at various Ranges.*

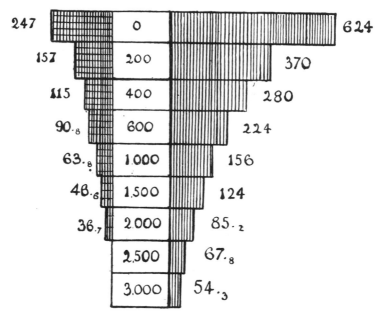

As concerns the 5-mil. bullets their striking force very
considerably exceeds that of the 7.66-mil. bullet.

What will be the effect of such projectiles when
employed in war by soldiers equal in equipment and
training it is difficult to foretell precisely. Nevertheless
such experiments and investigations as have been made
help us to form a very vivid picture of the future battlefield.

Experiments in the use of the 5-mil. Mauser rifle

against the carcases of horses gave the following results. From a distance of 27, 220, 550, 1100, and 1870 yards, the bullets penetrated 5, 4, 3, 2, and 1 carcases of horses, in each case preserving sufficient energy to penetrate to some extent the following carcase.

Number of Horses' Carcases Penetrated by the Bullets of the Mauser 5 Mil. Rifle at various Ranges.

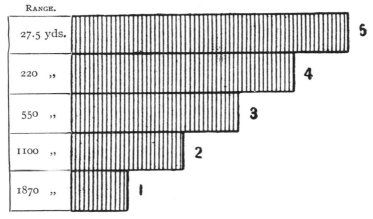

The enormous energy of such projectiles will for another reason cause an increase in the losses of war. Modern covered bullets are effective even in piercing metal. When the old round leaden bullets were used, a tree three inches thick or an earthwork twenty inches thick was an effective protection for soldiers. The modern small-calibre bullet will penetrate earth to the thickness of 78½ inches, pierce through a tree and strike those who shelter behind it. In olden times the second rank considered itself protected from danger by the first, the coward took refuge behind a companion. The modern bullet may not only penetrate soldiers in the first two, but even in the third rank.

From this we see that the number of victims of the modern bullet may be five times greater than that of the old.

x

In considering the degree of danger in battle the number of revolutions of a bullet has great importance. The following diagram shows the weight and rotation of bullets in use at various times.

Rotation and Weight of Bullets of Various Rifles.

Number of Revolutions.   Weight of Bullets in Grammes.

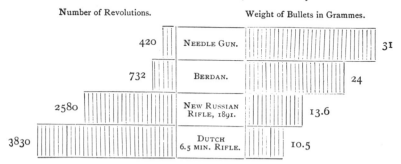

420	Needle Gun.	31
732	Berdan.	24
2580	New Russian Rifle, 1891.	13.6
3830	Dutch 6.5 min. Rifle.	10.5

This question has much importance, for upon striking something hard, such as the branch of a tree or a thick bone, the bullet takes an irregular position, and as its revolution continues it causes very serious wounds. It is for this reason that the intervention of a tree or a brick if it be insufficient to stop the bullet only makes it more dangerous. In Nirschau, in crushing the disturbances among the miners, but ten shots were fired, yet seven persons were killed and twenty-five wounded from a distance of from thirty to eighty paces. Many others slightly wounded concealed their injuries so as to escape legal prosecution. Each bullet struck from three to four men. This is explained by the thickness of the mob and the shortness of range. Of the wounded men six died, so that the percentage of death from wounds was 24 per cent., while in the war of 1870 it was only 12 per cent. The general mortality among those struck by bullets was 40.6 per cent.

It cannot be doubted that the immense increase in the penetrative force of bullets, and the gravity of the injuries inflicted, will be one of the most striking characteristics of a future war.   The effect of the deformation of bullets on striking hard substances will also be considerable, but concerning this we have no statistics.

The first quality of a rifle is accuracy of fire.   In this respect modern weapons possess qualities which ensure a number of casualties incomparably greater than in the past.   The bullet of the 6-mil. Mannlicher rifle for a distance of 750 yards will fly so close to the ground that it will strike everything in the line of fire for that distance. With the rifles employed in the war of 1870, the effective distance in a range of 650 yards was 30 yards for the Dreuze and 35 yards for the chassepot.   In other words the field of death has grown twenty times.   At a greater range than 750 yards the bullets of 1870 almost always struck soldiers on the point of fall ; at the present time the Mannlicher bullet aimed at a target 960 yards away, flies so low that it would strike a man for 110 yards of its flight.   Even at a range of 1300 yards it would be effective for 62 yards.   The following diagrams show this difference more plainly.

Zone of Effective Fire against Infantry (1 m. 70 cm. *in height*)
at various Ranges.

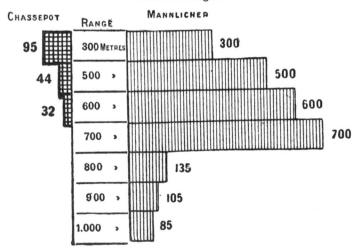

*Breadth of Zone of Effective Fire against Cavalry (2 m. 70 cm.
in height) at various Ranges*

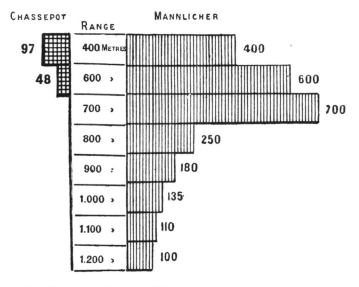

In all armies firing drill has been brought to perfection.
The quantity of cartridges expended in training is incomparably greater than before, and the most ingenious
methods have been devised for showing inaccuracy of fire
or nervousness.

It is easy to see how these circumstances will influence
future losses. At the present time the success of aim
depends only upon the proper holding of the rifle.
Raising the small-calibre rifle to the shoulder and firing
mechanically and horizontally, at the present day the
rifleman covers a space of 650 to 750 yards. Where in
1870 a special order was needed and attention had to be
paid to its execution, the mere mechanical use of the
weapon is now necessary. For this reason, too, the
range of useful fire, which will not involve waste of
cartridges, has immensely increased, as the following
diagram shows:

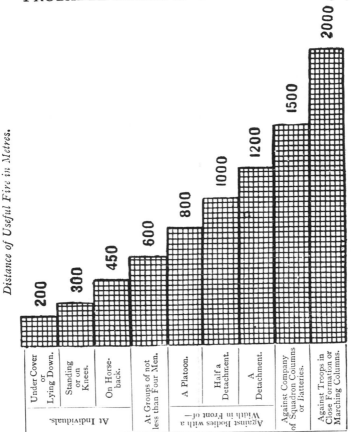

The effect of improved training may be shown by the following figures. In Russia up to 1874, at 650 yards range the accuracy of fire of a battalion was 25 per cent.; to-day, with improved training, it is as high as 69 per cent., or almost three times better. The modern rifle so nearly approaches perfection that a well-trained marksman almost certainly hits his mark. In the French and German armies the percentages of successful fire against an infantryman are shown by the following diagrams:

Percentage of Hits in Fire at One Infantryman.

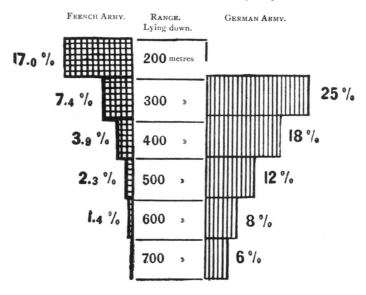

FRENCH ARMY.   RANGE.   GERMAN ARMY.
                   Lying down.

17.0 %	200 metres	
7.4 %	300 »	25 %
3.9 %	400 »	18 %
2.3 %	500 »	12 %
1.4 %	600 »	8 %
	700 »	6 %

Kneeling.

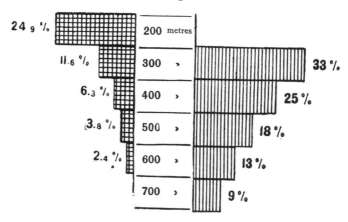

24.9 %	200 metres	
11.6 %	300 »	33 %
6.3 %	400 »	25 %
3.8 %	500 »	18 %
2.4 %	600 »	13 %
	700 »	9 %

Percentage of Hits in Fire at One Infantryman.

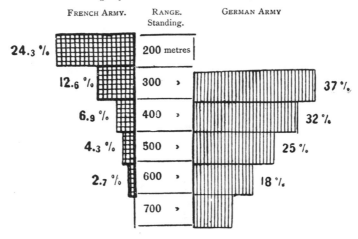

FRENCH ARMY.	RANGE. Standing.	GERMAN ARMY
24.3 %	200 metres	
12.6 %	300 »	37 %,
6.9 %	400 »	32 %
4.3 %	500 »	25 %.
2.7 %	600 »	18 %.
	700 »	

Besides these improvements in weapons all tending to the increase of casualties, the systems of measuring distances have been improved at the same rate. The improved instrument of Colonel Paskevitch adopted by the Russian army ten years ago measures up to 7000 yards in three minutes, while it weighs less than 72.6 lbs. The accuracy of this instrument may be seen from the following diagram :

Deviation of the Paskevitch Instrument in Metres.

At a Range of

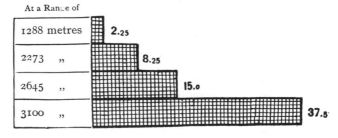

1288 metres	2.25
2273 ,,	8.25
2645 ,,	15.0
3100 ,,	37.5

In later years even more accurate instruments have been constructed.

The increase in the number of cartridges, already mentioned in another connection, carried by soldiers is another factor increasing losses. With the Berdan rifle a Russian infantryman carried 84 cartridges, with the new weapons 150 cartridges; with the 5-mil. rifle the number carried will reach 270.

Number of Cartridges carried by one Soldier with Different Rifles.

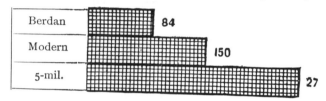

Berdan	84
Modern	150
5-mil.	27

With an even smaller calibre the number of cartridges carried will be from 380 to 575. If we assume that, without having recourse to the reserve, the number of cartridges now carried will be expended, it is easy to see how losses will be increased. The smokelessness of powder is another factor in increasing losses. But to this we have already referred more than once.

On the above statistics we have constructed the following table showing how the old loss of 18 per cent. from rifle fire will be increased, in all cases the lowest conceivable increase having been taken :

From increase of energy	7 per cent.
" " in revolutions and from deformation of bullet	4 "
" " in accuracy	18 "
" improved means of observation and measuring	2 "
" absence of smoke. &c.	2 "
" increase in quantity of cartridges	12 "

From which it appears that the general loss from rifle-fire will grow to 63 per cent. That this estimate is not exaggerated is shown by the Chilian war. Yet, as already stated in the beginning of this work, Professor Gebler gives even a higher value to the effectiveness of the new weapons :

Rifle of 1871	.	.	.	.	100 per cent.
French rifle of 1886	.	.	.	433	„
German rifle	.	.	.	.	474	„
5-mil. rifle	.	.	.	.	1337	„

In comparison with this our calculations appear very moderate.

Artillery.—Of the effect of artillery fire the past can give little idea. Such authoritative writers as General Wille, Professor Pototski, and Captain Moch declare that the quick-firing guns now built in France, Germany, and Russia are at least twice as effective as the 1891 type, of which Langlois said : " We have before us a whole series of improvements of the utmost importance, and must admit that war material has become entirely different from that employed in past wars." In addition to this the quantity of artillery has increased immensely.

In the present day as many projectiles can be fired in the course of a few minutes as were before fired during a whole battle, the best guns giving in the course of three minutes 83 shots and the worst 65. The accuracy of fire is no less remarkable. From a distance of 2000 yards guns have sent four projectiles into the same hole.

A comparison of the effect of 1000 rifle bullets fired by infantrymen attacking in open order with the effect of shrapnel showed that one round of shrapnel is effective over a space twice as long as, and not less wide than, the rifle fire. Experiments show that the fragments of these shells are thrown over a space 860 yards long and 420 wide.

On the basis of comparisons made by Langlois, it appears that the French gun of 1891 is twenty times more effective than that of 1870. In the same period the number of guns has increased from 780 to 4512. From which it appears that the French artillery of 1891 was 116 times more powerful than that of 1871. When the new quick-firing guns now being prepared—which in the opinion of specialists will be twice as effective as those of 1891—are completed, the French artillery will be approximately 232 times more effective than that employed against the Germans in 1870. It may be assumed that the losses will be correspondingly greater. The quantity of ammunition carried will be twice as great as was carried with the former arms. On the estimates of Langlois, in a future battle lasting only two days, every gun will require no less than 267 rounds of ammunition, while if the battle extend over three to four days 500 rounds will be required. With the 136–140 rounds per gun in the armies of the Triple and Dual Alliances, according to the calculations of General Müller, more than 11,000,000 men might be killed and wounded. With 267 rounds per gun 22,000,000 might be killed and wounded, and with 500 rounds 41,000,000. In consequence, it appears that artillery fire alone might exterminate eight times the number of the armies which could be placed on the battlefield. These figures seem absurd. Nevertheless, they are based on the detailed calculations of Langlois.

In the war of 1870 the losses from artillery fire amounted to 9 per cent. of the armies engaged. What they will be in a future war it is impossible even to guess. The quantity of artillery has increased, each gun being twenty times, and, since the introduction of the latest types, forty times more powerful than those of 1870. Even leaving the increase in the number of guns out of account, the losses of 9 per cent. would be replaced by losses of 180 per cent., though these new guns must in a short time give way to others more perfect. If we base our estimates on these new guns the results would be absurd, not through irregularity of reasoning, but simply because they would show that instruments had been prepared capable of destroying armies many times more numerous than could be placed in the field.

II.—Influence of Modern Tactics in increasing Losses.

In consequence of the use of long-range weapons and smokeless powder armies will be obliged to surround themselves, for a considerable distance, with commands of sharpshooters so as to render reconnaissance by the enemy difficult. The discovery and destruction of such commands will be a task of no small difficulty. In 1870 for the protection of the German rear 145,712 men with 5945 horses and 80 guns were employed. And since the strength of the infantry then operating was something over 455,000, it will be seen that a sixth part of the whole army had to be set aside to protect communications. Nevertheless the French sharpshooters more than once succeeded in cutting the German communications and causing confusion. If we bear in mind that these *franc tireurs* were exclusively on foot and had no military training, it will be understood what vast forces would have been required to guard communications from regular chasseur commands and cavalry.

In the present time, in all countries, an attempt is made to give some military training to all men who might be required for service in time of war. Such a state of affairs as resulted in France in 1870, when Paris was actually besieged, and yet hundreds of thousands of men liable to service continued to attend to their civil occupations, will not again be seen. At the very outbreak of war practically all the population liable to service will be either summoned to the operating army, or appointed to serve in the second and third strategical lines.

After this of course there will remain in the country a sufficient number of grown men for such work as the obtaining of information as to the enemy, and the burning of bridges and stores, &c. But generally it must be admitted that even partisan operations will be carried on by organised bodies, and systematically. A result of this will be that even a little war in the future will take a serious form.

During the manœuvres of the German army in Alsace-Lorraine attempts were made at transporting infantry in carriages for the purpose of doubling or even trebling rapidity of movement. Two experiments were made. The infantry either covered in one day a great distance, namely, 49¾ miles with halts for food and change of horses, or made two marches a day, one on foot and the other in carriages.

Military operations will begin in the form of a little war, considerable masses of cavalry being constantly maintained on frontiers, which will be immediately crossed, upon which reconnoitring detachments from both sides will come into contact with one another. It will be most important for such detachments to have light infantry with them in carriages. Of course their movements will be characterised less by regularity than by speed. But the command will be given to picked, experienced officers, and as a result such bodies will be much more dangerous than the French *franc tireurs* of 1870. At the present day a marksman from a distance of not more than 800 paces may pick off men at will, and as smoke will no longer betray his position his fire may be very deadly.

The losses suffered in attacks on fortified positions will constantly grow, side by side with improvements in arms. The attackers must advance in loose formation, taking advantage of inequalities in the ground, and of the light earthworks which they will throw up with the aid of trenching instruments. In the war of 1877 the Russian soldiers were imperfectly equipped, and ill-instructed in the making of such works. Yet, in spite of this, earthworks fully proved their value. It was such earthworks which prevented the Turks from driving the Russian army from the Shipka, notwithstanding the immense sacrifices they made. On the other hand picked Russian troops, with a numerical superiority of 25 per cent. and desperate bravery, for a long time failed to take the redoubt of Gorni Dubnyak although they got within a hundred paces of it. In the majority of unsuccessful attacks on Plevna the

Russian troops, after great loss, succeeded in getting within bayonet distance of the enemy; cases of nearer approach were very few.

Relying on the confidence with which the smokelessness and long range of his rifle inspire the soldier, commanders will stubbornly hold out in defensive positions, selecting natural cover and supplementing it with artificial defences. That earthworks will be had recourse to very often in the field is shown by the fact, that trenching instruments enter into the equipment of a certain proportion of all infantry. As further evidence, we might point to the instructions delivered to the Guards Corps in 1892 recommending defending bodies always to entrench themselves unless special orders be given to the contrary. It is interesting to see the degrees of equipment of European armies for such work.

Number of Sappers to 100 *Infantrymen.*

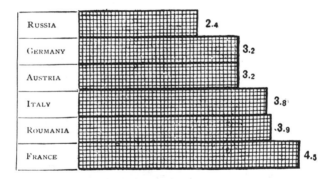

The Belgian authority General Brialmont considers that even the last proportion is insufficient. He declares that six sappers should go to every hundred infantry men. General Killichen goes even farther and would have a sapper for every thirteen infantrymen.

In former times every irregularity in the ground was

considered an obstacle in military operations. At the present day knowledge of how to take advantage of these irregularities is a great factor of success. This view has become so generally accepted within the last twenty-five years that all governments have undertaken the examination and measuring of all fields where a future battle might take place. This circumstance is very important. If a Plevna could spring up suddenly upon an unexamined and unprepared spot, what will be the case in a future war when every inch of frontier territory has been prepared for defence ?

In the opinion of the most competent authorities the war of the future will result primarily in a series of battles for the possession of fortified positions. In addition to field works, the attacking troops will have to overcome auxiliary obstacles of every kind near the regular fortifications, that is, at the place where they will run the greatest risk from the defenders' fire. Such obstacles will be constructed of beams, wire nets, and pitfalls. Their destruction will require immense sacrifices. The effect of artillery upon such defences is insignificant. Wire nets can only be destroyed by taking them to pieces by men acquainted with the methods of construction. But for this much time will be required. Meantime the foremost of the attackers will be under strong fire from the defence, and may very easily fall under the fire of their own artillery which will be supporting the attack.

Rifle fire over the heads of advancing troops will be practised more often than before, and may prove the cause of great losses. " Observe," says General Skugarevski, " the results of firing in peace time. The targets stand at some hundreds of paces away, yet bullets sometimes furrow the ground at a few decades of paces from the marksman. And this in time of peace. What will happen in war ? " Still more dangerous will prove artillery fire over the heads of troops, since want of coolness, a difficult locality, the distance of the enemy and other unfavourable circumstances may cause inaccurate fire from which advanced troops might suffer severely.

The amount of losses will depend more or less upon the skill or otherwise with which men are led. Yet even in peace times a deficiency of fully trained officers is felt. It must not be forgotten that a considerable number of the higher officers in modern armies have never been under fire. With the present composition, operating armies can never be properly officered, since the formation of new armies will so exhaust the reserve of officers of the line that a battalion at the front will have no more than eight out of thirty. Thus for every one of such officers there will be three from the reserve who will be inferior in knowledge, in discretion, and in applicability to conditions. Unskilful tactics will immediately react unfavourably on the amount of the losses. The deficiency in fully trained officers will be all the more felt as they will lose heavily in the very beginning of the campaign. The experience of the last wars, although smokeless powder was not used, and the rule that officers were to be first picked off was not generally accepted, shows how quickly the number of officers on the field of battle will diminish. As a guide in this respect the Chilian war may again be taken. Figures referring to two battles only show that while the number of men killed and wounded was 13 per cent. and 60 per cent. respectively, the number of officers killed and wounded was 23 per cent. and 75 per cent. But if officers are not there to give the example, men will not attack. Prince Höhenlohe, in his " Letters on Artillery," relates the following incident which occurred in the vicinity of Paris : " After driving the enemy from a village its graveyard was occupied by half a company from one of our best regiments. Quite unexpectedly the enemy made a new attack and regained possession of the graveyard, which we were obliged to capture anew. On this being done, I asked the men of the half-company how they could have given up the graveyard to the enemy. The soldiers answered naïvely : ' But all our officers were killed, there was no one to tell us what to do, so we also went off.' "

The German army in the war of 1877 lost considerably in officers, as will be seen from the following diagram :

Losses in the German Army in the War of 1870.

Killed.   Wounded.

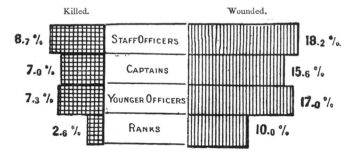

Killed		Wounded
8.7 %	StaffOfficers	18.2 %.
7.0 %	Captains	15.6 %
7.3 %	Younger Officers	17.0 %
2.6 %	Ranks	10.0 %

That is to say, the officers sustained twice as many in killed and three times as many in wounded as the lower ranks.

In consequence of improved means of destruction every meeting with an enemy will take a more threatening form than before, and every mistake, every delay, will have more serious consequences. The conditions of war have become enormously more complex. Yet for every hundred soldiers serving with the colours there will be taken from the reserves :

In Italy	.	.	.	.	.	.	260 men.
„ Austria	.	.	.	.	.	.	350 „
„ Germany	.	.	.	.	.	566 „
„ France	.	.	.	.	.	.	573 „
„ Russia	.	.	.	.	.	.	361 „

The majority of these reserves will have forgotten what they learnt in time of service. Of the officers also only a small proportion will be in a high state of efficiency. It would seem that with such conditions field instructions should be elaborated in times of peace, giving precise information as to tactical measures in every contingency. But, as we have already mentioned in another place, in this respect the different armies show deficiencies of various kinds. So far has the confusion gone that in the French army the expression is used "ordre, contre-ordre, désordre." And this is very natural when we bear in mind the want of experience of the new conditions.

Some writers express the opinion that it is a mistake to issue general instructions regulating tactics in a future war, as under certain circumstances their literal interpretation has the most disastrous consequences. In former times when fire was incomparably slower and weaker, and escape from the zone of fire could be effected quickly, the losses from mistakes in tactics were insignificant. But such are the conditions now that a mistake may lead to the extermination of a whole body of troops within a few minutes. The danger has grown immensely, while the factors of safety have diminished. Smoke will no longer betray the position of an enemy's troops, reconnaissance in the face of long-range rifles will be difficult, and the attacking troops will attempt to approach the defenders to within a short distance, at which the ballistic forces of projectiles can no longer receive development, from this distance the deciding weapon, as in former battles, being the bayonet.

But what will be the losses sustained by attacking troops before they get within such a distance? The advance, of course, will be carried out cautiously and in loose formation. Such an advance against an enemy occupying a strong position and firing over measured distances will be extremely difficult and may even require a two-days' labour.

It is not strange then that certain authors declare that battles will continue three, four, and even fifteen days. Other specialists find that we are returning to the epoch of sieges. Belgrade, Mantua, and Plevna may be repeated. It is very likely that the attacking army, finding decisive victory impossible, will attempt to lock up the enemy on the spot, entrenching itself and making raids for the stoppage of his supplies until the besiegers are starved out.

As we have already explained, the quick and final decision of future battles is improbable. The latest improvements in small arms and artillery, and the teaching of troops to take advantage of localities, has increased the strength of defence.   The modern rifle has immense power, and its use is simple and convenient. It will be extremely difficult to overcome the resistance of infantry in sheltered positions.   Driven from one position it will quickly find natural obstacles—hillocks, pits, and groups of trees—which may serve as points for fresh opposition.   The zone of deadly fire is much wider than before, and battles will be more stubborn and prolonged. Of such a sudden sweeping away of an enemy in the course of a few minutes as took place at Rossbach it is absurd even to think.   The power of opposition of every military unit has increased so greatly that a division may now accept battle with a whole army corps, if only it be persuaded that reinforcements are hastening to the spot. The case already cited, of the manœuvres in Eastern Prussia, when a single division sustained an attack from a whole army corps until reinforced, is sufficient evidence of this.   The scattering of immense masses over a considerable space means that a successful attack on one point by means of the concentration of superior forces may remain local, not resulting in any general attack on the chief forces of the defence.

In former times either of the combatants quickly acknowledged that the advantage lay with the other side, and therefore refused to continue the battle.   The result and the trophy of victory was the possession of the battle-field.   The majority of military writers consider the attainment of such a result very questionable.

From the opinions of many military writers the conclusion is inevitable that with the increase of range and fire, and in view of the difficulties with which assault is surrounded, a decisive victory in the event of numerical equality is possible only on the failure of ammunition on one side.   But in view of the number of cartridges which soldiers now carry, and the immense reserves in the ammunition carts, it seems more likely, that before all cartridges have been expended, the losses will have been so great as to make a continuation of battle impossible. To the argument that night will interrupt the battle we find an answer in the fact that, thanks to the adoption of electric illuminations, the struggle will often continue or be renewed at night.

In all armies attempts are made to inspire the soldiers with the conviction that a determined assault is enough to make an enemy retreat. Thus, in the French field instructions we find it declared that " courageous and resolutely led infantry may assault, under the very strongest fire, even well-defended earthworks and capture them." But the above considerations are enough to show the difficulty of such an undertaking.

Supposing even that the defenders begin a retreat. The moment the attacking army closes its ranks for assault partisan operations on the side of the defenders will begin. Indeed, it may be said that the present rifle, firing smokeless powder, is primarily a partisan weapon, since armed with it even a small body of troops in a sheltered position may inflict immense losses from a great distance. As the attackers approach, the thin flexible first line of the defence will retreat. It will annoy the enemy with its fire, forcing him to extend his formation, and then renew the manœuvre at other points.

While the first line of the defenders will thus impede the assault, the main body will have opportunity to form anew and act according to circumstances. The attacking army, though convinced of victory, finding that it cannot get into touch with the rear-guard of the enemy, which alternately vanishes and reappears, now on its flanks, now in front, will lose confidence, while the defenders will take heart again.

It is obvious that, with the old powder, the smoke of which betrayed the fighting front of the enemy and even approximately indicated its strength, such manœuvres were too dangerous to carry out. It would be a mistake to think that for the carrying on of such operations picked troops are required. The ordinary trained soldier is quite capable. Every soldier knows that two or three brigades cannot entirely stop the advance of an army. But seeing that the attackers may be so impeded that they will gain no more than four or five miles in a day, the defenders will have good cause to hope and wait for a favourable turn of affairs.

From this it may be seen how immensely smokeless powder has increased the strength of defence. It is true that in past wars we find many examples of stubborn rearguard actions facilitating orderly retreat. But even in those cases victory was too evident and irrevocable, and this encouraged the pursuers. The vanquished tried as quickly as possible to get out of fire. Nowadays with quick-firing and long-range guns the first few miles of retreat will prove more dangerous than the defence of a position, but the chain of marksmen covering the retreat may greatly delay the course of the attack.

It was Marshal St. Cyr who declared that "a brave army consists of one-third of soldiers actually brave, one-third of those who might be brave under special circumstances, and a remaining third consisting of cowards." With the increase of culture and prosperity nervousness has also increased, and in modern, especially in Western European armies, a considerable proportion of men will be found unaccustomed to heavy physical labour and to forced marches. To this category the majority of manufacturing labourers will belong. Nervousness will be all the more noticeable since night attacks are strongly recommended by many military writers, and undoubtedly these will be made more often than in past wars. Even the expectation of a battle by night will cause alarm and give birth to nervous excitement. This question of the influence of nervousness on losses in time of war has attracted the attention of several medical writers, and some have expressed the opinion that a considerable number of soldiers will be driven mad. The famous Prussian Minister of War, Von Roon, writing from Nikelsburg in 1866, said: "Increased work and the quantity and variety of impressions have so irritated my nerves that it seems as if fires were bursting out in my brain."

We have already referred many times to the probability of prolonged wars in the future. Against this probability only one consideration may be placed: the difficulty of provisioning immense armies and the probability of famine in those countries which in times of peace live upon imported corn. With the exception of Russia and Austria-Hungary, not a single country in Europe is in a position to feed its own population. Yet Montecuculli said : " Hunger is more terrible than iron, and want of food will destroy more armies than battles." Frederick II. declared that the greatest military plans might be destroyed by want of provisions. But the army of Frederick II. was a mere handful in comparison with the armies of to-day. It is true that ancient history presents examples of immense hordes entering upon war. But these wars were generally decided by a few blows, for there existed neither rapid communications for the purpose of reinforcement, nor regular defensive lines. Modern history shows many instances of prolonged wars. But it must be remembered that the Thirty Years' and the Seven Years' wars were not uninterrupted, and that the armies engaged went into winter quarters where they were regularly provisioned, and in spring recommenced operations resulting only in partial successes, the gaining of a battle, the taking of a fortress, followed by another stoppage of operations. Thus the long wars of modern history may be regarded as a series of short campaigns. In recent times, side by side with the long Crimean and North American Civil wars, we find the short campaigns of 1859 and 1866. Taking the last as example, the German military writer Rüstow jumps to a conclusion as to the " shortness of war " which is guaranteed by improved communications and arms. Such theorists were surprised by the fact that even the war of 1870–71 occupied seven months, although it, of course, may be considered as short having regard to the forces employed and the vastness of the results.

In the future, by virtue of concluded alliances, the whole populations of great states will take the field, every state having, in the course of years, made immense efforts to fortify its frontiers. In the last ten years France expended forty millions of pounds sterling on fortifications, the very nature of these having entirely changed. Instead of the old fortresses visible from afar and isolated forts easily passed or taken, we have fortified camps which can hardly be seen from a short distance, polygons with casemated quarters, where whole armies may be sheltered.

On whatever plans operations are founded the side which carries the war into an enemy's territory will meet with tremendous resources for defence. Uncounted millions have been spent to ensure that no great superiority of force can be attained by an invader whatever the difference in the time of mobilisation. Preparations have been made by all governments to stop the invaders, if not at the very frontier, then not very far in the interior of the country.

In the present condition of military organisation the responsibility for the supply of armies will rest upon the higher commanders who in times of peace have little to do with this affair. Meantime the more numerous the army and the slower its movements the greater will be the difficulty met with in supplying its wants. And in view of the long delays ensured by fortifications and defensive lines, the labour of provisioning troops will be immense. In former times it was comparatively easy to feed troops in time of war. Armies were small and moved rapidly from place to place. The present state of affairs is very different ; and delay in the provisioning of armies will not only cause great difficulties, but will have its influence in increased losses.

We have attempted elsewhere to treat briefly of the difficulties attendant on the care of the wounded in future wars. This question has also an important bearing on the question of losses, as the number of killed to a considerable extent depends upon the efficiency of the ambulance service.

The percentage of killed will grow considerably. The diagram opposite shows how modern small arms, not-

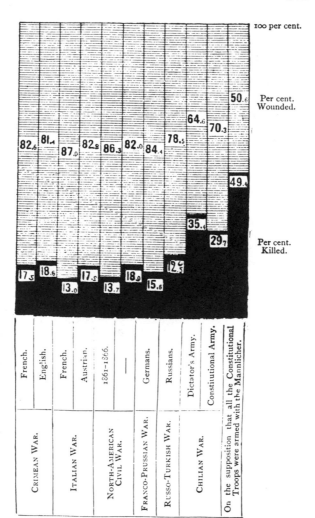

Influence of the Quality of Firearms on the Relations of Killed to Wounded.

withstanding their small calibre, are more dangerous than the old. Which shows that if all armies had been equipped with the Mannlicher rifle the proportion of killed would have been as high as 49.4 per cent., or practically equal to the number of wounded. This diagram has been formed from the general figures of losses, and to ensure accuracy it would be necessary to deduct the victims of artillery fire and cold steel. But as we have elsewhere explained an immense proportion of casualties are caused by rifle fire, so that the diagram is, probably, approximately correct.

The losses from wounds constitute but a small part of the total number of sacrifices. In past wars they have been but a fifth, the remaining four-fifths representing losses from sickness and exhaustion. Napoleon in the march to Moscow lost two-thirds of his army though he fought only one general engagement. The Russian armies operating against him, in the course of five months lost four-fifths of their strength. The losses of the Federal armies in the Civil War in two years (June 1861 to June 1863) amounted to 53.2 deaths in the thousand, of which only 8.6 were caused by wounds, and 44.6 by sickness. The mortality from sickness among the officers amounted to 22 in the thousand, while among the men it rose to 46. In the Franco-Prussian war the losses of the Germans were 34.7 per cent. from wounds and only 30 per cent. from sickness. But this is explained by the shortness of the campaign, and by the fact that, being greatly superior in numbers, the Germans were able to send their sick home. On the French side these proportions were reversed.

During the last war with Turkey the Russian armies, numbering in all 592,085 men, lost 16,578 in battle and 44,431 from sickness. In *L'Hygiène Militaire*, 1886, Morache draws up the following analysis of losses in modern wars :

War.	Strength of Army.	Losses.		Deaths in 1000 Men.	
		From Wounds.	From Sickness.	From Wounds.	From Sickness.
Crimean, French army . . .	309,268	20,240	75,375	64	236
Crimean, English army . . .	97,864	4,607	17,580	47	179
War of 1859, in French army .	128,225	5,498	2,040	42	15
Mexican, in French army . . .	35,000	1,729	4,925	49	140
Franco-German, in the German army	900,000	30,491	14,259	33	15
Russo-Turkish, in the Russian armies . .	737,355	36,455	83,446	49	113
Bosnian Expedition, in the Austrian army . .	260,000	1,326	2,168	5	8

In a future war, for many reasons, we must expect even more deadly results. Bad and insufficient food, in consequence of the difficulty of provisioning immense masses, will mean the increase of sickness ; and the overcrowding of the sick at certain points will complicate the danger both from sickness and from wounds, and thereby increase the mortality.

It is further necessary to bear in mind that modern armies will consist of soldiers less accustomed to marching and deprivation, while notwithstanding the lightness of his rifle, the infantryman has to carry a greater weight than before. The German writer Turnwald, who especially studied the question of the weight which the soldier can bear, finds that it ought not to exceed 57 pounds, that is, a third of his own weight. At the present time the infantryman carries 88 pounds. The weight of the equipment is undoubtedly a factor in causing the exhaustion and susceptibility to sickness observed among the soldiers during manœuv.res.   During manœuvres carried on by the garrison of Strasbourg no less than a third of the soldiers fell out, and the hospitals were filled with sick soldiers. It is true that this was in winter, and many cases were caused by frostbite.

Basing his judgment on the war of 1870–71, in which he took part, General Von der Goltz observes that "in a long and wearisome war armies undoubtedly deteriorate in quality.   Exhaustion and weariness may be borne for several weeks, but not for many months.   It is hard to remain a hero, ever ready for self-sacrifice, after daily battles and constant danger, after long marches through the mud, and nights passed on the wet earth ; all this has a bad effect on courage."

CHAPTER VII

MILITARISM AND ITS NEMESIS

THOSE who have considered the facts briefly set out in the foregoing chapters can hardly fail to agree that if European society could form a clear idea, not only of the military character, but also of the social and economic consequences of a future war under present conditions, protests against the present state of things would be expressed more often and more determinedly. But it cannot be affirmed that even this would bring about an amelioration of the present state of affairs. In all countries, with the exception of England, the opinion obtains that great armies are the support of government, that only great armies will deliver the existing order from the perils of anarchism, and that military service acts beneficently on the masses by teaching discipline, obedience and order.

But this theory of the disciplinary influence of military service is overthrown by the fact that, notwithstanding conscription, anarchism constantly spreads among the peoples of the West. It even seems that by teaching the use of arms to the masses, conscription is a far weaker guarantee than the long service of the professional soldier.

But the views of those interested in the present order do not extend so far, and are generally limited by considerations of safety at the present time. This safety the propertied classes see in large armies. As concerns the views of other orders of society, views which are expressed openly and constitute the so-called public opinion, these are too often founded only on those facts to which accident gives prominence. The public does not investigate and does not test independently, but easily gives itself up to illusions and errors. Such, for instance, is the conception of great armies, not only as guarantors of security, but even as existing for the encouragement of those industries which equip them, and those trades which supply them, with provisions and other necessaries.

It must be admitted that to decide the question whether militarism is inevitable or not is no easy task. We constantly hear the argument adduced, that there always have been wars and always will be, and if in the course of all the centuries recorded in history, international disputes were settled only by means of war, how can it be possible to get along without it in the future? To this we might reply that not only the number, equipment, training, and technical methods of armies, but the very elements from which they are constructed have essentially changed.

The relations of the strength of armies in time of war to their strength in time of peace in former times was very different. Wars formerly were carried on by standing armies consisting mainly of long service soldiers. The armies employed in future wars will be composed mainly of soldiers taken directly from peaceful occupations. Among the older soldiers will be vast numbers of heads of families torn from their homes, their families and their work. The economic life of whole peoples will stand still, communications will be cut, and if war be prolonged over the greater part of a year, general bankruptcy, with famine and all its worst consequences, will ensue. To cast light on the nature of a prolonged war from all sides, military knowledge alone is not enough. The study and knowledge of economic laws and conditions which have no direct connection with military specialism is no less essential.

Consideration of the question is made all the more difficult by the fact that the direction of military affairs belongs to the privileged ranks of society. The opinions expressed by non-specialists as to the improbability of great wars in the future, are refuted by authorities simply by the declaration that laymen are ignorant of the subject. Military men cannot admit to be unnecessary that which forms the object of their activity in time of peace. They have been educated on the history of warfare, and practical work develops in them energy and capacity for self-sacrifice. Nevertheless, such authorities are not in a position to paint a complete picture of the disasters of a future war. Those radical changes which have taken place in the military art, in the composition of armies, and in international economy, are so vast that a powerful imagination would be required adequately to depict the consequences of war, both on the field of battle and in the lives of peoples.

Yet it cannot be denied that popular discontent with the present condition of affairs is becoming more and more keenly noticeable. Formerly only solitary voices were raised against militarism, and their protests were platonic. But since the adoption of conscription the interests of the army have been more closely bound with the interests of society, and the disasters which must be expected under modern conditions have been better appreciated by the people.

It is impossible, therefore, not to foresee the constant growth of the anti-military propaganda, the moral foundations of which were not so indisputable in the past as they are to-day. To this moral sentiment has lately been added a consciousness of the complexity of the business relations threatened by war, of the immense increase of means of destruction, and of the deficiency of experienced leadership and the ignorance and cloudiness now prevailing on the subject of war.

All these tend to make the people see in war a misfortune truly terrifying. And if, even in the past, it was found that the sentiments of peoples are more powerful than any force, how much more so now, when in the majority of states the masses indirectly share in the government, and when everywhere exist strong tendencies threatening the whole social order. How much more significant now are the opinions of the people both directly as to the system of militarism and in their influence on the spirit of armies themselves!

It is impossible here even to outline the energetic struggle against militarism which is being carried on in the West. It is true that the advocates of the settlement of international disputes by peaceful means have not attained any tangible success. But success, it must be admitted, they have had if the fact is taken into account that the necessity of maintaining peace has been recognised by governments, and that dread of the terrible disasters of war has been openly expressed by statesmen, and emphasised even from the height of thrones.

As a chief factor tending to preserve the system of militarism the existence of a professional military class must be considered. It is true, that the changes which have taken place under the influence of conscription and short service have given to armies a popular character. On the mobilisation of armies a considerable proportion of officers will be taken from the reserve: these officers cannot be considered professional. Nevertheless, a military professional class continues to exist, consisting mainly of officers serving with the colours.

It is natural that the existence of such a numerous and influential class, which—in Prussia, for instance—is partly hereditary, a class in which are found many men of high culture, should be one of the elements supporting the system of militarism, even independently of its other foundations. Even if the conviction were generally accepted that it is impossible to carry on war with modern methods of destruction and in view of the inevitable disasters, yet disarmament would be somewhat delayed by the existence of the military caste, which would continue to declare that war is inevitable, and that even the decrease of standing armies would be accompanied by the greatest dangers.

It must be admitted that from the nature of modern life, the power and influence of this class will tend to decrease rather than increase. The conditions of war are such that military life is much less attractive than it was of old, and in the course of a few years will be even less attractive. In the far past the military class preponderated in the state and the very nobility, as in Rome, and at the beginning of the Middle Ages was formed of knights (Equites, Ritter, Chevaliers). The carrying on of constant wars in the period embraced by modern history created anew a military profession enjoying a privileged position.

But changes which have taken place in political and social conditions, the increased importance of knowledge, industry, capital, and finally, the immense numbers of the military class, considerably reduced its privileges in society. Rivalry in the acquisition of means for the satisfaction of more complex requirements has caused the majority of educated people to see in military service an ungrateful career. And, indeed, there is no other form of exacting activity which pays so badly as the military profession. Owing to the immense growth of armies, governments cannot find the means for improving the position of officers and their families, and a deficiency in officers is everywhere felt.

Thus, insufficient recompense will inevitably result in the military profession losing all its best forces, all the more so because the fascination for society of persons bearing arms has departed. The movement against militarism leads to views diametrically opposite. Modern ideals every day see less to sympathise with in the old ideals of distinction in battle, and glory of conquest. Everywhere the idea spreads that the efforts of all ought to be devoted to the lessening of the sum of physical and moral suffering. The immense expenditure on the maintenance of armies and fleets and the building and equipment of fortresses, acts powerfully in the spreading of such sentiments. Everywhere we hear complaints that militarism sucks the blood of all—as it has been expressed, "in place of ears of corn the fields produce bayonets and sabres, and shells instead of fruit grow on the trees." Those who adopt the military career are, of course, not responsible for these conditions, which they did not create and which react injuriously on themselves. But popular movements do not analyse motives, and discontent with militarism is inevitably transferred to the military class.

It might be replied that scholars, too, are often ill rewarded, notwithstanding which they continue their work. But every scholar is sustained by the high interests of his work, by the hope of perpetuating his name, and finally, by the chance of enriching himself upon success. The position of officers is very different. For an insignificant salary they bear the burden of a petty and monotonous work. Year after year the same labour continues. Hope of distinction in war is not, for none believe in the nearness of war. For an officer with an average education the limit of ambition is the command of a company. The command of a battalion little improves his position. For the command of regiments and larger bodies of troops, academical education is required.

But even among those officers who console themselves with the thought that war will break out, presenting occasion for distinction, there is little hope of attaining the desired promotion. We have had many opportunities for conversing with military men of different nationalities, and everywhere we were met with the conviction that in a future war few would escape. With a smokeless field of battle, accuracy of fire, the necessity for showing example to the rank and file, and the rule of killing off all the officers first, there is but little chance of returning home uninjured.

The times are passed when officers rushing on in advance led their men in a bold charge against the enemy, or when squadrons seeing an ill-defended battery galloped up to it, sabred the gunners, and spiked the guns or flung them into ditches. Courage now is required no less than before, but this is the courage of restraint and self-sacrifice and no longer scenic heroism. War has taken a character more mechanical than knightly. Personal initiative is required not less than before, but it is no longer visible to all.

It is true that warfare and the military profession will

continue to preserve their attractions for such restless, uncurbed natures as cannot reconcile themselves to a laborious and regular life, finding a charm in danger itself. But even these will find that the stormy military life and feverish activity of battle are no more surrounded by the aureole which once set them above the world of work.

It is notable that the younger and the better educated they are, the more pessimistically do officers look on war. And although military men do not speak against warfare publicly, for this would be incompatible with their calling, it cannot escape attention that every year fewer and fewer stand up in defence of its necessity or use.

As the popularity of war decreases on all sides, it is impossible not to foresee that a time will approach when European governments can no longer rely on the regular payment of taxes for the covering of military expenditure. The extraordinary resource which has been opened by means of conversion of loans—that is, by the lowering of the rate of interest—will soon disappear. In 1894 a sum of five hundred and twenty millions of pounds sterling was converted, meaning for the proprietors of the securities, a loss of four millions seven hundred and sixty thousand of pounds. To defend themselves against this, capitalists have rushed into industry. In Europe, in recent times, industrial undertakings have immensely increased, and a vast number of joint-stock companies has been formed. The Conservative classes, considered as the best support of authority, foreseeing the loss of income, dispose of their Government securities and invest in industrial securities, which bring a better dividend. State securities tend to fall more and more into the hands of the middle classes— that is, the classes which live on incomes derived from work, but who are nevertheless in a position to save.

These changes tend to make the economic convulsions caused by war far greater than those which have been experienced in the past. The fall in the value of Government securities at the very time when, owing to the stoppage of work, many will be compelled to realise, must cause

z

losses which will be intensely felt by the middle classes and cause a panic. And, as out of the number of industrial undertakings some must reduce their production and lose their profit and others altogether cease to work, the richer classes will suffer great losses and many even ruin.

A detailed examination of the vexed questions of Europe would lead to the conclusion that not one is of such a nature to cause a great war. France has no ally in an offensive war for the recovery of her lost provinces, and single-handed she cannot be assured of success. From an offensive war over the Eastern question neither Russia nor Austria could draw compensatory advantages, and such a war, which in all probability would involve the participation of England, France, Germany and Italy, would lead only to exhaustion of forces. Germany cannot think of attacking France, while out of an offensive war with Russia she could draw no profit.

Of new territory in the West, Russia also has no need, and a war with Germany would involve such immense expenditure as could hardly be covered by an indemnity, all the more so because, exhausted as she would be by a struggle with Russia, Germany could not pay an indemnity corresponding to the case. Generally, the political question for Russia lies in the Far East and not in the West.

As concerns other possible pretexts for war, examination would show that, in the present conditions of Europe, none are of sufficient gravity to cause a war threatening the combatants with mutual annihilation or complete exhaustion, nor need those moral misunderstandings and rivalries which exist between European states be seriously considered. It cannot be supposed that nations would determine to exterminate one another merely to show their superiority, or to avenge offences committed by individuals belonging to one nation against individuals belonging to another. Thus a consideration of all the reasonable causes of war would show that not one was probable.

But even if peace were assured for an indefinite time, the very preparations made, the maintenance of armed forces, and constant rearmaments, would require every year still greater and greater sacrifices. Yet every day new needs arise and old needs are made clearer to the popular mind. These needs remain unsatisfied, though the burden of taxation continually grows. And the recognition of these evils by the people constitutes a serious danger for the state.

In our time both military and political affairs have ceased to be high mysteries accessible only to the few. General military service, the spread of education, and wide publicity have made the elements of the polities of states accessible to all. All who have passed through the ranks of an army have recognised that with modern weapons whole corps and squadrons may be destroyed in the first battle, and that in this respect the conquerors will suffer little less than the conquered.

Can it be possible that the growth of expenditure on armaments will continue for ever? To the inventiveness of the human mind and the rivalry between states no limits exist. It is not surprising therefore that the immense expenditure on military aims and the consequent growth of taxation are the favourite arguments of agitators, who declare that the institutions of the Middle Ages—when from thousands of castles armed knights pounced upon passing merchants—were less burdensome than modern preparations for war.

The exact disposition of the masses in relation to armaments is shown by the increase in the number of opponents of militarism and preachers of the Socialist propaganda. In Germany in 1893, the opponents of the new military project received 1,097,000 votes more than its supporters. Between 1887 and 1893 the opposition against militarism increased more than seven times. In France the Socialist party in 1893 received 600,000 votes, and in 1896 1,000,000.

Thus, if the present conditions continue, there can be but two alternatives, either ruin from the continuance of the armed peace, or a veritable catastrophe from war.

The question is naturally asked: What will be given to

the people after war as compensation for their immense losses ? The conquered certainly will be too exhausted to pay any money indemnity, and compensation must be taken by the retention of frontier territories which will be so impoverished by war that their acquisition will be a loss rather than a gain.

With such conditions can we hope for good sense among millions of men when but a handful of their former officers remain ? Will the armies of Western Europe, where the Socialist propaganda has already spread among the masses, allow themselves to be disarmed, and if not, must we not expect even greater disasters than those which marked the short-lived triumph of the Paris Commune ? The longer the present position of affairs continues the greater is the probability of such convulsions after the close of a great war. It cannot be denied that conscription, by taking from productive occupations a greater number of men than the former conditions of service, has increased the popularity of subversive principles among the masses. Formerly only Socialists were known ; now Anarchism has arisen. Not long ago the advocates of revolution were a handful ; now they have their representatives in all parliaments, and every new election increases their number in Germany, in France, in Austria, and in Italy. It is a strange coincidence that only in England and in the United States, where conscription is unknown, are representative assemblies free from these elements of disintegration. Thus side by side with the growth of military burdens rise waves of popular discontent threatening a social revolution.

Such are the consequences of the so-called armed peace of Europe—slow destruction in consequence of expenditure on preparations for war, or swift destruction in the event of war—in both events convulsions in the social order.

INDEX

AGRICULTURAL Class (see names of Countries)
Algiers, French Army in, defective ambulance arrangements, 155
Alsace-Lorraine :
    Loss of, ultimate economic benefit to France, 277, 278
    Russian Alliance, probable effect on, of return of provinces by
    Germany, 90
Aluminium, vessels constructed with, impenetrability alleged, 102
Ambulance work (see title Wounded)
Ammunition (see title Artillery)
American Civil War:
    Armoured ships, final supersession of wooden ships, 96
    Expenditure, 130
    Losses, 343 345
    Overcharged rifles found on field of battle, 21
    Wheat, rise in price. 295
Anarchism, spread of, effect on militarism, 347, 356
Arms, Small :
    Bayonet, reliance on, impossible in modern warfare, 33, 34
    Chassepot, effectiveness of fire compared with modern rifle, 5,
    323
    Improvements in, 4 :
        Increased number of casualties resulting, 319-329
    Renewal in time of war, 307
    Rifles (see that title)
    Russia, manufacture in, 242, 243, 307
Artillery and Artillery Ammunition :
    Amount effective for war, 63
    Bombs:
        Illuminating, used in night attack, 52
        Improvements since Franco-Prussian war, 9
    Coast batteries, fire from, ineffectiveness, 104
    Destructiveness, calculations as to possibilities, 20
    Electric projectile used in night attack, 52
    Entrenchments, time taken in construction, 45
    Explosion, premature, danger of, 20, 21, 22
    Fire over heads of advancing troops, dangers attending, 334
    Gases, extent of direct action, 22

Artillery and Artillery ammunition (*continued*) :
  Guns :
    Cost of firing, 99, 100
    Effect on future warfare, 8
    Number of rounds required, 20
    Russian factory at Obukovsk, 308
  Improvements in, 7–19, 38, 329
  Nerves, strain on, in dealing with highly explosive ammunition, 21
  Preliminary action, before infantry attack suggested, 32
  Rôle in future warfare, 17–23
  Shells :
    Decreased use of, in future warfare, 9
    Increase in destructiveness since Franco-Prussian war, 9
    Premature explosion, danger of, 20
  Shrapnel :
    Area of dispersal, 8
    Destructiveness, 8, 9, 329
  Wounds caused by artillery fire, 148, 149, 152
Attack :
  Artillery, losses inflicted by, 10
  Cavalry, 50
  Difficulties under modern conditions, 337–340
  Direct, rarity of, 45
  European armies, comparative efficiency, 62
  Infantry, defects of modern tactics, 25–34
  Loose formation, 5
  Night attack, 50
" Auf der Schwelle des Kriegs," statement as to food supplies in time of war, 302, 303
Austria :
  Agricultural Class ;
    Earnings, 314
    Proportion of population, 317
  Attack and defence, efficiency in, 62
  Bachelors, percentage, 290
  Coal supply, 306, 307
  Crime, convictions, 232, 237
  Danish war, expenditure, 130
  Declaration of war improbable, 354
  Drunkenness, statistics, 229, 230
  Expenditure on Army and Navy, 133–138
    Future war, estimates, 142, 143, 144
  Fires, losses by, 192
  Food supply, sufficient in event of war, 302
  France, war with, expenditure on, 130
  Frontier defences, expenditure on, 57
  Grain Supply :
    Home production and import, 295, 296, 297

Austria (*continued*):
  Grain Supply:
    Inequalities of harvests, 301
    Oats, home production, 297, 298
    Price, rise in, probable, in event of war, 141
  Horses for military purposes, statistics, 316
  Infantry, re-armament, estimated cost, 5
  Kerosene supply, deficiency, 305, 306
  Marriages, statistics, 208
  Meat supply, superfluity, 303, 304
  Military strength, 36, 63, 318
  Naval expenditure, 133, 137, 138
    Russian compared with, 125
  Officers, proportion possessing good preparatory training, 43
  Population, increase, 292
    Old men and children, percentage, 289
    Town and country, comparison, 193
  Reserve, proportion to be drawn upon, 42, 336
  Revenue, distribution, 145, 146
  Rifle, calibre adopted, 319
  Russo-Austro-German war of the future (see that title)
  Salt supply, superfluity, 304, 305
  Sappers, number in army, 333
  Securities held in Germany, 275, 276

BACHELORS, proportion to population in leading European States, 290
Baker, Sir F., on probable effect of war on people of England, 313
Baltic Fleet, introduction of steam, 95
Bardleben, Professor, on destructiveness of modern rifles, 151
Battles:
    Accidental, description of, 46
    Area, increased by modern conditions, 5, 39
    Descriptions of future battles, 47, 48
    Duration, prolonged, 52, 337, 338
    Indecisive, probable increase in number, 49, 338
    Opening from great distance, 5
Bayonet, reliance on in modern warfare impossible, 33, 34
Beck, Dr., on humanity of modern bullets, 150
Belgium:
    Crime, statistics, 232
    Drunkenness, 229, 230
    Fires, losses by, 192, 193
    Frontier defences, expenditure, 57
    Rifles, experiments with, 4
Berdan Rifle:
    Cartridges, number carried, 328
    Range of fire, 6

Beresford, Lord Charles, on food supply in England, in time of war, 313

Bilroth, Professor, on aid to wounded, 156

Bircher, experiments in rifle fire, 152

Births :
    France, low rate, 288, 292
    Illegitimate, statistics, 225
    Russia, rate compared with other countries, 207, 208

Bismarck, Prince :
    Russian designs against Germany, report spread by, 136
    Sea and land victories, statement as to comparative importance, 122

Black Sea Fleet, composition, 95

Blockade of ships in ports and harbours, 104, 105

Bombardment (see Naval Warfare)

Bombs, 9, 52

Boots, defective, supplied in the Russo-Turkish war, 158

Bones, penetrative power of bullets, 153

Botkin, Professor, on defective ambulance arrangements in Russo-Turkish war, 154

Brest-Litousk, strategical importance, 71, 79, 80, 82

Brialmont, General, on :
    Fortresses, investment, 55
    Franco-German War of the future, 65
    Russia :
        Economic effect of war, 163
        Route of attack by Austro-German Army, probable, 76, 78
    Sappers, number required in army, 333

Brisant shell, destructiveness, 9

Bruns, Herr, on modern bullets, 150, 151

Bullets :
    Penetrative power, 3, 6, 149, 319
    Revolution and deformation, destructiveness affected by, 322, 328
    Wounds (see title Rifle Wounds)

Bunge, M. N. H., on fluctuation in Russian securities, 166

Burleau, M., on abandonment of investigation of economic conditions accompanying war, 91

CANADA, losses by fires, statistics, 192, 193

Captains, importance in modern warfare, 38

Cartridges :
    Explosion, premature risk of, 21, 22
    Supply carried by modern soldiers, 5-7, 328

Casualties, increase in, 5, 319-346

Cattle-breeding, 303, 304
    England, 254-256
    Russia, 198-201, 303, 304

Cavalry, rôle in modern warfare, 11
    Attack, 14, 50
    Losses under fire, comparison with infantry, 14
    Pursuit, rôle in, 16
    Reconnaisances, 11, 12, 16
    Rifle fire against, effectiveness, 324
Chassepot, effectiv ness of fire, 5, 323
Chasseurs, artillery hampered by, 18, 19
Chilian War :
    Losses, statistics, 343
        Officers and men, comparison, 42, 335,
    Rifles, modern deadliness proved by, 6, 29, 329
    Torpedoes, use in, 101
China, foreign trade with, 125, 126
Coal supply of European States, comparison, 306, 307
Coast batteries, ineffectiveness, 104
Commander-in-Chief, position in modern warfare, 38, 39, 46
Commissariat, difficulties of, 37. 300, 301, 303, 341, 342
    Rise in price of provisions in event of war, 140, 141, 143
Companies, Joint Stock, in England, 262
Conscription :
    Anarchism, increase since introduction of, 347, 356
    Defects of system, 35, 36, 37
Consols, holders of, statistics, 260, 261
Corea, possession of, unde-irable for Russia, 126, 127
Corn supply, effect of war on, 141, 294-303, 313, 314, 318
    (See also Names of Countries, sub-heading Grain Supply)
Coumés, Professor, on difficulties encountered by modern officers, 38
Crete, bombardment, ineffectiveness of fire from war-ships, 118
Crime, statistics, 228-240
Crimean War:
    Armoured ships, introduction, 96
    Black Sea Fleet, composition, 95
    Casualties, 148, 343-345
    English national debt increased by, 265
    Expenditure, 129, 168
    Provisions, rise in price, 143, 295
    Success of invading fleets, Van der Goltz on, 119
Cronstadt, committee to consider defence of, 97

" DANDOLA," guns carried by, 99
Danish War (1864), expenditure, 130
Death statistics, 209-213
    Drunkenness, 230
    Killed, in proportion to wounded, in modern warfare, 342-345
    Typhoid, death from, in Russia, 224
Declaration of war by any European Power improbable, 354

Defence :
   Advantages on side of defensive force, 63
   European armies, comparative efficiency, 62
   Strengthening necessitated by modern arms, 5
Dementyeff, E. M., on condition of industrial class in Russia,
   185-187
Doctors :
   Army medical work (see title Wounded, aid of)
   Civil, statistics, Russia compared with other countries, 220,
   221
Dragomiroff, General, on advantages of night attack, 51
Dreuze rifle, range of effective fire, 323
Drunkenness, crime, suicide, and insanity resulting from, 226-228
Düppel, Battle of, casualties resulting from rifle fire, 148
" Duilio " :
   Cost of construction, 98
   Guns carried by, 99
Duration of battle, statements as to, 52, 337, 338
Duration of war, probably prolonged by modern conditions, 341

ECONOMIC effects of war, 61, 91, 92, 348, 349, 353
   England, 251-265
   France, 277-293
   Germany, 266-276
   Naval warfare, effects, 110, 112
   Russia, 163, 242, 250
   Summary of effect on vital needs of people, 294-318
Education :
   Crime in relation to, statistics, 238
   Expenditure, contrasted with that on war, 139
   Russia, condition in, 216-219
Efficiency of armies, elements constituting, 61, 62
Electric projectile for use in night attack, 52
Emigration of Germans to America, decline in, 274
England :
   Bachelors, percentage, 290
   Companies, Joint Stock, 262
   Consols, holders of, statistics, 260, 261
   Crime, convictions, 232, 237
   Drunkenness, 227, 229, 230
   Economic effect of war, 251-265
   Expenditure on Army and Navy, 133-138, 263, 264
      Russian Naval expenditure compared with, 125
   Factories, large proportion of people engaged in, 262
   Fires, losses caused by, 192, 193
   Food:
      Production and importation, 251-258
      Supply in time of war, probably inadequate, 313

England (*continued*) :
  Grain Supply:
    Harvests, inequality, 301
    Importation and home production, 251–254, 295
    Insufficiency of local products in time of war, 296
    Oats, home production insufficient, 297, 298
  Horses for military service, statistics, 316
  Income Tax, statistics, 259, 260
  Marriages, statistics, 208
  Meat, importation, 254–256
  National Debt, increase owing to past wars, 264, 265
  Navy :
    Expenditure, 125, 133–138
    Increase, 123, 124
    Superiority over other nations, 111
  Poor Law Relief, number of people receiving, 261
  Population :
    Distribution between town and country, 262
    Increase, statistics, 292
    Occupation, 258, 259
    Percentage of old men and children, 289
  Potatoes, cultivation and importation, 254
  Revolution, possibility of, as result of war, 263
  Rifle, calibre adopted, 319
  Savings banks, deposits in, statistics, 261
  Wages and incomes, probable effect of war on, 258–263
Entrenchments :
  Dead bodies cast out of, 157
  Importance in modern warfare, 10, 11, 332–334.
  Sappers, number of in different armies, 333
  Tactics in relation to, 26–33, 45
Envelopment, varying opinion as to value in military tactics, 30, 34
Equipment, weight carried, 36, 345
Expenditure, Military :
  Comparative statement as to expenditure on armies and navies, 111
  Future wars, estimate, 140–146
  Past wars, 128–139
  (See also names of Countries)
Explosives (see title Artillery and Artillery Ammunition)

FINLAND, crime, statistics, 236
Fires, losses by, statistics, 192, 193
Food Supply :
  Armies (see title Commissariat)
  Effect of war on, 294–305, 313–315, 318
  Three Great European Powers only in position of independence in event of war, 302
  (See also title Grain Supply)

Fortresses :
Auxiliary obstacles used in defence, 334
Declaration of war, probably followed by immediate breaking
through frontier defences, 57, 58
Losses during siege, probable increase, 332–334, 342
Strength of investing force, modern requirements, 55
Time probably required for siege, 55
Use in modern strategy, 52, 113
Fougasse cartridges and shells, danger of premature explosion, 20,
21, 22
France :
Agricultural Class :
Effect of war on, 287
Incomes, 313, 314
Percentage of population, 284, 285, 287, 317
Wages, 286
Algiers and Tunis, armies in, defective care of wounded, 155
Alliance with Russia, probable effect on of return of Alsace
and Lorraine by Germany, 90
Artillery :
Effective in event of war, amount, 63
Improvements in, 19, 329, 330
Assistance given to poor, statistics, 287, 288
Bachelors, proportion to population, 290
Coal supply, 306
Crime, statistics, 232, 236, 237
Debt, National, growth of, 281, 282
Declaration of war, improbable, 354
Drunkenness, 227, 229, 230
Economic effects of war, 277–293
Efficiency in attack and defence, comparison, 62
Estates passing by legacy and gift, statistics, 282, 283
Expenditure on war, statistics, 133–139
Future war, estimates, 142–144
Past wars, 128, 130
Revenue, distribution with regard to, 145, 146
Fires, losses by, 192, 193
Foreigners engaged in industry, 283
Franco-German War (see that title)
Frontier defences, 57, 342
Grain Supply :
Harvests, inequalities, 301
Insufficiency of local production in time of war, 296, 297
Import and home production, of wheat, barley, and rye,
295
Oats, home production insufficient, 297, 298
Horses for military service, statistics, 316
Imports and exports, 278–281, 283, 295, 303–305
Incomes, statistics, 286, 313
Insanity resulting from drunkenness, 227

France (*continued*) :
Kerosene supply, deficiency, 305, 306
Marriages, statistics, 208
Meat supply, deficiency, 303, 304
Militarism, attitude of people towards, 355
Military strength, statistics, 36, 63
Mobilisation of army in time of war, expense estimated, 141
Navy :
    Armoured ships, introduction, 96
    Expenditure, 133, 137, 138
        Russian compared with, 125
    Increase, 123
Officers, proportion possessing good preparatory training, 43
Paris (see that title)
Population :
    Birth-rate, low, 288–292
    Distribution according to industry, 284
    Town and country, comparative growth, 193
    Value of growth, comparison with Germany, 293
Re-armament, estimated cost, 5
Reserve forces, 42, 336
    Defective training proved by manœuvres, 37
Revenue and Expenditure, 281
Rifles :
    Calibre adopted, 319
    Effectiveness :
        Comparison with other nations, 4
        Diagrams illustrating, 325-327
Russo-Austro-German war of the future (see that title)
Sappers, number employed, 333
Savings-banks, deposits in, 282
Socialist propaganda, 288
Tactics, defects of, 25
Tonkin War, torpedoes used in, 101
Unemployed, proportion of population, 287, 288
Women, active share in industry and trade, 287
Franco-German War, 1870 :
    Economic condition of country, improvement resulting from, 277–283
    Fortresses captured, 54
    Improvement in arms since :
        Artillery, 9, 19, 78, 329, 330
        Small arms, 4, 5, 323, 324
    Losses, statistics, 130, 131, 343–345
    Metz, battle indecisive, 49
    Mobiles, second day's attack generally necessary for dislodgment, 53
    Navy, unimportant part played by, 120, 121
        Moltke, statement as to improbability of attack on German coast, 117

Franco-German War (*continued*):
Night attacks, 51
Officers :
  Disablement, adopted as principle in battle, 42
  German :
    Losses, statistics, 335, 336
    Superiority in independence and self-reliance, 46
Paris. siege of, number of men required for investment, 55
Sharpshooters, important part in, 331, 332
Wounded :
  Ambulance arrangements, defective, 154, 155
  Cold steel, wounds by, percentage, 148
  Explosive bullets, charge as to use of, 150
  Shells and bullets, wounds by, percentage, 149
  Total losses, 131, 343-345
Franco-German War of the future, 63
  Distribution of troops, 64
  Effectiveness in attack, comparison, 66
  Invasion of France by Germany, 65
  Invasion of Germany by France, 67
  Paris, siege of, difficulties attending, 66
  Strength of forces, almost equal, 65
Frontier defences, 52, 57, 58
  Franco-German, 65, 66
  Russian, 73, 75

GEBLER, Professor, on effectiveness of modern rifle, 4, 5, 329
Gerbinus, on movements initiated by the masses, 60
Germany :
  Agricultural Class :
    Earnings, 314
    Effect of war on, 267, 314, 316
    Percentage of population, 266, 268
  Artillery :
    Increase in power, 19
    Strength in 1896, 63
  Bachelors, proportion to population, 290
  Coal supply, 306
  Crime, statistics, 232, 236, 338
  Danish War, expenditure of Prussia on, 130
  Drunkenness, 227, 229, 230
  Economic effects of war, 266-276
  Efficiency in attack and defence, 62
  Emigration, decline in, 274
  Expenditure on future war, estimates, 142, 143, 144
  Expenditure on maintenance of Army and Navy, 133-138
  Fires, losses by, 192, 193

Germany (*continued*) :
  Franco-German War (see that title)
  Franco-German War of the Future (see that title)
  Frontier defences, expenditure on, 57
  Grain Supply :
    Harvests, inequality, 298, 299, 301
    Home production and import, 295
    Insufficiency in time of war, 296, 297, 299, 302
      Plans for remedying, 302, 303
    Oats, home production insufficient, 297, 298
  Horses, number required for military service, 314-316
  Incomes, distribution, 269, 270, 272, 308
  Industrial classes, effect of war on, 266-275
  Infantry :
    Carriages used for transport during manœuvres, 332
    Re-armament, estimated cost, 5
  Kerosene supply, deficiency, 305, 306
  Manœuvres, 45, 332
  Marriages, statistics, 208
  Meat supply, imports and exports, 303, 304
  Militarism, attitude of people towards, 355
  Military strength :
    Proportion of population engaged in army, 318
    Total, 36, 63
  Military writers, caution of, 26
  Navy :
    Expenditure, 125
    Increase, 123
  Officers :
    Hereditary class in Prussia, 350
    Proportion possessing good preparatory training, 43
  Population :
    Distribution by occupation, 266, 268
    Growth, 290-293
    Town and country, growth in compared, 193
    Old men and children, percentage, 289
  Production of necessities of life, decrease in time of war, by withdrawal of men for military service, 315
  Reserve, statistics, 42, 336
  Revenue, 145, 146
  Rifles :
    Calibre adopted, 319
    Effectiveness, 4, 326, 327
  Russian designs against, report spread by Prince Bismarck, 136
  Russo-Austro-German War of the Future (see that title)
  Salt supply, superfluity, 304, 305
  Sappers, number in army, 333
  Savings of people, inconsiderable, 269, 271, 309, 310

Germany (*continued*):
  Securities, effect of war on, 275, 276
  Socialist propaganda, activity, 271, 311, 312
  Wages, low standard, evils of war increased by, 308–311
  Women, effect of war on wage-earning class, 272–274
Gilyarovski, P., on condition of children in Russia, 211
" Gloire," construction, 96
Goltz, Van der, Quotations from :
  Accidental Battle, description, 46
  Deterioration of armies during long war, 346
  Importance of reinforcements, 45
Gorni-Dubnak, night attack on, 51
Grain supply, effect of war on, 141, 294–303, 310, 313, 314, 318
  (see also names of Countries)
Grardimay, defective ambulance arrangements, 156
Great Britain (see England)
Gulletta, defective ambulance arrangements, 156
Guns :
  Field guns (see title Artillery, subheading Guns)
  Naval, 99, 103

HEDZVETSKI, V. I., on insufficiency of grain supply for German
  Army on Russian frontier, in event of war, 300
Hoenig, F., Quotations from :
  Night attacks, 51
  Sieges, in modern warfare, 52
Höhenlohe, Prince, on :
  Franco-Prussian War, incident in, 335
  Shrapnel, destructiveness, 8
Holland :
  Fires, losses by, 192
  Rifle, calibre adopted, 319
Hornby, Admiral, on insufficiency of food supply in England in
  time of war, 313
Horses, use of for military service, 315, 316
  Russia, large supply available, 240–242
Hungary :
  Bachelors, percentage, 290
  Crime, statistics, 232
  Grain production, 295
  Population, percentage of old men and children, 289

ILLUMINATING bomb for use in night attacks, 52
Incomes, Statistics :
  England, 259
  France, 286, 313
  Germany, 269, 270, 272, 308
  Russia, 314

Infantry :
  Attacking party, number, proportion to defenders, 31
  Bayonet, reliance on in modern warfare impossible, 33, 34
  Carriages, use for rapid transport, 332
  Cavalry, attack on, 15
  Enveloping, varying opinions as to, 30, 34
  Equipment, weight, 36
  Losses, estimates, 14, 27-32
  Marches, endurance required, 25, 36
  Officers, great ability required, 27
  Reconnaissance, duties in relation to, 12, 13, 24
  Re-armament, estimated cost, 5
  Rifle fire against, effectiveness, 323, 326, 327
  Rôle in future warfare, 23
  Tactics, differences of opinion as to modern system, 25-34
Inkerman, battle of, casualties caused by bullet wounds, 148
Instructions as to tactics, elaboration in time of peace desirable, 336, 337
Iron and steel manufacture, working of in Russia, 242, 243, 307
Ironclads :
  Aluminium, vessels protected by, alleged impenetrability, 102
  Boilers and engines, protection of, 102
  Cost of construction, 98
  Guns and ammunition, 98, 99
  Introduction, 96
  Machinery, complexity, 106
  Thickness of armour, 98
  Water-tight compartments, 102
" Italia " :
  Cost of construction, 98
  Guns and ammunition carried by, 99
Italy :
  Crime, statistics, 232, 236.
  Drunkenness, deaths from, 230
  Efficiency, comparative, in attack and defence, 62
  Expenditure on war estimates, 133-139, 142-146
  Frontier defence, expenditure, 57
  Future war, distribution of troops, 64
  Marriages, statistics, 208
  Grain Supply :
    Harvests, inequalities, 301
    Home production and importation, 295
    Insufficient in event of war, 296, 297
    Oats, home productions. 297, 298
  Horses for military service, statistics, 316
  Infantry, re-armament, cost estimated, 5
  Kerosene supply. deficiency, 305, 306
  Losses in war with Austria, 343, 345
  Meat supply, superfluity, 303, 304

2 A

Italy (*continued*) :
    Military strength, total, 36, 63
    Navy, expenditure on, 133, 138, 139
        Russia compared with, 125
    Population, rate of increase, 292
    Reserve, proportion to regular army, 25, 42, 336
    Revenue, distribution, 145, 146
    Rifle :
        Calibre adopted, 319
        Effectiveness, 4
    Salt supply, superfluity, 304, 305
    Sappers, number in army, 333
    Securities held in Germany, 275, 276.

JANSON, General, on :
    Infantry attack, 32
    Officers in Franco-Prussian War, independence of, 46
Japan :
    Foreign trade with, 125, 126
    Russia, relations with, 124, 125, 127
Jung, General, on mobilisation of French Army in time of war, 141

KAGARETCH, night attack on, 51
Kars, night attack on, 51
Kef, defective ambulance arrangements at, 156
Kerosene supply, 305, 306
Killed, proportion to wounded in modern warfare, 342-345
Killichen, General, on number of sappers required by army, 333
" Koenig Wilhelm," cost of construction, 98
Königsberg, sections of bridges, and materials for railways stored
    at, 83
Kotié, S. N., on effect of war on price of corn in Austria, 141
Kovno, strength of fortress, 79
Kuropatkin, General, night attack advocated by, 51

" LA POUDRE SANS FUMÉE " :
    Battle described in, 47
    Night attack advocated in, 51
Langlois, Colonel, statements as to artillery fire :
    Effectiveness, 7, 8, 329, 330
    Number of rounds required for one field-piece, 20
Le Mans, night attack on, 51
" Le Progrès Militaire " on cost of naval weapons, 99
Leer, General, on :
    Duration, probable, of war with Russia, 315
    German Army on Russian frontier, statistics, 300
Liebert, on difficulties of pursuit under modern conditions, 50

INDEX

Lissa, destruction of Italian fleet at, 120
Losses, probable, in future wars, 319-346
Luzeux, General, on modern teaching of tactics, 26

" MAGENTA," cost of construction, 98
Makarof, Admiral, on machinery of the " Rurik," 106
Malshinski, Mr., on growth of population in Russia, 190
Mannlicher rifle, effectiveness of, 323, 324, 343, 344
Manœuvres, information obtained from, incomplete and unsatisfactory, 41
Maps and plans, Russo-Austro-German War of the Future :
    Prussia invasion by Russia, 89
    Russian defensive system, 74
    Vistula-Bug-Narev theatre of war, 77, 78
Marches, endurance required, 25, 36
Marriages, statistics, 207, 208
Mauser Rifle :
    Effectiveness, 4, 320, 321
    Number of shots fired per second, 4
Mayence, investment difficulty, 67, 68
Meat Supply Statistics :
    Continental Powers, 280, 303, 304
    England, 254-256
Melinite, danger of premature explosion, 20
" Merrimac," exploit of, 96
Mexican war, losses in, analysis, 345
Mignol, Colonel, on French tactics, 25
" Militärische Essays" ; statements as to cavalry in modern warfare, 14, 15
Militarism, opposition to, 347-356
Mobilisation :
    French Army in time of war, estimate of cost, 141
    Rapidity of modern methods, 36, 64, 65
Moltke, General Von, statement as to possible invasion of German coast by French Navy, 117
" Monitor," battle with " Merrimac," 96
Monteculli on effect of insufficient food upon troops, 341
Morache, analysis of losses in modern wars, 344
Moscow, attempt to occupy, possibility, in event of war, 84-87
Movements of enemy, observation of :
    Auxiliary instruments for, 10
    Cavalry and infantry, duties in relation to, 12, 13
    Sharpshooters, duties, 331, 332
Müller, General, on effectiveness of modern artillery, 20, 31, 330
Murder, convictions, statistics, 232

NAPOLEON I :
    Moscow campaign, strength of French and Russian armies at Smolensk and Moscow, 86

Napoleon I. (*continued*) :
    Plan of battle, allowance made for accidents, 45, 46
    Success in battle, statement as to chances of, 44
Naval Warfare :
    Accident, strong element in, 108, 109
    Austrian Navy, expenditure on, 133, 137, 138
        Russian expenditure compared with, 125
    Blockade of ports, 104
    Bombardment of towns, 103, 118, 119
        Undefended towns not to be bombarded, principle not
            acknowledged, 103
    Coast batteries, ineffectiveness, 104
    Cruisers : Light and swift, preference for, 100
    Destructiveness, increase in, 105
    English Navy (see England)
    Expenditure entailed, 98, 99, 110, 111, 113, 133–138
    French Navy (see France)
    Future of naval warfare, 93–112
    German Navy, expenditure, 123, 125
    Guns, 99, 103
    Ironclads (see that title)
    Italian Navy, expenditure, 125, 133, 138, 139
    Ordnance, improvements in, 97
    Privateering, 109, 295
    Result of battle between fleets of equal strength, 107
    Russian Navy (see title Russia)
    Shells :
        Cost of, 99, 100
        Destructive power, 99, 106, 108
    Social and economic results, 110, 112
    Steam, adoption, 95
    Torpedoes, 100–103
Nerve of soldiers :
    Artillery fire, effect of, 10
    Deterioration, 52, 340
    Rifle fire, effect of, 6
    Strain in dealing with highly explosive ammunition, 21
Night Attack :
    Effectiveness, difference of opinion as to, 50–52
    Nerves of soldiers affected by possibility of, 340
Nigote, Captain :
    Battle described by, 48
    Duration of battles, 52
Nirschau riots, casualties caused by rifle fire, 322
Norway marriage statistics, 209

Oats, home production insufficient in Central European States,
    297, 298

Obukovsk, ordnance factory at, 308
Officers:
Decline of popularity of military profession, 350
Disablement of, chief aim of enemy, 41, 335
Efficiency under modern conditions questioned, 27, 34, 37, 335
Militarism supported by, 350

PARIS:
Siege of (1870), number of men required for investment, 55
Siege of, in Franco-German War of the Future, difficulties, 66
Unemployed in, 288
Workmen trained to light trades, incapacity for heavy tasks, 272
Paskevitch, Colonel, instrument for measuring distances of rifle fire invented by, 327
Peroxylene, danger of premature explosion, 20
Pestitch, General, on cost of firing naval guns, 100
Peterhead, bombardment threatened during naval manœuvres, 103
Pigorof on :
Defective care of wounded, 154
Frost-bitten feet caused by defective boots, 158
" Piotr Veliki," guns carried by, 97
Pistols, Mauser, rate of fire, 4
Plans of campaign in future warfare, 63
Plevna, siege of, 54
Poland:
Crime, statistics, 231, 236, 238
Population, town and country, comparative growth, 193
Strategical importance in event of Russo-Austro-German War, 82-85
Pont de Fahs, defective care of wounded at, 156
Populace:
Attitude towards militarism, 347, 353
Effect of war on vital needs of, 294
Porth, Dr., on defective care of wounded, 153, 157
Potatoes, cultivation and importation into England, 254
Powder, smokeless, effect of, 3
Artillery, 17, 18
Assault, difficulties increased, 337, 339
Battle described in " La Poudre sans Fumée," 47
Cavalry attack favoured by, 15
Deadliness of modern warfare increased, 6
Infantry action, 24
Night attack aided by, 51
Reconnaissances, difficulty increased, 12
Sound of shot, distance of penetration lessened, 24
Prisons, expenditure on, in Russia, 239
Privateering in future warfare, 109, 295
" Prokhor," guns carried by, 97, 98

Propaganda against war, effect on minds of soldiers, 30
Prussian needle-gun (1870), range of effectual fire, 6
Psychological aspect of war, 59
Pursuit:
   Cavalry, rôle in, 16
   Difficulty under modern conditions, 50
Puzuirevski, General, on night attacks, 51

QUARTERS for soldiers, difficulty of procuring, 37

RECONNAISSANCES:
   Cavalry and infantry, duties defined, 12, 13, 24
   Sharpshooters, employed for prevention of, 331
Reger, Dr., on modern bullets, 150
Reserve Soldiers:
   Drawbacks to employment of, 25, 27, 37, 340
   Officers, efficiency doubtful, 27, 37, 42, 335
   Statistics, 42, 336
Retreat:
   Cavalry pursuit, 16
   Dangers under modern conditions, 340
Revenue, distribution in different countries, 145, 146
Revolutionary movements, effect of war on, 91, 356
Rhine, probable difficulty of crossing, in Franco-German War of
   the Future, 67
Richter, Professor, on defective care of wounded, 155
Rifle wounds, 148
   Explosive character of bullets fired at great velocity, 150, 151
   Increased number of casualties, 150, 152, 319
      Penetrative power of bullets, 3, 149, 319
      Proportion of killed to wounded, 342
Rifles:
   Accuracy increase, 6, 7, 323, 324
   American Civil War, over-charged rifles found on field, 21
   Artillery fire, comparative destructiveness, 148
   Calibre, diminished, advantages, 5
   Cartridges, number carried, 5-7, 328
   Chilian War, deadliness of modern arms proved by, 6
   Effectiveness of modern weapons, 3, 319
      Diagrams illustrating, 321, 343
      Rate of increase in power, 38
   Fire over heads of advancing troops, dangers of, 334
   Measuring distances, instrument for, 327
   Penetrative power of bullets, 3, 6, 149, 319
   Random shots, losses from, 29
   Range of effective fire, 3, 324
   Rate of fire, 4, 45
   Revolution and deformation of bullet, destructiveness effected
      by, 322, 328

Rifles (*continued*) :
  Self-loading. made of alloy of aluminium, 4
  Shrapnel fire, comparison with, 8, 329
  Sound of shot, distance of penetration lessened by use of
    smokeless powder, 24
Rohne, General, on :
  Attack on fortified position, 10
  Sharpshooters, use of, 19
Roon, Von, on strain on nerves, 340
Roumania :
  Army, number of sappers in, 333
  Harvests, inequalities, 301
"Rurik," machinery of, 106
Russia:
  Agricultural Class, 196–203
    Conditions subsequent to Crimean War, 114
    Earnings, 314
    Effect of war on, 249, 317
    Indebtedness of peasants, 203
  Arms and ammunition, manufacture, 242, 243, 307
  Births :
    Illegitimate, 223, 225
    Proportion, compared with other countries, 207
  Cattle supply, 198–201, 303, 304
  Character of population and country, 163, 203, 214
  Children, condition of, 209–213
  Chinese trade, 125, 126
  Coal supply, 306, 307
  Corea, possession of undesirable, 126, 127
  Cotton, wool, skins, and linen supply, 307
  Crime, statistics, 228
  Crimean War (see that title)
  Death-rate, 209
  Declaration of war improbable, 354
  Defensive war, advantages in, 246
  Doctors, number, comparison with other countries, 220
  Domestic animals, 198
  Drunkenness, 227
  Duration of war, probability, 315
  Economic effects of war, 163
    Summary, 242, 250
  Education, popular, 216
  Efficiency in attack and defence, 62
  Expenditure on justice and prisons, 239
  Expenditure on War :
    Comparison with other States, 133, 245
    Daily, in time of war, 142, 143, 169, 248
    Decrease, probable, 249
    Future war estimates, 142–144, 169, 248

Russia (*continued*):
Expenditure on War:
Increase, 133, 134-139, 169
One inhabitant, expenditure by, 169, 170
One soldier, cost of maintenance, yearly, 136, 169
Past wars, 131, 132, 168
Revenue, distribution, 145, 146
Families of soldiers, contribution towards support during time of war, 169, 171, 314
Finances, 115
Difficulties attending war, 247, 248
Fires, losses by, 192-195
Food supply, sufficient, in event of war, 302
Germany, Russian designs against, report spread by Prince Bismarck, 136
Grain Supply:
Effect of war on prices, 249
Harvests, inequalities, 301
Oats, yearly exports, 298
Sufficient in time of war, 297
Horses for military service, 240, 316
Incomes of people, effect of war on, 314
Indebtedness of population, 203
Infantry, re-armament, cost estimated, 5
Iron and steel, working and manufacture of, 242, 243, 307
Japan, danger from improbable, 127
Kerosene supply, 305, 306
Marriages, proportion compared with other countries, 207, 208
Meat supply, 303, 304
Medicine, outlay on, per inhabitant, 222
Military strength, 36, 63
Proportion of population engaged in army, 318
Navy:
Armoured ships, introduction, 97
Expenditure, 124, 125, 133-139
Increase, 116, 124
Need of, questioned, 113
Shipbuilding works executed in England, 116
Steam introduction, 95
Nerve of soldiers, probable superiority, 52
Officers, proportion possessing good preparatory training, 43
Population:
Distribution, 190
Effect of war on, 188
Growth, 114, 115, 189, 190, 193, 206, 207, 292
Posts and Telegraphs, expenditure on, 181
Renewal of army, circumstances affecting, 240
Reserve, proportion to regular army, 25, 42, 336

Russia (*continued*):
Revenue, distribution, 145, 146
Rifles :
Accuracy, improvement in, 325
Calibre adop'ed, 319
Paskevitch instrument for measuring distances, 327
Salt supply, 304, 305
Sapper-, number employed in army, 333
Savings, inconsiderable, 193, 196, 314
Securities :
Depreciation in event of war, 166–168, 247, 248
Germany, securities held in, 275
Settlements, average number of houses in, 191
Sickness, prevalence, 223, 224
Siberian railway, 124, 126
Statistics, official, compiled first under Nicholas I., 164
Suicide, statistics, 225
Towns, growth of, 193
Trade, effect of war on, 172, 244, 249
Exports, 172
Imports, 177
Manufacturing crisis probable, 182
Maritime trade, 125
Undertakings in 1892, 180
Wages, 186, 314
Wounded, care of, reforms needed, 158
Russo-Austro-German War of the Future :
Allies of Germany, weakness, 70, 71
Distribution of troops, 64
Defensive attitude of Germany, 72, 73
Economic and social conditions, affecting, 91, 92
France, probable change of attitude in the event of return of Alsace-Lorraine, 90
Invasion of Austria by Russia, 85, 87, 90
Invasion of Eastern Galicia by Russia, improbable, 90
Invasion of Germany by Russia, 87
Bombardment by fleet, small cities only accessible, 121
Invasion of Russia, improbable, 82, 85, 117–120
Maps and plans, 74, 77, 78, 89
Moscow, attempt to occupy, 74, 84-87
Number of men available, 63, 75, 76, 79, 80, 81, 85, 86
Plan of campaign, 69
Poland, strategical importance, 72, 73, 82-85
Prolongation of war, advantageous to Russia, 86
Results, probable, 90
St. Petersburg, attempt to occupy, 84
Vistula-Bug Narev District, operations in, 73, 76, 84, 85, 86
Plans, 77, 78
Winter, difficulties of advance in, 87

Russo-Turkish war :
    Entrenchments, value proved in, 332
    Expenditure, 131, 132, 168
    Frost-bitten feet ascribed to wet boots, 158
    Industrial production of Russia at time of, 182
    Losses, statistics, 343-345
    Nerve of soldiers, 52
    Night attack, 51
    Revolutionary movement strengthened by, 91
    Torpedoes, use in, 101
    Wounded :
        Cast out of trenches, 157
        Defective care of, 154
        Steel weapons, 148
Rüstow, on probable duration of future campaign, 341

St. CYR, MARSHAL, on composition of a brave army, 340
St. Petersburg, German occupation possibly attempted in war of
    the future, 84
Salt supply, Russia contrasted with Western Powers, 304
Sappers, number required, 333
Sardinia, war (1859) expenditure on, 130
Saur, General Von, on attack on fortresses, 56
Saxony :
    Grain production, 299
    Incomes, amount and distribution, 270
    Population, town and country, comparative growth, 193
Scheibert, Major, on Russo-Austro-German War of the Future, 72,
    82
Schultze-Gävernitz, Dr. Von, on low standard of wages in
    Germany, 309
Scotland, population distribution, 262
Securities, Government, probable effect of war on, 353
Servia :
    Harvests, inequality, 301
    Securities held in Germany, 275, 276
Sharpshooters :
    Artillery-men hampered by, 18, 19
    Use of in future warfare, 331, 332
Shells :
    Decreased use in future warfare, 9
    Explosion, premature, danger of, 20
    Increase of destructive power, 9
    Navy, 99
        Destructive power, 106, 108
    Wounds caused by, 148, 149, 152
Shrapnel :
    Area of dispersal, 8

Shrapnel (*continued*) :
    Chief artillery ammunition of the future, 9
    Destructiveness, 8, 9
    Rifle fire compared with, 8, 329
Siberian railway, important only as means of transport, 124, 126
Sickness, losses from, in armies, 344
Sieges (see title Fortresses)
Sinope, battle of, cost of firing guns, 100
Size of armies, difficulties of warfare increased by, 36
Skugarevski, General, on :
    Attack by infantry, 31, 32
    Rifle fire, 334
Smokeless powder (see title Powder)
Social conditions, effect of war on, 59, 91, 110, 112, 163, 347
Socialism, development in Germany, 311
Sokolovski, Mr., on indebtedness of Russian peasant, 205
Spain :
    Crime, statistics, 232
    Rifle, effectiveness, 4
Steel Weapons :
    Casualties caused by, 148, 319
    Russia, manufacture of, 307
Stein, on provisioning of army, 141
Strasburg, siege of, sickness amongst soldiers, 346
Suicide, statistics, 225
Supporting bodies in attack, deadliness of artillery fire to, 10
Sweden :
    Crime, statistics, 236
    Fire, losses by, 192
    Marriages, statistics, 108
Switzerland, frontier defences, expenditure on, 57

TACTICS :
    Deadliness of warfare, increased by modern system, 331
    Differences of opinion as to, 25
Tchernaya, battle of, bullet wounds in, 148
Torpedoes, 100-103
Trenches (see title Entrenchments)
Tunis, French Army, defective care of wounded, 155
Turkey :
    Revenue expenditure, 145
    Rifle, calibre adopted, 319
    Russo-Turkish War (see that title)
    Securities held in Germany, 275
Turnwald, on weight of equipment, 345
Typhus, death from, frequency in Russia, 223, 224

UNITED STATES :
    Chilian War (see that title

United States (*continued*) :
  Civil War (see title American Civil War)
  Fires, losses by, 192, 193
  Food supply, independence in time of war, 302
  Population increase, 292
  Rifle :
    Calibre adopted, 319
    Effectiveness, 4
Universal Service :
  Anarchism, increase since introduction of, 347, 356
  Defects of system, 35-37

VARISCHOEFFER, Inspector, report on wages in Germany, 310

WAGES :
  Agricultural population, proportion of national income earned
    by, 314
  England, 258
  France, 286
  Germany, 272-274, 308-312
  Russia, 186, 314
" Warrior " :
  Cost of construction, 98
  Shells carried by, 99
Werner, Admiral, on character of modern naval warfare, 109
Wheat (see title Grain Supply)
Wissenberg, battle of, defective care of wounded at, 154
Women, Economic Position :
  France, 287
  Germany, 272, 273
Worth, battle of, dead and wounded soldiers cast out of trenches,
  157
Wounded :
  Aid to, 147, 152
    Defective arrangements in recent wars, 154
    Difficulties, under modern conditions, 30, 156
    Reforms needed, 152, 156
  Artillery fire, 148, 149, 152
  Character of wounds, effect of improvements in firearms on,
    147
  Killed, proportion to wounded in modern warfare, 342
  Rifle wounds (see that title)
  Steel weapons, casualties caused by, 148, 319